MANAGING PUBLIC ORGANIZATIONS

MANAGING PUBLIC ORGANIZATIONS

Lessons from Contemporary
European Experience

Edited by

Kjell A. Eliassen and Jan Kooiman

SAGE Publications
London · Thousand Oaks · New Delhi

First published 1993

SAGE Publications Ltd
6 Bonhill Street
London EC2A 4PU

SAGE Publications Inc
2455 Teller Road
Thousand Oaks, California 91320

SAGE Publications India Pvt Ltd
32, M-Block Market
Greater Kailash – I
New Delhi 110 048

ISBN 0-8039-7714 X
ISBN 0-8039-7715 8 pbk

Printed in Great Britain by The Cromwell Press, Melksham.

CONTENTS

NOTES ON THE CONTRIBUTORS

Carl Böhret *Postgraduate School of Administrative Sciences Speyer*
Hans-Ulrich Derlien *University of Bamberg*
Kjell A. Eliassen *Norwegian School of Management*
Brian W. Hogwood *University of Strathclyde, Department of Government*
Gerard Gerding *SUG*
Torben Beck Jørgensen *University of Copenhagen*
Hans Keman *Vrije University Amsterdam*
Jan Kooiman and Martijn van Vliet *Rotterdam School of Management*
Jan-Erik Lane *University of Oslo*
Les Metcalfe *European Institute of Public Administration*
Guy Peters *University of Pittsburg*
Sue Richards *Office for Public Management, London*
Jeremy J. Richardson *University of Warwick*
Torodd Strand *University of Bergen*
Rune J. Sørensen *Norwegian School of Management*
Aaron Wildavsky *University of California at Berkeley*
Vincent Wright *University of Oxford*
Paulus Yntema *OECD*

PREFACE

It is a great pleasure for us to be able to present the second edition of *Managing Public Organizations*. We hope that it will be as well received as the first edition. In the years between the two editions, the issue of public management in Western Europe has not diminished in prominence. In fact, in many Western European countries, the need to bring administrative systems up to date is still high on the political agenda. The nature of what falls under the heading 'public management' differs considerably from country to country in terms of both the items for reform and the scope of reform. However, as far as we can see, reform in the area of public management is being carried out in all Western European countries. This is understandable in that the major reasons behind the need for reform have not diminished in importance. On the contrary, it could well be argued that the need for reform has in fact increased in the past years and it will stay with us in the years to come. What is interesting here is that the evidence to support this supposition is not directly apparent. As a result, political interest in administrative/management reform has never been great and it probably never will be. Most Western European political systems, of which administration/management is an integral part, are still suffering from low popular support and highly ineffective performance. Politics bears the brunt of the blame for this because, for the citizens at large, it looks as if there is not much which can be done about the standard of administration in the public sector. Where research data are available on this topic, it can be seen, time and time again, that the administrative side of government suffers from a level of dissatisfaction bordering on disillusion.

On the other hand, in many governmental systems, there does exist a limited awareness with regard to internal shortcomings (such as duplication of work and inefficiency) as well as knowledge about external failings (such as limited access and little responsiveness). This had lead to efforts to design and try out new ways of carrying out public tasks (see the OECD report on recent trends in public management, 1992).

It is against the background of developments such as these that we have produced this second edition of *Managing Public Organizations*. The basic structure remains the same but we have tried, in this new edition, to pay more systematic attention to developments within the public sectors of our societies and the way in which they are related to the questions, the tasks and the roles involved in public management.

The revision of this book has been carried out as part of a research project financed under the program for Research on Organization and Steering (LOS), directed by the Norwegian Research Council for Applied Social Sciences. We are grateful for this organization's support in this project and we hope that the book will contribute to the understanding of national political and administrative challenges in Western European countries.

We would like to express our special gratitude to Jan-Erik Lane who has been a great inspiration in setting the tone of the second edition. Not only has he made many of the suggestions as to how the book could be updated but he has also been involved in the administrative and editorial tasks.

We would also like to thank both the contributors to the previous edition and those authors who have so kindly responded to our call for their participation in this edition, despite almost all of them having extremely heavy work loads.

Finally, we would like to thank a number of individuals who helped in the initial editing, layout and translation of the book. These people include Audun Iversen, Bård Kuvaas, Gillian Kennedy, Esben Oust Heiberg and Tom Edwin Manshaus, all employed at the Center for European Studies, The Norwegian School of Management, Oslo.

Oslo/Rotterdam
May 1993

Kjell A. Eliassen
Jan Kooiman

1

INTRODUCTION

Kjell A. Eliassen and Jan Kooiman

One may approach public management by a general distinction between two levels of analysis. First, there is the overall management of the public sector as a whole, embedded in its social and physical environment. One face of public management is orientated towards the external governance of bureaux in their immediate social, political and administrative contexts. Second, another face of public management is the internal running of public organizations where the role of public managers as leaders is crucial. Each level of analysis – external and internal management – deserves its own analysis calling for different concepts and models. Here we have a typical characteristic of the public sector: its double principal-agent structure. In external management the politicians as the principal attempt to guide and monitor the provision units as agents in the public sector, whereas in internal management the leaders of the provision unit, e.g the bureau become the principal and the employees – administrators and professionals – the agent.

It used to be the so-called 'public administration' that offered interpretation and understanding in the conduct of research concerning public organizations of various kind and public officials as leaders or employee of bureaux. Yet, the world in and around the public sector has changed much. In many respects public resource allocation and public regulation have problems and difficulties not anticipated in the traditional public administration framework. The public sector in the large welfare state of the 1990s calls for an understanding of how its institutions might be brought in more harmony with the variety of interests that surround state and local governments. Institutional evaluation and reform is the chief perspective now on the public sector, but the welfare state analysis must include the variety of interests of politicians, administrators, professionals and citizen groups.

There are clearly many connections between developments in society at large and the shape of the public sector generally. This holds in particular for the management of public organizational units at the ministerial level. Social developments, the shifting roles of the state, the dynamics of the boundaries between state and society or the public and the private as well as the time perspectives in such transformation process call for a reorientation of the management of the public sector, both in its totality and its individual parts. These change processes have common features such as the move from steering to guidance, the orientation of policy demands from popular to unpopular issues and the search for new forms of legitimacy for public decisions. Looking at the consequences of such trends for the management of public organizations, some scholars take an optimistic view of the capacity of public bodies to adapt themselves to new opportunities, whereas others underline the risk for a pathology of public institutions at the present (Hogwoord and Peters, 1985).

A more sceptical view about the capacity of public institutions to handle important problems in the external governance of state bureaux and local governments relates to the crisis in the welfare state where there appear to be general difficulties of identifying institutional solutions that are compatible with all the interests that cluster around public institutions. The maturing of the welfare state creates enormous challenges for the political-administrative system. Unfortunately, most public programmes learn slowly, meaning that necessary adaptations do not take place when time is ripe, except in extreme circumstances for wrong reasons. Change in management increasing adaptivity and flexibility is primarily a cultural phenomenon based on learning processes. There is reason to doubt if the cultural and structural conditions of the modern welfare state are such that various kinds of resistance to change can be overcome. Experience shows that interests play a heavy role here, as even when intentions are good, the real political and administrative will to put changes into operation may be lacking.

In many respects public organizations and their principals handling the external management of the public sector are responsible for the growth, in some parts even explosion, of public activities. Several management problems in the public sector and its organizations have to do with the ambition to broaden the scope of the delivery of public goods and services and with promoting the production of rules, regulations, subsidies and other public outputs at the negligence of the costs or the revenue side of the public household. Structure, process and culture in public sector organizations operating in networks of a public and semi-public nature set limits to what external management can do when it comes to 'getting more out of the public pie'. It must be pointed out that external demands may create such difficulties that so-called garbage can processes take place in one or more public sector programmes at the state or local government (March and Olsen, 1976).

Several factors contributing to the problematic state of the public sector are of a more internal nature (Wildavsky, 1979). In internal management the responsibility for the state of affairs of public programmes rests with administrators and professionals. The basic procedures and techniques used by public managers to steer and guide their organizations are very important for effectiveness and efficiency in public resource allocation and public regulation. The change from a legalistic and administrative culture to a managerial one underlining benefits versus costs is certainly on its way, but it will have to face many obstacles to be overcome during the 1990s. In particular, not only external but also new internal management is required when the problems of a welfare state in crisis are to be handled. Pointing to the fundamental nature of these problems in the wider social and political context should not conceal the often occurrence of internal problems of public organizations.

Are external problems more difficult to change than internal problems? Some major difficulties for public bodies and their managers are deeply embedded in the historical roots of public institutions, whereas other large scale problems stem from present day national, social and political conditions. Yet, in several respects management problems in public organizations can be explained by looking at internal factors such as a lack of interest from leaders, poor training for management responsibilities, a tendency to neglect criticism or a fear of outsiders. Within internal management there is both scope and need for pragmatic solutions to public sector problems, but for the solution to external management problems we must not look only at the public managers as agents, because here the responsibilities are shared with the principals: politicians. However, we must ask to what extent external or internal management in the public sector can find and implement first-best solutions to problems in public resource allocation and public management.

CONCEPT OF PUBLIC MANAGEMENT

What does the term 'public management' mean? What role could a concept of public management play in the reform process of the public sector in democratic countries? Does it make sense to talk about it as something different or something new in relation to the traditional public administration approach? Two distinct but related aspects of the concept of public management may be identified when one attempts to identify the criteria for a definition of the term:

1 The relevance of the public-private distinction.
2 The blend of the theoretical and practical approach.

The concept of management has been used in so many different contexts and with so many conflicting definitions that it is difficult to indicate any general definition. The confusion about the concept increases when the prefix 'public' is added. In spite of the growing interest in the problems of management and leadership in the public sector, few attempts have been made to elaborate the implications of the concept of the public for management. On the contrary, both in public debate and in scholarly writing the vague concept of management in the private sector has been borrowed uncritically.

Looking at various definitions one can place a few distinctions under the following headings: Those that are based primarily on a scholarly or disciplinary background; those that are concerned with the typical activities or functions of public management; and finally those that stem from based on the distinction between public and private organizations.

If 'public management' was just another label for traditional public administration, then it would belong more to political science than to business administration: 'It makes a lot of difference if one puts an accent on the word public or on the word management.' The public administration focus would stress elements such as equity, fairness and the rule of law in handling so-called cases. The business management aspect would talk about effectiveness, efficiency and cost-benefit analysis. It is obvious that any effort at defining 'public management' would be essentially contested as it opens up Pandora's box of disciplinary beliefs, preconceptions and even of prejudices. Public management, on the one hand, has to be seen in the context of basic constitutional principles, especially in connection with the 'rule of law'. It must guarantee that the administration of the state is in accordance with political objectives and rules. On the other hand, public management must deliver goods and services where the demand and supply of these often shift rapidly. In the welfare or the post welfare state a public manager has different functions when compared with the civil servant in the traditional public administration role. The various definitions of 'public management' may be stated either in theoretical and analytical terms or be outlined on a practical or normative basis. Both ways may be useful in understanding public sector operations. The kind of prescriptive definitions which merely reflect a professional or scholarly bias are to be avoided.

One could also emphasize functional qualities. The notion of necessary prerequisites in organizations could mean a search for such basic functions that can be manifested through specific roles'. Here, one mode of presentation is to state broad and general functions like the identification of the goal function or the derivation of technology. Another mode could be to look at specific functions like budgeting or implementation. Public management can be analysed in either a descriptive language or a normative language. As there is a choice in the conduct of research on public management to employ a theoretical perspective as different from a practical one, it is vital to see their differences both in terms of cons and pros.

Although one may contrast these approaches as exclusive alternatives – understanding versus recommendation – we argue that there is room for both ways of looking at public organizations and their management This is the reason we asked authors in both 'traditions' to contribute to this book. This may be a sound decision, because significant contributions in both the theory and practice of public management have been. By focussing on the understanding of public middle managers, one may suggest a number of measures that could improve public managerial effectiveness both of inter-organizational tasks and in terms of individual persons.

PUBLIC VERSUS PRIVATE MANAGEMENT

It is worth while to attempt to reveal some of the differences between the conditions for and practices of management in the state and local government as compared with those in market orientated organizations. Such differences could in turn be used as a point of departure for an investigation into alternative ways of handling the management functions in public organizations of various kinds, e.g. from those who mainly exercise authority in relation to single persons all the way to those that operating full scale on a market.

In the literature there are two polar arguments. At one extreme there are those who strongly oppose the proposition that there are principal differences between public management and private management. The adherents of view are to be found among people involved in private management or in private consulting firms. Thus, the standards of 'good' and 'bad' management in business matters have been employed in first and foremost recommendations on the reform of structures and processes in public organizations. Normative considerations are strong in this corner.

The opposite view states that public management differs not just marginally but in basic principles from private management. The adherents of this argument can be found within people in the public sector or in the traditional public administration circles. The principal differences include the following: one of the main differences is that public managers share their authority for managing their organization, *viz* authority is shared with democratically chosen political functionaries who exert a decisive influence on the organization and its direction. The public interest in compulsory taxes (cost) and obligatory policies (benefit) is another important difference of the public organization. Public managers operate in a fish-bowl: they have to legitimate their purposes and actions before they can go on with their task: organizational design, efficiency improvement and control as well as evaluation.

A third position stands somewhere in between the two polar arguments, as there are those who think the truth to be somewhere in between the two extremes. They see differences as well as similarities. This group include both empirical and normative orientated arguments such as: they may not differ in fact but should differ from a normative point if view. Or those who entertain the view that differences are as a matter of fact real, but it would be to prefer that they are diminishing. Let us combine these distinctions in a 2 x 2 Table (Figure 1).

As is apparent from the Figure, there are four possible arguments about the relationship between public and private management. The classical Weberian standpoint would be type IV, whereas the Simon bounded

Figure 1   *Public and private management differences*

		Normatively	
		Similarity	Dissimilarity
In Reality	Similar	I	II
	Different	III	IV

rationality argument or March and Olsen's garbage can model would closer to type I or type II. Much of the reform zest in the public sector to-day hinges on the feasibility of type III.

This very question, the comparability of management of private and public organizations, runs through this volume. Here, it is approached not only from a theoretical point of view but also with reference to empirical data. The debate between the various positions, I–IV, is by no means outdated, because these distinctions are highly relevant in the recent discussions about the need for reforming big government. To deal with the distinction between public and private organizations and their management in a systematic manner we follow the public-private distinction on the systems level and on the actor level in the volume. Let us move from here to the external perspective, mentioned above.

IMPLICATIONS OF THE ENVIRONMENT

One systematic focus on public management deals specifically with the environmental characteristics of public organizations. Thus, one may argue that a key difference between public and private organizations is the greater complexity of the environment which public managers face, even compared with the largest and most diverse private organizations.

Empirical data support the conclusion that public managers look upon their environment as predictable but complex, whereas private managers are more inclined to report that their environment is simple but highly changing. Such attitudes to the environment have consequences for the functioning of organizations and their management (Pugh and Hickson, 1976). One may ask whether it is the actual environment that means most or whether is is the way the environment is looked at that is more important.

The vulnerability of the leaders of public organizations must be mentioned. It seems that responsibility for the external threats but also for the opportunities that the environment offers cannot be the sole responsibility of the administrative head of such bodies. External vulnerability should be the shared responsibility of administrative and political leadership of public organizations. Handling the environment is team work in public management.

Whatever may be the particular responsibilities of the political and administrative leaders, one finds that at the top of most public organizations, these external factors have consequences for the roles of public managers. The tentative conclusion would be that the differences between private and public leadership, although hardly of a fundamental kind but in terms of more or less similarity or dissimilarity, has to do with the different types of environments.

One cannot just analyse the elements of the internal structure of public and private organizations as one has to include the typical external differences such as the level of environmental complexity and fluctuations. Thus, one set of things to emphasize when public management is confronted with private management includes the emphasis on rules and regulations, legal and administrative procedures and especially interorganizational patterns. But another set of differences stemming from the environment must also be underlined: the ambition to plan ahead, the failure to cope with sudden changes, but the stronger commitment to long-term transformations. It has been stated that resilience matters also in the public sector (Wildavsky, 1989), as public organizations have to camp on the seasaws (Hedberg, Nystrom and Starbuck, 1976).

Yet, we must also look at so-called third sector organization, as these elements would also differ in respect of the character of private organizations. Private organizations with a non-profit character are much more alike public management in internal or external structural characteristics than private organizations with the overarching profit goal.

It can be hardly be a matter of dispute that structural factors are important in distinguishing public and private organizations. What are the consequences for the management of such bodies? First and most dominant is the principle of structural design. The need for predictability and due process makes the formal design of the organization one of the important tasks that public managers have to face. Deciding on the formal structure of the bureaux or the local government bodies is a source of both predictability but also involves a risk of rigidity (Crozier, 1964; Blau, 1974; Scott, 1987).

At the same time structural design is not simple to carry through in public organizations, because it touches upon the inertia of political decision-making and may be become caught up in opportunistic strategies on the part of myopic leaders. The formal firmness of structural arrangements in the public sector sets limits to the administrative tools available to reform in the management of public organizations.

When we look at the distinction between public and private organizations in terms of their basic processes turning revenues into the provision of goods and services, there are bound to be significant dissimilarities. However, it remains to spell out what this means for management. One may point to the need for role mixes of the middle managers, but the full statement of the management consequences are important questions for further research (Figure 2).

Thus, we end up with a 2 x 2 table that summarizes the argument in this volume that public and private management tend to be different, because there are both internal and external factors that are conducive to variation. According to the standard view, both internal and external factors make public management very different to private management (Type I versus IV). However, one must look at other combinations, as public and private management are not miles apart both with regard to environmental exigencies or in relation to the organization of tasks.

CONCLUSION

Most of the contributions in this volume extend the traditional boundaries of political science, public administration and business administration. This applies to the subjects taken up, to the analytical schemes used, the data presented and to the normative conclusions with which several authors conclude their chapters. Here is a combination of functionally general and organizationally specific features, of the systems and actor approaches as well as of the internal and external dimensions. Broader environmental factors influencing public management are clearly connected with developments in a number of factors: political, social, economic and technological factors in the societies of which it is an integral part. System characteristics and role aspects comprise the use and development of management tools, just as the external and internal dimensions of public management involve inter-relationships. Working towards a 'new' conceptualization of what public management is and what it could mean for the functioning of governments in Western Europe, especially for a better functioning of government in these countries, is the aim of this volume.

Public management should not be considered as a remedy, and certainly not for all public illnesses. Public management involves both risk and opportunity, as it may be a tool for efficient resource allocation and public regulation, but there is always the risk for garbage can process. Public management is a phenomenon which has always been present in some sense at the systems and actor dimensions of public sector organizations. But it should be seen as a phenomenon with a rationale of its own. In practice we see public management functioning and public managers at work in the top and middle levels of public sector organizations, acting more or less differently from traditional civil servants, and leaders of

Figure 2   *Conditions for management differences*

		External factors	
		Public M	Private M
Internal factors	Public M	I	II
	Private M	III	IV

private organizations. Public and private management differences are expressed in matters such as the emphasis placed on the dynamic versus the static aspects of organizations in relation to their environments; furthermore, in the identification of role conceptions and in the innovation in the use and development of tools to be used in leading such organizations. Moreover, there are the crucial questions about motivation, incentives and efficiency.

We take a pragmatic view on how extensive are the differences between public and private management; similarly it is much too early to state a full-blown definition specifying exactly what public management is. This point of view is in line with other social science experiences which show that it is often more practical and fruitful to regard the arrival of a definition as something which happens at the end of a long road of conceptual searching and empirical substantiation. The same can be stated about the relation between the different perspectives used in this volume. Again for reasons of presentation, we divided the book into four parts but fortunately the authors went beyond these confines and handled their subjects more comprehensively than we had asked them or expected from them. Such distinctions as the ones needed to build a book are artificial, and should not be carried to extremes.

This second edition of the volume contains new material on Western Europe and also additional material on the American experience with public sector management.

PART 1

GOVERNING IN THE PUBLIC SECTOR

Managing public organizations concerns both the management of the public sector as a whole and the internal management of public institutions. These two levels of management are closely linked. The ambitions of politicians, the principal actors in public organizations, and their handling of external affairs, are often the factors which are responsible for the internal management problems of the public sector. At the same time, the culture, the functions, the organization and the processes of public agencies have important implications for the overall governing capacity exercised in the public sector.

It is important to analyse both types of management, the governing or steering of society at large and the leadership of managers in public agencies, in order to understand the particular characteristics and the future challenges facing the public sector. All of the chapters in this section deal with this relationship.

Hans Keman, in his chapter on *Proliferation and Organization of the Welfare State*, raises the question of the consequences of the proliferation and institutionalization of the welfare state for the contemporary public sector and its management. He focuses both on the welfare state development and the proliferation of the welfare state across nations and time. The consequences of the organization of the welfare state are also discussed in relation to the socio-economic development of the different countries. He shows that there are alternative ways for public organization and societies at large to cope with problems related to needs and welfare in capitalist democracies.

In *Public Management and Politics*, Hans-Ulrich Derlien raises the classical questions concerning the relationship between politicians and administrators and between the logic of politics and the new emphasis on managerialism in public bureaucracies. He looks at the top level problem created by the role of the politicians in contrast to the role of the administrators, and the consequences in modern bureaucracies of the managerialism of the 1980s and 1990s on recruitment patterns, role understanding and political governance of the system as such. The problems of politically controlling the public sector will by no means diminish because decentralization is colliding with the notion of ministerial accountability. At the same time, he argues, important new problems are created for both recruitment patterns and role understanding.

Guy Peters in his chapter, *Managing the Hollow State*, extends this attitude of scepticism even further by questioning whether the new economic conceptualization of government really helps to improve management. At the same time, he argues that '... it tends to substitute one narrow concept of efficiency for the more fundamental values of accountability and responsiveness that should be inherent in a democratic system'.

Jan Kooiman and Martijn van Vliet in their chapter, *Governance and Public Management*, relate the concept of public management to the problems of governing in modern societies. The West European welfare states, characterized by growing complexity, dynamism and diversity, have experienced a reduction in their capacity to govern effectively, combined with an increased need for collective problem solving. This chapter tries to develop criteria which illustrate the way in which modern public management copes with these features of contemporary societies and thus contributes to 'good governance'.

In *Economic Organization Theory and Public Management*, Jan-Erik Lane uses the concepts and theories of neo-institutionalism in order to redefine the traditional problems involved in managing the public sector. He discusses various institutionalist approaches and transaction costs and he analyses the public management problems in terms of the principal-agent relationship. Understanding the public sector requires a focus on specific interests and institutions, as well as on the role they play in the formation of strategies among the actors in state and local government. In the area of 'big government' this requires the use of neo-institutional paradigms.

2

PROLIFERATION OF THE WELFARE STATE

Comparative Profiles of Public Sector Management, 1965–90

Hans Keman*

One of the few undisputed facts of comparative research on political economy and public policy analysis is the growth of the public sector in highly-industrialized democracies. This development is by and large a result of the growth of welfare programmes (Flora and Heidenheimer, 1981; Wilensky, 1975; Castles, 1989; Kohl, 1984; Flora, 1986). Hence the 'welfare state', as the nexus between welfare programmes, its implementation and (intended) effects is commonly called, is one of the paramount features of the contemporary organization of the production and supply of public services by means of the public sector. Not only the scope and range of the goods and services rendered has grown over time, but also the number of people involved, be it as policy-makers (politicians and bureaucrats) or as policy-takers (those who are affected by or depend on welfare programs; OECD, 1985b; Esping-Andersen, 1990).

The proliferation and institutionalization of the 'welfare state' is thus an important aspect of the contemporary public sector and its management is becoming quite complex and extensive. The principal aim of this chapter is to describe by means of cross-national evidence over time to what extent and in what way the 'welfare state' has developed between 1965 and 1990 as part and parcel of the public sector. By presenting a comparative description of the public sector related to welfare provisions, it will be shown to what extent public sector management of welfare affects society in terms of allocation, distribution and regulation of its resources as well as the related societal outcomes in terms of performance.

In the first section the welfare state as a part of the public sector will be discussed conceptually and its comparative development described empirically. Subsequently, we focus on the proliferation of the welfare state, both cross-nationally and across time. I will then go on to discuss the public-private link by means of the so-called 'Extraction-Distribution Cycle' (Goldscheid and Schumpeter, 1976). Finally, the consequences of the organization and development of the welfare state related public sector are discussed with reference to the socio-economic performances of the countries under review.

THE DEVELOPMENT OF THE WELFARE STATE: CONCEPTUALIZATION AND DESCRIPTION

The scope, range and goal-orientation of the 'modern state' in 'mixed economies' is a continuing topic of debate among students of public administration and political economy (see, for example, Lane, 1985; Keman and Lehner, 1984; Peacock and Forte, 1981; Heald, 1983; Lane 1993; Castles et al., 1988). Most contributors to this debate mainly focus on the causes and consequences of the growth of the public sector in terms of expenditures only (OECD, 1985a; Kohl, 1984) and view this as the salient indicator of state intervention in a modernizing world. Questions then arise to what extent this growth of the public sector is an inevitable development (Lane and Ersson, 1990: 146), whether or not differences in the growth of public expenditures yield different societal effects (Keman, 1988), and, in what way the extension of the public sector affects economic development (Cameron, 1985; Maddison, 1982; Gough, 1979). Hence central to the study of the public sector is the relation between markets and states and thus the interaction between *politics* (i.e. organisation of collective decision-making that leads to a binding allocation of societal resources by the 'state') and *economics* (i.e. the process of re-allocating and redistributing of commodities mainly by means of exchange on the 'market'). Viewed in this way, the size and development of the public sector as well as its cross-national variations over time will tell us more about the relation between state-intervention and socio-economic development. In other words: the way the public sector is managed is a crucial variable for understanding the present interaction between politics and economics and its effects on society.

The focus of attention is on the so-called *Welfare State Sector*, i.e. those public sector activities that are intended to solve collective problems that emanate from socio-economic developments. On the one hand this concerns the production and provision of public services related to social welfare (e.g. social security benefits, education, health care, etc.). On the other hand, it involves public policies that can best be circumscribed as maintaining and enhancing economic welfare (e.g. regulation of the market-economy by means of fiscal and monetary instruments; Alt and Chrystall, 1983; Keman, 1993).

Social and economic welfare 'statism' have doubtless been one of the main factors contributing to the growth of the public sector. The very same 'statism' is often considered as a source of the uneven and unstable development of mixed economies of late (Lane, 1993). Yet, at the same time it is undeniably a necessary feature of modern society. That is to say, managing the public sector, and in particular the social and economic welfare state, should not to be discussed in terms of whether or not it is possible or desirable, but rather in terms of how much (scope), to what extent (range), and in which direction (goal) it has developed.

To this end we shall develop *profiles* of public sector activities in 18 OECD-countries, representing the variation in the mix of social and economic welfare statism for each country. They are developed not only in terms of expenditures but also in terms of revenues. For too long the study of welfare statism has hinged upon *social expenditures* alone, disregarding the *economic policy* function altogether (Alt and Chrystal, 1983; Hicks and Swank, 1984; OECD, 1985b; Keman et al. 1987; Schmidt et al., 1988; Lane and Ersson, 1990; Dunleavy, 1991). However, it is clear that managing the mixed economy implies the study of the welfare state as a *dual purpose* project. On the one hand we must examine the relationship between the supply and provision of social welfare related public services, and on the other the regulation and redistribution of economic welfare related public policies. In addition to this there is another side to managing the public sector: organising the fiscal *inputs* in relation to the redistributional *outputs* (Keman, 1988; 1993). Researching the proliferation of the welfare state without taking into account the so-called *Extraction-Distribution Cycle* of the public sector would render the analysis incomplete and insufficient to consider the effects of public management in relation to its development. This line of reasoning can be captured in the following typology of *Welfare Statism* as a form of the public management of societal welfare:

Following the conceptualization in the introduction to this book, this typology is another example of how the public sector can be operationalized. For instance cells 1 and 2 concern those public policies that reflect the way civil society contributes to financing the public economy, whereas the cells 3 and 4 indicate how social services and economic policies are distributed. The vertical dimension represents the available 'welfare mixes' in terms of inputs and outputs. These combinations have in common that they result from political choices in which various decision-makers are involved (e.g. voters, parties, and interest groups). This *external* governance is supposed to direct the public management of the welfare state and is almost exclusively expressed in the form of public policies. The inherent tension of welfare-related policy-formation is that they are not distributed at random, but are directed at certain groups and/or goals (e.g. benefits for the elderly

Figure 1 *The management of the social and economic welfare state*

Public sector	Provision of Welfare	
management	*Social Services*	*Economic Policies*
Extraction	1	2
Distribution	3	4

and unemployed, as well as toward goals like economic growth and avoiding inflation). Furthermore, the production is often organized on the basis of more or less unequal criteria (e.g. the relationship between direct and indirect taxation) and is apparent in the above typology (i.e. the cells 1–4 and 2–3). Such an inherent tension creates great problems for the management of social *and* economic welfare simultaneously, which is – inter alia – why the 'welfare state' has become such a disputed topic (Keman et al., 1987; Lane and Ersson, 1990; Esping-Andersen, 1990). The reason may be that most public programmes, in particular welfare-related ones, are hardly learning from past experiences and often slowly adjust to external changes. This means that it is quite important to understand how, why and in which way the social and economic welfare state has proliferated in capitalist democracies.

THE DEVELOPMENT OF THE WELFARE STATE: GROWTH, SIZE AND PROLIFERATION

Although the operationalization of the public sector by means of expenditures and its scope and range is problematic (see, for example, Hoogerwerf, 1977; Lane, 1993), the best indicators that we can avail ourselves of show with a certain accuracy the relative scope of state intervention. The functional distribution of public expenditures indicates fairly accurately which preferences have priority in terms of policy-formation (Flora, 1986; Whiteley, 1986: Ch. 2; Keman, 1987). In short, they reflect the growth of the welfare state.

The development of welfare statism

One can observe certain patterns of development of the public economy during this century (Rose, 1976; Kohl, 1984; Flora, 1986). In the period before the First World War not only the level of public expenditure was lower, but also the functional distribution was quite different. For example, in Germany the size of the public economy has more than tripled since 1900 when compared to the present, in France it has doubled over the same period, and in the smaller countries (Belgium, Denmark, the Netherlands, Norway and Sweden) public sector spending runs at an average of 4 to 5 times more than in 1900 (Kohl, 1984: 220–221; Flora et al., 1983). In the countries outside Europe this development has been less rapid and drastic.

During the first phase of the development of the 'modern' state (i.e. before 1914) the functional distribution of government outlays involved primarily internal and external security as well as infra-structural provisions (e.g. roads, railways and transport) which had priority over other functions.[1] The interwar period is characterized to a greater extent by

Table 1 *Historical development of the welfare state in European capitalist democracies, 1900–75*

Country	Public economy in:				Social welfare in:				Economic welfare in:			
	1900	1930	1950	1975	1900	1930	1950	1975	1900	1930	1950	1975
Austria	—	12.9	12.0	23.5	—	4.1	5.4	10.8	—	1.5	2.1	4.2
Belgium	—	23.1	19.2	33.0	—	5.4	5.2	15.8	—	2.7	3.5	6.5
Denmark	4.7	6.3	14.5	35.3	1.0	2.7	6.0	24.6	0.6	0.6	0.2	4.0
Finland	—	14.7	18.4	28.1	—	4.1	4.0	12.6	—	3.6	1.8	9.5
France	9.9	19.0	26.2	18.7	—	4.9	8.9	9.2	—	1.4	8.8	2.8
Germany	4.2	9.8	13.9	15.7	0.2	4.0	6.8	6.7	0.1	0.5	1.5	1.9
Ireland	—	14.6	22.4	37.3	—	6.2	11.1	13.8	—	2.8	6.2	9.2
Italy	13.6	19.2	21.1	27.9	0.5	2.5	5.7	9.2	2.8	2.7	5.6	7.7
Netherlands	8.6	11.6	26.4	31.3	—	3.8	4.5	17.2	1.6	2.2	4.8	3.8
Norway	5.7	7.8	16.8	24.2	1.2	2.2	7.4	9.5	1.0	1.2	3.9	6.8
Sweden	5.5	6.7	14.5	31.1	1.0	1.7	5.6	17.6	0.6	1.4	2.6	3.7
Switzerland	—	7.4	8.4	9.7	—	1.1	1.5	2.9	—	1.3	1.1	2.9
UK	9.7	15.6	26.9	34.0	0.7	5.6	10.7	15.0	0.1	0.4	3.4	3.8
Average	7.6	13.0	18.5	26.9	0.8	3.7	6.3	12.7	1.0	1.8	3.5	5.1

Note: Public economy concerns expenditures by central government since these figures are available at more points in time in most countries. All figures are expressed as % of GDP. Social welfare concerns expenditures on transfers payments, housing, education and social insurance; economic welfare concerns budgetary allocations regarding industry and commerce, agriculture, transport and communication.
Source: Flora et al., 1983: 349–490

cross-national variation and quite volatile developments. In 1930 one can observe that the larger countries (e.g. Great Britain, France and Germany) spent more on social welfare (and on warfare) than most smaller countries (Zimmermann, 1986), a situation which, with the exception of Switzerland, has been reversed since the 1960s. The development of respectively social and economic welfare also changed considerably. Before 1914 approximately the same amount was spent on these functional categories of the public economy, whereas later on the trends show a divergent trajectory, social welfare growing twice as much as economic welfare (OECD, 1985a).

Since 1945 the growth of the public economy has been tremendous and cannot be explained solely by the well-known Wagner's law or by the 'displacement' thesis alone (Whiteley, 1986: 40–42; Hoogerwerf, 1977).[2] To put it more strongly, there is little evidence that such economic explanations, which have some plausibility in the long term, are helpful for explaining the cross-national variation in public expenditure (Maddison, 1991; OECD, 1985a).

The period, starting in the mid-1960s, can be characterized as the heyday of the development of the mixed economy and welfare statism. Most of the countries under review here were halfway through a period of two decades of unprecedented economic growth at the same time social welfare programmes were developing (Maddison, 1982: 166–176; Armstrong et al., 1984: 181–198). Public sector growth was now widely viewed as both a means and a necessary consequence of economic expansion accompanied by an extension of social welfare. The state was in a position to divert resources away from the private sector and to provide welfare services that were often the result of a deliberate political choice. On the one hand, the state was able to create a range of redistributive instruments, that were intended to increase living standards that could be shared by the whole society. On the other, fiscal instruments were assigned a pivotal role in the management of the economy, aiming at sustained full employment. In addition infra-structural needs such as communication and transport were also met by the state or now seen as almost genuine public goods (e.g. railways, airports, harbours and often also airways).

The last 25 years have been characterised by an accelerated growth in the degree of government involvement in all the countries under review.[3] This overall view of the growth of the public sector not only shows its immense development, but in particular that the so-called Extraction-Distribution Cycle is becoming increasingly unbalanced over time. It implies that the state creates more and more a 'fiscal crisis' or – as Tarschys (1983) calls it – a 'scissors crisis in public finance'. As we shall see below, this scissors crisis developed in the 1970s, creating great problems for public sector management throughout the 1980s, leading to attempts to introduce new finance techniques in order to control the gap between outlays and receipts.

A major reason for this 'scissors crisis' and the related problem of controlling it has been the development of the provision of social welfare. Table 2 demonstrates that the expenditures related to the state apparatus itself (i.e. government consumption) did not grow at the same pace as the overall expenditures. Two underlying causes can be mentioned: firstly,

Table 2   *Average growth and size of the public sector between 1965 and 1990 (N=18)*

	1965	1990	1965–90
Total outlays	31.8%	47.7%	15.9%
CV	0.19	0.20	0.18
Total receipts	28.5%	39.8%	11.3%
CV	0.18	0.18	0.18
Government consumption	14.0%	18.1%	4.1%
CV	0.18	0.23	0.21
Government employment	14.9%	19.7%	4.8%
CV	0.28	0.38	0.33

Note: Instead of the Standard Deviation (S.D.), the Coefficient of Variation (CV) is used as a measure of dispersion since the range is quite high among the cases included.

the establishment of welfare *programmes* that are either linked to per capita expenditures or are a consequence of economic recession; secondly, the economic recession itself that reared its ugly head after the breakdown of the Bretton Woods system in 1971 and the steep rise in oil prices after 1973 and 1979 (Armstrong et al., 1984; Alt and Chrystal, 1983). The recession resulted in needs that destabilized the public sector economy and broke down the relationship between government revenues and disbursements in most countries. Both the actual figures in Table 2 as well as the change of CV clearly shows this development. To put it succinctly: the development of the public sector over the last 25 years is a story of a *dialectical* nature: extending the welfare state created problems of control that were the result of maintaining it whilst simultaneously attempting to adjust to 'objective' developments, such as demographic effects, international economic interdependence, as well as a growing demand for employment, e.g. of women and highly qualified young people (Wilensky, 1975; Maddison, 1982; Esping-Andersen, 1990; Cameron, 1982, 1985; Flora, 1986).

There exist several explanations concerning the growth of the public sector as well as its contradictory development since the late 1960s (OECD, 1985a, b; Taylor, 1983; Tarschys, 1975; Castles et al., 1988; Keman, 1993). Lane and Ersson (1990: 146–148) categorize these in terms of demand-side and supply-side oriented ones in which the political organization (i.e. parliamentary democracy) on the one hand, and the public sector organization (i.e. bureaucracy), on the other, of the welfare state is seen as a cause and consequence of these contradictory developments and the scissors crisis (Dunleavy, 1991). From this it appears to follow that the organizational features of the welfare state are considered to be related to the extent and way of proliferation of the public production and provision of welfare related public policies and services. In addition, as the growth of the public sector is mainly due to a pursuit of social and economic welfare, we must focus on the provision of these public policies and how they are financed. We examine this process by analyzing the developments in three separate periods which reflect by and large the change in the external economical environment that is common to all the countries under review here: 1965–1973; (first oil crisis) 1974–1981; (second oil crisis) 1982–1990.

The rise of social welfare provision

Although the rise of the public sector in most OECD-countries has prevailed, there are large differences in how much and what they provided. This can be shown by examining the development of the public expenditures in respectively health care, education and transfer payments (Table 3). Even a cursory glance makes clear that both across nations as between periods the variation is not only large but also of a different nature.

Table 3   *Expenditures on social welfare provision*

Country	Level (percentage) 1965–73	1974–81	1982–90	Change (percentage) 1965–81	1974–90
Australia	12.8	19.9	21.0	7.1	1.1
Austria	21.6	26.8	30.3	5.2	3.5
Belgium	23.0	32.4	35.6	9.4	3.2
Canada	18.0	21.8	24.8	3.8	3.0
Denmark	18.2	26.3	31.5	8.1	5.2
Finland	17.8	21.4	22.9	4.4	1.5
France	21.7	32.5	35.9	10.8	3.4
Germany	21.4	28.1	27.5	6.7	–0.6
Ireland	18.4	25.7	30.5	7.3	4.8
Italy	21.8	26.8	29.8	5.0	3.0
Japan	11.3	18.2	21.2	6.9	3.0
Netherlands	26.4	38.0	38.3	11.6	0.3
Norway	21.7	27.6	29.8	5.9	2.2
Sweden	22.2	30.8	34.1	8.6	3.3
Switzerland	15.4	23.5	25.4	8.1	1.9
UK	17.6	22.0	24.3	4.4	2.3
USA	14.8	20.2	21.7	5.4	1.5
Average	19.1	26.0	28.5	6.9	2.5
CV	0.21	0.20	0.19	0.28	0.15

Note: Figures represent the total expenditure on education, health care and transfer payments as a percentage of GDP. Change is first differences. See also Table 2.

Between 1968 and 1981 the difference between the leading nation (i.e. the Netherlands) and the one at the bottom of the distribution (i.e. Japan) is increasing, whereas afterwards the range between top and bottom decreases. Secondly, it must be observed that there is a clear distinction in terms of the growth of the social welfare state. Before the 1980s the high level social welfare states keep on growing in comparison to the others, but after this a reverse trend develops: apart from Denmark and Ireland, all countries appear to stop the upward development, with Germany even decreasing its effort on social welfare! Thus, it can be concluded that social welfare programmes have been developed everywhere at a certain level – which is different for each country, but at the same time, it can also be observed that the inherent incremental change of those programmes is transformed into a certain platform (Dierkes et al., 1987). This indicates that the supply and position of social welfare during the 1980s becomes *institutionalized* at certain levels. The social welfare state is built up during the 1960s and 1970s and develops its *national* profile during the 1980s. This observation is supported by the relations between the levels of welfare provision and change over time: between 1974 and 1981, $r = 0.73$ and between 1982 and 1990, $r = 0.25$.

The social welfare profile in most countries concerns in particular the extent to which transfer payments (to households) is an institutionalized part and parcel of it. Examining the relationships between the composite

Table 4   *The relations between social welfare and change in expenditure on education, health care and transfer payments (N=17)*

Change in:	Level of Social Welfare in:		
	1965–73	1974–81	1982–90
Education	–0.07	0.16	–0.28
Health care	0.41	0.31	–0.26
Transfer payments	0.53	0.58	–0.08

Note: Pearson Product Moment Correlations. New Zealand is missing case.

measure of social welfare and respectively health care, education and transfer payments, it appears that the level and change in education expenditures is not significantly related to social welfare expenditures. Health care expenditures are, albeit less than transfer payments. Table 4 reports the correlations between the level in social welfare and the change in public expenditures on education, health care and transfer payments:

There is no systematic relation between education and the 'social welfare state', meaning that this 'merit good' is differently organized in the countries under review. The basic difference is the fact that – contrary to health care and transfer payments – it is in many countries organized through the market rather than provided by the state, although, this does not imply that it is not regulated by the state. The provision of health care in terms of expenditure, however, is a welfare programme that can be characterized as a public service and has been subject to adjustment and cutbacks (Heidenheimer et al., 1983; OECD, 1985b; Dierkes et al., 1987).

Yet, the most striking observation is that after 1981 the supply-side explanation of public sector growth is not supported by our analysis. This may indicate that the production and provision of social welfare is sensitive to changing circumstances. It also means that – given the 'scissors crisis' – the organisation of the public sector is indeed open to adjustment and that the scope and range of the social welfare programmes can be altered notwithstanding political and societal demands (as e.g. Castles et al., 1982; Wilensky, 1975; Tarschys, 1983 believed). Rather, the conclusion must be that the development of social welfare is a curvi-linear one and that although the *levels* of provision vary cross-nationally, the *change* in the production of these programmes, both up and downward, tends to become more or less uniform across time. On the basis of our inspection of the size and developments of the public sector in OECD-countries, and in particular of the role of social welfare related programmes, it may be concluded that the management of the public sector appears to be subjected to both *internal* pressures (political and societal demands) and *external* developments (fiscal and macro-economic room for manoeuvre). In order to understand the development in the proliferation of the welfare-related public sector more fully, we must investigate the relationship between the production and provision of social and economic welfare as has been depicted in Figure 1: the Extraction-Distribution Cycle.

MAKING BOTH ENDS MEET: THE EXTRACTION-DISTRIBUTION CYCLE

The interdependent relation between fiscal extraction and re-allocation by means of policy-making was already analyzed by Rudolf Goldscheid (1917) and Joseph Schumpeter (1918). It is remarkable that in most studies of public sector development this interaction between politics and economics is not taken into account (see however: Gough, 1979; Schmidt, 1983; Cameron, 1985; Keman, 1988; Lane and Ersson, 1990). Yet, understanding the cross-national variation in levels and growth of the public sector, and in particular its most dynamic part: social welfare programmes, makes it inevitable and necessary to investigate the relations between the 'Tax State' and the 'Welfare State'. In terms of the typology described in Figure 1 it means that we focus on the relations between the cells 1 and 3, and between cells 2 and 4.

Providing social welfare: public services and income maintenance

The first relation can be labelled as the Tax-Welfare State and it examines the extent to which welfare-related public goods and services are paid for by means of *individual* contributions, either through direct taxation or by means of social security levying. In other words: the direct relationship between what the citizen contributes and what he or she may get in return is analyzed. Here public sector management can be considered as an intermediary agency that redistributes authoritatively values in a society. One could consider this type of public sector management as a collective insurance and as a service organization.

The *political* dimension is represented by the fact that policy decisions influence the level and organisation of (re-)distributive measures: for instance, on the basis of a means-tested principle, or on the basis of flat-rate contributions (Esping-Andersen, 1990; Heidenheimer et al., 1983; Peacock and Forte, 1985; Castles, 1985).

The *policy* dimension of the Tax-Welfare State is manifested in the way the public services are allocated: a difference between social welfare states which are characterized by a redistribution by means of transfer payments and those that emphasize social services (Dierkes et al., 1987; Castles et al., 1989; Keman, 1988).

In Table 5 both dimensions underlying the relation between who pays for what concerning the provision of social welfare are examined on the basis of factor analysis. On the one hand, the level of direct taxation and social security contributions (of employees and employers) are used as items, on the other hand, the provision of Social Welfare, i.e. expenditures on education, health care and transfer payments (see Table 3) is taken into

Table 5   *The Extraction-Distribution Cycle of social welfare, 1965–90*

Country	1965–73	1974–81	1982–90
Australia	−1.07	−1.19	−1.28
Austria	1.38	0.72	0.90
Belgium	0.96	0.72	0.80
Canada	−0.91	−0.63	−0.50
Denmark	−0.88	−1.09	−1.16
Finland	−0.86	−0.90	−0.98
France	2.26	1.73	1.76
Germany	1.09	0.92	0.78
Ireland	−0.24	0.01	−0.02
Italy	−0.03	0.67	0.41
Japan	−0.37	−0.51	−0.28
Netherlands	1.38	1.73	1.70
New Zealand	−1.36	−2.04	−2.07
Norway	−0.24	0.25	0.19
Sweden	−0.49	0.36	0.36
Switzerland	−0.15	−0.08	−0.12
United Kingdom	−0.19	−0.35	−0.24
USA	−0.28	−0.34	−0.23
Median	−0.24	−0.03	−0.07

Note: Based on Varimax-rotation (one factor solution) of annual data of public revenues concerning levels of direct taxation, social security contributions of employers and employees, and disbursement regarding education, health care and transfer payments to households.

The average factor loadings are:

Item:	1965–73	1974–81	1982–90
Direct taxation	−0.466	−0.555	−0.633
Social security contributions	0.815	0.840	0.809
Education	−0.366	−0.190	0.023
Health care	0.141	0.337	0.404
Transfer payment	0.875	0.876	0.857
R^2	40.3%	43.1%	46.6%

account. On the basis of the factor-loadings, the emerging 'profile' can be interpreted as follows: in countries with a positive factor-score the level of social security levying is high and strongly related tot high levels of transfer payments. A negative factor-score indicates that levels of direct taxation coincide with more emphasis on expenditures on education and health care. Hence, we can observe two types: the *Tax-Return State* (+) and the *Tax-Service State* (−). Countries that are in between and close to the median can be considered as mixed types.

This profile clearly indicates in what way and to what extent the social welfare related public sector is organized. In New Zealand and Australia for instance, social security levying is absent and transfer payments to households are means-tested. Direct taxation is thus the only source of income of the state and is mainly directed to social services and merit goods (Castles, 1985). In France and the Netherlands, the provision of social welfare is a system of redistribution based on transfer payments which is mainly financed by means of social security contributions.[4] In most other countries the Extraction-Distribution Cycle regarding the provision of social welfare is of a mixed complexion.

It should be noted that the Scandinavian countries with their reputation of being welfare states (Stephens, 1979; Korpi, 1983; Esping-Andersen, 1985; Korpi, 1983) can be typified as Tax-Service States. However, over time, this situation has changed slightly towards a Tax-Return position. Such a change can be observed in most countries, except in Australia and New Zealand. Apparently, the 'scissors crisis' due to the economic recession have forced governments to rearrange their management of social welfare production, either to the direction of the market (i.e. privately organized income maintenance), or by shifting the financial base of social welfare benefits. The latter option appears to have been chosen in many countries.

Whereas change in direct taxation remains in the same way related to the Tax-Return State, the relation between the change in social security contributions shifts from an equal share of employers and employees to the latter. The level of transfer payments becomes stronger related to the contributions by the working population (r = 0.42 for 1965–73; 0.36 for 1974–81; 0.54 for 1982–90). In other words, public sector management becomes increasingly again a *re*distributing agency rather than producing public goods and services on the basis of equity. The leading principle being a cost-benefit calculation, which is, however, paid by and large by the working population itself or is partially privatized (Esping-Andersen, 1990; Schmidt, 1989).

It seems plausible therefore to suggest that these developments are the result of political *choices* which have been influenced by economic pressures after 1974 and have led to policy *changes* concerning the role of the public sector. Let us therefore turn now to the second relationship of the Extraction-Distribution Cycle that could be deduced from Figure 1: the supply and production of Economic Welfare (cells 2 and 4).

Producing economic welfare: the size of the public sector

As the macro-economic performance in most, if not all, OECD-countries deteriorated and remained generally poor after 1973, this affected the climate of opinion concerning the role of the public sector. In particular, the conventional wisdom that governments could offset cyclical perturbations in the economy through active fiscal and monetary policy intervention was seriously questioned (Lindberg and Mayer, 1985; Keman et al., 1987). This led to a re-assessment of the extent to which, and the direction of, fiscal policy-formation. The growth of the public sector came to be seen more as an obstacle rather than an essential complement to a healthy economy. It was felt that fiscal expansion had proceeded to the point where the influence of welfare-related programmes needed to be restrained in order to control its impact on the economy (OECD, 1985a; Whiteley, 1986). Hence, the question became: how to alter the overall Extraction-Distribution Cycle of the state in such a way that an *optimal* relation could develop between revenues and expenditures. Or else: how to avoid the secular nature of deficit-spending without grossly abandoning the provision of social welfare as well as curbing the growth of public spending?

In Table 6 we have developed a 'profile' of the production of economic welfare (again by means of factor analysis). The items used are, on the one hand, outcome related, i.e. the budgetary size and its balance (deficit-spending or not), as well as its allocative branch (growth of Government Consumption and Employment). On the other hand, the profile consists of items indicating the size and proportion of its revenue base: total taxation and total contributions to social security (including contributions by the state, if any).

The results can be interpreted as follows (on the basis of the factor loadings): a *positive* score implies a large state in terms of the size of its public economy and relying on tax and social security income; a *negative* score indicates the opposite and also that in these cases the rate of deficit-spending is relatively slow. In particular, social security contributions by the state are either absent or very low in the latter category. Hence, the differences in Table 6 are caused by the size of the public sector and the extent to which social welfare programmes are financed via the state and coincides with the degree to which the budget is more or less balanced (i.e. more or less deficit-spending).

The emerging profile shows that the 'reputed' social welfare states have high positive scores notwithstanding their organizational profile in terms of a Tax-Return or a Tax-Service State, as epitomized by respectively the Netherlands and Sweden. Conversely, Australia and New Zealand, Japan and Switzerland are minimal states in terms of the level of extraction and avoiding large deficits.

The developments over time should also be noted: in a number of countries a rise in the Extraction-Distribution Cycle can be observed (Belgium, Denmark, Italy), whereas in other countries the opposite development can be seen. This is the case for example in Austria, Germany, Norway, the United Kingdom and the U.S.A. These observations indicate that the public sector can be managed effectively, i.e. contrary to what, in particular, the supply-side explanation suggests, namely that the public sector is inflexible or is only influenced by institutional sclerosis or incrementalism (Tarschys, 1975; Olson, 1982). This finding does *not* imply, however, that changes in the relationship between extraction and (re-)distribution are optimal in terms of providing social and economic welfare. Nor can we conclude that these changes will, in the end, produce a satisfactory degree of economic welfare. However, the conclusion that can be drawn from this analysis is that the size and, in particular, the growth of the public sector appears to be more *manageable* than is often assumed. This appears to have been particularly the case during the 1980s. If we correlate the profiles of the 'tax-spending' state to the change of its components, the results shown in Table 7 emerge.

These findings can be interpreted as support for the argument that the size of the public sector is not necessarily related to huge deficits or an to an unbalanced development (Cameron, 1982; Keman, 1993). On the contrary, the role and size of the public sector is apparently open to

Table 6   *The Extraction-Distribution Cycle of economic welfare, 1965–90*

Country	1965–73	1974–81	1982–90
Australia	−1.31	−1.14	−1.09
Austria	0.65	0.49	0.50
Belgium	0.46	0.70	0.81
Canada	−0.04	−0.32	−0.25
Denmark	0.54	0.84	1.05
Finland	−0.23	−0.40	−0.44
France	0.66	0.43	0.83
Germany	0.66	0.61	0.24
Ireland	−0.16	−0.04	−0.06
Italy	0.12	−0.28	0.23
Japan	−1.91	−1.60	−1.50
Netherlands	1.21	1.20	1.07
New Zealand	−1.95	−1.88	−1.85
Norway	0.81	0.95	0.56
Sweden	1.25	1.87	1.91
Switzerland	−1.38	−1.02	−1.18
United Kingdom	0.57	0.19	−0.05
USA	0.06	−0.58	−0.78
R^2	49.7%	48.0%	47.4%
Median	0.29	0.08	0.09

Note: See Table 5 for explanation.

Average factor loadings are:

Item:	1965–73	1974–81	1982–90
Public Economy	0.894	0.882	0.888
Deficit-spending	−0.097	−0.089	−0.295
Social security contributions by the state	0.659	0.715	0.623
Total taxation	0.851	0.876	0.882
R^2	49.7%	48.0%	47.4%

change in the way it is organized. In other words: the size and growth of the public sector seems to be more manageable than is often taken for granted.

On the basis of the typology (see Figure 1) we have examined the proliferation of profiles of public sector development in OECD-countries. Point of departure was the contention that such a profile should rest on the distinction between social and economic welfare on the one hand, and on the relation between extractive and distributive measures of the state, on the other. The investigation has demonstrated that there are two types of social welfare provision that are simultaneously related to the so-called Extraction-Distribution Cycle. The Tax-Return State, in which the public sector acts as an *intermediary* agency redistributing individually based extraction across society more or less in favour of those in need of income maintenance. The Tax-Service State, in which the public sector plays a more *interventionist* role transforming revenues into certain public services such as education and health care.

It is clear that the proliferation of these activities of the welfare state has grown over time everywhere, however large the differences between countries in terms of levels of provision may be from a comparative perspective. Yet, more relevant to the subject of this book is the fact that both the size and the way the public sector organizes these welfare-related activities varies cross-nationally considerable and are open to change. Hence, contrary to what is often contended, social welfare programmes and their financial implications can apparently be managed to a certain extent.

The evidence presented in this section across periods demonstrated that, in particular in times of economic recession and related changes in the climate of opinion about the role and size of the public sector as a whole, the scope and range of the welfare state changes. Hence, contrary to the views that the public sector can hardly be controlled and is characterized by incremental change, we have shown that the Extraction-Distribution Cycle is a crucial variable for a better understanding of the working and organization of the welfare state. It became clear that there are two types of organizing economic welfare: large spenders with high levels of taxation and small spenders. The former type indeed appears to be more inclined to produce unbalanced budgets and thus deficits.

Table 7 *Degree of taxing and spending in relation to the development of budgetary balance and size of public sector, 1974–90*

Change in:	1974–81	1982–90
Budget Deficits	–0.09	–0.37
Government Consumption	0.34	–0.35
Public Sector	0.50	–0.29

Note: Pearson Product Moment Correlations. N=18.

However, our analysis also showed that this is not a strong relationship and that the differences in 'welfare statism' is directly influencing the economic performance in one way or another.

PUBLIC SECTOR GROWTH AND ECONOMIC PERFORMANCE: DOES IT MATTER?

In this section we address the important and much discussed topic of to what extent the size and growth of the public sector matters regarding economic development. We shall draw on available evidence in attempting to evaluate a number of economic effects of government activities. In other words: the relation between the state and the market (Lane, 1985; Castles et al., 1988; Keman, 1993). In particular, we focus on the relation between the Extraction-Distribution Cycle and measures of economic performance indicated by rates of economic growth, inflation and unemployment. In addition we shall take into account labour market developments as this can be considered as an important indicator with regard to the management of the Extraction-Distribution Cycle in terms of both social and economic welfare.

Economic performance and welfare statism

Most of the literature concerning political economy emphasizes the relation between the size of the public sector and economic growth, inflation and unemployment (Alt and Chrystal, 1983; Whiteley, 1986; Schmidt, 1988; Lane and Ersson, 1990; Keman, 1993). An oversized public sector, particularly if it is mainly directed toward providing social welfare, is considered to be disadvantageous to the economic performance. In addition, it is suggested that tax pressure and social security levying is a burden on the market economy creating a disincentive for economic growth (Olson, 1982; Mueller, 1989 Maddison, 1991). Conversely, it is put forward that without publicly organized income maintenance programmes and other social welfare measures political consensus is not feasible, the economic climate in a country would be jeopardized, forestalling economic recovery as well as erode the tax-basis of the Extraction-Distribution Cycle (Peacock and Forte, 1985; Keman et al., 1987; Scharpf, 1987; Castles, 1989). Hence, the management of the public sector is faced with a dilemma: reducing its size and curbing its growth may enhance economic performance; yet, simultaneously, if this occurs at the cost of social welfare it could imply a loss of aggregated demand, wage demands and inflation, eroding the tax-base of the state. Let us first examine the overall relationship between the social and economic welfare state and economic performance.

The findings of Table 8 do not support the widely held belief among economists and many politicians, that the size and growth of providing welfare-related public services are almost by definition detrimental to

Table 8   *Economic Performance and Social and Economic Welfare Provisions*
(1965–90)

Extraction-Distribution	Economic performance		
	1965–73	1974–81	1982–90
Social welfare	0.13	0.15	–0.17
Economic welfare	–0.20	0.07	–0.29
Size public sector	–0.14	–0.07	–0.36

Note: See for explanation preceeding Tables. Economic performance is a composite index of the average rates of economic growth, inflation and unemployment for each period (source: OECD, 1992)

the economic performance of a country. Neither do they corroborate the argument that highly developed social welfare programmes and a large public sector are conducive to sustaining economic performance.

One lesson can be drawn from this analysis if we look back on some of the findings of the preceding section. We found that the production and provision of social and economic welfare is not a linear development nor a fixed-sum game, but that its direction and size appears to vary over time. In particular after 1981, the public sector growth related to social welfare could be arrested. It seems therefore plausible to conclude not only that the public sector is a manageable entity, but also that the relation between the production and provision of public goods and services in terms of high-powered welfare statism is not necessarily jeopardizing the working and viability of the market economy.

Yet, at the same time, it should be noted that the cross-national differences in economic performance are considerable. For instance, Canada, Ireland, Italy and the United Kingdom have consistently bad records, whereas some other countries such as Austria, Germany, Japan, Norway and Switzerland show an above average record of economic performance. In other words: the relationship between the extent of state-intervention and economic performance is not a linear one, nor a fixed relation. It may be useful therefore to look more closely at the functioning of the labour market. For here the goals of the public sector in terms of social and economic welfare are highly intertwined: on the one hand it is provided to produce economic welfare (i.e. more employment) and on the other to reduce the need for supplying social welfare benefits (i.e. less unemployment).

Labour market performance and the Extraction-Distribution Cycle

The question is whether or not the differences in economic performance in relation to the public sector also affect the labour market performance of a country. If this is the case, than a tax-welfare backlash can be expected: the lower the proportion of the economically active labour population, the less revenues will be yielded and the more social welfare-related disbursements will be necessary (Castles et al., 1988; Esping-Andersen, 1990): a vicious circle could very well develop.

The first category (EDC) demonstrates the working of the vicious circle (see Table 9): when the economic going is good, that is before 1974, the relation between labour market performance and the welfare state is harmless, albeit that the production of social an economic welfare is apparently associated with growing budget deficits.

Since the breakdown of the existing international money system (Bretton Woods) and the rise of the price of oil, a negative relationship develops between the welfare-related part of the public sector and the functioning of labour markets. If it is performing well, this is at the cost of welfare provision, or if the level of welfare is maintained, it negatively affects a proper working of the labour market. Either way, the Extraction-Distribution Cycle is off balance, which completes the vicious circle.

As Manfred Schmidt (1988) showed in his analysis of the politics of labour market policy there are two roads to Full Employment: a conservative one (restrictive state) and an Keynesian one (state interventionism). The difference is the political choice between regulation through the market or by the state.

If the market forces are considered to be the main agents for steering the economy this implies a 'small' state in terms of the size of the public sector, in particular in terms of income maintenance programmes (see the preceding section). Examples that illustrate this point include Australia, Japan, New Zealand and Switzerland. If the state is the chief agent and organizes its attempts to improve the economic and labour market

Table 9   *Relations between labour market performance and the tax and welfare Extraction-Distribution Cycles*

| | Labour market Performance | | |
	1965–73	1974–81	1982–90
1. EDC:			
Social welfare	0.25	–0.38	–0.40
Economic welfare	0.24	–0.51	–0.42
Budget deficit	0.25	0.30	0.59
2. Expenditures			
Transfer payment	0.29	–0.46	–0.53
Government outlays	–0.40	0.26	–0.45
3. Revenues:			
Social security	0.54	0.11	0.20
Taxation	0.40	–0.48	0.40

Note: Labour market performance is a composite index of the average rates in the growth of employment, government employment and rate of unemployment as a % of the economically active population (OECD, 1992).

Figure 2a *The Extraction-Distribution Cycle of economic welfare in relation to labour market performance, 1982–90 (based on Tables 6 and 9)*

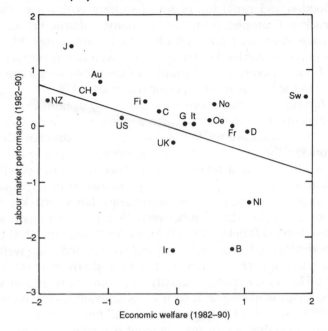

Figure 2b *The Extraction-Distribution Cycle of social welfare in relation to labour market performance, 1982–90 (based on Tables 5 and 9)*

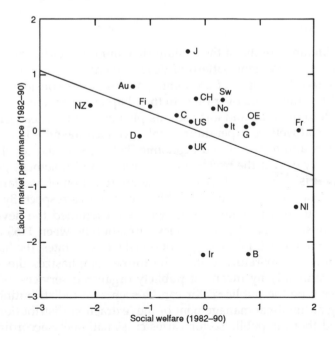

performance through the public sector, it appears that those countries characterized as a 'Tax Service State' (see Table 5) are able to combine the production and provision of social welfare with a well-performing labour market. Examples comprise Germany, Austria, France and Sweden. Welfare states that are typically 'Tax Return States' like Belgium, Ireland and the Netherlands, clearly do less well in this respect. In Figure 3 the relations between the two profiles of the public sector are presented in relation to the labour market performance after 1981.

These figures show that there are indeed two options in times of economic adversity in order to produce a positive labour market performance. Both options are related to the way the Extraction-Distribution Cycle works: either the public sector is managed on a small scale and directed towards limited services, or it concerns countries with a large scale public sector which is by and large managed in terms of services (like job-qualifying education and stimulating labour market access). In most other cases, i.e. those in-between 'fiscal restrictivism' and 'state interventionism', (Whiteley, 1986; Scharpf, 1987; Keman, 1988) the labour market performance has deteriorated and has created a tax-welfare backlash either through tax-erosion or due to a sharp increase in transfer payments. Hence, it appears crucially important how and in what way the public sector is managed. It seems less relevant to discuss whether or not the public sector is too large or too small, but more important to ask whether or not public sector management is effective in solving societal problems such as an economic recession and meeting the needs that are caused by this.

CONCLUSION

The proliferation of the of the welfare state in highly industrialized countries shows a divergent pattern of development. The provision of social services and the supply of economic policies varies considerably across the OECD-nations and over time. In this chapter we have used a different approach to describe and analyse this phenomenon. Instead of focusing on the social welfare expenditures only, we have taken into account the way states aim at social and economic welfare simultaneously as well as how they extract the necessary fiscal means to implement policies. In this way it is possible to investigate the organization of 'welfare statism' and in particular the role of the public sector in this respect. By means of the 'Extraction-Distribution Cycle' we have examined the development of welfare state related public policy formation between 1965 and 1990. We found that there are two types of social welfare states: the 'tax-service state' and the 'tax-return state'. The former emphasizes the provision of welfare mainly by means of publicly organized services, whereas in the latter type the public sector can be seen as a redistributing agency. Looking at the fiscal management of the 'extraction-distribution cycle' it appeared that the public sector varies cross-nationally according to size and its sources of income. Big spending states rely on taxation and social security levying, whereas small spending states tend to rely more on taxes as a means of extraction.

Contrary to widespread ideas that both the development of the welfare state and the growth of the public sector are difficult to control let alone to change we did not find evidence to sustain this argument. Neither did we find conclusive evidence for the contention that the size and organization of the public sector is indeed hazardous to economic development. On the contrary, the analysis of the public sector by focusing on the 'extraction-distribution cycle' rather demonstrated that its development and growth can apparently be influenced and is not necessarily jeopardizing economic performance. At the same time it must be concluded that the way the public sector is organized does matter with respect to labour market performance. Hence, it makes sense to analyze the public sector from the viewpoint employed in this chapter since, it sheds light on the alternative ways of how to cope with societal problems related to needs and welfare in capitalist democracies.

Notes

* I am grateful for the assistance of Jaap Woldendorp and the useful comments of Jan-Erik Lane whilst preparing this chapter.
1 It should be emphasized that the figures presented in Table 1 are only *illustrations* of the development of the public economy. The categories used are rather crude indicators and particularly because of differences of definition, cross-national comparisons across countries *and* time remain hazardous.
2 Wagner's law contends that there is a positive relation between the growth rate of National Income and public economy; the 'displacement' thesis (cf. Peacock and Wiseman, 1961) holds that external shocks (e.g. wars) cause an increase in public spending which is not decreased later on. See for this: Kohl, 1984: 26–46.
3 i.e. Australia, Austria, Belgium, Canada, Denmark, Finland, France, Germany, Ireland, Italy, Japan, the Netherlands, New Zealand, Norway, Sweden, Switzerland, the United Kingdom, and the United States; N = 18. It should be noted that all the data reported in this chapter are based on OECD-statistics and have been collected on an annual basis from which the computations and transformations have been derived. In this way the composite indicators used are reliable both across nations and time.
4 In France completely financed by employees and employers, which explains its extreme position in Table 5.

3

PUBLIC MANAGEMENT AND POLITICS

Hans-Ulrich Derlien

Central government personnel usually await the advent of a new minister with curiosity as to how long it will take them to educate the minister to lead the bureaucracy and to accept departmental policy views. When dealing with the relationship between public management and politics one is immediately caught up in the intricacies of political theory, constitutional traditions and orthodox administrative science views, which customarily treat the problem under consideration in the framework of the institutional politics-administration dichotomy. Although most administrative scientists today might agree that this classical framework is a descriptively misleading conception of two separate realms of politics and administration, we can hardly abandon the dichotomy for theoretical reasons, as we might run into difficulties when trying to draw organization charts with horizontal lines to indicate hierarchical relationships or having top executives sit on the ground floor of their office building and the clerks on the top.

In this chapter I shall take as a first vantage point the traditional conceptualization of the politics-administration dichotomy relating to Max Weber, using it to analyse empirically some aspects of the complicated functional relationship between top administrators and executive politicians and the predominance of rather classical or political, even managerialist role understanding. First, it is useful to draw attention to the historical differentiation of the polity that brought about the institutional separation of powers and led to the emergence of a distinct politician and a *classical* administrator role, often under pre-democratic regimes. Second, in a functional analysis, the implicit means-end and facts-values dichotomy will be confronted with empirical findings revealing the degree of objective involvement of top administrators in the democratic political process, thus suggesting a rather *political* role understanding. Subsequently, I shall deal with a widespread development induced by politicians since the 1970s: party politicisation, interpreted as a mechanisms for politically controlling bureaucracy. Finally I shall discuss if the managerialist revolution in some countries in the 1980s has once again affected the role understanding of top administrators, and if so whether a *managerialist* role understanding is helpful in solving the perennial political control problem or rather tends to disguise it.

POLITY DIFFERENTIATION AND THE EMERGENCE OF
THE CLASSICAL ROLE UNDERSTANDING

The politics-administration dichotomy is intellectually rooted in the doctrine of separation of powers as a system of political checks and balances, in which the executive branch draws its legitimacy from Parliament. It is not merely a normative theory which has a strong bearing on most civil service codes and in particular implies that the neutral execution of written law should guide administrative decision-making. But it also reflects the change undergone by most Western political systems during the last two centuries: the coming into existence of Parliaments and political parties, organized interest groups and mass media. The absolutist state on the continent was transformed and the polity differentiated into various subsystems, among which bureaucracy remained as but one, albeit important, power centre exposed to an increasing number of conflicting interests and rivalling expectations.

The absolutist bureaucracy, for instance in Prussia, was occasionally far from being merely the obedient servant of the king's 'personal regime' but was itself rather an agglomeration of conflicting provincial and societal interests. With the advent of constitutional monarchy, even more within republican states and competitive party systems, the relationship between 'political master and staff for domination', to put it in Max Weber's terms, became more complicated. Whereas under absolutist rule top administrators were often politicians and ministers juridically civil servants, roles became formally differentiated as (at least prime) ministers were elected and supported by a parliamentary majority and stayed in office for a limited number of years. The by then tenured, professionally trained, appointed and salaried full-time civil servant who went through a career to the top of the administrative hierarchy, faced the elected party politician and transitory amateur as his political master, who after the introduction of equal suffrage sometimes came from the working-class. The ministerial bureaucracy, predominantly recruited from the nobility and still monarchist in orientation, as in Germany after 1919, adhered to the classical role model of neutral execution of the law, particularly when they saw themselves serving 'the state' and mediating partial interests as wardens of the commonweal.

On the other hand, both groups of politico-administrative actors have become assimilated, since politicians, as Max Weber had already observed, increasingly tended rather to 'live from politics than to live for politics'. Despite this professionalization of politicians, the career path of both elite groups remained quite distinct with a predictable career and job security in the one case and more 'entrepreneurial', competitive, uncertain political careers and transitory maintenance of top positions in the case of politicians.

There are, though, marked national differences in the degree to which there is horizontal career mobility between the realms and arenas of politics and administration, depending basically on the institutional safeguards developed to secure the neutrality of the civil service. Whereas some countries practise total ineligibility and even non-affiliation with political parties as a norm (Great Britain and the United States), others allow public servants to become members of political parties as their civil right and even to run election campaigns while formally in office (e.g. in Germany and France). However, these different recruitment patterns for political positions do not necessarily have a direct influence on a classical versus a more political role understanding of top administrators if these continue to be recruited from the career service. For, where bureaucracy, like in central Europe, is historically older than democracy (and not the other way round like in the US), there is still a strong tendency to emphasize expertise bread in a career civil service over political responsiveness.

Obviously, there exists a goal conflict between preserving neutrality, non-partisanship (historically: incorruptibility) and expertise in particular with respect to executive agencies, and, on the other hand, securing the political responsiveness of the ministerial bureaucracy to leading politicians. This is at the roots of party politicisation of personnel policy I am going to deal with below. Also, to the extent the notion of linkage rather than separation of powers applies better in systems of parliamentary government, the actual threshold between politics and administration is located somewhere below the top executive position; the exact borderline, again, depends on the extent to which political criteria may be or actually are applied in staffing these positions.

TOP ADMINISTRATORS AND POLITICIANS IN THE POLICY PROCESS

What in an institutional perspective means the separation of powers or – more generally speaking – differentiation of the polity, in an organizational perspective it implies the emergence of at least two distinct types of positions and actors. Weber (1919) in particular pointed out that politicians act in public and in Parliament as their arena, while administrators stay in offices and on boards; that politicians' medium is voice, whereas bureaucrats rely on the written word and records; that politicians' imperative is the fight for power as opposed to the obedience of disciplined officials working 'sine ira et studio'. Furthermore, Weber regarded the typical politician as an actor who tries to persuade and to convince people, with passion and occasionally with charisma; the administrator, on the other hand, was supposed to argue, to be a scientifically trained problem-solver opposed to the preference changer; and s/he – in principle – would play this role impassionately and impersonally.[1]

Clearly, these characteristics refer to the policy process and to the functioning of both groups of actors in politics. Rather than the original Weberian theory of political domination, organization sociologists have emphasized an additional implication: politicians are regarded as the goal-setters, while administrators are supposed to select adequate means to achieve those goals and to implement political visions. In other words: politicians cope with what may be called *normative complexity*, while the function of civil servants can be seen as reducing *factual uncertainty* by relying on routines and applying professional expertise stored in the records. In this view only politicians are in a position to bring about *substantive rationality*, whereas civil servants produce at best *formal rationality*.

The means-ends and facts-value dichotomies are, however, logical distinctions highly inappropriate for conceptualizing the interaction between politician and administrator. They reflect the logic of legitimating administrative decisions rather than depicting the legitimating process. Nevertheless, this does not exclude that administrators perceive themselves in these terms. Together with the policy-administration distinction and the facts-value dichotomy the means-end distinction is obviously at the core of the classical role understanding.[2] In its reference to the decision-making paradigm, it can serve us, however, also as a starting point from which to shed some light on the mutual functioning of political and administrative actors in the decision process, irrespective of self-perception and beyond those characteristics Weber had regarded as typical.

A good deal of what a ministry does – apart from policy implementation and control of the implementation process – is devising new policies and programmes, which often have to be legislated. Given that these new policies are innovative, that they are incremental or pre-programmed by previous decisions, the initiatives for dealing with a problem, defining it and devising (alternative) ways to solve it, often originate in the operative sections at the bottom of the ministerial hierarchy. Of course, to a certain degree, the decision-making process is fuelled by problems and policy proposals from party and election programmes; but already government declarations are regularly a *mixtum compositum* of political initiatives and bureaucratic suggestions. In any case, political initiatives from above and bureaucratic proposals from the bottom have to be mediated into the operating units and on to the political layer, respectively. Gearing each side to the other is basically the function of the two top administrative levels in the hierarchy. For top administrators this means either to operationalize policy goals, to specify the basically normative decision premises, and to anticipate constraints as well as political feasibility, or to filter initiatives from below through perceived or anticipated decision premises of the minister. Even routine matters, which normally would not involve the minister but are decided by officials, have to be evaluated with respect to potential political repercussions.

Matching political preferences and administrative professional and procedural expertness requires vertical communication. Contrary to the classical mechanistic model of hierarchical top-down decision-making and bottom-up reporting, the process of adjusting normative and factual decision premises is a dynamic, iterating process (Mayntz and Scharpf, 1975: 100). In addition, it is highly selective, as the intensity of vertical communication varies with each stage in the process and with issue salience. While entire divisions in a ministry may work on 'auto-pilot' (Rose, 1985: 3), there are always issues that attract particular political attention, that is those for which the minister is held accountable, with which he identifies, and through which he wants to become renowned as a competent policy-maker. In these instances the intensity of communication between division heads and minister will increase.

Not only are top civil servants more involved in internal vertical communication, but the frequency of external contacts with other ministries, including the office of the head of government, to parliamentary bodies, interest group representatives and press relations, increases the higher the rank of the civil servant (Aberbach et al., 1981: 209 ff). The arena of policy-making changes, too, as we move up the hierarchy: whereas the operative units basically communicate with sections in other departments or with subordinate authorities and exchange information, top administrators are more likely to be engaged in parliamentary or cabinet committees (often accompanied by section heads to assist them) or – depending on the political culture – occasionally to appear in public; even more so does, of course, the politician. A German minister often spends only one-third of his working hours in his department (Wagener, 1971: 6). While his function is predominantly representing and 'selling' departmental policy in order to reach a consensus and secure party support as his most important political resource, the top civil servant is rather involved in resolving conflicts, which are engendered in lower-level internal and external communications. The mechanism to shift controversial matters up the hierarchy, which is well known from the process of settling budgetary disputes, also shifts power upwards. So far the decision patterns follow the management-by-exception model. As the typical form of conflict resolution, bargaining implies changing the political preference structure. Thus, this power shift mechanism (Downs, 1967) serves politically to control lower-level co-ordination and transports consensus building on to hierarchical levels, which are normally more informed about the politician's willingness and limitations to compromise, and are better legitimized to bargain.

Only the most essential matters then are referred to the minister for decision, whereas issues of minor political importance are accomplished by top administrators. This function of filtering the vertical flow of information presupposes that top administrators have developed the sensitivity to recognize what might be of political importance and should be reported to the political top.

There is, however, not merely a gradual, but also a qualitative difference between top administrators and politicians when it comes to managing a department with respect to organizing, staffing and budgeting. Not taking into account those ministries which are functionally specialized within government to deal with budgeting (Finance, Treasury) or staffing (Civil Service Department) as their professional policy field, management tasks within a department are to fulfil subsidiary functions for policy development and long-term maintenance functions for the effectiveness of the apparatus, independent of specific governments and their policies. It might be a generalization to say that politicians are involved in management functions merely in cases which again are defined as exceptional (setting overall budgetary priorities or bargaining a percentage of budget cut-backs with the finance minister) or which formally have to be authorized (major reorganizations). Of course, there are differences between ministers with respect to their management capabilities and interests, but in general the initiatives originate in the department and proposals are elaborated in close contact with the top civil servant before a minister is informed or gets involved.

It is, one could say, the privilege of the permanent top administrator as opposed to the parliamentary secretary of state or the minister, to control management decisions implying the maintenance of administrative resources. Only to the extent that these questions have an important bearing on substantive policy matters is the minister asked for a decision or takes an active stand in them, although it is questionable whether politicians care about organizational matters for more than symbolic reasons (March and Olson, 1983). Complementary, it is rather the top administrator who considers the resource implications of substantive policy issues. Undoubtedly, though, politicians are seriously concerned with the appointment of their closest collaborators, the top administrators.

The importance of management decisions in shaping the role of the top administrator does not mean that such administrators are preoccupied with management problems; their involvement in policy development is regularly too time-consuming to specialize solely in the 'administration of administration'.

This so far stylized picture is more complicated in reality, taking into account that often there can be more top actors involved in the running of a department. Owing to the increasing number of public tasks and the expansion of central government departments in most European countries, the number not only of top administrative but also of political positions has grown. Some German departments acquired additional secretaries of state in the late 1960s, and in Britain deputy secretaries of state were introduced. Furthermore, staff units occasionally fulfil important co-ordinating functions instead of top line administrators, most prominently so in Belgium and in France (Thuillier, 1982).

When staff units take over co-ordinating functions or more top political positions are installed, departmental management tends to deviate from the classical monocratic model. The function of, say, a German secretary of state as departmental co-ordinator might change into that of a super-division head, occasionally even allowing the parliamentary secretary of state to concentrate on management functions in the narrow sense (Mayntz and Scharpf, 1975: 86). As the relationships at the top of a ministry are seldom formalized and co-operation to a great extent depends on the personalities of the actors, formally monocratic political authority can in fact be transformed into colleagual modes of leadership. When the configurations become more complex, formal positional differences are blurred and the qualification of actors as rather political or bureaucratic is even more difficult in terms of their empirical function in the policy process.

Whatever the actual configuration, top civil servants have a broader range of political discretion than would have been attributed to them in the classical notion (Mayntz, 1984a; b). Empirical evidence available also from opinion surveys among the administrative elite shows that the ministerial bureaucracy in toto and the role of the top administrator are functionally political. Although the majority of the administrative elite in Bonn, in 1987 as well as 17 years before, perceive their role as rather distinct from that of politicians, the majority in 1987 liked the inevitable political aspects of their job very much (78.5 per cent), as opposed to only 45.2 in 1970 (Mayntz and Derlien, 1989: 394). This political role understanding coincides with tolerance for politics and a low level of technocratic thinking (Aberbach et al., 1990).

POLITICAL CONTROL BY PERSONNEL POLICY

Is the high compatibility of subjective role understanding of top administrators and (parliamentary) politicians brought about by their operating in a functionally politicized context? Is political role understanding, so to speak, automatically produced once ideologies and myths have become unbearable? Presupposing such an automatism, which would result in pre-stabilized harmony of both sets of actors, could lead us to underestimate the problem of politically controlling a huge bureaucratic apparatus like a government department and preventing it from emancipating itself from its political master. Even when excluding from our consideration cases of bureaucratic disloyalty or sabotage, information leaks and withholding information from a minister, the political responsibility of a minister today cannot be fully exerted, as the complexity of tasks and openness of decision-making prevent him from knowing everything that goes on in his department. The law of requisite variety limits his attention and information-processing capacity vis-à-vis an apparatus of overwhelming expertise, renders political control necessarily selective, and enables the bureaucracy to become politically self-controlling, as Max Weber had already observed. The politician, therefore, will tend to broaden his control capacity.

One way to do this is to build up staff units; the French *cabinets ministeriels* are the prototype for a structural solution to increase political control capacity. However, they have resulted in an impairment of the top executive's line authority. In most European countries and the United States, furthermore, the staff solution can rather be observed on the level of the chief of government in order to secure inter-departmental co-ordination (Rose and Suleiman, 1980).

Another solution observable in a number of countries consists of super-imposing more genuine politicians on to a closed civil service career system with immobility of top executives. The politically neutralized, although not apolitical, Whitehall bureaucracy then might function quite smoothly, because there is a great number of MP's appointed to political executive positions; certainly, the sixty sub-cabinet positions and thirty-six unpaid parliamentary private secretaries also serve a patronage function for the parliamentary faction (Rose, 1980: 6), but they do enable ministers to delegate external relations and to broaden the internal political control capacity. Increasing the number of political appointees in the executive branch may, however, create co-ordination problems as well as problems of balancing the division of labour in departmental management mentioned earlier.

A functional alternative as well as an additional device to enhance the control capacity of ministers over their bureaucratic staff is the selective promotion of political trustees within the civil service career system. Be it in staffing the ministerial cabinet, or in appointing top line administrators, ministers all over the world try to select those candidates whom they regard as valuable collaborators in the policy process, because they supposedly share normative convictions with the minister. This congeniality reduces the need to communicate normative political decision premises and allows the politician to rely on the candidate's political self-control. Selective, politically motivated promotion is possible even in a closed career system, as the post-1979 change in personnel policy in Whitehall indicates (Ridley, 1985; Rose, 1988). The widest range of politically motivated staffing is notorious in the American spoils system (Heclo, 1977; Fesler, 1983; Mackenzie, 1987) where political appointees as well as the senior executive service can be removed from office and new trustees appointed to vacancies from within and without the career service.

Countries like France and Germany know merely the 'political civil servants', who can be temporarily retired, an institution that is particularly made use of after changes in government (Derlien, 1984; 1988). Here vacancies are predominantly, though not exclusively, filled with insiders. Of course, with public employees instead of tenured civil servants (as is partly the case with the personnel in French cabinets) it is even easier to purge important positions. The most modest form of gearing top career civil servants to the political requirements of the day is to reshuffle them and bring those looked at with disgrace into politically less sensitive positions. If reshuffling is not possible because of strict immobility, new

positions might be established and filled with trustees in order to circum-
vent or control mistrusted office-holders.

These are not only the basic mechanisms for practically substituting
communicated political decision premises by socialized convictions; in
my view they also contribute to an explanation of why top administrators on average fit into a functionally politicized environment and
exhibit a role understanding which is, notwithstanding recognition of
basic functional difference, compatible and partly congruent with that
of politicians. The wide range of informal devices available for political
control by personnel policy could also help to explain why there are
hardly any national differences in the subjective role understanding of
top civil servants despite different formal prescriptions for recruitment
into top administrative positions (Putnam, 1973; Aberbach et al. 1981).
But it is also arguable that strong involvement of civil servants in the
democratic policy process, i.e. *functional politicisation*[3] per se furthers a
political role understanding irrespective of party patronage.

Pointing out the functional relationship between party politicisation
and the development of a political role understanding, must though not
lead us to overlook the potential negative long-term systemic impact
of universal increasing party patronage on recruitment, motivation and
expertise of a career civil service.[4]

POLITICAL CONTROL, MANAGEMENT TECHNIQUES AND MANAGERIALISM

Having elaborated the political environment of top administrators, their
functional involvement in the policy process, their concomitantly accepting a more or less political role understanding, and various mechanisms
of personnel policy which to a certain extent might have brought about
a fit between these elements, we return to systemic questions. From a
functionalist point of view, we can clearly observe a high degree of
interpenetration of the legislative and the executive subsystems of the
polity (Mayntz, 1983). The more politicians hold functions in both of the
systems, the more top administrators subjectively and objectively share
segments of their role with that of their minister, the more they engage
in political parties, gain parliamentary mandates and are appointed as
top administrators because of these very properties, the more politics
and ministerial bureaucracy (formerly differentiated systems socially and
career-wise) become de-differentiated. At least, the borderline between
the two systems has shifted deeper, downwards into the executive
branch. To the extent that party membership over-rides expertise as
the decisive criterion for recruitment into top administrative positions,
one could even state a regression of the system towards neo-feudalism
akin to its eighteenth-century state, when ascribed properties like social
class or family bonds were dominant recruitment criteria.

On the other hand, it is arguable that the systems are still being kept separate, as political and administrative careers are distinct and inter-sectoral mobility is low or one-sided, as long as (junior and lower) civil servants enter politics. What may have appeared as de-differentiation or regression, then, could also be interpreted as a state of the system, in which internal complexity has been increased by mutually incorpo-rating elements of the other system in order to cope with the increased complexity of the administrative and political environment, respectively. Functional role differentiation within Parliament (bureaucratic skills and positions) and within administration (political roles and skills) require yet more complex forms of information processing.

It is within this context together with the general trend of expanding state activities that the various attempts to improve the manageability of the executive branch since the late 1960s are rooted and can be understood. Integrated planning and budgeting systems of the PPBS type, cost-benefit analyses, and programme evaluation were meant to rationalize policy and policy-making in order to replace traditional piece-meal engineering, incrementalism and adhocracy by goal-oriented, comprehensive and long-range planning. Management by objectives, performance appraisal, payment schemes and new recruitment and staffing procedures have been brought about by civil service reforms aimed at increasing productivity in government. These reforms (Caiden and Siedentopf, 1982), however, often failed, were implemented half-heartedly or later reduced, leaving the traditional system basically as it was before – except for the increased number of staff positions as well as analytical specialists in these positions. Among the multiple reasons for the failure of most reform attempts, two are of theoretical significance here. Planning systems, which follow the logic of decision-making and aim at comprehensiveness, were bound to fail within a turbulent political environment creating contradictory and unstable normative preferences incompatible with established executive plans. Secondly, organizational models and instruments for personnel policy as well as decision tools were often borrowed from business administration and followed the logic of hierarchical, closed decision-making inappropriate to the open system of politics and the cognitive uncertainties and fragmented powers operating there. There-fore, the hope of coping with the problem of politically controlling the ministerial bureaucracy by introducing management techniques and by moulding the role of the top administrators towards the model of the manager in private industry was shattered. Top administrators remained 'reduced' politicians, and these management techniques, as far as they were perpetuated, were carried out by people in staff units. The dilemma still is that, on the one hand, they strengthen the control capacity of the top vis-à-vis the apparatus, and on the other hand the control problem is duplicated, although to a lesser degree, in the ancient question of who is to control the controllers.

Nevertheless, in the 1980s civil service reforms were launched and car-ried through, which in some countries were part of the broader strategy of 'rolling back the frontiers of the state' by emphasizing economizing the public sector, decentralization and privatisation – in other words: reducing complexity. This new *'managerialism'* (Aucoin, 1988; Hood et al., 1988) is controversial not only for the privatisation aspect but also for its potential unforeseen consequences exactly for the relationship between bureaucracy and polity. In particular, questions of role definition (budgetary responsibility and political accountability) in a more decentralized structure are raised. Of utmost practical concern seem to be also payment questions and the declining attractiveness of the civil service in Britain (Rose, 1988) and even in France (Rouban, 1989; Montricher, 1991), as it had been in the US since the introduction of merit pay and with increasing politicisation (Levine, 1988).

Leaving the higher civil service for an economic career is more likely today owing to the managerialist role model and to relative pay deficiencies, where the social status of the civil service is losing its former exclusiveness. Motivational reactions of civil servants toward a changing working climate and impaired civil service morale as results of these policies seem to be inevitable (Peters, 1991). Although it is not exactly clear what is rhetoric of civil service policy and initial reception in the service and what its lasting effects on the basic features of the system are, it appears that those top administrators who were involved in implementing privatisation and QUANGOization policies did so adopting a managerial role model to meet deadlines, targets and market conditions. Yet, this particular emphasis did not necessarily imply the emergence of a 'third kind' of role understanding, for these policies had to be devised and implemented in an environment politicized as ever.[5] That managerialism in the ministerial bureaucracies could be a temporal phenomenon, would explain why, according to recent reports,[6] things have less dramatically changed than initially expected.

However, the introduction of performance pay systems based on individual contracts with top administrators in particular in large public enterprises in most European countries is an indication of changing career patterns; recruitment of private managers and transfer of public managers into private – and preferably recently privatized – enterprises becomes more likely and could fundamentally change role understanding – less so on the classical-political dimension, but rather on the so far unquestioned dimension of public versus private orientation of top administrators. Most importantly, though, the problems of politically controlling the public sector will by no means diminish; decentralization is colliding with the notion of ministerial accountability, and individual performance contracts pose the well-known problems of performance measurement (Laegrid, 1993). The experience with management techniques in the 1970s should be reason enough to be prepared for instrumental failures. Like the previous reforms engendered lasting structural effects, the recent managerialist experiments could have unforeseen consequences as well in altering recruitment patterns and role understanding.

Notes

1 Max Weber in 1917 opposed the recruitment of ministers from the ranks of bureaucracy (Beamtenherrschaft) and in that took a stance totally different from what Woodrow Wilson intended for the USA at about the same time: to secure the emerging professional bureaucracy independence vis-à-vis the democratic spoils system.

2 This corresponds to 'images' 1 and 2 in Aberbach et al. (1981: 4–9), while their other two 'images' derive functions in the policy process. Aberbach and Rockman (1988), in revisiting the 'pure hybrid' (image 4) emphasize that they conceptualized this type also with a view at atypical recruitment and staffing of novel positions. It should be noted that Putnam (1973) developed his juxtaposition of classical and political bureaucrats from attitudinal measures of tolerance for politics, programmatic commitment and elitism. Therefore, as a methodological consequence in this ongoing debate one should carefully distinguish the levels of self-perception and attitudinal orientations from functional descriptions and objective recruitment patterns.

3 See, for the distinction between party and functional politicization as well as a subjectively political role understanding, Renate Mayntz and Hans-Ulrich Derlien (1989).

4 However, it is advisible to distinguish between facts and fables of the phenomenon (Derlien, 1985; Stahlberg, 1987).

5 Indicatively, despite some emphasis on privatisation in Germany, a managerial accentuation of administrative role understanding similar to that in the Commonwealth countries was not observed (Derlien 1991).

6 As to the UK, Fry (1988) stated a good deal of stability despite the Thatcher reforms and Wilson (1991) envisages a return to the pre-Thatcher civil service likely.

4

MANAGING THE HOLLOW STATE

B. Guy Peters

Beginning in the mid-1970s and continuing through the 1980s and into the early 1990s governments in the industrialized democracies have brought about tremendous changes in their own state structures and in the relationship between the State and society. In the United States and the United Kingdom we refer to the 'Reagan revolution' and the 'Thatcher Revolution', but the changes have been no less profound in other countries. These have included countries such as France and Sweden with very large and well-respected public bureaucracies. In other countries such as New Zealand the reforms have been even more extensive and have altered fundamentally the nature of the public sector (Boston, Martin, Pallot and Walsh, 1991). While these changes in the nature of government are well-known and well-documented (Olsen, 1991; Bodiguel and Rouban, 1991; Jones, 1988), their implications for the implementation and management of the public sector have not been explored adequately, especially in comparative context. To the extent that the implications have been discussed it has been primarily in the context of the 'new managerialism' but the changes really extend much more deeply into the process of governing and the manner in which the State relates to society.

This chapter will be a step in the direction of more fully ramifying the nature of the changes, using the phrase 'the hollow state' to capture the changes that have occurred. The paper will attempt to look at what has been happening in government, as well as at the implications for the future of the State, and for 'statecraft' (Malloy, 1993) in contemporary democracies . That statecraft, by which the policy initiatives of government are linked to the lives of citizens must continue to be a central element in the design of governments, but often has been ignored in the rush to reach fashionable political goals. If government is to continue to be a positive force in the future, then that craft must be fostered and mobilized rather than ignored with contempt.

THE HOLLOW STATE

As we will employ the term 'Hollow State', it can have three meanings, each representing different levels of power and State influence, and different degrees of connection to quotidian issues of policy and management. It is important to consider and understand all three meanings of the term, because rushing in to cope with problems created by one interpretation may mask or even exacerbate problems associated with the others. Indeed, although the changes identified have been occurring contemporaneously in most countries, they are not the same, and must be conceptualized differentially if appropriate advice is to be given to State officials. Similarly, different countries may experience change along one dimension while the other two continue very much as they have in the past, perhaps changing at later date if ever. Like most revolutions, this one affects different countries and different segments of society at different times and in different ways, if at all.

The macro-level: loss of legitimacy

Some years ago Richard Rose and I wrote of the threat to governments of a loss of legitimacy as a result of their continuing increases in revenue extraction from the public (Rose and Peters, 1978). Our vision then was not so much of revolution and blood running in the streets as it was of a quiet loss of confidence of the public in the capacity of the State to govern, and with that a loss of the real capacity of the State to enforce its laws and extract its taxes. The difference between what has occurred and the scenario we depicted then is that there has been active political intervention that has identified and profited from public concerns about the State. It may not be clear if popular distrust of government preceded the success of the Reagans, Thatchers, Perots and Glistrups of the world, or whether those leaders were able to mold popular movements to meet their own political purposes. Given the differences between the more radical strategies of Glistrup and Perot and of the other three leaders some of both is likely, but what is clear is that all these leaders found a very receptive audience for their views of government and the need to reform government.

The fundamental point here is that the apparent loss of legitimacy for public action in many states, again even those with long histories of active and effective governments, may require some reconceptualization of the nature and role of public administration within those states. No longer will it be sufficient for government to launch innovative and potentially expensive programs if it perceives a problem in the economy or society. Rather, there will need to be a more careful conceptualization of the appropriate relationship between State and society, and perhaps of how to fashion the least intrusive intervention possible. One school of 'policy instrument' scholars, for example, has argued that the most important characteristic explaining the choice of interventions is (and should be) the extent to which they intrude into the normal workings of economy and society (Woodside, 1986; Howlett, 1991).

The meso-level: decentralizing program delivery

At the second level, the State has been hollowed by the tendency to move programs away from direct provision by the State. The 'mixed economy welfare state' had been the principal means through which the industrialized democracies had legitimated themselves during the post-war period, but that concept of the State as an important service provider has now been weakened substantially (Eisenstadt and Ahimeir, 1985). Privatization and deregulation have been the buzz words of the 1980s for the public sector, and continue to be important shibboleths into the 1990s. Governments have become extremely creative in the manners in which they have chosen to reduce their direct involvement in service provision, while still maintaining some semblance of control over the economy and society (Hood and Schuppert, 1988). Even when programs remain provided by the public sector, they are often moved to lower levels of government, or to quasi-governmental organizations. This at once hides the costs of those programs from taxpayers considered government costs at the national level, and diffuses responsibility for the content and provision of the programs. Program content may be determined nominally by one set of actors at the national level, with service provision (which generally defines the true nature of the program) occurring at another level of government, or through some form of partnership with the private sector.

This increasing use of private or quasi-private means of service provision is important for preserving the financial stability of the state, but at the same time may pose tremendous problems of legitimacy as well as more ordinary problems of actual service delivery. The citizens of industrialized democracies tend to be schizophrenic about government. On the one hand citizens vote for politicians who promise to maintain or lower tax levels, while on the other hand they also vote for candidates who promise more services. Sometimes, a single candidate will promise to do both things for the public. Thus, a government that attempts to reduce services may encounter difficulties, even if it lowers taxes at the same time. A fundamental problem in the logic of hollowing out the state has been that states must continue to provide public services but are severely constrained in their ability to extract realistic levels of taxes to do so.

Further, both management and legitimacy are threatened when actors perform tasks in the name of the state but do so without the controls associated with being a servant of the state. Again, we encounter a fundamental schizophrenia on the part of citizens in contemporary democracies. On the one hand they demand efficient, non-bureaucratized public services while on the other they want to have the responsiveness and accountability usually associated with public servants. Indeed many of the 'reforms' implemented, and still being implemented, in the public sector involve increased accountability to clients for public servants at all levels of government (OECD, 1987; Manion, 1991).

Finally, privatizing or utilizing quasi-governmental means of reaching policy goals may require a strong State, albeit one of a different sort than is being replaced. To be able to privatize often means that the State must intervene with a wide variety of regulations and incentives in order to ensure that the public interest is protected. Similarly if contracting is to be used as the means of service provision there must be adequate means of enforcing the contracts and monitoring performance to prevent fraud and abuse. Once involved, the State may find it extremely difficult to withdraw fully from the society and economy.

The micro-level: the roles of civil servants

The above description of the demands for accountability on the part of civil servants leads to the third level at which the State has been hollowed out in many contemporary democracies. This is the extent to which the role of the civil servant in these societies has been attacked and made less meaningful in the policy making process. The diminution of the position of civil servant has come from two directions, but both have attempted to reduce the power and discretion available to the civil servant. First, as noted above, there have been pressures to make civil servants more like the employees of private businesses, concerned about satisfying the 'customer' and being responsive to the needs and wishes of those customers. Few people, in or out of government, would argue that civil servants should not be courteous and polite when dealing with the public, or that they should not take citizens' wishes into account when making decisions. The problem is that civil servants also have legal and ethical responsibilities to serve the State and to make decisions that at times are not what the citizen would want. These increased pressures for service make the role of the civil servant in exercising his or her discretion more difficult and tend to reduce the role of judgment, decision making and even personal values in the role of the public servant (Peters, 1991). The role of the civil servant has been hollowed-out from above as well as from below. Politicians as well as citizens have been demanding greater control over the civil service, and the concept of a neutrally competent civil service has become an anathema to many politicians on the political left as well as the right. The public bureaucracy has been more politicized in many Continental governments during recent memory (Meyers, 1985; Derlien, 1988) than it has in Anglo-Saxon countries. There have been, however, strong pressures and real political movements to make the civil service more political in the Anglo-American democracies that have clung to the concept of neutrality. Political allegiance has (apparently) become more of a factor in the appointment of civil servants, and also political appointees have intervened more directly in decisions that might have been made by career civil servants. Politicians appear to feel that their civil service can not be trusted and that much tighter political control must be exercised if their mandates are to be achieved.

The basic effect of this politicization of the civil service has been to reduce the power and discretion of career officials and to reinstitutionalize in many ways the old politics-administration dichotomy that has been pronounced dead so many times. That dichotomy was always somewhat more acceptable in the real world of government than it was in academic circles, but we now must all reconsider seriously our concept of the relationship between the career and non-career components within the governing apparatus of the State. The practice of contemporary governance may be to make civil servants into 'mere managers' and to attempt to assign all significant policy decisions to political leaders.

That attempt at separation may be only just an attempt, given the importance of even the most minute administrative decisions during implementation to the effectiveness of policy. Further, there is the real possibility of conflicts between the demands of politicians for greater control over administration and the concurrent demands of citizens also for greater control. The civil service runs the risk of being caught in the middle between two forces, each expressing their legitimate claims to greater influence over decisions. This can only make the job of the civil servant at once more difficult and less rewarding.

Summary: a changing state

The above description paints a very different description of the State and its role than has been popular for most of the post-war era, especially within Western Europe. The success of the Welfare State in these societies now has become to some extent a perceived problem rather than a solution. Politicians and citizens alike are seeking to redefine at least in part the nature of the State. In so doing they have presented the individuals charged with managing the State and its relationship with the society a formidable task of redirecting their activities and changing their style of coping with social problems. Any return to the *status quo ante* by political means appears unlikely, as many citizens have become more accustomed quickly to a smaller role for the State, especially somewhat lower taxes. Therefore, any subsequent government–whether from the political right or left–may well have to adopt some of the same strategies for governing that the neo-liberal governments have employed. Furthermore, we need to think rather carefully about the options for governance, and especially the role of the public bureaucracy in supplying governance in this changed environment.

THE CHANGING ROLE OF THE PUBLIC BUREAUCRACY

The dismantling of the State is not as pronounced in Western Europe and the Anglo-American democracies as it is in Eastern Europe and the former Soviet Union. Most civil servants in place before the 1980s are still doing their jobs, or have been replaced by new people rather like themselves who will continue to perform those same tasks. Still, there has been a transformation of the meaning of public activity, and following generations of civil servants may not do the same jobs, or at least will be less likely to do them in the same ways. These changes then are challenges for governments, as well as for the institutions which will train those future public servants. Although our analysis and prescriptions will doubtless be incomplete, there are some points that should be made about the nature of the public bureaucracy in States in transition. Most of these admonitions, however, are in defence of the traditional role and conceptualization of the public bureaucracy, and express the need to find politically acceptable means of reinforcing that role.

The charisma of routine

The first point to be made is that if government is to succeed, it will need its civil servants, and need them perhaps more during a period of change than during a period of greater stability (Peters, 1992). This is true whether the change is the building of the Welfare State or if it is dismantling it, or at least slowing the pace of its development. This is a rather mundane statement, but expresses a point that appears to have been forgotten by many political leaders responsible for implementing change. Indeed, if one source of popular complaints about the State is its lack of competence and/or responsiveness, then political leaders will need better bureaucracies, rather than attempting always to dismantle the existing structures of governance. To produce that competence and responsiveness is not easy, and the practice of denigrating the civil service may be a self-fulfilling prophecy.

The need for a (relatively) stable and technically proficient civil service is manifested in several ways. One is that there is no Republican, or Christian Democratic, or Socialist way to perform many of the tasks that contemporary governments perform. Indeed, many of the governments undergoing massive change in Eastern Europe, Latin America and elsewhere have found the need to retain many employees of the former regime simply to keep government functioning as it needs to on a day-to-day basis (Piekalkiewicz and Hamilton, 1992). Loyalty and political correctness are important for civil servants, but service delivery may be more important for creating legitimacy.

Increasingly the tasks of government are technical rather than the paper-shuffling tasks usually attributed to the public bureaucracy. Given the character of the jobs, governments need experts as much as they may need political dedication and commitment. This argument has not prevented governments from attempting to impose a particular view on science and technology policy, especially when it is couched in other programs such as environmental protection, but still there often is the need to foster expertise at the possible expense of short-term political goals. Managerial techniques such as performance evaluations may offer one means of creating efficient and responsible government, but require a tremendous investment of time and effort.

Not only is advice on policy important, but the simple ability to keep government running is also important. Managers brought in from outside often begin by assuming that people in government are there because they cannot do anything else, but soon find that running a government is at least as complex as running a private enterprise and that they need the skill and experience of the careerists to be successful. The difficultly is that these simple truths may not filter up to the leadership of government that continues to denigrate the career service in the name of political goals and the presumed quality of the new team that is attempting to manage the State. Politicians and civil servants need each other, but the marriage that is created is often an unhappy one unless they understand their mutual dependence.

Efficiency is not the only goal

Much of the thrust of the new managerialism in the public sector has been to stress efficiency over other goals for the public sector (Pollitt, 1990). The version of efficiency advocated is often a caricature of what might be understood to be efficiency in a business school, but the idea parades under that banner nonetheless. The efficiency effort often appears to be to make government function more as would private enterprise, and to make civil servants into line managers, with political leaders retaining (or recapturing) primary responsibility for policy (Kemp, 1990). While we scholars can easily critique this reinstitutionalization of the old politics-administration dichotomy, many people functioning in the real world of government never fully abandoned the notion and some would like to have it restated more clearly. Those favouring the restatement would be primarily politicians, but some administrators might also like to have their responsibility for policy clarified, and diminished.

The problem in attempting to reinstate the old dichotomy is that the world of government is now more complex than that for which this differentiation was created. Separating policy from administration is less easy to do, and government needs rather desperately the expertise of its civil servants in areas such as science policy, health, and the like (Barker and Peters, 1992). Effective management is certainly needed, but so too is dispassionate and far-sighted policy advice. Issue networks, epistemic communities or whatever are better prepared to provide such advice than they once were, but the role of civil service must still be in part to 'speak truth to power' about policy. Civil servants should, and generally do, provide a perspective on policy that may extent beyond immediate political goals to look at the broader public interest and the values that strong state policies may bring to the policy area. We do not want to beatify civil servants, but neither should they be demonized as they have been by many contemporary politicians. Finally, it must be noted that at the same time that governments are attempting to make senior civil servants into line managers, they are attempting to transfer more and more line functions out of government to private profit and not-for-profit organizations.

We must also remember that many of the programs in the public sector are there precisely because they do not lend themselves easily to market provision. This is certainly true for classic public goods and many common-pool goods, but is also true for some seemingly more private goods. For some public services – education, social services, tax advice – citizens want highly personalized and decentralized services that are seemingly 'inefficient' to provide well but which to some extent define the relationship between the state and its citizens. This may extend from some of the rather simple and traditional services of the state such as fire protection and mail delivery to many of the social services provided by governments, such as education and counseling. This contrast taps one of many prevailing schizophrenic views of government, in which it is at once expected to be caring and nurturing, and brutally efficient.

Efficiency may not even be maximized by the Hollow State

We have so far granted the assumption that a more privatized form of program provision may be more efficient for governments. That may not, however, be the case once we begin to look at all the aspects of efficiency in the public sector. It may well be that as is so often the case as one aspect of efficient management is enhanced, another may suffer as the structures of the state are 'reformed' in an attempt to make them function better. One of the most obvious factors that arises here is that definitions of 'reform' and 'better' will differ markedly depending upon the political and administrative ideologies of individuals.

One of the most obvious examples of this maxim of efficiency can be seen in the impact of 'hollowing', whether by decentralization and deconcentration or by the utilization of quasi-governmental providers, on administrative outputs such as coordination among programs. One of the persistent problems of public management is the coordination of programs. For example, the 'bottom-up' school of implementation and administrative analysis (Milward and Walmsley, 1985) is based in large part upon the difficulties of coordination and the consequent need to focus on interactions occurring at the service delivery level. It would appear that while this 'hollow' approach to management reflects some of the realities involved in that school, it also assumes that the necessary coordination will take place in an efficient and effective manner, an assumption that does not appear well-supported by the available evidence.

Indeed, the possibilities for effective policy coordination may be diminished by using private or not-for-profit organizations rather than using public sector organizations. There is an academic literature arguing that agencies in the public bureaucracy are utility maximizers (Niskanen, 1971; Bendor, 1990), and that view is widely accepted among the public. The evidence on this behavior by public organizations is spotty at best (Peters, 1992), but it is certainly widely available for the private sector. This type of maximizing behavior is in fact the leitmotif and justification for the private sector, and is assumed to be what makes it efficient. If that is the case, then the competitive motivations of the private or quasi-private participants in a policy network would make them less amenable to coordination than would be public sector actors having some responsiveness to the stricter hicrarchies within government. This may be as true of not-for-profit organizations competing for grants and contracts as it is of for-profits competing for the same financial rewards from government (Provan and Milward, 1991).

Market incentives are not the only tools for government

Following from the above, we should point out that market incentives are not the only effective tools available to the public sector in reaching its policy goals. The spate of writing about the use of the market to achieve the goals for government as well as private industry might make the unwary citizen or scholar believe that all else has been proven to be inadequate. That is not the case, and the variety of tools that Kirschen (1964), Hood (1986) and others have some thoroughly catalogued over the years still exist at the disposal of the leader willing to use them. The difficulty therefore may well be in the political will to exercise authority, or to use treasure (in Hood's terminology), rather than in the inherent inadequacy of the instruments available.

The task for political leaders and for managers, therefore is to exercise appropriate choice over public policies and the means for achieving public ends. There are instances in which market forces may have as much of a distorting influence over policy outcomes as the use of regulations would have over other outcomes. The difficulty will be in overcoming the dominance of free market ideology in government, often now even among parties of the political left (Crozier, 1987), in order to make realistic judgements that will enhance the effectiveness and even efficiency of programs by using non-market instruments for implementation. The advocates of market tools have made an important corrective to the inertial tendency in government to always 'throw money at problems' or to use command and control regulations; what is needed now is a means of performing non-ideological analyses about the appropriate use of all these instruments in the achievement of public purposes.

The trick in the selection and implementation of policy instruments may be to find tools that can exploit the more positive features of the mixed environment in which they will be employed. That is, if the service is to be provided by a hollowed out state and will almost necessarily involve a large private element, we need to design better means of providing the service almost privately, while still maintaining the relevant public features of the program. Likewise, we need to think of means that provide maximum leverage over individuals while maintaining the maximum appearance of freedom in the market or quasi-market. This must be done while also maintaining a sense of authenticity and honesty in dealing with clients and the autonomous service providers. This rather difficult balancing act must be done, however, by officials in the public sector whose morale is likely to have been shaken by the continuing assaults of free-market advocates. This will be no easy task. Contracting appears to offer something approaching this balance, but the experience of contracting by government other than for rather tightly specified goods, and some rather simple services, is not promising.

Confused responsibility may be no responsibility

One of the 'proverbs' of conventional public administration has been that there should be clear lines of authority and clear responsibility for actions within the public sector. While it is easy to denigrate these bits of conventional wisdom, these proverbs do have substantial utility in directing our attention toward possible problems in the design of administrative structures within the emerging 'hollow' state. In particular, we must be concerned with the extent to which the complex structures linking the public and private sectors, designed to provide programs in as efficient a manner as possible, actually mask responsibility and add to the problems of citizens of understanding and influencing the actions of their governments.

Cost and inefficiency are not the only complaints being registered about the public sector. Not only do citizens object to the 'prices' they are forced to pay for public services through the tax system, but they also object to the quality of service being provided and the seeming lack of connection between service providers and their 'clients' (OECD, 1987; Day and Klein, 1987). The problem program designers face here is that the remedies selected for solving one problem may indeed exacerbate the other. Thus, very much as in Simon's (1947) analysis of the proverbs of administration, most decisions about administration are true dilemmas in which the selection of either horn produces some undesirable results on the other. We may be able to please citizens with (somewhat) lower costs for services but then displease them when responsibility and accountability are confused. Privatizers may not even be able to please them with lower costs, given that the efficiency benefits of privatization are often overstated by its advocates.

Even if the responsibility for delivering a public service is entirely in the hands of a private agent, with government playing only the role of the principal, these problems of accountability may still arise. The accountability problems arise first in a financial sense, with public money being expended without the types of controls that might normally be required for funds expended directly by the public sector. They may also arise around more substantive policy and administrative issues, with many of the procedural and ethical guidelines mandated in the public sector not being required for private programs. For example, governments often encounter difficulties with private contractors or grantees (including unfortunately many universities) expending money in ways that are, if not manifestly illegal, certainly unethical and impermissible in the normal conduct of public business (Rehfuss, 1991). Even when there are attempts at institutionalizing controls over the activities of the public sector, e.g. the Citizen's Charter in the United Kingdom, these are now often phrased in terms of the rights of *consumers*, rather than as the more extensive political and legal rights that presumably would accrue to citizens. It is important for the public sector to remember that their money, and ultimately their power, in democratic societies comes from *citizens*.

CONCLUSION

Both political leaders and citizens appear to be exerting pressures to reduce the powers of the central state and to create a diminished, 'hollow' state. Those pressures are manifestations of some real failings and excesses of governments in the post-war era, but also are potentially dangerous over-reactions to those problems. The greater visibility of the problems of government, simply because governments are public, and its functioning more in a fishbowl of publicity, make the failings appear worse. Further, critics of the public sector assume, although it is by no means clear why, that the private sector might have done better in providing superior services at a more reasonable cost. These pressures point toward a future for government that is very different from its past.

The option of pursuing more privatized means of service provision and an indirect, principal-agent relationship between government and service-providers is attractive to many critics of government, but threatens some of the most fundamental values of the public sector in democratic systems. It tends to substitute one narrow conception of efficiency for more fundamental values of accountability and responsiveness that should be inherent in a democratic system of government. An economic conceptualization of government also tends to replace values of public service with those of the market. It also may not even be able to reach the efficiency goals valued so highly, given difficulties in coordination and control. The future of the public services may be in using highly decentralized and privatized modes of provision. Such a mode of production will require, however, much greater attention to means of enforcing accountability, controlling competition, assuring coordination, and ensuring that public services are for the public. These are many of the same requirements that provoked the movement away from the dreaded bureaucracies and toward these presumably debureaucratized means of serving clients.

5

GOVERNANCE AND
PUBLIC MANAGEMENT

Jan Kooiman and Martijn van Vliet

The development of welfare societies in North-Western Europe can be described in terms of their growing complexity, dynamics and diversity. These characteristics put governing political and social institutions for great problems. Their usual interventions, methods and policy instruments are not suited for these new problems why their effectiveness and legitimacy have come under great pressure. These fundamental patterns of change have led to a strongly diminished faith in the governing capacities of governments but not to a diminished need for collective problem solving. Basic social needs have been satisfied in these societies for the majority of the population (standard of living, education, health care and housing) but new collective problems emerge based upon the complex, dynamic and diverse character of these societies: environmental pollution, return of massive and long-term unemployment. But also new and qualitatively different governing needs appear having to do with the growing internationalization of the Western (and especially) European economies.

In our opinion trends such as internationalization, disturbance of ecological equilibria, developments in technology and cultural individualisation are expressions of the growing complexity, dynamics and diversity of our societies. This means that the relations between states and their environment, between citizens, governments, business and private initiative are changing considerably. The presence and character of these problems exclude in our opinion the feasibility and attraction of on the one hand a government which withdraws unilaterally and just negates these governing needs, or on the other hand the belief in the self-governing capacities of other social subsystems. Hence we are searching for alternative modes of governing and governance in which interactions between government and society, between public and private actors are central and in which politico-administrative interventions and social forms of self governance correspond (Kooiman, 1993).

In this chapter we conceptualize the tasks, roles, demands and criteria for public management as a basic part of such interacting governments. We start with a sketch of three 'theoretical traditions' in public administration and political science from we which we derive some ideas to give meaning to a new concept of public management as interaction between governance and governing. We call this a moving perspective.

MOVING PERSPECTIVE

Recent theories on public management

The attention to management in the public sphere has two major sources. The first one is the mainly from the US coming idea of applying management techniques developed for business firms in public sector organizations. The experiences in this realm have had widespread and incidental adjustments, but certainly have not led to new more comprising theoretical concepts. The second source at first gave more reason to such an expectation, because of its political-ideological colouring, that is to say the neo-conservative re-appraisal of the market as a guiding principle for the society as a whole. From that source we see initiatives such as deregulation, privatization and contract-management. In other words a withdrawing government which moreover should be run as a company. This management impulse has certainly in many West European countries had effects. And somewhat in a conceptual sense. But in the words of Les Metcalfe: 'much imitation and little innovation' (Kooiman, 1993). And as far as this conceptual imitation went, it was mainly concerned with emphasizing (internal) efficiency of public management; it had much less an external emphasis.

Accordingly our plea for a changing perspective starts with a much more central place for an externally directed attention for an effective tackling of – especially new – collective problems; much more than in the just mentioned public management approaches where the focus is internal. The major difference then is not to reason from inside to outside, but from outside to inside.

Rigthly Metcalfe and Richards write that public management is not (yet) a fully developed concept (1987: viii). What presents itself as Public Management is more a collection of practice-in-use in which ideological, scientific and practical considerations are mixed with a considerable leaning towards concepts borrowed from private management. That such as mix of ideas and concepts can not lead towards a clear conceptualization several authors in the first edition of this volume noted (Kooiman, 1987). There is a definite need for a new conceptualization for public management to which we want contribute in this chapter from this moving perspective.

What is the crux of the conceptualization problem? In our opinion the Public Management concept is usually defined too poorly and too narrowly. According to Metcalfe and Richards the enrichment of the concept depends on developments in the following 'themes': information, decentralization, line management, spend to save, interorganizational management, role of the centre, accountability, human resources management (1987: 217–). This enrichment however has not yet a clear structure or direction. It is a mixture of internal and external elements. In our opinion a renewed conceptualization of the internal and external elements could be the core of the enrichment of the public management concept. The greatest problem is not so much the internal functioning of the governmental organization. No doubt there are shortcomings there also, but the main conceptual shortage is in the relation between the external and the internal because governments have great difficulty coping with growing complexity, dynamics and diversity of social reality. When collective goals are less straightforward, external factors are less predictable and central tasks of governmental (but also business) organizations become less routinized, then the attention has to be shifted from the internal to the relation between the external and the internal. A starting point for such a new conceptualization could be a combination of what Metcalfe calls 'the responsibility for the performance of a system' (Kooiman, 1993: ch. 14) with the conceptual distinction made in the first edition of this volume between macro, meso and micro levels of public management (Kooiman, 1987).

Recent pluralism theory

Starting from a more externally oriented approach the question arises what this external 'looks like' conceptually and how this 'external' presents itself to the government and public management in a social-political context. For an answer on questions as these, we take the 'pluralism debate' as a point of departure. In the view of Smith (1990: 307) borrowed from Luhmann, pluralism can be considered as' the dispersal of power in modern industrial society', which can be seen as the result of social complexity and interdependence in combination with an open political system (idem: 306). The pluralism debate is of importance because pluralists, neo- and reformed pluralists debate about questions such as: how are power and influence distributed across different social actors, and especially: how scattered or cumulative sources of power are? How 'open' is a political system for special interests and how more open for certain interests than for others? Which normative judgement can be given to such a pluralist order? For our argumentation the answer to such questions are important because they might give clues to the 'external orientation' of public management in terms of the new conceptualization we aim at.

In this debate which is being carried on for several decades we see rather extreme pluralist as well as rather extreme 'corporatist' concepts and all kinds of forms in between, which can be best characterized as ideal models. We can find ourselves in the conclusion of Jordan who sketches the theoretical menu as 'Some form of competitive pluralism versus sectoral or meso-corporatism/corporate pluralism look like the options with most relevance for western political systems. But there is a growing range of work which says that our conclusions are likely to be different sector by sector; that we cannot draw conclusions about 'the' system as a pattern of sectorally different processes exist' (Jordan: 300). For our particular purpose – the conceptual relevance for elaborating a concept of public management – two versions of 'competitive pluralism' within this debate should be looked at a bit more in detail, indicated as reformed pluralism and neopluralism.

In the 'reformed' variant it is recognized that government-interest relations often are institutionalized and that some groups will be excluded. The concepts of policy communities and issue networks play a role here; relations between government and social groups can vary from corporate pluralism (rather strictly structured forms) to issue networks (less structured, volatile and time bound). The state in this theoretical framework is an autonomous actor, although rather stabile networks can make the boundaries between the state and 'external' blurred. A distinction between 'primary' and 'secondary' policy communities makes sense as 'circles' of admitted or permitted influence exertion. Neo-pluralists have especially an eye for the consequences of unequal distributions of social power sources in the society for the the functioning of modern Western democracies. These are hampered because unequal cumulation of resources will be used to keep certain issues from the political agenda (Bachrach and Baratz, 1970), others point at the favoured position of the business community (Lindblom, 1977) or point at social-political inequalities (Dahl, 1985). 'Improvement' of the public sphere is in the eyes of neo-pluralists strongly connected with the improvement of the measure of 'openness' of the political system. This pluralism debate is in a broad sense important for our purpose because it gives some clues as to how we might conceptualize the 'external' for a new public management orientation. In this perspective we are able to combine efficiency and effectiveness goals of public management with the way in which social reality is organized or self-organizes itself in terms of the government in which also normative aspects are important. The pluralism debate shows that normative judgements about public management are not separate from a judgement about social reality itself, the character of its power distribution and the way governments organize themselves to interact with the world around them.

Recent normative theory

In a recent paper Lehning makes a plea for a sincere integration of normative political theory and public administration. He sketches an 'architecture of government intervention' in which normative political theory formulates an order of feasible rules of the game to which institutions should bind themselves (1992: 10). He distinguishes in this architecture four institutional levels: pre-constitutional, constitutional, law giving and law implementation; for each level normative principles apply. What is of importance in our context is the link he establishes between the normative in administrative management and the broader normative political context. One could speak of a 'normative hierarchy', where from social-political debates and argumentations norms and criteria can be derived which are applicable to other levels. The other way around, in the daily practice an externally oriented public management time and again will be confronted with choices and dilemma's in which these broader normative discussions can be tested. This underlines the dynamic character of the work of and the context in which public management operates. Lehning, however, limits himself to a sort of procedural normativity. This in itself is important and relevant for the pluralist character of the external structures and processes in which Public Management manifests itself in the moving perspective. But there is also an independent normative input in such a changing perspective. According to Aquina and Bekke this is explicitly necessary in a pluralist-democratic context, because of the constant dilemmas inherent in such an order (Kooiman, 1993).

For such a normative input Gawthrop offers certain clues. This author reasons that there is an intricate relation between Public management, systems and ethics (1984). He is of the opinion that classical public administration models fail because of the great variety, dynamics and complexity of the environment (idem: 4). A new conceptualization of public management has to develop a critical (systems) consciousness and an ethical design in which the usual 'from process to purpose' is turned around into 'from purpose to process' (idem: 122). What is needed is a change in 'civility' from individual ethics to systems ethics where the concepts of responsibility and relatedness are central. With this normative conceptualization we can give substance to what Metcalfe and Richards mean when they talk about responsibility and accountability (1987). Substantive communication and not communication as process is a necessary condition reflecting the discussion between Luhman and Habermas about communication as an exchange of information and communication as a means to come to a shared understanding.

Combined with the normative 'architecture' in the sense of Lehning, such a purposive communication can change level by level. The normative criteria to which public management has to adhere can change form intervention level to intervention level. Because of the growing variety and the context of social differentiation, these have to be imbedded in a pre-constitutional 'governance' perspective that offers the normative context in which meso (network) and micro (public manager) behaviour relate in a dynamic manner. The democratic-pluralist character of the social-political order can – up to a point – guarantee the openness of these ethical debates and the constitutional level can take care that important outcomes will be translated into generally accepted and legitimatized rules and procedures. Interacting public management is a central and indispensable actor in these debates, because in the practice of modern government in the Western world it takes part in the majority of the actual interactions between public and private, between government, its social partners and citizens individually. That makes for the predominant importance of the development of an ethics for public management on the macro, meso and micro levels. It even could lead to a model for 'bureaucratic morality' (Dunsire, 1988) or could be related to the four public management roles Strand develops in this book (chapter 12). In our context of a more external orientation for public management in particular the 'entrepreneurial role' would need such a more normative, ethical or even moral 'code'.

Trends in perspective

In the foregoing we gave a brief presentation of three theoretical discussions with relevance for the development of some new ideas on public management. Basically the line of argument is that there is a need to structure all kinds of new notions and ideas about public management. In our opinion the starting point should be a much more focal external orientation, from which internal concepts can be developed. In contrast to more traditional approaches, some recent theorizing on public management gives a basis for this. To come to grips with this external orientation, the pluralism debate gives some clues as to how 'the world looks on the outside', a world with which modern Public Management has to deal in order to cope with modern problems translated into complex, dynamic and diverse governing needs. This debate asks special attention for uneveness in power distributions, unequal access to public institutions. As a consequence of this there is definite need for concepts which help in overcoming an uneven representation not only of interests but also of aspects of societal problems. For an effective public management it is of the greatest importance to have a fair in stead of an uneven representation because otherwise problem solving or opportunity catching will be inefficient and ineffective, and quite probably also illegitimate and unjust. This last point becomes especially clear if we add a third source of needed ideas, that is to say the normative aspect. Here the conceptualization has to take into consideration that substantives debates certainly have to be stretched to the outside world. Only within the context of a continuous debate between 'insiders' and 'outsiders' will it be possible to develop a coherent, up to date and flexible set of values and norms that will enable Public Managers to cope with a constant stream of dilemmas with which they necessarily will be confronted. The traditional 'solution' saying that this is matter for politics, does not hold any longer, because of the dynamic, complex and diverse character of modern society. Public

Managers are central actors in this in all respects.

GOVERNANCE AND MANAGEMENT

Governance can be considered as the pattern or structure which comes into existence – 'becomes' – in a social-political system as the common outcome of efforts in intervention by all actors concerned. This pattern can not be reduced to the acting of one actor or one group of actors in particular: 'political governance in modern societies can no longer be conceived in terms of external governmental control of society but emerges from a plurality of governing actors' (Mayntz & Marin, 1991). The governance concept points to the creation of a structure or an order which can not be externally imposed but is the result of the interaction of a multiplicity of governing and each other influencing actors. This order is a restricting but also an enabling or reinforcing condition for social-political action. In practical action there exists a continuous interaction between those conditions and the use and implementation of those conditions. A governance structure has to free and coordinate sufficient transforming capacities in order to cope with modern governing needs. The 'purpose' of governance in our societies can be described as coping with the problems but also the opportunities of complex, dynamic and diverse modern societies.

Complexity, dynamics and diversity has led to a shrinking external autonomy of the national state combined with a diminishing internal dominance vis à vis social subsystems. Modern governing should primarily be seen as efforts to activate and coordinate social actors in such ways that public and non-public interventions satisfy the need of coping with complexity, dynamics and diversity. This specific task of modern government expresses itself in the sort of 'network' constructions of administrative and societal arrangements. Governments will be hold responsible for direct political-administrative action as well as for the quality of the political-administrative order (part of the broader social-political governance structure). This responsibility we consider to be the main public governing task. Governments try by exerting direct forms of influence on social interactions to reach their own goals, albeit that conditions for 'central control' no longer are present. Governing in modern society is predominantly a process of coordination (Kaufman et al.) and influencing social, political and administrative interactions (Kooiman, 1988) meaning that new forms of interactive governing are necessary (Kooiman, 1993)

Governing in an interactive perspective is directed at the balancing of social interests (Dunsire, 1993) and creating the possibility and the limits (Mayntz, 1993) of social actors and systems to organize themselves. Central in this is the question how cooperation in practice can be directed towards the enhancement of common goals, and situations be created in which political governing and social self-organization can be made complementary.

Public Managing

Public management can be seen as the professional substantiation, the actual implementation of the direct care for public governing. The fact that the government (politically and administrative) will be held responsible for the quality of this direct care (governing) as well as for the quality of the social-political order (governance) means that recent public managing is not a sinecure. In modern society with all its new problems and opportunities (due to complexity, dynamics and diversity), the traditional Weberian distinction between the political system and the administrative apparatus no longer can be contained. In societies where policy making and policy implementation are interactive and can be seen as co-products of governmental agencies and their clientele groups, public managing is more and more 'political' in the traditional sense. Also the civil servant sets the agenda, promotes or hampers consensus, wins social support and makes bargains.

That the traditional conceptualization of politics and administration no longer holds and is contrary to reality is common knowledge. However conceptualizations which are closer to reality but at the same time satisfy certain normative considerations are scarce. The public manager is sometimes administrating and sometimes dealing with politics; the politician (certainly those in executive functions) sometimes prepare, sometimes implement decisions. It is absolutely unclear what this means for the tasks and norms of public managing. Offe (1985) describes as the central dilemma for public management in the modern (welfare) state the contradiction between legal-bureaucratic rationality (guided by rules and regulations) without making any distinction between persons (output: compliance to official norms), and a rationality which emphasizes goals to be reached and aims set (output: achievement of tasks).

This free floating politicization of the administrative function and the connected politicization of the the civil service have in most parliamentary democracies led to a great discrepancy between the reality as perceived at the outside and that experienced on the inside. No fundamental consideration of this – almost schizophrenic – quality of modern public management (note the changing in wording) can be developed without the social-political context in which it exists. Pekonen (1993) argues in favour of acknowledging the politicization of the task of public managing and take care that public decision-making processes are organized in such a dynamical way (by manifold feedbacks) that at least all or most social-political 'realities' are represented. Here the normative solution is mainly procedural. But much more difficult are conceptualizations not with procedural but of substantive normative priorities. Probably no general rules can be given so long as no new conceptions have evolved and situational solutions should be promoted as learning experiences. It will be clear from the foregoing that such solutions will not be 'technical' but 'dilemmical' and will be put within the context of governing experiences and governance practices.

TASKS OF PUBLIC MANAGEMENT

The argumentation so far has been that social changes have brought out new governing needs which have to be answered by new governing capacities. These changes do not say anything about a diminishing or a growing need for collective problem solving or about the role of governments in this. Our reasoning is that governing needs now are different from those before; we presume that the answer is more in the direction of 'doing things together', of interaction, than everybody on its own or steering from one central point. In this paragraph we carry the conceptualization a bit more specifically about the role of governments in this and the changing tasks and roles of Public Management as a partner. In a general sense then the objective of modern government in a governance perspective could be defined as to activate and coordinate social actors in such ways that the social-political order (the governance structure) which emerges from the presence of many actors satisfies the demands made by coping with complexity, dynamics and diversity. The position of governments in this is such that they can be hold responsible for the quality of both requirements: the quality of the broader social-political governance and the quality of its own governing. Public management is an integral part in and instrument of both objectives.

Tasks of public management

A first effort at classifying the tasks of government in a governance and governing perspective may comprise those shown in Figure 1.

These are taskfields with a combined responsibility of the 'elected' and 'nominated' parts of governments. These responsibilities can somewhat be specified by saying that for the 'elected' the perspective is more from the governance than the governing angle; for the 'nominated' the other way around. From this distinction more specific tasks for public management (the 'nominated 'part) can be – conceptually at least – inferred.

With (de)-composition we mean that with every problem or opportunity a new one has to judge which social parts and processes are involved

Figure 1   *Governmental tasks*

Coping with	tasks
complexity:	(de)composition and coordination
dynamics:	collibration and steering
diversity:	integration and regulation

and the relations between those involved (a complexity requirement) That depends mainly on the way a problem or an opportunity is defined: this definition process basically is a process of decomposition and composition of parts, processes and interaction patterns. The rules according to which this (de)composition game – as de Leeuw (1986) calls this – is played are in the realm of governance; the actual (de)composition more in the realm of governing. Here insights from the 'pluralism debate' may help in conceptualizing these governing practices and the 'normative' angle on the governance requirements. When a problem situation or an opportunity has been defined (and this not a static but a dynamic affair with actors being added or dropping out) the coordination 'game' will start. This could be seen as a task more specifically in the realm of governing, and in that respect more a typical public management task. However, the two tasks closely hang together and are basically complementary. No coordination without (de-)composition and vice versa. Here, a difference exists between the governance and the neo-corporatist approach: in the last one actors involved are rather precisely defined and coordination takes place within well organized structures.

Steering and collibration are ways to govern the dynamics of modern societies. Steering is the definition of a norm and indicating the means with which these norms can be reached. (Kooiman, 1988). Collibration is the influencing of (social) power relations in such ways as to move social developments in a preferred direction (Dunsire, 1993). Steering is the more common form of governing, but considered by many to be 'implementation-intensive' and 'enforcement-expensive' (idem). Collibration will – also by us – be seen as an attractive complement of steering. The attraction of collibration is its relative simplicity with which already existing (political, administrative or social) processes can be guided without being forced to specify in advance what has to happen.It makes use of already existing (natural) feedback processes by amplifying or reducing them. Governing by positive or negative feedback is more simple than feedforward in terms of the knowledge and information needed beforehand: one of the great difficulties in steering and other forms of feedforward in coping with dynamics. We speak of the complementarity of steering and collibration because both are basic government tasks. It seems primarily a question of a) knowledge and information needed beforehand (such as in situation where equality before the law is a high norm as in judicial procedures) or where uncertainties are great (such as in specifying conditions under which economic or environmental investments should be made). But again somewhat of a differentation between the 'elected' and the 'nominated' can be made. The rules according to which collibration and steering take place can be seen as a more /governance' oriented task (responsibility of the 'elected'); the tasks themselves – although certainly not exclusive by definition more a governing (public management) task. The development of feedback and feedforward mechanisms and controlling or monitoring techniques are more in the realm of public management tasks.

Integration and regulation are two tasks directed at coping with the diversity of goals, demands, ideals and interests in modern societies. Integration points at the need for togetherness or meaning in spite of diversity. E.g. health care will denaturate if it is only an addition of specialisms; the integrative task of the doctor (general practitioner) becomes almost impossible indeed. Regulation aims at overcoming the negative effects of each individual (sub-system) on another; environmental regulation: countering unwanted side effects of producing and consuming; regulation of data processing: countering negative privacy aspects.

Integration and regulation are again complementary tasks. Integration is working on a more fundamental level: in a well integrated society enterprises more can easily be approached for negative side effects and privacy aspects are more easily understood and accepted. This seems to be more closely related to governance (more a taskfield for the 'elected') Regulation is a more technical taskfield, which should be developed 'when other governing efforts are not effective'. In this sense it is the less fundamental, more governing one and in that sense belongs more in the realm of public management. If integration works better, regulation is less necessary. The Data Protection Registrar in the UK defines his work as 'a massive educational exercise which is trying to change attitudes as practices of the whole nation' (Raab, 1993) and as such sees his task more as an 'integrator' than as a 'regulator'. It certainly belongs next to the more traditional regulation task of Public Management to organize and develop communication structures in which meaningful debates and information exchanges take place in order to enhance integration.

CRITERIA

After this conceptualization of public management tasks in a new context we want to formulate a number of criteria, with which those tasks can be evaluated. To do this we make use of the fact or presupposition that our Western societies are becoming more complex, dynamic and diverse. We want to say something about dilemma's with which public management will inevitably be confronted. In the tradition of management fit criteria like effectiveness and efficiency; in the pluralism debate we find criteria such as representativeness and selectivity; and in the normative literature we find criteria like justice and legitimacy. These can be applied to the way complexity, dynamics and diversity can be handled (see Figure 2).

Handling complex problems or opportunities means in a governance/governing perspective the care for a 'representative iteration' between the taking into account of interactions of wholes and parts of the problems and the opportunities. The same can be said for selectivity of participating actors. Without giving a judgment about the measure of such iterations, one could say that from an evaluative point of view at least once a full cycle of the (de)-composition game

Figure 2   *Criteria*

	Governance	Public management
complexity:	wholes/parts	representativity selectivity
dynamics:	cybernetics	learning effectiveness
diversity:	quality	fairness/justice legitimacy

has to be played; and for the selectivity can be said that at least a fair representation of the 'secondary policy community' should be present in the governing/governance process. For public management these criteria are especially applicable in regard with the (de)composition game itself (governing); for the 'elected' especially in terms of an evaluation of the rules with which the (de)composition games are played in a certain (sector of) a society.

In the same manner coping with dynamics can be evaluated in terms of learning and effectiveness. The emphasis on evaluating the way governance structures handle dynamics could be in terms of the willingness to 'learn' either from past mistakes or from new insights. This is certainly not common place if we look at the inertia so characteristic of many public organizations or (public-private) interorganizational networks. And stressing effectiveness as a criterium for coping with dynamics has to do with the well-known phenomenon of feedback processes which 'run behind the facts', resulting in the opposite effect of what was meant. One could say that 'learning' is a measure for the use of feedback mechanisms; effectiveness is a measure of how the insights from learning are applied 'in the next round or cycle'. Effectiveness and the related criterium of efficiency used in the above described sense become dynamic concepts, in stead of their static application as we find so often in public administration literature.

For coping with or handling diversity we propose the usage of justice, with an emphasis on evaluating governance; and legitimacy with an emphasis in evaluating governing. These more substantive criteria which should definitely be situationally specified, at the same time form the closing piece and the starting point for the other four criteria. They are in our opinion not independent of the others. Otherwise they easily become empty shells i.e.interesting for discussion, but neglected in the practice of governance and governing. Justice (governance) and legitimacy (governing) used in this sense become also complex but especially dynamic evaluative criteria and standards. Their normative 'power' helps and underpins the normative quality of the other criteria. Public administration should be much more seriously integrated with disciplines such as normative political theory. This certainly applies to the field of public management as a scholarly discipline and the practical applications promoted by it.

DILEMMA'S OF AND RESPONSIBILITIES FOR PUBLIC MANAGEMENT

The aim of this chapter has been to develop criteria for the performance of 'modern' public management, that is public management that copes with the central features of contemporary advanced (western) society: increasing complexity, dynamics and diversity. We conclude that high quality public management in '(post-) modern times' is public management that contributes to 'good governance'. Good governance refers not only the quality of the governments own actions alone but also to the quality of the politico-social order as a whole and the process of governance that is resulting from that order. The importance of the extra criteria we developed in the earlier paragraphs is not so much within the quantitative extension of the performance criteria for public management but in the manifestation of the dilemmas that face modern public management today. These dilemmas confronts contemporary public management with the task to re-model its responsibilities towards societies and its citizens. In our opinion, it is the confrontation between a perspective 'from inside out' with a perspective 'from outside in' that makes the public management task a difficult one.

With regard to dynamics, the task of public management is to relate effectiveness and efficiency measures more to learning and learning capacities. Effectiveness cannot be measured on basis of fixed *ex ante* objectives alone. In a dynamic context one must reckon with changing circumstances that can develop in changing problem definitions, better solution methods and fresh insights that can develop over time. Learning, the capacity to learn and the capacity to develop learning capacities must be part of new definitions and conceptions of effectiveness and efficiency. Management of problems, which are dynamic in character such as environmental problems, have to sail between two forms of failure. On the one hand there is the risk that new insights are continuously translated into new problem definitions en new targets so that governing and other social actors do not where they stand and what they are supposed to do, with the result that developments stop and usual criteria of effectiveness and efficiency are not met. On the other hand the risk is that not incorporating new insights could mean that the achievement of *ex ante* determined objectives is less or not at all useful at the time of accomplishment.

Diversity seems to be the most difficult factor to deal with in contemporary society. Rules and regulations in a constitutional state are based on the principle of equality for the law. However, in a diversified society the equality principle is less applicable if everyone is 'different'. Implementation of social security regulations in the Netherlands shows us that, due to an increasing diversification in living situations, rule-implementation without interpretation is increasingly difficult and is often regarded as not justified. On the other hand more freedom of interpretation in the hands of implementing personal could lead to (a sense of) arbitrariness. Governmental action in a diversified world seem to depend more and more, neither on 'impersonal' application of general rules on special cases, nor on the personal but arbitrary choice of implementing (executive) public officers but on the the development of communication structures in which reasonable argumentation leads to acceptable and legitimate governmental intervention. 'Reasonable argumentation' means that there is an (ongoing) interaction between 'general rules' and 'special cases' within the government itself and between government and society. Within this interaction process governments and social actors have to consider governmental action and its intended and unintended consequences.

Public management must create time and room for 'self-reflection' but it must also support society and its citizens in its consideration on public action. In Reich's (1985; 1988) opinion the responsibility of public managers is not only taking decisions in the public interest but also in helping the population to deliberate about the collective decisions that should be taken: 'Thus the public manager's job is not only, or simply, to make policy choices and implement them. It is also to participate in a system of democratic governance in which public values are continuously rearticulated and recreated' (Reich, 1988: 124).

In a society that is increasingly complex, dynamic and diverse, 'the' government is not capable of deciding alone in which direction society develops. Societal development is necessarily a result of interactive social forces. The fact that societal developments are dependent on the actions of a variety of social actors, however, does not mean that public management does not have a special responsibility. On the normative level it has the responsibility to stimulate public debate about public values, governmental tasks and collective decision-making through which government's role in society is being legitimized and a public 'purpose' is given to governmental action. On the level of the political-governmental process the public management has to take care that all involved interests, also wide-spread and/or interests difficult to organize interests such as the interest of future generations, are represented or take part in public decision-making. On the level of implementation public management must innovate and experiment with new instruments of public management, such as public – private partnership for infrastructural investments, and urban development, negotiated rule making in environmental issues, and forms of (semi-) autonomization of public services.

CONCLUSION

Within this chapter we have developed the idea that modern societal development described by means of increasing complexity, dynamics, and diversity, leads to new collective and social needs that only can be answerd by newly developed forms of governance. These governance forms have to take into account the *Eigendynamik* of society in social subsystems directed to the development of processes of interaction in which political-governmental interventions and social self-organization are co-ordinated. The government has to take care of both the performance and quality of its own actions/interventions as the performance of the evolving governance structure. In the governance perspective public management as the form giving and executive part of governing is set for the task to implement these governmental responsibilities by supporting and making possible 'responsible' decision-making within and between social organizations and citizens, by 'balancing' social forces so that develop as much as possible in a desired direction, and by making use of innovative public management instruments.

6

ECONOMIC ORGANIZATION THEORY AND PUBLIC MANAGEMENT

Jan-Erik Lane

Whenever human interaction involves considerable transaction costs due to the intertemporal nature of the interaction as well as the complexity of the agreement involved, principal-agent problems arise. Principal-agent relationships may be seen as constitutive of the public sector in a democracy with regard to the making and implementation of policies. A few critical problems in public management may be stated within such a theoretical perspective.

At heart of the policy process and at the implementation stages is the attempt of the politicians as the principal to monitor the efforts of bureaux as the agents to live up to the terms of the contract agreed upon. Public contracting stretches from the election arena over to the parliamentary theatre to the bureaucratic setting. Management contracts involve principal-agent interaction, the logic of which will be highlighted in this chapter by a combination of a public choice perspective and the neo-institutionalist approach.

Starting from the interests that people or various groups bring to political institutions in an effort to further these by various state activities the public choice approach underlines *motivation* in the conduct of public sector analysis (Mueller, 1989). At the same time neo-institutionalist frameworks imply that it is vital to separate the *rules* or the public institutions from the egoistic – personal and collective ones – interests, which figure in public institutions. In order to understand the logic of public management we need both interests and institutions, motivation and rules.

Broadly conceived, institutions are the humanly created constraints on the interaction between individuals (North, 1990). They are the rules and norms – formal or informal rights and obligations – which facilitate or regulate exchange by allowing people to form stable and fairly reliable expectations about the actions of others (Moe, 1984; 1990; Powell and DiMaggio, 1991).

In public management there is bound to be serious problems of ambiguity about the rewards to be given to the manager, about the desired actions to be taken by the manager, about the causal link between actions and outcomes, as well as about what the consequences of the environment for the feasibility of public policy-making and implementation could be. What are the main institutional responses to the principal-agent problems in the public management setting?

INSTITUTIONALIST APPROACHES

Neo-institutionalism embraces a variety of new ideas, but two general versions of the institutionalist argument can be identified, one sociological version and one economic version. The sociological version of the new institutionalism looks upon institutions as more than constraints on choices. The identities and conceptions of the actors, perhaps even the notion of an actor itself, are formed by the institutional structures. The distinction between interests and institutions is not underlined. In sociological neo-institutionalism, institutions seem almost to assume the role as actors, which could lead to reification or the fallacy of misplaced concreteness. In this perspective, interests are endogenous, as the individuals' conceptions are formed in the institutional context they live within (March and Olsen, 1989).

Economic neo-institutionalism embraces two different perspectives: neo-institutionalist economics and the new institutionalism. What phenomena are to be called 'institutions' is not entirely clear. Matthews (1986) distinguishes between institutions as property rights, as conventions, as types of contracts and specifically as contracts about authority or governance structures like the firm or the bureau. Williamson (1985: 15) concentrates on the latter approach, whereas North (1990) stresses the importance of distinguishing conceptually between the rules of the game (institutions) and the strategies (organization) the players in the social game find it advantageous to adopt (1990: 5). Three levels of institutional analysis may be identified in relation to public management.

Operating choices: the actors pursue their interests within a given institutional framework. The institutions are the rules of the game which shape the interaction between the actors. The rules of the game such as a Weberian bureau and the self-interests of various actors determine the social outcome of the interaction. Institutions serve here as a source of explanation for outcomes.

Institutional choice: the institutions are no longer a source of explanation, but are themselves to be explained. The focus is on understanding the processes by which institutions are formed. Economic neo-institutionalism recognizes that an individual may pursue his/her interests in a better way by making an effort to change the institutional constraints he or she faces rather than simply adapting to the institutional structure as if it was unsusceptible to change. The producer operating within the constraints of perfect competition may attempt to get favourable regulation by the government in order to avoid threatening competition. Or the prevailing structure of bureaux may have to altered in order to make programme changes effective. Such a rule conscious strategy could be directed towards both explicit and implicit institutions, comprising constitutional rules as well as operating rules of the game such as corporatism, iron triangles and policy-networks (Jordan, 1990).

Political actors know that the institutional structure matters and act accordingly by pushing for institutional change when the institutions are unfavourable to their interests. Yet, the institutional structure that results over the years, however, may not reflect explicit and rational design, because opposing interests, opportunistic behaviour and uncertainty imply complexity.

Meta-institutional decision-making: This is the constitutional stage, where problems with regard to the rules for the making of institutional choice are discussed and sometimes resolved. It is an eminently political arena – the arena where the basic rules of the state are laid down (Kelsen, 1961).

In the economic approach to institutions there is a clear distinction between the interests of the actors on the one hand and the institutions that regulate their interaction on the other. Most interests are exogenous in this perspective, as they are not to be explained with reference to institutional phenomena, but the actors may develop institutional interests, i.e. rational expectations about which institutions best serve their interests. Public management involves activities on the first operating level as well as on the second level, i.e. institutional choice, the last one of which we focus upon here. Why is the bureau the typical institution in the public sector?

TRANSACTION COSTS

Neo-institutionalism implies a theory about the role of the state in defining the basics of contractual arrangements, depending on existing technologies and natural endowments. As technologies or endowments change, there is initiated a process towards new equilibrium contracts in which the state may play a profound role in institutional innovation. Group interests whether in the form of self-interests or broad collective interests not only enter public institutions at the first level as the building blocks of public decision-making and implementation. Such interests at the second affect the choice of public institutions prior to ongoing policy-making. Neo-institutionalism may be based on the rational choice or the bounded rationality model deserves attention in political theory.

In neo-institutional economics political institutions may be chosen rationally by means of deliberations about which rules are appropriate for patterns of interaction in society. Instead of treating institutions and interests as given, the institutionalist approaches in economics attempt to endogenize what has traditionally been regarded as exogenous. Various stands in economics organization lead up to the development of a theory of institutions that is highly relevant to the interpretation of the public sector (Hodgson, 1988; Bromley, 1989; Hargraves Heap, 1989; Eggertsson, 1990).

The neo-classical decision theory describes individual choice and action as based upon stable preferences and a rational consideration of alternatives and their consequences where the alternative yielding the highest level of expected utility is chosen. The process of choice takes place within a given institutional structure of fully defined and enforced property rights. This basic choice model is retained within neo-institutional economics, examining how various institutional arrangements influence outcomes, and how institutional arrangements themselves arise as the outcome of interaction between various actors rationally pursuing their interests (Matthews 1986: 903).

Basic in the application of the neo-classical decision model onto organizations is the concept of transaction costs in this literature. Within a defined system of property rights it may be conceived as all the costs involved in the transfer of sets of property rights. More specifically, transaction costs are conceived as all the costs involved in establishing, monitoring and enforcing a contract. The costs of negotiating a contract include the costs of searching for contractual partners, acquiring information and concluding an agreement.

Economic organization theory departs from the neo-classical economic model which assume that the costs of transacting when engaging in exchange is zero. Ronald Coase argued that the initial assignment of property rights does not affect resource allocation outcomes in the economy when transaction costs are zero, although it may have distributional consequences (1960). Formulated more generally, when the cost of transacting is zero, institutions, e.g. systems of property rights do not affect allocative outcomes. The implication is that the neo-classical model does not recognize the importance of transaction costs and thus fails to pay adequate attention to the existence of institutions.

Minimizing the costs of transaction arises thus as the goal in the choice of institutions. Coase argued that allocative outcomes will tend towards efficiency through voluntary exchange if transaction costs were negligible. Voluntary exchange can be trusted more extensively if the state minimizes the transaction costs, e.g. by creating or clarifying property rights. Developing this argument from private sector organizations to public sector organization, the bureau or the state could be interpreted as a rational device for handling transaction costs. Taken to its conclusion the economic theory of public institutions ends up in economic constitutionalism.

New institutional economists, e.g. Oliver Williamson have gone a step further by introducing the concept of bounded rationality. With this alternative model of choice, Williamson addresses the same basic question that neo-institutionalists deal with: how does an institution emerge? Governance systems regulate contracts. The governance system that minimizes the costs involved in establishing and enforcing contracts will be chosen by the contractual partners.

Williamson (1975; 1986) looks upon a hierarchical system in a comparative institutional framework as an arrangement that in certain organizational contexts is the most transaction cost efficient way of handling exchange. The basic question is under what circumstances a firm should organize an exchange internally or through the market assigning governance structures to the most cost efficient framework with the aim of reducing the cost of transacting.

As a matter of fact, this basic hypothesis is equally or even more relevant for political institutions, because the issues brought to the public agenda are social problems with high transaction costs involved – issues which could not be resolved by private contracting in a simple voluntary exchange approach. The public sector employs two basic institutional mechanisms – public resource allocation by means of bureaux and public regulation in terms of regulatory regimes. Both involve transaction costs which derive from the interests of the actors. Two human factors and two environmental factors which when combined help explain the relative higher cost of writing and enforcing contracts in the market compared to internal organization.

Bounded rationality: it refers to the limited ability of man to receive/process information as well as to communicate it. Individuals are not typically capable of handling large amounts of information making it difficult to foresee all contingencies in a complex and changing environment.

Opportunism: it refers to self-interest behaviour through deliberate manipulation of information about attributes of the object of exchange as well as own preferences and intentions.

'Uncertainty' derives from the environment of organizations which is complex and changing offering risks but also creating opportunities.

Small numbers: it means that only a few actors participates in the exchange.

The combination of bounded rationality with uncertainty means that writing contracts that cover all contingencies that may occur over a long period of time is impossible. Any attempt to approach the goal of rational decision-making will tend to be very costly. The market solution to this coordination problem would be an incomplete long-term contract or recurrent short-term contracts. However, both these alternatives are subject to the problems that appear when opportunism is paired with the small numbers condition. This condition secures that competitive pressures do not eliminate the potential gain of opportunistic action. The bureau is a more appropriate institutional response to the problems of coordination in public management than individual contracting for each task to be completed.

Incomplete contracts may leave room to behaviour contrary to the intention of the contract when unforeseen contingencies arise. The need for adjustment and amendment of the contract leads to the consideration of short-term contracting. Short-term contracts invites the strategies involved in the negotiation between bilateral monopolists. Each party has an incentive to realize the gain potential by engaging in cooperation, but also to capture the largest possible proportion of this potential in exchange.

Even though a small numbers condition do not obtain at the outset, this condition tends to evolve as the contractual partners invest in *transaction-specific* capital and acquire transaction specific skills. This process makes maintenance of the contractual relation all the more important for the parties to the contract, as the consequences of termination become severe. Market contracting becomes risky as the pay off resulting from hold-up strategies increases. Again, the proper institution in the public sector is the bureau with its internal and hierarchical organization rules.

The relative advantages in the public sector of relying on internal or vertical organization instead of market contracting consist of the attenuation of incentives by subgroups in an organization to behave opportunistically, as their behaviour can be monitored more closely and an incentive system be designed to further the interests of the organization. In addition, disputes may be more easily settled within an organization than across markets. As for bounded rationality, the advantages include the possibility of a step-by-step approach to problem solving in the exchange process, as well as a process of convergent expectations serving to reduce uncertainty. However, internal or vertical organization in the public sector by no means creates rational public management.

PUBLIC MANAGEMENT PROBLEMS IN PRINCIPAL-AGENT TERMS

The principal-agent model starts from a contractual perspective. Agreements establish a hierarchical relationship between the contractual parties where one part in return for compensation agrees to follow the directions of the other. One party, the principal, is given the right to instruct the other, the agent, whereas the agent promises to work for the promotion of the interests of the principal. Such relationships are established when it is impossible to specify all the details in a contract, and at the same time it is risky to leave room for discretion.

Public contracts, pervading the state and local governments, involve the principal's task to design a governance system which gives the agent incentives to act in accordance with the principal's interests, that is to act as the principal would have done had he/she had the capacity and competence to do it him/herself. The principal-agent perspective highlights the possibility for contractual failure and implies a search for mechanisms to be established in order to control whether the agent lives up to the terms of the contract, and sanctions to be employed to enforce the contract.

The governance problem is non-trivial except under exceptional circumstances. First, there must be conflict of interest between the principal and the agent. If the agent anyhow wants to do what the principal wants him/her to do, there would be no reason to create institutional constraints on the agent's choice of action. Second, the agent must have information that is relevant to the principal which the principal can not obtain without incurring costs. If the principal had the same information base as that on which the agent acts, and if he could monitor the actions of the agent easily, then the principal can easily design and enforce a short-term contract. *Asymetric information* in combination with conflicts of interest creates the potential for two different types of governance problems in the public sector.

Adverse selection: it arise at the time when the contract is established when the agent has information about the services the agent will render which is inaccessible to the principal. The agent may misrepresent the fundamentals of contract negotiation to obtain better contract terms than he would otherwise have been able to secure. When the principal comes to realize this, he/she may design terms according to the expected performance of the would-be agents discouraging better-than-average candidates and encouraging worse-than-average candidates.

Moral hazard: it may arise even though the principal has the same information as the agent at the time when they bargain over the contract. The problem is that the principal is unable to observe the actions taken by the agent, and consequently has to base his evaluation of the agent's contract performance on the results of those actions. If the result depends on unobservable random variables beyond the agent's control, the principal can not make reliable inferences about the activities of the agent by monitoring the results of those activities alone. It allows the agent to disobey the terms of the contract without being revealed. Adverse selection arises when the agent has hidden information while moral hazard arises when the agent can hide his actions. Contracts have to be made between the state and civil servants stipulating what the state expects in return for remuneration. Due to the transactions costs involved in hiring and monitoring public officials, the state typically employs the bureau model for handling various state activities – compare Coase's derivation in 1937 of the firm as an attractive institutional set (Coase, 1988; Muller, 1986). In accordance with neo-institutionalist theory, vertical integration is chosen ahead of voluntary exchange . Basic to the operation of the bureau is hierarchical principal-agent relationship between politicians on the one hand and civil servants be these administrators or professionals on the other hand. The bureau has the same status as the basic institution in the public sector as the form occupies in the private sector. Is the bureau such a formidable instrument for rationality in public management as the Weber tradition claims?

Using the bureau as the unit of analysis, adverse selection arises ex ante the policy decision when these units supplies information about the current situation in their area of responsibility, for instance in budgetary requests. Moral hazard can be related to the implementation of public policies. There may be reasons to believe that the potential for moral hazard problems ex post is even greater in public hierarchies than in private hierarchies for which the principal-agent theory originally was developed.

The Niskanen theory of the budget maximizing bureau is one way to model the second principal-agent relationship. It emphasizes the asymmetrical information involved in the interaction between politicians and the bureaux, but it assumes a passive political principal (1971). If one assumes more of symmetry, then the conclusion that the public budget will always be much large than the optimal one does not follow.

The very same problems crop up when the state employs public regulation in stead of public resource allocation.

Trying to control actors by means of regulatory schemes give rise to the inefficiency problems stated in the so-called capture model (Stigler, 1988). The generalized model of public regulation in the form of the model of rent seeking points out that there is no way for the government but to pay a rent for the information advantage that those regulated possess (Tollison, 1982). Implementing optimal solutions by means of public regulatory schemes is impossible due to information asymmetry and moral hazard.

MOTIVATION AND EFFICIENCY

There is bound to be ambiguity in the double principal-agent relationships in the public sector. Bounded rationality, small numbers problem and strategic behaviour give rise to opportunistic tactics that were not recognized within the traditional public administration and welfare economics approaches.

The two basic tasks in state and local government of resource allocation and public regulation are entrusted with public managers. Public managers have to operate under the rationality requirement. It may well be the case that public organization fail to deliver goods, services or regulatory schemes that are efficient, but there is the demand for efficiency in resource allocation and in public regulation from the principals of the public managers, i.e. either the politicians or the population. A crucial question in economic organization approach to the state and local government is whether public institutions may be devised that minimize the scope for opportunistic behaviour.

One may employ a very simple model to illustrate the difficulties of reaching first-best solutions in resource allocation in terms of the bureau as well as in public regulation. Failing to find the optimal solutions to allocative and redistributive problems, one has to move to the next critical question: are there second-best solutions that can be identified and implement by public managers. Total demand for a public programme may be written as:

(1) $$TD = ax - bx^2,$$

and total supply as:

(2)
$$TS = cx + dx^2.$$

The first best solution would be derived from the price equals marginal cost condition. Thus, we have:

$$Qopt = \frac{a - c}{2d + 2b}$$

Rationality or efficiency in the public sector boils down to finding the institutional set up that implements the optimal solution. Either government employs a bureau to produce the quantity of the good or service itself. Or government employs an entrepreneur with the task in accordance with a regulatory scheme.

The main problem in public management is that its two fundamental institutions – the bureau and the regulatory regime – will not automatically find and implement Qopt. Figure 1 portrays three solutions, which all bear on the question of efficiency in public management (Figure 1).

Suppose that the state is to provide some good or service and that it may employ two mechanisms: public resource allocation by means of bureau or a public regulatory scheme that entrusts an entrepreneur with the task of supplying the good or the service. Suppose that the first-best solution given citizen preferences (willingness to pay = D) and the available technology (marginal cost curve = S) is the provision of a quantity Qopt in Figure 1. How is government to identify and implement Qopt?

If it builds up a bureau for the purpose of supplying the good, then there is the risk of a Niskanen budget-maximizing choosing the Qnis solution, which is inefficient, because to the right of Qopt all solutions involve that the marginal cost is larger than its value. The bureau decides upon the output by means of the decision-rule that TS = TD, which involves that

$$Qnis = \frac{a - c}{d - b}$$

However, if government wishes to hire an entrepreneur to provide the good under a regulatory scheme, then there is the risk for monopoly behaviour or rent-seeking. This means that the quantity supplied will follow from the condition that marginal revenue equals marginal costs. i.e. the solution will be to the left of Qopt, or some solution to the left e.g. Qmon, i.e.

$$Qmon = \frac{a - c}{2d - 4b}$$

Figure 1   *Efficiency losses in public regulation and budget allocation*

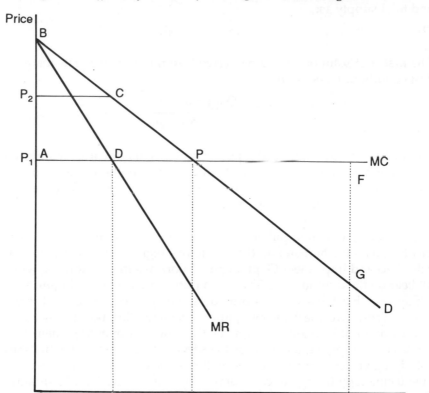

The difficulties in public management derive from the uncertainties and opportunism involved in the principal-agent relationship between the overall the political body and their agents in bureaux and in regulatory schemes. How is a contract to be framed which enhances the probability that bureau will find and implement the first-best solutions to allocative and regulatory problems?

Asymmetric information characterizes the public contract between politicians and public managers, as the latter group has much more information about demand and supply than the former group. However, the asymmetry makes it the more important that the public institutions are framed in such a way as to reduce the negative consequences for the possibility of reaching efficiency. The only way to make for more of symmetry between politicians and public managers is to create institutional mechanisms such that the agent reveals his/her information to the principal. Such mechanisms imply that interests and institutions be harmonized, which creates a need for various kinds of institutional reforms in the public sector: contracting, bidding and benefit taxation (Figure 2).

By moving the public sector towards type IV from the traditional type

Figure 2   *Public sector reform direction*

		Supply	
		The Bureau	The Firm
Demand	Taxes	I	II
	Charges	III	IV

I would mean that public managers get the correct incentives for operating efficient. It is vital that public managers have a self-interest in the employment of his/her knowledge, i.e. somehow the principal must come up with a reward system that minimizes the effects of opportunistic behaviour. The institutional response to budget maximizing bureaucrats and rent-seeking is to increase choice and competition within the public sector.

CONCLUSION

The different neo-institutionalist paradigms bypass the two prevailing approaches to the analysis of the public sector in an era of big government, viz. the traditional public administration framework with its Weberian conceptions of hierarchy, division of labour and public interest motivation on the one hand and the welfare economics framework with its traditional policy criteria of market failures. Understanding the public sector requires a focus on interests and institutions as well as how they interact in the making of strategies among the actors in state and local government.

The bureau has been sen as the proper institutional response to the problems of coordination in the public sector. It is true that the occurrence of bounded rationality, opportunism, uncertainty and the small numbers problem makes vertical organization more rational in the public sector than horizontal short-term contracting of public managers. However, the bureau with its hierarchical institutions do not solve the problem of rationality or efficiency in the public sector.

The bureau whether employed in public resource allocation or in public regulation do not offer institutions that identify and implement first best solutions in the public sector. To counteract the tendency towards budget maximizing behaviour and rent seeking new institutional responses have to be found such as contracting, bidding and benefit taxation which increase choice and competition in the public sector.

PART 2

MANAGING THE PUBLIC ORGANIZATION

The internal management of the public sector can be analysed, not only through the use of a large variety of concepts, approaches and theories as shown in the preceding chapter, but also at several levels within the organization itself. In this section we focus on the management of the organization as such. This involves dealing with the structures, the culture and the resources which are aimed at developing a more effective and efficient provision of public services, either within existing public organizations or outside in private suppliers such as public utilities.

In his chapter, *The Tools of Public Management*, Carl Böhret discusses public management and management reform from a more general perspective than the other authors in this section. His point of departure is the challenges likely to face public management in the future. He describes the post industrial and post modern societies and tries to analyse the public management tools employed in the different types of society.

In the chapter, *Evolving Public Management Cultures*, Les Metcalfe and Sue Richards argue that changes and developments in the type of management used is a cultural phenomenon based on learning processes. They have serious doubts as to whether the cultural – and structural – conditions present in the modern welfare state are such that the embedded resistance to change, inherent in public bureaucracies, can be overcome.

Jeremy J. Richardson, in his chapter on *Public Utilities Management*, discusses how economic orientation and more especially, privatization, foster a different type of managerial culture in the companies where they are implemented. The shift is linked to the introduction of market mechanisms: prices, competition and a reward system based on consumer satisfaction and profit. His concludes, however, that the level of public regulation is not necessary less, but in some cases even greater for private utilities than public. Without public ownership the need for regulations seems to increase.

Financial Management in the Public Sector is a chapter in which Torben Beck Jørgensen concludes that financial management also has to be understood within a cultural framework. The ability to optimize the composition of resources instead of maximizing growth, reduce client expectations instead of playing on them and break down vested interests, all necessitate a shift towards a more business oriented culture. However, this, in turn, raises questions of political responsibility and public security.

7

THE TOOLS OF PUBLIC MANAGEMENT

Carl Böhret

The need for new tools of active administration (public management) and their type and usage is determined by the management and leadership requirements rising from the development of society at the end of the twentieth century. These requirements can increase or decrease in quantity for the public sector, depending on which social scenario is considered. In any case, however, they will increase in *quality*; because with increasing complexity, insecurity in decision-making also increases and therefore, the level of conflict, as well as the pressure of responsibility rises. This is because a turbulent development, characterized by additional ('new') shortages, must be reckoned with rather than with a stable one. In any case, a twofold demand is made upon the tools: they must help public management to react to environmental changes and must take into consideration the inherent complexity of management in the face of relatively reduced resources.

The conditions for the success of traditional or newly-shaped tools arise from the tension between the demands made by social changes (adequacy of the tools) and the realities of institutions (effectiveness and suitability of the tools for implementation). It is the combination of the correct problem-solving tool and the correctly-employed (accepted) tool that ensures a successful result which fulfils expectations. Both dimensions of effectiveness must be considered and 'improved to an optimum'.

If social development demands extensive and new achievements in guidance and control from public management, then different tools will need to be employed in different ways than in cases where development requires a rather more conservative policy. In this latter case, usual and well-tested remedies can be resorted to.

The question as to which tools will need to be employed or even developed for public management at the end of the eighties and during the early nineties depends on the assumption as to which social developments are likely to take place. Hence such differential conditions, based on different societal scenarios are to be fixed before all else. Future demands made upon public management will be derived from them. From these scenarios the tools which appear most suitable can be found out, described and assessed, in each case with a view to their external and internal orientation.

TWO DIFFERENT DEVELOPMENT CONCEPTS (SCENARIOS)

Society in the year 2000 will be obviously more or less different to that of the present day. Depending on which development trends established today are strengthened, for example through public management, either the 'post-industrial' or the 'post-modern' version of society can become predominant. Elements of both versions will, however, remain 'interspersed' in realities (Böhret, 1988).

Post-industrial society and its consequences for public management

The post-industrial society undergoes a gradual and virtually unbroken development out of highly industrialized societies. It is founded upon an optimistic expectation based upon further scientific-technological development. The tension between changes in needs and signs of shortage can be relaxed in the course of technological progress. In post-industrial society, researchers and scientists are the leading figures in contrast to businessmen in an industrial society. Daniel Bell calls central control and sysematisation of theoretical knowledge the predominant 'axial principle' of this version of development. Extended education and management competence, as well as 'think tanks' are the core of innovation in this society. Its central phenomenon are:

– progressive development towards a society of service and recreation with an *enlargement* of the education and *management sector*;
– further increase in productivity with a surfeit of material goods and at the same time an exchange of manufacture by means of intensive work and capital for production backed by intensive knowledge;
– a strengthening of the trend towards a society of information (towards a 'technocratic and biotronic' society);
– an opening-up of new fields of innovation (traffic, deep-sea, information and communication technology, as well as bio-technology, economic use of outer space etc.);
– dominance of specialists and organizers referring to the matter (management of innovations with a tendency towards the 'technocratic dominance of an elite');
– And there will be growing function of the State:
– as a 'fellow-player' in the economy (guidance services, research aid, conveying sense, stabilisation of the economy; simultaneously increasing neocorporatist tendencies);

– as a 'stabiliser' of society like psychological aid for new fringe groups: the 'victims of welfare' of a hedonistic society);
– as 'responsible for the protection of society' (protection through a strong order state in the interest of the new middle classes = mediocrity) against growing lack of norms of disorientated groups of non-experts.

Two central components of development determine the organization of public management: (1) The 'cores of innovation': research and technotronically-oriented development, together with innovation management and the dominance of specialists in 'thought-factories' as well as planners and organizers. (2) The flexible steering function of the State (encouragement of innovation and protection) with a high intensity of adjustment control. The necessary tools of public management are to be found in the adaption and further development of processes that are principally known within the management cycle: definition of problems and goals, development of processes (measures, costs), assessment (with test of conclusions) and choice between alternatives, implementation (with development of organization and staffing), valuation (examination, control, revision). It is the range of application that are extended and the intensity of the operation is increased.

Post-modern society and its consequences for public management

The concept of *post-modern* society aims to offer a qualitative alternative to the development in post-industrial society. In important aspects (technology, production method and consumption, political decision-making and administrative organization, pre-eminence of ecology, an emancipated concept of achievement etc.) it adopts a clear counter-position, even a 'counter-culture', which certainly bears features of a 'new-fashioned Middle Ages' (modern living and working communities with a style of life geared towards the community – 'return to the human dimension'). The post-modern society presents itself as a combination of plural, dominance-free institutions, horizontal interaction ('equality') and diversified structures of living (self-realization). The basic pattern is formed by the 'change of value' from the predominance of the materialistic to that of post-materialistic values, whereby close reciprocal effects are acknowledged.

Standing at the head of non-materialistic values are self-realization, solidarity/humanity, friendship, participation, decentralization, environmental and nature protection, as well as careful treatment of resources. The 'ethics of voluntary simplicity' or a new inner-worldly ascetism (against the exploitation of objects) are post-modern ideals. This society will gradually free itself from the traditional dominance of the economy (growth of economic values, demonstrative consumption). Instead chief stress is placed upon: middle 'soft' technologies and ecologically tolerable methods of production ('small is beautiful'), ecology and protection for prosperity as guidelines for technology and economy, more lasting products which spare resources, adjustment of work to people according to time and place (type of performance required, diversified forms of job-sharing).

Priority of decentralization as a state *and* a social principle of organization: the consequences of which are 'small social networks', new neighbourhoods, 'elective affinities', local culture; promotion of social experiments (new forms of working and living included) in order thus to strengthen individual expressions of life, stimulation of small political units ('communities') and a high degree of (unconstrained) participation; radical abolition of bureaucracy and regulations.

Moreover, there is a quite different adjustment in post-modern societies to those of a post-industrial version. Predominant amongst them are: care of resources and humanly dignified production as well as the distribution of (lasting or permanent) 'goods' such as the 'generalization' (socialization) of services; the promotion of decentralization, self-government, self-realization (aid towards self-help), participation of everyone in public affairs. In addition: denationalization is brought about as a *joint* venture (= *social self-government*), soft ('open') planning, pre-eminence of contact, communication, co-ordination, co-operation (the four useful 'c's'), flexible institutions.

The tools of public management will be of a quite different nature and of a new form of quality than those procedures and techniques at present available. The new instruments must at least expand the traditional ones. Information, discourse and techniques of creativity which involve participation stand in the foreground. Planning basically means the 'co-ordination' of the individual activities of decentralized units of decision-making. Finding consensus becomes more important: negotiating, bargaining, participating, assessing and convincing will, in future, be the central tools of public management. Thus the focal points of adjustment of the tools is to promote creativity, form compromises and consensus as well as the valuation of opening-up procedures.

Both versions of society have only been described very roughly here and only with a view to their *typical* components. Diverse overlappings and intersections are possible, especially in the passages and transfers into new forms. Thus, the respective tools of public management can also only be classified as 'ideal-typical'. The transitions are fluid in the development towards the post-modern version of society. Tools of planning and government which take precedence for *present* public management will be exchanged over the more 'soft' instruments designed for the purpose of finding a consensus among decentralized units which are more typical of the *other* version of society ('people'-oriented management).

TOOLS OF PUBLIC MANAGEMENT IN A POST-INDUSTRIAL SOCIETY

Use and adaptation of traditional tools

In the post-industrial version of society, those tools of planning and decision-making aid which have hitherto been tested are further developed and augmented. The usual, generally well-known tools are to be mentioned here merely as examples (Voelkner, 1992). As relevant as ever are:

– heuristic procedures (such as brain-storming, Delphi-method and morphology),
– target lists ('trees') and assessment of targets,
– decision-making structures (decision-trees, decision-tables),
– simple techniques of prognosis (extrapolation, analysis of regression),
– estimation of costs and examination of costs/benefit/efficacy,
– studies into interdependence (including cross-impact analyses).

Many of these individual techniques will be used more frequently than hitherto as an aid to the improvement of both task and finance planning and of programme budgeting applying to areas of great importance (target budgeting).

The penetration and solution of complex problems becomes more urgent in post-industrial society. Thus, *system and risk analysis relating* to efficiency is of exceptional importance. This type of analysis is suited for penetrating into the whole structure of connections, as well as for assessing subsequent side-effects and consequences. The aim of system analysis is principally to help grasp, present and assess the general connections of all components. The more complex the field of effect (the interlacing network) is, the more side-effects and risks may become apparent; the longer-termed the regulations and the programme is to remain in effect and to remain effective, the more unforeseen results are likely to appear. System analysis is thus a tool that allows a comprehensive analysis of whole contexts and, at the same time, for the recording of certain aspects of a problem area that need settling. System analysis also constitutes the basis for system-simulations with which alternatives can be tested by public management. Figure 1 represents a condensed overview of risk analysis which complements system analysis (Böhret, 1990).

It is only possible to draw attention here to adequate tools of organization and staffing development. The same applies to inner-organizational implementation studies and further development of management (leadership) concepts. Notice a remarkable tendency in the personnel sector: Recently tools for the increase of performance in inner-administration

Figure 1   *Risk analysis*

Action by consequences	
security	that consequences occur, also when and where, is known
risk	probably consequences are objectively and subjectively known
uncertainty	that consequences can occur, also possibly totally new ones, is known
Risk assessment and risk appraisal	
risk assessment	possible (negative) consequences of a project x probability
risk appraisal	are the respective risks allocable, are they reasonable (today/tomorrow) for the concerned parties

have been increasingly discussed and developed. Although maintenance of performance in spite of shortage of cash has been the primary concern, nonetheless the rising cases of situations of 'superfluity' have also been considered under the aspect of maintenance of performance; i.e. consideration of possibilities of *non-monetary* incentives.

DEVELOPMENT OF TOOLS UNDER PRESSURE OF PROBLEMS

Precursory checking of legal regulations

In post-industrial societies, control-checking like laws and administrative regulations tends towards increase. At the same time,the areas of regulation become more important: distribution, safeguarding and stabilising norms are the types of rules. In post-industrial society, new regulations in many areas often only take effect somewhat 'retardedly': side- and consequential effects must be taken into consideration and, if necessary, reduced by public management. Hence experimental tools of 'precursory checking' of legal-type programmes are determined by laws of short duration (policy termination/sunset legislation), law tests and methods of execute-checking (for bills).

The use of test methods is above all advisable when bills or relevant excerpts are to be tested in context as if they have already become a law. The application of test methods lends itself, above all, at the stage of drafting of legal regulations and when analysing individual aspects of a legal regulation. Especially in the case of complex regulation material, public management could settle for such experiments; backhaul automatism and follow-up studies that are fixed in time are of great service when planning and carrying-out programmes of legal character (Böhret and Hugger, 1980).

Environmental compatibility test

This concept, which stems from the USA, is designed to achieve as comprehensive, early and systematic an assessment of the consequences of planned projects on the whole ecological situation as possible.

The main idea behind the environment compatibility test (Umweltverträglichkeitsprüfung UVP), is to facilitate a decision involving the execution or abolition of a programme or measure when ecological criteria play a significant role. With the instrument of an environment compatibility test, plans and individual projects are to be tested as to whether or what kind of damage is likely to be caused to the environment before they are put into practice and whether better solutions exist in the interests of environmental conservation. Environment compatibility tests are to be carried out in such a manner that all fields of environment are systematically examined as to whether the planned projects could be harmful.

In the Federal Republic of Germany, principles of environment compatibility were drawn up in 1975. The principle of provision for the environment is valid: test requirements (relevance for and compatibility with the environment) have been drawn from it early. Since the middle of 1985, a guideline has been in existence in the European Community, which in the Federal Republic of Germany, for example, was converted into national law through a statute concerning environmental impact assessment (EIAL, 1990). Until administrative regulations have been issued, the procedural steps of the EIAL act as guidelines: preliminary determination of the scope of the investigation, participation of special government agencies and the public, summary statement and assessment of the environmental impact. At each step, appropriate remedies or management techniques are employed; currently, benefit analysis and marginal value assignment bring the most common (Cupei, 1986).

Technology assessment

An important form of analysis of effects and consequences that currently exist, and will continue to do so in the near future is the widely-established 'technology assessment' (Böhret and Franz, 1982). In several European countries, technology assessment was introduced, following the American example, as a tool of public management, but also as a political aid to decision and partly institutionalized. Technology assessment is a tool used for the multiple identification, analysis and valuation of the consequences and side-effects of technology and technics. Technologically political decisions and measures are to become improved, even 'more intelligent'. Besides technological information, economic, social, political, ecological, legal, demographic, anthropological, socio-cultural and administrative effects or contacts respectively are to be investigated as to their relationship to one another (cross-section) and their development (longitudinal cross-section).

By means of early recognition of extremely diversified effects of technological innovation, a network pattern of thought that is orientated towards the future, as well as a long-range control of technological change is to be stimulated. There are already many examples of applied TA in rather different areas and with methodically diverse characteristics.

Analysis of impairment (cost-constraint analysis)

In post-industrial versions of society, the actions undertaken by public management are also subject to the critical observation and valuation of the citizens. Although technological progress and economic prosperity are principally accepted, social and ecological fears (lack of concrete goals, excessive welfare, on the one hand, and unemployment, destruction of environment on the other) grow at the same time. The limit of consensus, as far as new projects are concerned, drifts on to higher levels. However, because the structures of decision and participation do not *fundamentally* change, public management must deal with more 'weighty' oppositions in the matter. The more meritocratic structures develop, however, the less these problems of acceptance become. The difficulties lie in two areas: in the system of political determination (government, parliament, political parties) and in the system of political participation (social organizations, alternative movements, media).

The customary techniques of planning, but also the more costly, large-scale system analysis are still too seldom concerned with such conditions of establishment and implementation.

For predominantly political assessment of consequences and for the investigation into expenditures needed to reduce political opposition in the system of decision, public management could make use of 'cost-constraint analyses'. Implementation restraints of a project and the costs needed to 'resist', neutralize or reduce drawbacks can be found out and weighed in the balance with the expected political benefit. The amount and nature of political expenditures that are to be – or can be – made in order to put a desired programme into practice, even in the face of obstructions (opposition, delays), can be determined. Five operative steps need to be taken in order to carry out a 'cost-constraint' analysis: identification of the impairment, valuation of the costs required to resist or neutralize the impairment, determination of the benefit to be obtained from resistance or neutralization respectively, appraisal of the programme analysed in such a manner, and selection of a politically satisfying (and pacifying) programme.

The danger of manipulation is present, just as, at the very end, all influence and intervening measures of political guidance show a tendency to operate in a dominant way. In post-industrial societies, it depends on

the currently realizable counter-pressure of social interests as to whether
– and how far – social acceptance can be obtained at all, or how far the
planned projects require alteration in content or procedure.

Public regulations and commitments as a tool of guidance and control

The debates about the appropriate regulation of economy and especially
of large enterprises have led to two directly opposed positions and respective measures:

1 Refraining from interventions (stop and go) leads through principles of
   market economy back to 'self-regulation'; therefore deregulation and
   the rendering private (for example of public enterprises) is necessary.
2 Increasing market failure exerts for itself the strengthening of public
   intervention going as far as diversified forms of nationalization and
   socialization of enterprises or branches.

There is, however, a very subtle tool that is available to public management 'in between': the so-called public regulations, ties and commitments
of enterprises. Basically this means that the enterprises of a branch of
economy are subject to sovereign special provisions which restrict free
market activity for a certain length of time. Supervision and direct control are taken over by certain offices/institutions of public management
(Thiemeyer, 1983).

Undesirable effects such as ecological and social effects of enterprise
activity upon a wider circle of individuals are to be avoided – or desirable
advantages are to be obtained in the interest of the public. It is therefore
through such 'public regulations and commitments' that protection aims
can be pursued. Suitable tools of such regulations and commitments
are: legal regulations (prohibitions, requests, conditions of permit), recommendations, appeals, and duty to report to and inform the public.
The following can constitute sanctions: public 'denouncements', fines,
shutdown of works or parts of works, and positive: incentives towards
different (the actually desired) actions. Public management can make use
of specific centres of control, such as the setting-up or expansion of boards
of control or supervisory commissions.

TOOLS OF PUBLIC MANAGEMENT IN POST-MODERN SOCIETY

New social attitudes and forms of legitimation, such as will be typical in *post*-modern society, demand quite different tools as well-known
resources will at least be employed in a different manner. To a certain
extent a guideline for the type of tools and their use are the ties with
joint and decentralized planning and decision-making processes of a non-
bureaucratic nature. The predominant concerns are:

1 To explore desirable developments, humane needs and social as well as ecological compatibility.
2 To obtain a wide acceptance of planned programmes or measures.
3 To spread widely participation in even complicated decision-making processses (e.g. through the use of 'layman's competence').
4 To use human-social debates as an important means of convincing rather than tactics of persuasion; thereby, mediation techniques will be employed to a greater degree.
5 To employ tools equally appropriate to public management itself (such as communicative and laissez-faire management, rotation of office, temporal management positions, etc.).

Exploring and evaluating

On the way to post-modern society, it will be necessary for public management to look ahead and anticipate potential developments. Desirable tendencies are to be advanced while undesirable ones are to be prevented or at least moderated. To do so, it is necessary to know which processes and phenomena appear desirable or still endurable in the first place. This form of qualitative exploring ought to be characteristic and relevant for post-modern ways of thinking, whereby early communication with concerned parties and with a widely-distributed expert competence is advisable.

The ideal of post-modern society rests upon appropriate developments which do justice to mankind and to attain a 'balance' that is socially and ecologically tenable. Past- and future-orientated investigation is required, as well as investigation of desirable goals, of 'backgrounds' (i.e. of 'good' traditions), effects and potential consequences. New tools are to be developed, whereby the peculiar nature of decentralized participation as a fundamental idea is to be taken into consideration.

Tables of values can, for example, be drawn up in order to explore the goals and expectations of certain social groups which help to fix priorities and posteriorities, as well as to social acceptabilities. Such trees of values and similar points of departure can be integrated into more complex tools. Two of these larger-scaled methods are 'desiderative scenarios' and the 'FAR method'.

Desiderative scenarios

Scenarios of this nature are used to describe *desirable* situations or models of society, i.e. 'possibilities' neither existing in the past nor the present so that, for this very reason, *no data* is *yet* available for extrapolation purposes and therefore no quantitative trends can thus be ascertained! Hence a 'retrograde' method lends itself to analyses relating to time. One moves, so to speak, from the desired future that is described in the

Figure 2   *Tools of consequence analysis and consequence anticipation*

Newer methods of prognostication	Delphi and long-term predictions, dynamic innovation studies, improbability analysis
Methods of consequence estimation	system analysis, consequence estimation/assessment, cross-impact analysis and morphology, chance-risk assessment; consequence balance sheets, defensive output, production analysis/production consequence estimation, compatibility tests
Model-building and simulation	ex-post simulation (including the 'unoccurred story', the genesis of consequence), causal, model-building, computer-supported planning games, simulation

scenario backwards into the present: the adequate *path of development* is discerned. If the path is possible (able to be 'produced') then the desired future situation ought to appear. If the reality of the current state of affairs (present) and the (uninfluenced) developments established within it are also taken into consideration and, moreover, the historic conditions of these developments are taken stock of, then a plausible path from here towards a fairly desirable future can be described.

Public management would then have to carry out, in a participatory mode, the respectively appropriate interventions by means of suitable socially acceptable tools in order to minimize deviations from the path.

The FAR-method

The Field-Anomaly-Relaxation (FAR) Method (O.W. Markley and R.F. Rhyne) could be employed as a tool for the supervision of deviations. By means of descriptions, sectors and factors, alternative lines of development are described, valued and presented in development tables ('Trees'). If now, for example, variant Y represents the suitable way towards the attainment of the state of affairs presented in the desiderative scenario without meeting any surprises, then it is the duty of the 'new' public management to detect, through constant observation of society, deviations for example towards a variant X, and to take counter-measures (for example, certain methods, rules, programmes) using consensus-forming processes.

Tools of consequence analysis and consequence anticipation

These tools are concerned with new methods of prognostication, model-building and simulation, as well as with tools of consequence analysis and assessment which have yet to be developed or improved upon. Four assumptions concerning consequence-orientated prognostication are given: (A) Generally, speaking, there are alternative futures; i.e., degrees of freedom do exist. (B) To a certain extent, it is possible to visualize such futures (controlled 'fantasy', intuition, thinking in scenarios). (C) Path (corridors) of alternative futures can be demonstrated; we are not drifting back and forth in a tide of times and events. (D) There is a political (and moral) duty to use the ability to prognosticate and to draw consequence-orientated conclusions from it. Figure 2 gives an overview of consequence-orientated tools of prognosis.

In this connection, the 'product-line analysis' must also be mentioned. It begins with the planning and development of products and their manufacture and especially examines the 'life-cycles' of a product, from raw material extraction, through the actual production and marketing, to consumption and the elimination of residual wastes (Böhrct, 1990).

Budget distribution struggles being intense and the budgetary procedure remaining sluggish, the possibility of a partial budget flexibility should be considered in view of the new consequence dimension. A kind of 'second budget' should be created for areas of grave importance. This 'second budget' should combine the often-discussed elements of period transgression and the contingency budget, with incentives for innovation. One cannot wait for 'money' when the collapse of the ecological system is to be expected.

Basically, this means that the political-administrative 'management of consequences' must not be allowed to run aground due to financial bottlenecks. Therefore, a part of the overall budget of a one or two-year budget should be placed quasi 'outside of the brackets' and, under supervision, allocated, although not fully appropriated, for the treatment of unforeseen

Figure 3   *Aspects of flexible budgeting*

Keyword	Predominant orientation	Budgeting method	Example
multi-period budgeting	action-orientated	a budget item is allocated for consequence-orientated expenditures, i.e. with material and temporal transferability from item to item and year to year	reduction of forest damage
contingency budget	problem-orientated	an additional item is allocated for unexpected and belated manifestations of consequences (with transferability to the 'multi-period budget')	overcoming the effects of chemical accidents
100-x-budget	innovation-orientated	to encourage consequence-reducing/consequence-preventive projects, a budget item is allocated to 'idea suppliers'/implementors ('competition budget')	development of new methods of residual waste reduction (e.g. contamination)

(negative) consequences. In Figure 3, three aspects of such 'consequence-orientated, flexible budgeting' are presented (Böhret, 1990).

Convincing

The sooner the basic principles of post-modern society are clearly formed, the sooner orders, instructions, directions and allowances in the *internal system* will be repressed. These traditionally bureaucratic methods of introspective management contradict the rather more decentralized and participative lines of 'post-modern' management. This management requires appropriate delegation, with decision-making responsibility, reciprocal information *and* consultation.

However, the *external relations* of public management will also require alteration. More personal advice-offering contact with individuals of equal statues and spontaneously-formed groups will take the place of 'letting people know' according to instructions, decisions made in the absence of the client and more formal, written methods. For both developments, discussion and exchange of information will increasingly take the place of directing, sanctioning and contradicting forms of communication: thus, integrating instead of merely instructing, convincing instead of directing, and also allowing oneself to be convinced.

'Institutionalized publicity' will more often be complemented by spontaneous dissemination of information and partly also 'rectified'. Public management must continually inform itself, be informed and inform others (public relations work). Only in this way is it possible to obtain a wide social acceptance for public action. This acceptance, however, is an important aspect in the *formation of consensus*, which in turn represents a central feature of the post-modern version of society. Information about possibilities of informing based on computers that have future perspectives is to be found elsewhere. In order to provide examples, 'new forms of negotiation', participation ('structured participation') and transparency through communication (media, citizen and layman's competence) will be treated.

New forms of bargaining and negotiating

Special importance ought to be accorded to a new style of bargaining and negotiating. Bargaining and negotiating activities are especially required in post-modern society. Although the different valuation of benefits and individual aims are to a large extent well-known (due to a society-oriented policy of information), they are not yet harmonized nor even put into effect. In negotiations, information is 'published' for the first time. As a form of 'compensating substitute', negotiations as well as bargaining procedures must lead to fair solutions, as long as *discursive* formation of consensus is not yet possible – or only possible over too long a period of time. Three typical aspects form the point of departure for new forms of bargaining as an important tool of public management:

– The negotiating partners have *two basic interests*: maintenance of personal relation *and* an optimal solution of a 'practical issue';
– the bargaining partners are *firstly* human beings and not mere abstract representatives,
– it is easier to change the *process* of negotiation and bargaining than the *people* involved; thus it is also more correct to concentrate on interests than on positions or stands. Only in this way can: the rules of the game that are acceptable to all partners be united, the method 'objectified' and thus 'equalities' created, and sufficient benefit be obtained for all participants. It is a question of developing alternative solutions for oneself and one's 'partner', which are also of service to others: (to one's 'contemporaries' and the environment) – or at least do not harm them (a sort of 'holistic Pareto-principle').

For the process of bargaining and negotiation this means being firm in the matter which is designed for the social benefit of all and being 'soft' with partners. Emotions are included as positive expressions; symbolic gestures ('mutual approach and recognition') are important. The feedback is particularly relevant in communicative bargaining situations: have I understood you correctly?

This form of negotiating as a tool of public management in 'post-modern situations' is also always directed towards a superior situation: not only reciprocal advantages are to be guaranteed, but also insight into the expediency of a whole benefit is to be given and, at the end of the day, a social awareness to be conveyed.

As a part of participation and consensus negotiating, the mediation procedure has attained increasing importance. Decision-making and conflict resolution are made easier through the inclusion of a neutral mediator in the reconciliation process. In this way, problem-centered, consensual solutions by fair means are supported over irreconcilable power positions, hostilities and dogmatism. A lot depends on creating a good climate and a common sense of responsibility, as well as attaining a communicative, procedural arrangement and mutual acceptance of the partners. On this basis, negotiated solutions and extended programmes can be achieved. Good results with the mediation procedure are especially respected in environmental protection (Fisher and Ury, 1984).

New forms of participation

The new forms of negotiating logically presuppose sufficient participation of individual groups that are orientated towards consensus. Being present and participating are demands made upon *everyone* in the post-modern version of society. Public management can only be successfully shaped – when important public affairs are involved – through the processes of participation. Planning and development of programmes are not among the last items to be concerned, especially since these are to come into being in a *decentralized* manner.

Participation in planning and projecting (the formation of projects and plans)

1 *Workshops for the future*

Even in a more post-modern version of society, a minimum of imagination, planning and co-ordination is required. This, however, is not reserved for 'superior' specialists and bureaucrats alone. On the contrary, all citizens are, if possible, to be included so that they may reflect upon their future, or also think about fully concrete plans and projects, and have a say in deciding on chances of putting them into practice (Jungk and Müllert, 1981). The typical pattern of events commences with criticism of drawbacks and deficiencies by those potentially concerned and proceeds to the realization of novel ideas.

2 *Planning cells*

Similarly set up (but even more concretely orientated towards the individual projects of those concerned) is the functioning of 'planning cells' (Dienel, 1978). Planning cells are instruments of participation and political advising. Following the principle of coincidence, groups of about twenty-five participants are selected to solve a clearly outlined task. The participants are remunerated for their work (loss of earnings). The results of the 'layman's competence' in understanding the matter are summarized in a 'citizen's opinion' which is, above all, directed towards the decision-makers in public management. In this process, 'concerned' or 'representative' members of society are involved in important phases of decentralized decision-making processes: co-operation and co-responsibility are employed as *qualitative* tools.

Both processes of participation are therefore to include as many people as possible in the processes of public management, and to render it 'public' in the first place. The idea behind this as a well-founded acceptance which is created by participation in the discovery of ideas and the valuation of alternatives. Such processes, depending on their participative and decentralizing tendencies, especially coincide with the ideals of post-modern society.

Innovation alliances

A top priority for public management in the post-modern version of society is to obtain social acceptance for important projects. This means, above all, the general agreement among the population with socially-compatible, technological change promoted by public management, and the economic realization of that change.

This requires continual communication between the political-administrative and social forces, that is, communication far beyond cooperation in planning processes. Innovation alliances between administrative management, science and lay expertise, as a kind of 'quality circle' of political-administrative management will be established (Böhret, 1992).

Despite diverse backgrounds and knowledge, the members of the innovative alliance are convinced that the creativity and chance for implementation stem from their common cooperation. They rely on continual communication and reconnection with their institutions of origin and, at the same time, with the alliance partners ('network'). These 'active' innovation alliances are not fixed in a concrete, institutional form. On the contrary, they are made up of political inventions which must be continually created, using existing elements in new compositions. In the management-related area, it is possible to create a varying combination of internal and external expertise, to stimulate consequence-orientated thinking among political-administrative actors and to push forward a corresponding personnel development, to develop foresighted methods (management models) and steering instruments, and to set a time-limit on political programmes when critical consequences are not sufficiently assessable.

Beyond this, the inclusion of 'lay experts' is of considerable importance. The starting-point of these considerations is that most of the trend-setting problems are no longer revealed to specialized, scientific experts, or even to professional politicians. The new lay experts are included quasi as a 'second type of knowledge' (surmising, exploring, assessing) in the actual development of policy, especially in its preparation and evaluation.

Change in internal organization

Administrative internal organization is also supported in the post-modern version of society by motivating methods which include and stimulate colleagues, especially since 'job rotation', too, exists in the external-internal relationship. Managers who are increasingly appointed for a limited time are rather dispersers of information and 'stimulators', 'go-betweens', 'negotiators' as well as coordinators and moderators, than traditional heads of authorities, describers of targets, instructors and controllers. Leadership is rather an 'ideal' of promoting cooperation; it takes its course through the awakening and stabilizing of insight and intrinsic motivation.

Four specifically 'post-modern' aspects for internal, system-orientated management are to be high-lighted here, namely the successful transfer into public management of: the modified rotation principle, the communicative or even laissez-faire management style, the quality management, and the 'double' time management.

'Job rotation' here means that the occupants of individual positions are frequently changed: even in top-management there exist 'top positions of limited duration'. Expert knowledge is less important than the prevention of official authority, the development of bureaucracy and routines. Rotation should, at the same time, offer incentives: the new activity allows for new social experiences of the individual, it enriches comprehensive knowledge positions.

In contrast to the cooperative style of leadership, a communicative, or even laissez-faire, style is criticized because of its tendency towards 'non-leadership' and disorganization. This open, situation- and individual orientated leadership lends itself, however, especially to post-modern versions of society. Leadership becomes 'each person's handling of himself' in an intention free from rule or leadership. Of course, the 'primus inter pares' endeavours to obtain a consensus concerning goals, activities and results; he must learn to 'let go'.

Even if this extreme form is not suitable for every situation, this style of leadership ought nevertheless to become an ideal: in connection with other elements of the leadership system, such as incentives, means of leadership, development of personnel, coaching as well as rotation principle and new forms of negotiating, interesting prospects of a socially appropriate treatment of people by the administration-manager arise.

The public sector is exposed more and more to the double pressures of economical job performance and 'customer orientation', i.e., the products and services of the administrative system must be 'sold' and/or made available to the private sector (citizens, business firms) in an efficient, useful and cost-accountable manner. The change to participatory quality management, in which co-workers are included in a responsible manner in 'quality circles' in order to improve efficiency, range of performance, the method of production of goods and services, and included also in quality production and quality assurance, is indispensable.

Dealing with time ('Time Management'): Consciously dealing with the scarcity of time is becoming increasingly important. Alongside personal time management stands the strategic employment of the time-factor in planning, steering and coordinating decision-processes. Above all, it deals with early recognition and handling of a problem, a pre-drawn timetable ('script') for the coordination of individual measures and activities within a complex decision-process, assessment of the correct time for certain measures, and observation of the course of the process in order to speed up or slow down, if necessary.

In the main, time management on the personal level must serve to create 'space' in which the administration-manager acquires distance from routine business and has the opportunity to develop innovative ideas and fundamental concepts, as well as to integrate his work and that of his co-workers into inter-connected parts of a whole.

CONCLUSION

Leadership and guidance demands on public management will increase on the way into the twenty-first century. The type of demands made and their concrete features are, however, for the most part dependent on which form of society prevails as 'ideal'. There are many indications of a

Figure 4　*Tools of public management in different types of society*

Predominant type of society	Resulting predominant public tasks	Typical tools of public management
predominantly post-industrial	technologically-orientated innovation management ('thought' factories, furthering of high tec)	heuristic methods, methods of target-finding and decision-making, prognostics, etc.
	planning and co-ordination on state level: stabilizing/ securing developing	cost-benefit analyses, intermediate planning procedures, systems analysis, UVP and Technology Assessment
	directing; also by legal norms	precursory control of legal regulations, impairment analysis, incentive systems (staff), implementation studies, public regulations
	PASSAGES　　　–　　　TRANSITIONS	
predominantly post-modern	soft planning, consequence analysis	desiderative scenarios, value tables, FAR simulation, consequence anticipation
	resource management	product-consequence estimation, consequence balance sheets, new budget types
	furthering of self-government, decentralisation, self-help	workshops for the future, planning cells, participative negotiating, innovation alliances
	diminishing of bureaucracy, communicative steering	participative direction, time and quality management, job rotation

'transindustrial society' as a mixture, with a slight tendency towards the post-modern version, of both post-modern and post-industrial forms.

No matter which version of society develops predominantly, in any case public management must be able to employ the correct tools in order to be able to handle, both inwardly and outwardly, the often turbulent passages from one to another. Figure 4 attempts a synopsis and classification of outlined tools for both lines of development.

A prerequisite of efficacy is that the tools must be suitable to the problem and socially adequate: cost-benefit-analysis and analysis of impairment ought to constitute suitable and 'accepted' tools of public management in post-industrial versions of society. Desiderative scenarios, workshops for the future and partnership negotiations correspond rather more to the post-modern version. Test of compatibility with the environment and assessment of the consequences of technology can serve as expedient tools in both versions. Their classification would then depend on their either more technological or more participative character.

Finally, it is significant that outwardly-directed tools and developments in inner administration are, as far as possible, parallel: the use of partnership negotiating or bargaining in contact between public management and social groups also requires an inwardly open direction with laissez-faire or emphatically cooperative forms, as well as the use of 'innovation alliances'. The employment of heuristic and system analytical tools requires bordering incentive systems and measures of further education in the inner-administrative system of post-industrial society.

Personally, I am convinced that we must count on mixed versions of social development over longer periods of time. This requires a 'mixed' use of tools of public management in the process of development and a careful, judicious application and adaptation of these tools, involving, in some areas, intensive participation.

8

EVOLVING PUBLIC MANAGEMENT CULTURES

Les Metcalfe and Sue Richards

Public management is an idea whose time has come (Kingdon, 1983). Force of economic circumstances and political doctrine are combining to push European governments into seeking ways of improving the performance of public organizations. At least some of the attempts to reduce costs, increase efficiency and improve resource utilization have moved from ad hoc cuts to management reforms. The anxieties of the 1970s about governmental overload and economic failure have crystallized into reform efforts directed towards reducing governmental demands on scarce resources and increasing the value for money obtained from resources actually deployed. Various approaches have been adopted to try to squeeze more output from fewer resources. Some reform efforts aim at making savings or improving performance in limited areas. Some involve introducing widespread organizational changes such as decentralization or tighter financial management. Others seek more general cultural changes to inculcate values conducive to greater cost consciousness, a stronger service orientation or greater willingness to accept responsibility for results among civil servants.

The variety of lines of attack is symptomatic of the fact that the problems are both complex and ill-defined. Simple slogans, such as value for money or modernization, attract widespread assent. But useful prescriptions for action require a more searching diagnosis of the real problems than superficial assertions that government is out of control and some universal panacea can correct this. As Herbert Kaufman pointed out, this raging pandemic is a disease with several distinctly different strains (Kaufman, 1979). The popular appeal for tighter control of public bureaucracies not only means several different things but may also be quite misconceived. To manage is not to control (Landau and Stout, 1979), and many reforms have foundered in the past because they applied control solutions such as Programme Planning Budgeting System (PPBS) to management problems.

The radical prescription for these ills is massive privatization and deregulation. But the scope for government to divest itself of functions is politically constrained. In general, politicians show a marked reluctance to cut services and allow their opponents to claim they are defaulting on commitments. For the foreseeable future improving the performance of large, complex and highly interdependent public organizations will remain a crucial task. Better public management is a vital route to economy, efficiency and effectiveness in both the short run and the long run. There is certainly scope to do this. Because standards of public management have not been high in the past, improvements can be made by eradicating waste. Initiatives aimed at limited targets may produce relatively quick results – especially economies in the form of staff cuts and financial savings. Cutting inputs concentrates the minds of officials and forces them to take the difficult decisions they have been putting off. More broadly based improvements in efficiency and effectiveness depend on fundamental changes in the way public organizations are run. Hence the current interest in public management.

As in the past, much of current thinking about public management is derivative rather than original. It draws heavily on models and techniques developed for managing in the private rather than the public domain. Formerly, this interest might have led to proposals for reform aimed at introducing specific private sector techniques into government. PPBS is the prime example. Management by Objectives is another. They led to proposals to bring about more rational distributions of responsibilities among departments and transformations of departmental structures into more logical forms. To an excessive degree the same solutions are being proposed now, but they seem dated. The success rate of transplants from business to government is low both for techniques and for individual managers. Successful businessmen rarely make the grade in the public sector.

Of late the emphasis has changed from technique to culture. The new philosopher's stone, or perhaps management consultants' meal ticket, is organizational culture. In an uncertain world people need more general points of reference to guide them and a firm belief in the value of what they are doing. A strong organizational culture offers a means of inculcating the motivation and sense of purpose that more mechanistic management techniques have failed to provide. Current interest in cultural change as a means of improving performance owes a great deal to fashionable private sector interest in corporate culture. This interest was stimulated by Peters and Waterman's (1982) much vaunted and much criticized book *In Search of Excellence*. Putting on one side methodological doubts about their claims to have found strong relationships between business performance and corporate culture, there are familiar difficulties in transferring their principles from private to public organizations. It is far from certain that 'excellence' in public management means the same as it does in business. For example, 'closeness to the customer' sounds straightforward, but government deals with the public in many different kinds of relationship: as clients, taxpayers, subjects, claimants, inmates and patients among others.

Nevertheless, the meaning of excellence – reaching for and achieving high standards of performance – is very important for the future development of public management. However the content of excellence is specified, it raises aspirations from the level so long accepted as the norm for administrative behaviour (Simon, 1957). In addition, it can help provide a clear public image and a legitimate political profile for public management. Without a clear image and defensible standards, public management is vulnerable from two directions.

It is vulnerable to the counterattack of established administrative cultures which tenaciously impose obsolete limitations on the beliefs, values and theories of organization that public officials are expected to espouse. More seriously perhaps, it is vulnerable to the intellectual imperialism of business management which seeks to mould government in its own image. While there is much to be learned from business that is relevant to the improvement of the familiar management functions, personnel, finance, purchasing, as well as at the general management area, governments should select what they learn on the basis of a diagnosis of public management needs.

OBJECTIVES

The main objective of this chapter is to try to define the distinctive characteristics of a public management culture; to differentiate public management from current concepts of business management and from traditional ideas about public administration. The title 'Evolving Public Management Cultures' defines a task and states a thesis. The task facing European governments is to make a transition from existing administrative cultures to public management cultures. Governments must discard their obsolescent administrative cultures as they evolve public management cultures. The transition may involve gradual evolution or an evolutionary discontinuity. Current reform efforts may be viewed as part of that evolutionary process.

The thesis contained in the title is prescriptive. In order to cope with newly emerging problems and cope with rapid change, public management must become an adaptive evolutionary process. What should distinguish public management cultures is the value they place on capacities for organizational learning, adaptation and flexible response to new problems and priorities. The pace of change with which governments are confronted calls for a succession of policy responses. Public management is not just the management of change, it is a learning process. The capacity for evolving new solutions and learning from experience provides the core values and assumptions round which a concept of excellence in public management can develop.

The task and the thesis are linked. Evolution towards and evolution within public management cultures are related. The ease or difficulty of transition from an administrative culture depends on where we are as well as where we are going. At present our knowledge of each is inadequate. As the Irishman said, it would be easier to get to our destination if we did not have to start from here. On the other hand, coping with the stresses and strains of transition can contribute to building the learning skills and adaptive competences that public managers will need in the future.

LOYALTY AND CULTURE

It is not easy to place the cultural dimension of public management in the contemporary scheme of things when there are such strong political pressures to treat management as a tool for cutting back on expenditure and resources. A useful point of departure is Hirschman's (1970) analysis in *Exit, Voice, and Loyalty* of how firms, organizations and states respond to faltering performance. His analysis of ways in which different feedback mechanisms activate responses to decline and stimulate efforts to improve performance has a hidden relevance.

Most of *Exit, Voice, and Loyalty* is devoted to exit and voice as, in Hirschman's phraseology, 'impersonations' of economics and politics. Exit and voice represent endogenous forces of recovery, environmental signals and sanctions to businessmen and politicians that organizational performance is slipping below acceptable levels. Dissatisfied customers exit; they take their business elsewhere . Dissatisfied citizens voice complaints; they direct protests at those in office to draw their attention to shortcomings. 'Exit and voice that is, market and non-market forces, that is, economic and political mechanisms, have been introduced as two principal actors of strictly equal rank and importance' (Hirschman, 1970: 19). Loyalty, if not left waiting in the wings, had to accept a lesser billing. Hirschman discussed loyalty mainly as customer or member loyalty, a moderating demand-side influence on exit and an encouragement to exercise the voice option. To forge a link with organizational culture, loyalty can also be considered as a supply-side phenomenon. Instead of a cultural influence on the exercise of voice and exit, it may be regarded as the combination of commitments to standards of service that determine how producers respond to the exercise of exit and voice. This interpretation of loyalty links it closely with the present discussion of public management cultures. Loyalty is an impersonation of public management.

In the present phase of transition it is no accident that the loyalty of public officials is a political issue in many contexts. Governments are currently exploiting the traditional loyalties of civil servants to the limit. More is being expected in terms of performance and less is being offered in terms of resources, income, job security and career prospects. Meanwhile, civil servants are under attack through political channels and experiencing the effects of the exit option through privatization and contracting out. Even if some of this is unavoidable as an accompaniment to overdue adjustment to hard times, it is only an early phase of a process that has a long way to go. The unfreezing of established loyalties should be a prelude to change to be followed by refreezing round a new and more relevant set of loyalties.

As business discovered after the turbulence of the 1970s, the painful process of cutting back has a searching effect on organization and management. It exposes weaknesses and deficiencies that could be masked and tolerated in more benign conditions. But the real challenge is remedying the weaknesses, and a demoralized and demotivated staff is not likely to rise to the challenge. The reason why In Search of Excellence caught the mood of the times was that it pointed a way forward. It provided guidelines and established a new faith round which managers could rebuild their confidence and begin to look ahead rather than looking back. As with business in the 1970s, government is now undergoing an adjustment which will require a phase of cultural renewal and culture-building. Our main premise is that the evolution of public management cultures will be successful only if it creates a framework of values and concepts that incorporates traditional concerns of public administration and relates them to governments' future tasks and environments. A new set of loyalties is needed to guide public management.

THE CRISIS OF THE STATE

One of the dangers in the current situation is that reform efforts and perspectives are too narrowly focused on current issues. Political imperatives call for solutions tomorrow to today's problems. Yet, it is normal for significant changes in management systems and organizational structures to take years to bear fruit in improved performance and productivity. The time-scale of cultural change is even longer. In forming a public management culture the values and concepts should relate to future challenges. Although it is present problems of governmental overload and economic stagnation that have prompted reform efforts, more deep-seated forces are at work. Karl Deutsch (1981) asserted that we are experiencing a crisis of the state which should be understood in broad historical perspective rather than as a result of short-term cut-backs.

In the present-day world, the state – and this is typically the more or less sovereign national state – is both indispensable and inadequate. It is an indispensable instrument to get many things done and to deal with many real problems. But it is inadequate to cope with an increasing number of other problems of life and death for many of its inhabitants. (Deutsch, 1981: 331)

The inadequacy of the nation state has an internal and an external aspect, both of which can give rise to crisis. Internally, decisionmaking power is less concentrated and central control less easily established.

But within the dictates of traditional administrative cultures, evidence of disintegration and fragmentation frequently produces feverish and ineffective efforts to assert central control. Externally, many problems of security, defence, ecological balance and economic progress are international. But in crisis conditions, governments are prone to withdraw from inter-governmental cooperation and supranational policy-making rather than to move positively into closer collaboration. The stalling of European integration is symptomatic of the withdrawal from international collaboration. It remains to be seen whether the agreements emerging from Luxembourg in late 1985 will break the log-jam.

Deutsch suggested further that the existing welfare states of western Europe are obsolescent; along with the administrative theories embedded in their cultures. Looking ahead, the role of the state – and the concepts of public management appropriate to it – will be different from those prescribed to deal with current problems.

What of the state of the near future, say about 2000 AD? In today's highly developed countries, it may have to put heavy stress on adaptive social learning, together with the power to implement its results, followed by a heightened concern for integration and coordination. (Deutsch, 1981: 338)

As the key values of future public management, social learning, adaptive implementation and integration have far-reaching consequences. Yet, they have not gained much prominence in recent discussion of modernization and administrative reform. The bulk of attention has gone to more urgent if not more important problems of cutting spending and managing resources more efficiently. It is questionable how far this contributes to building a public management culture which can help to deal with the crisis of the state in the long term. To take a familiar example, one of the dominant themes of current reforms aimed at greater operational efficiency is transforming government departments into responsibility centres or accountable units which have clear objectives and as much autonomy as possible. But in an increasingly interdependent world putting these precepts into practice may reinforce centrifugal tendencies rather than foster capacities for integration. As we argue later, it is the management of interdependence that is a critically important feature of public management. There are considerable dangers in introducing a management culture that makes the assumption that governments and their constituent organizations are loosely coupled systems.

Evolving from administrative culture to management culture

The present analysis is unavoidably speculative. We cannot look to other countries to find ready-made models or solutions. We all have our array of national stereotypes, but there is little comparative work that draws out cultural similarities and differences between the administrations of European countries in a systematic way. One can glean some information from studies such as Aberbach et al.'s (1981) comparative investigation of the roles of bureaucrats and politicians in France, Germany, Italy, The Netherlands, Sweden, the United Kingdom and the United States. The collection of national studies of policy style in western Europe edited by Richardson (1982) also highlights cross-sectional differences. But discussion of administrative culture tends to rely upon statements about bureaucracy in general or observations of individual cases. There is no general concept of public management against which to test and evaluate practice. Guy Peters, while asserting the impact of cultural variables on public administration, added that 'assessment of this impact had to remain in a somewhat impressionistic level because of the lack of much hard evidence' and went on to point out that one of the main difficulties with the idea of culture as an analytical tool 'is that it generally tends to be a vague and amorphous concept that can be twisted to include virtually anything a researcher wishes' (Peters, 1978).

We have argued elsewhere (Metcalfe and Richards, 1984) that organizational cultures provide theories of management incorporating the values which guide action and legitimize the exercise of power. Culture is the theoretical dimension of organization which provides participants with 'a view of itself, its role within some large system, the nature of its environment, its own operation and the norms which govern its behaviour' (Schon, 1971). All of these basic assumptions are habitually taken for granted and are extremely difficult to change. Beliefs are deeply entrenched and protected by disbelief systems which reject alternative views and protect orthodoxies. With due allowance for differences between countries, we make the assumption that, at present, governments have administrative cultures which give a high priority to procedural conformity rather than management cultures which give a high priority to achieving results. It is possible to add other pairs of values to extend the range of contrasts between an administrative culture of procedural conformity and a management culture of performance. For example: a culture of subservience versus a culture of responsibility; a culture of continuity vs a culture of innovation; a culture of propriety regardless of costs vs a culture of cost consciousness; a culture of stability vs a culture of progressive improvement.

Of course, these are not absolute distinctions. They provide a rough guide to broad differences of orientation and indicate the general direction of cultural change now being sought – a move towards taking responsibility for the performance of public organizations. Furthermore, they suggest pointers to the directions that should be taken in the pursuit of excellence in public management.

THE PROSPECTS FOR REFORM

Sceptics might argue that this amounts to nothing more than playing with words, attributing positive qualities to go-getting public management and negative qualities to old-fashioned public administration. For obvious reasons, observers of administrative reform have acquired a strong sense of deja vu. The record of administrative reform is poor. Its political appeal is much greater than its administrative impact. March and Olson's (1983) observation about administrative reorganization in the United States during the twentieth century has more general validity: reforms are more attractive as proposals than effective as programmes. Early enthusiasm evaporates once the magnitude of the task and the obstacles to progress become apparent.

Part of the explanation of past failures lies in the area of electoral propaganda and political tactics. Politicians can promise more if they claim that increases in efficiency will keep costs down and help curb public spending. They can also trade reform proposals for agreement on substantive policy. But the main explanation of reform failure lies in the conceptual and practical difficulties of managing the required changes successfully. Management has such strong association with business and commercial practice that the mere mention of the word prompts reflex responses among some civil servants that owe more to ideology than analysis. Another factor, already referred to, is that reformers mistakenly equate public management with private management. They select targets for reform because they fit the solutions available, rather than develop new solutions to fit public problems. Private sector practice is not irrelevant to public management reform. In some instances it is clearly appropriate and useful. As argued elsewhere in this volume, contracting out, pricing of common services and designing information systems and cost centre structures are examples. But private sector practice cannot provide criteria for its own use in the public domain. A concept of public management is needed which addresses the distinctive problems of government and points to when and where business practice should be used and where fresh thinking is needed.

There is a recurring tendency to brush these difficulties aside and to argue that resistance to change can be overcome by summoning up sufficient political will. However, political will is a necessary, not a sufficient condition for reform to succeed. It provides the motivation but not the direction of reform. Formulating a concept of public management is a necessary part of creating a public management culture as a credible and defensible alternative both to traditional administrative cultures and private management cultures. In the process of formulating this concept we shall consider what constitutes excellence in public management. More generally, we shall consider by what criteria public management should be judged. There are certain respects in which management is management. All organizations have ways of dealing with personnel problems, finance, making judgements about, if not measuring, performance and so on. But in other respects public management is distinctive. The standards that should be applied are different from and more stringent than those applicable to private management. If private management standards are applied inappropriately, instead of promoting effectiveness, the results are likely to be suboptimal or even counterproductive.

PUBLIC-PRIVATE: INSTITUTIONAL OR ANALYTICAL DISTINCTION?

Public management implies a meaningful public-private distinction between different kinds of institutions or different kinds of problems. Stressing the cultural dimension in the transition of public management has the important advantage of side-stepping the sterile problem of drawing an institutional boundary between public and private sectors. The field of public management is better defined analytically than institutionally. No clear institutional distinction can be drawn. Every attempt to do so fails to produce a demarcation that is either sharp or behaviourally significant. There are always gradations, hybrid cases and grey areas. The ambiguous status of 'quangos' as semi-autonomous, semi-public bodies exemplifies more general uncertainties. The rhetoric of current privatization presumes a sharp distinction which is not found in reality. Government's management responsibilities are being redefined to span the boundary rather than being eliminated. Some of the theoretically interesting public management problems arise at or beyond conventional institutional boundaries.

Public and private management are more usefully distinguished analytically as inter-related levels of policy-making than as mutually exclusive spheres of activity. The distinction does have an institutional origin in the structure of modern governments. Governments are not unitary hierarchical structures. They are multi-organizational systems. They consist of networks of interdependent organizations. The critical area of public management is the management of organizational interdependence, for example, in the delivery of services or in the management of the budgetary process. Public management is concerned with the effective functioning of whole systems of organizations. The public-private distinction is important analytically in situations where attempts by individual organizations to pursue their own (private) aims independently of what others are doing is both self-defeating and counterproductive from the (public) point of view of the performance of the system of which they are the parts.

Logically, the public-private distinction is important in situations involving a fallacy of composition. The whole is not simply the sum of the parts. Individually rational actions interact to produce a collectively irrational outcome. There are many familiar examples. No one thinks that watering their own garden during a drought will make a significant impression on the water supply, but if everyone does so the combined effect on water reserves could be serious. No one thinks that their minor tax evasions or excursions into the black economy have any great importance. But once evasions become the norm rather than the exception this is not true. The managerial implications of this logical dilemma have not been fully explored although it has been considered from other angles.

A number of familiar social science analyses centre on the problem of disparity or contradiction between the separate (private) interests of the constituents of a system and their common (public) interest. They include the prisoners' dilemma game, the tragedy of the commons, the social psychology of panics, the logic of collective action and turbulence in organizational environments. The common feature of these analyses is that the situation in which the participants interact creates structural obstacles to the realization of common interests. Even if common interests are clearly recognized in principle, in practice, co-operative action to realize them is blocked because of mutual mistrust, the dominance of incentives to compete rather than co-operate, failures of communication, or other structural obstacles to co-ordination.

The most extensive exploration of these problems is probably in public choice economics. But because much of the work starts from reductionist assumptions of individualism, rationality and self-interest that economists work with, it largely fails to contribute usefully to our understanding of real world public management problems. Public choice economics virtually builds an expectation of failure into its assumptions. By giving an over-riding priority to internally defined goals it neglects the dependence of goal achievement on environmental conditions. But environmental conditions are not just external givens, they are products of interaction among the constituent organizations. The environment is a network of organizations.

Reviewing these various analyses, Buckley et al. (1974) proposed a more constructive line of attack. They emphasized the necessity of isolating structural problems from more routine incremental problems and the need for concerted action to deal with them. Structural problems require systemic solutions. If the degenerative tendencies inherent in the situation are to be checked, collaborative action is required to restructure the situation – to remove those elements that obstruct the realization of common interest and establish conditions favourable to their achievement in the future. What distinguishes public management is explicit acknowledgement of responsibility for dealing with structural problems at the level of a system as a whole.

This should not be taken to mean that there is no role for private management (in the analytical sense used here) in governmental organizations or that private sector management techniques are of no value. On the contrary, they can have an important role and one contribution of this analysis is to clarify the nature of that role. Private management methods can be used to best effect in situations where structural problems do not arise or where provision for their resolution through public management processes is adequately made. In short, their effective use requires a relatively stable set of environmental conditions, which it is the task of public management to sustain and create. These restrictions on their use should be recognized, otherwise misapplication of valuable but limited tools will discredit them.

The focus on structural problems is the first distinguishing feature of public management. Whereas private management treats its operational situation as an externally given set of opportunities and constraints and formulates policies within it, public management cannot make *ceteris paribus* assumptions. Instead it treats the total situation as a network of relationships among organizations which can be modified through co-ordinated action. Public management is concerned with setting the framework within which private management functions. A public management culture recognizes the strategic importance of coping with structural problems and rewards co-ordinated action to deal with them.

The search for common interests is a core value of a public management culture. In many respects this may seem an old fashioned idea – the common good, the public interest, the national interest are concepts which are apt to make hard-bitten practitioners look askance. The reason for their scepticism or cynicism can often be traced back to a record of failure in dealing with structural problems rather than excellence in performance. Serving common interests sets a standard of excellence that is difficult to live up to, and one way of coping psychologically with failure is to reject the standard as impossibly idealistic or unrealistically high or simply as not practical politics.

This general concept is developed in three ways in the following sections, to clarify the meaning in the context of modern government and to spell out other core values: the first considers public management as a macro-process; the second as a learning process; and the third as a process of political design.

ASPECTS OF PUBLIC MANAGEMENT

Public management as a macro-process

The foregoing analysis abstracts severely from the richness and complexity of public organization. But it poses some key questions about how to improve public management with important and uncomfortable practical implications.The implications are important because they recast the task of public management so as to emphasize the interdependence of organizational and political processes in dealing with structural changes. Public management involves the exercise of public power and decisions about how public power should be used. Instead of separating policy and management, and subordinating the latter to the former, as the administrative tradition does, public management assumes close interaction and mutual feedback between them. Management does not begin where policy-making ends. The implications are uncomfortable

because they set standards of excellence for public management which
are above much current practice. They are also above the standard of
achieving pre-set objectives. Administrators typically feel their primary
loyalty is to a particular organization and see their role as 'fighting
their own corner' in dealings with other organizations. Reform efforts
usually take increasing the internal efficiency of public organizations as
the main target. But in a changing environment such efforts are likely to
produce disappointing returns and may even be totally misconceived, if
they uncouple operational efficiency from broader long-term questions of
effectiveness. Unless the process by which objectives are set is included as
part of management there are no clear performance criteria.

To make reform efforts productive and worthwhile, new macro-
processes of public management are required at the inter-organizational
level. The core values of a public management culture centre on managing
structural change through improved inter-organizational co-ordination.
Modern governments consist of complex networks of organizations
which are frequently large and closely interdependent. Governmental
organizations are very diverse in form and function. They deal directly
with individuals as citizens and subjects, customers, clients, claimants,
employees, tax-payers, patients, inmates and in many other roles.
However, the environment of a particular governmental organization
consists of other organizations within government and outside. Public
policies are formulated through interaction among organizations. Services are delivered through multi-organizational systems. The networks
involved in public policy formulation and implementation may be
intergovernmental and supranational as well as intra-governmental and
national. The seductive simplicity of a standard of excellence such as
'close to the customer' loses a good deal of its appeal, to say nothing of
its prescriptive force, once the conflicting objectives, roles and interests of
several different organizations are taken into account.

Thus the public-private distinction is a distinction between micro- and
macro-management processes. Individual organizations are the unit of
management at the micro-level while at the macro-level the unit of management is a network of organizations. Private management in this sense
is the mutual adaption of organizations to each other in the process of
securing resources and pursuing their separate objectives. Public management is the macro-level process concerned with steering the behaviour
and performance of interorganizational networks (Metcalfe, 1974). Both
contribute in different ways to effectiveness.

Four sets of variables influence the effectiveness of individual organizations and whole networks of organizations: intra-organizational
processes, input transactions, output transactions between organizations
and their environments and, finally, interactions within the environment
itself – the causal texture of the environment (Emery and Trist, 1965).
This ordering roughly corresponds to the priority given to different
ways of improving performance. Tightening internal systems is the

first priority, next comes controlling inputs, after that improving outputs and the environment – where resources come from and where problems arise is last. But in public management as a macro-process the appropriate distribution of attention is reversed. The greater the level of organizational interdependence, the more frequent the occurrence of structural changes which require management at the macro-level rather than incremental changes requiring increased operational efficiency at the micro-level. Structural problems arise from actual or potential failures of inter-organizational co-ordination. The role of public management as a macro-process is to foresee and cope with structural problems which damage performance by eroding the conditions of inter-organizational co-operation.

The need for specific processes at the macro-level arises because the causal texture of the environment is a macro-phenomenon. From the standpoint of any one organization, the environment is an external set of constraints and opportunities to which it must adapt. The configuration of the environment is something it can influence but not control. The more complex the environment the greater the extent of organizational dependence on external forces that are increasingly difficult to anticipate or adapt to. The difficulty encountered in many fields of public policy, whether at the national or international levels, is that centrifugal forces of organizational self-interest are stronger than the centripetal forces of public management. When structural problems occur the co-operation and goodwill needed to overcome them is hard to generate. Nowhere is this more obvious than in the budgetary process and the management of public expenditure. But reform efforts typically give priority to squeezing resources at the departmental or subdepartmental level rather than redefining the basis of co-operation between departments.

Public management as a learning process

The traditional values associated with public administration emphasize stability, predictability, continuity and certainty. They are closely associated with the machine concept of bureaucracy. Typically, the role of public organizations is defined in apolitical, instrumental terms. The conventional critique of this conventional theory emphasizes bureaucratic rigidity, inertia and resistance to change. Proposals for reform generally recommend alternative structures to the ones that exist. But the transition from an administrative culture to a public management culture is not a move from one structure to another structure, from stable state to stable state; it is a move towards management processes that are flexible and adaptable enough to match changing circumstances and capable of evolving at a pace which is consonant with the rate and type of social change that advanced societies are likely to encounter in the future. Donald Schon's observations on public learning and government as a learning system are particularly apt:

If government is to learn to solve new public problems, it must also learn to create the systems for doing so and to discard the structure and mechanisms grown up around old problems. The need is not merely to cope with a particular set of new problems, or to discard the organizational vestiges of a particular form of governmental activity which happen at present to be particularly cumbersome. It is to design and bring into being the institutional processes through which new problems can continually be confronted and old structures continually discarded. (Schon, 1971: 116)

Public management should take account of this evolutionary requirement, which gives enhanced importance to cultural values that guide action and reduces dependence on particular structures created to serve them. Public organizations in this perspective are temporary structures created to perform a function. The values associated with public management are learning, adaptation, resilience, resourcefulness and flexibility. The emphasis in reform proposals should be on building capacities for managing change rather than installing a permanent structure.

Treating government as a learning system calls for a model of learning which is complex enough to represent the different kinds of response required by different types of change. Incremental change may be absorbed by individual organizations or by mutual adaptation among organizations at the micro-level. But structural changes require more fundamental reorganization of whole networks of organizations. A model for learning which incorporates this macrolevel process is Ashby's (1960) multi-stable system. In a multi-stable system the constituent parts may adapt to small frequent changes independently, but if faced with large-scale changes they pool their adaptive resources and undertake a whole system reorganization, thus supplementing and amplifying the adaptive behaviour of the constituent parts. Instead of simply aggregating a series of adaptive responses which would be insufficient to deal with structural changes, in the multi-stable system the constituent organizations interact directly with each other to redefine common problems and co-ordinate the search for solutions (Metcalfe and McQuillan, 1977).

PUBLIC MANAGEMENT AS POLITICAL DESIGN

The emphases on structural change, on public learning and on creating a context within which more operational management processes can function effectively, brings out a third distinguishing feature of public management. Public management should include a process of political design. Despite the scorn that is so often heaped on 'tinkering with institutions', questions of organizational design and broader issues of the distribution of power have a significant impact on performance. By political design, we mean the process of reconstituting and redistributing organizational power and responsibility. Political design in this sense links traditional public administration concern about constitutionalism and public accountability with more recent developments in the field of organizational design. It goes beyond the details of internal structure to defining the roles and mutual relations of interdependent organizations.

In keeping with the evolutionary perspective, political design is not a once-and-for-all allocation of functions: instead it is a continuing top management responsibility. The problem of political design is to create institutions for effective co-ordination of organizations which have a vital role to play in the execution of public policy and to design arenas in which competing interests seek to resolve differences and arrive at agreed policies (Anderson, 1977). Thus, political design is a process of setting the rules of the game within which organizations involved in the public policy process work. Although it does not determine policy outcomes, political design is concerned with establishing appropriate distributions of organizational roles and responsibilities; providing institutions for conflict resolution and establishing procedures for accountability.

From the cultural standpoint the design of accountability processes deserves special mention. Accountability is widely regarded as an obstacle to effective performance in public management rather than a positive contributing factor. One reason for this is that accountability processes do impose structural constraints on what public organizations can do. The issue here is whether the constraints imposed are appropriately designed, given the form and function of the organizations concerned. Often, rigid and inappropriate accountability procedures are imposed without sufficient regard to their effects on performance – ostensibly to check the abuse of power.

In addition to checks and balances against abuse of power, accountability processes at the cultural level can be designed to guide and motivate the legitimate use of power. They do so by embodying the right to manage in doctrines of legitimacy. Doctrines of legitimacy are public statements of internalized beliefs about the exercise of managerial authority. They may invest public managers with hierarchical authority but may also cast them in different roles, for example as professionals interpreting the needs of clients and subject to peer group evaluation of performance as distinct from hierarchical evaluation (Metcalfe, 1981). Designing the cultural framework of accountability not only has important motivational implications in providing the moral basis for managerial action, but it also provides the ground rules for determining how performance criteria should be set. Once more, this leads to differentiation to take account of diverse public management tasks and functions. By so doing it raises the issue of a subcultural variation within an overall public management culture.

SUB-CULTURES IN PUBLIC MANAGEMENT: MATCHING CULTURE TO FUNCTION

The discussion of public management, thus far, has been at a high level of abstraction and refers to a correspondingly high level of practice. Public management as we have defined it focuses on strategic issues. Frequently, these are the issues that elude the grasp of policy-makers because they are conceptually difficult and politically demanding. Despite lip-service to concepts such as the public interest, integration and cordination, public organizations are not notably effective in overcoming the limitations of departmentalism. Hence, in the evolution of public management cultures the main challenge is to establish a recognition of the need for public management as a macro-process, as a learning process and as a process of organizational design.

Nevertheless, public management is not just a high-level process conducted in a rarified atmosphere where strategic issues are considered without reference to the underlying organizational realities. Indeed, to make a useful contribution to organizational effectiveness, the public management process at the macro-level must be linked into micro-level policy processes in both the policy formulation and policy implementation stages. These interactions are implicit in the emphasis on public management as a learning process and a design process. However, their implications for organizational culture at the micro-level of individual organizations need specific consideration.

Government consists of a complex network of inter-related organizations which share a common culture but also generate their own subcultures. Given the heterogeneity of public organizations it would be unrealistic to expect and counterproductive to prescribe cultural uniformity across the whole of government. In a comparative perspective, finance ministries concerned with public budgeting and financial control, foreign ministries, or education ministries display recognizable similarities of outlook and orientation which national differences in administrative culture modify but do not mask or suppress. Such differences are conditioned by the roles and tasks these bodies undertake and the values they espouse.

However, accepting the legitimacy of differences in organizational culture cannot and should not lead to the kind of cultural relativism which presumes that there is some justification for any and all cultural differences. A more critical attitude to subcultures in public management is essential. Whatever is, is not always right. The difference between the present situation, where subcultures emerge ad hoc in specific organizational contexts, and the future may be a more deliberate effort to plan the development of appropriate cultures. As Schein (1985) pointed out, conscious effort to manage cultural change may be the most important task of organizational leadership. Instead of being culture-bound and reacting defensively to changes that threaten the integrity of the existing organizational culture, public managers should see cultural change as a major source of organizational flexibility.

For this to happen, public managers must know what options are available and what criteria would be employed in choosing between them. They must begin to think in terms of matching culture to function. Unfortunately, at present there is little readily available information on which to base judgements and decisions. Governments have not made good use of their varied and wide-ranging experience to develop systematic ideas about the appropriate choice of organizational culture. What information is available in general organization theory owes a good deal to business experience but is still useful as a starting point. For example, the schema originated by Harrison (1972) and elaborated by Handy (1981) is a good place to begin. In Handy's terminology distinctions can be drawn between four types of organizational culture: role culture, task culture, power culture and personal culture. Each type is considered briefly below and then the utility of the schema is discussed.

The *role culture* corresponds to the dominant stereotype of public organization, the large complex bureaucratic machine. Government performs many tasks which require routine and programmed activities to be carried out continually on a massive scale. Systems for collecting taxes and delivering benefits are prime examples. The culture appropriate to organizations charged with such tasks is a role culture. In a role culture people expect tasks to be precisely defined and responsibilities to be demarcated; career progression is regularized and governed by explicit criteria and set procedures, usually with security of tenure and many rules and regulations to order behaviour. Organizational structures conform to a hierarchical model and subordinates are socialized into compliance with superiors. Role cultures are found in business as well as government. Large banks, insurance companies, manufacturing and retailing companies frequently adhere to the familiar and, for the customer, frustrating model of business bureaucracy. Nevertheless, machine bureaucracies guided by a role culture are indispensable instruments of modern government.

The *task culture* differs in important respects from the role culture. It gives priority to performance and achievement of objectives as against procedural regularity. In order to get the job done, people are encouraged to mobilize the requisite resources and establish teams, project groups and task forces. The task culture strongly values flexibility and adaptability and emphasizes the kind of conformity that is central to the role culture. Within the task culture, non-hierarchical structures such as matrix organization are created by bringing together the appropriate mix of people at the right organizational level and then letting them 'get on with it'. Identification with a team which has clear and specific objectives focuses energies and motivates the commitment needed to produce innovation. Such groups have a finite life and organizations with task cultures consist of a changing assemblage of semi-independent teams.

Task cultures are important for managing internally or externally generated change. New political objectives require new policies and new structures to develop and implement them. New problems call for responses that the established structures may have difficulty recognizing, let alone dealing with. Taking initiatives depends upon having people accustomed to giving shape and substance to ideas that are initially poorly defined or resolving problems that are ill structured. When governments encounter new or unanticipated problems they often resort to a task structure but then staff it with people who do not subscribe to a task culture and are therefore poorly equipped to make a success of a new venture. They allow old loyalties to over-ride new ones.

The third type of culture is the *power culture*. Power lies at the centre of a web and is exercised in a very personal and sometimes arbitrary way. The power culture is focused on satisfying the objectives and needs of the person or people at the centre of power. In order to do this priority goes to responding promptly to the demands of the centre even though this may mean riding roughshod over others or executing U-turns in policy.

The power culture places great store in loyalty to leaders and commitment to serving and protecting their interests. Because personal loyalty is greatly reinforced by personal contact power cultures have difficulty in extending their web of influence across large organizations. However, in government they may be significant in ministers' cabinets and private offices and in the higher echelons of departments.

Handy labelled his fourth type the personal culture because he was mainly thinking of private organizations. For the public domain we choose to redefine it somewhat and call it a professional culture. Within this culture professionals, experts and specialists regard the organization as an administrative support system to facilitate their work, rather than as a source of authority that governs and directs their activities. Within broad parameters they expect to exercise professional autonomy and use their skills. Self-control and self-regulation are important elements of the professional value system and lead to claims for peer group evaluation of performance. The needs of clients rather than the orders of superiors provide the guidelines for assessing effectiveness.

Governments employ large numbers of people in professional and quasi-professional roles. Some such as lawyers, architects, scientists and engineers have links with outside professions. Others such as tax inspectorates are professions in government. The numbers and diversity of professions in government are considerable. But the extent to which this is reflected in existing administrative cultures appears to vary considerably.

It would be too much to expect that these four cultures – roles, task, power and professional – would map neatly and precisely on to different public organizations. Perhaps administrative life and organizational design would be more straightforward – though more constrained – if they did provide off-the-peg answers to specific organizational questions. They are not templates to be applied slavishly, but reference points to be used in diagnosis. They are analytically distinct but in particular empirical cases they are combined. Indeed, some of the recurrent conflicts and persistent dilemmas of public management can be framed as problems of reconciling norms and values of disparate subcultures within, as well as between, organizations. For example, the tension between generalists and specialists or the conflict between accountability and initiative may arise from the disparate values of the role culture and, respectively, the professional and task cultures.

CONCLUSIONS

Cultural change is increasingly seen as a means of improving the efficiency and effectiveness with which the business of governments is conducted. But a clearly defined pattern of culture appropriate to the future tasks of government has been lacking. This chapter has sought to fill the gap by proposing an evolutionary concept of a public management culture. The core values round which public management cultures should develop include learning, experimentation, adaptability and flexibility. The need for these values arises from the rate of change with which governments will have to cope in the future The standards of excellence to which public managers should aspire are linked to the performance of large systems, often composed of several inter-related organizations. Effectiveness in public management depends on managing interdependence. The combination of a rapid rate of change and high levels of interdependence produces structural problems that not only require concerted action to resolve them but also call for skills in political design to redefine organizational roles and interorganizational relations. Political design also sets the framework of accountability within which performance criteria are set and actual performance is assessed.

In summary, public management cultures should be general enough in concept to embrace public management as a macroprocess as well as a micro-process; public management as a learning process as well as a process of serving predefined objectives; and public management as a design process as well as an executive function. It is within this context that governments can draw on business experience in an intelligent and discriminating way and identify areas where they must innovate or learn from each other rather than imitate business practice.

9

PUBLIC UTILITIES MANAGEMENT

Jeremy J. Richardson

One of the problems in discussing the management of utilities is that there is no agreed definition of what a utility is! Moreover, utilities are sometimes publicly owned, sometimes privately owned and are often rather hybrid organisations, almost impossible to classify in terms of conventional public/private distinctions. Thus, we need to be conscious of the fact that a category of organisation where boundaries and status are ill-defined may be especially subject to the same shifts in political and public perception as are public services more generally. In the latter case, most western European states have been subject to changes in the financing and management of public services and to broader shifts in 'policy fashions' regarding what is an acceptable level of publicly funded provision. The 'marketisation' of the public sector – including public services and public utilities – is perhaps one of the main characteristics of the 1980s and 1990s. However, we should be cautious in discussing trends as though they apply only to public organisations. The kinds of economic and resourcing pressures that have characterised public sector management in the past decade or so are also very familiar to private sector organisations. For example, the 'contracting out' of services, a characteristic of British public sector management since 1979, has also increased in larger private sector organisations and multi national companies. Similarly, the increased pressure for monitoring and evaluation, development of performance indicators, development of separate cost centres, greater responsiveness to social and consumer pressures etc. are trends that cut across the public/private divide. In a sense, changes in managerial fashion know no boundaries – be they national or sectoral.

In particular, the central feature of the management of public utilities – namely regulation – is increasingly a central feature of the activities of private organisations. For example, is the regulatory burden on, say, public or private electricity generators or telecommunications operators, significantly different in its managerial impact from the range of regulations under which, say, a chemical company operates in Germany? The growth in employment of corporate lawyers in the private sector is itself an important indication of the enormous impact that public regulation of private sector activities has in the modern state. It is true, of course, that utilities are commonly subject to particular forms of regulation not usually imposed on private sector organisations – such as price capping or rate of return regulations – (and that the degree of regulation may be particularly high) but the fundamental managerial task of running an organisation in the context of a strong regulatory environment may not be so different between the public and private sectors. For example, in early 1993, British banks mounted a campaign against what they considered to be 'costly and disruptive' plans proposed by the Government, to require auditors of financial institutions to report to regulators anything of 'material significance' (See *Financial Times*, 9 March 1993). The response from the banks could well have come from a privately owned utility, complaining about excessive monitoring of its activities – 'We think that auditors may feel the need to deluge regulators with information they don't need'. In particular, the implementation of the Single European Act (SEA) has meant an enormous increase in 'state' regulation of companies operating within the EC. For example, there are now quite detailed regulations governing the need for food retailers to display information in a language which can be easily understood by customers; toy importers/manufacturers may need to have their products independently tested before going on sale, and the EC had by 1993, introduced over 200 environmental measures, many of which have a direct effect on the operation of private organisations. Similarly, EC competition and public procurement laws have a major impact on company activities, as do the hundreds of technical standards under which firms now operate. (This is why firms participate so intensively in standards setting bodies such as CEN).

Finally, political ideas on what should be public and what should be private have changed quite radically in some western European states, alongside radical shifts in views on appropriate regulatory regimes, irrespective of ownership. Thus, the British case, on which this chapter draws quite heavily, (in view of the radical nature of British policy experimentation), is an important model in the sense that most of the utilities have either been transferred from 'public' to 'private' or will be transferred in the near future. Relatively little research has been done so far by social scientists on just what happens to the management of these organisations when their constitutional status is changed so radically, and when the societal expectations and value systems under which they operate are also subject to major change. In the 1980s and 1990s many utilities have seen their constitutional status changed, have seen new regulatory regimes introduced, and have begun a managerial revolution which has yet to run its full course.

THE CONVENTIONAL MODEL OF PUBLIC UTILITIES

Traditionally, utilities have been regarded as monopolies or quasi monopolies. The central 'policy problem' has been, therefore, to secure adequate benefits for consumers, for the shareholders (often the national government or regional/local governments, but also, especially in the US and now the UK, private shareholders), and to secure economic efficiency in terms of the efficient allocation and use of resources. Balancing these often conflicting objectives has proved to be a major growth industry for academic economists and regulators alike! In terms of public policy processes and institutions, the core activity has been, of course, regulation. In theoretical terms, the public policy dilemma was captured perfectly by George Stigler over twenty years ago, as follows:

> The central tasks of the theory of economic regulation are to explain who will receive the benefits or burdens of regulation, what form of regulation will take place and the effects of regulation upon the allocation of resources (Stigler, 1971).

In terms of public policy instruments, typical forms of regulation include price controls, profit or rate of return controls, controls on entry and, of particular importance of late, performance targets related to quality of service and customer satisfaction.

To these visible (and sometimes quantifiable) controls, we need to add the controlling effect of public expectations of how utilities should behave. For example, the perception that citizens have of water are quite different to their perceptions of, say, cars as commodities. In reality, water is just a product like cars, but public expectations regarding the behaviour of the suppliers of these two products – and of the price they are prepared to pay – is quite different. This became very evident in Britain in the early 1990s as the price of water rose rapidly in order to make up the backlog of investment and to meet tough new European Community regulations. Similarly, when the privatised water companies began to behave more like any other private company supplying a good, there was often a strong public reaction (e.g. regarding the salaries paid to Executives). Basically, utility managers have generally been subject to much more social control than managers of other industries, although this gap has narrowed considerably as the private sector has come under more pressure to behave responsibly. Thus, we have seen a rapid development of the corporate responsibility function in private companies (Moore and Richardson 1988). The need to maintain organisational and managerial incentives in public utilities has been a central concern of both theorists and regulators alike. Regulating rates of return and profits and controlling entry to the industry via licensing, run the obvious risk of removing incentives to increase efficiency. Paradoxically, the development of more sophisticated performance targets can have the same effect. With all of these policy instruments, the risk is that managers will act in ways to reach the set targets but will have no material incentives for going beyond these. Thus, 'under perfect, frictionless regulation, the regulated firm has absolutely no economic incentive whatever to minimise its costs'

(Schmalense 1986: vii-2). It then falls to the regulator to be sufficiently well informed and resourceful in devising new regulations, and above all to know what performance is possible and what could, therefore, be demanded of the utilities. Usually, there is a marked imbalance in expertise and resources between regulators and regulatees, and a resulting tendency for regulators to underestimate what could be achieved by an organisation such as a public-utility. One has to look only at comparative telephone charges, cross-nationally, to realise that the variation in management efficiency is quite enormous, not withstanding that all telecommunications services are subject to some form of state regulation and have the same technological opportunities. Regulation is like taxation – the more sophisticated legislators are at devising taxation regimes that widen the tax base – the more inventive accountants and taxpayers are at avoiding the tax! As Schmalense notes, 'Commissions can generally observe a firm's actual costs, for instance, but they cannot directly observe the level of management effort or the quality of managers' discussions' (Schmalense, 1986: vii-2).

The record in practice has been problematic, in part because regulation is, at its most basic, usually about controlling profits. As one observer has noted:

> Legislatures and administrative agencies have, by and large, chosen to regulate profits in the effort to assure reasonable prices. This has been done primarily through rate-of-return regulation, specifying an allowable rate of profit to be applied to a utility firm's equity capital. This potentially leads to a distortion in the firm's incentives ... (Nowtotny 1989: 21).

The attempt by regulators, on both sides of the Atlantic, to generate other incentives appears to have been a failure, in most cases. Thus, Strasser and Kohler argue that:

> Traditional utility regulation has been largely unsuccessful in motivating improved company performance. Traditional regulation creates a number of incentives for inefficient operation, and controls efficiency only crudely; some counterbalance is needed. When regulators have tried to use performance incentives in rate cases, the results have been terrible. The goal of incentive plans should be to motivate better utility management performance (Strasser and Kohler 1989: 168).

The problem of securing a good performance from utilities is not simply a technical question, however. It is in large part political, in the sense that there is always a political process – in the setting up of a regulatory framework, in the formulation of regulations, and in the detailed implementation of regulations. The utilities themselves are active players in this process. They are not simply recipients of the regulatory process, treating regulation as an independent variable beyond their control. They are active participants in a dynamic process of interchange between themselves and the regulators. Thus a key function of management in utilities is managing the regulatory interface. Ultimately, this interchange can result in regulatory capture. Consumer interests, particularly in the US, but increasingly in Europe, have long argued that the traditional form of regulation was ineffective. For example, Nowotny quotes the Nader study group as follows: 'In the area of economic regulation, the verdict is in. Academics and advocates of varying persuasion nearly all have pronounced the ICC, FCC, FMC, CAB and FPC 'guilty' of favouring their regulated clientele over consumer interests' (Nowtotny, 1989: 15).

Similarly, Stigler concluded that regulation was actually the result of the political power of business and was a matter of supply (the coercive powers of the state) and demand (the need of firms to restrict entry and price competition) (Nowotny, 1989: 15). Similarly, Barbara Barkovich has argued that 'The utilities will always be a central interested party in utilities regulation. They dominate the regulatory process under traditional regulation' (Barkovich, 1989: 151). Yet the picture is not uniform. As Berg and Tschirhart argue, 'neither public interest theory, nor capture theory, can claim strong support from observation of actual regulatory behaviour' (Berg and Tschirhart, 1988: 286). Certainly, British Gas, to take one current example, would be amazed if anyone suggested that it had managed to capture its regulator, OFGAS. By 1993 it was open warfare between the two organisations!

In Western Europe there has been noticeably less discussion of regulatory capture, either by the utilities or by other public and private organisations. In the case of European utilities, this is largely due to public ownership. The fact of public ownership of many of the utilities almost removed the capture issue from public debate. Until privatisation and deregulation (see discussion below) the European regulatory style was best characterised as the private management of public business (Richardson and Jordan 1979). This was in sharp contrast to the overtly adversarial regulatory style in the US. The conflicting objectives, discussed in our introduction, were largely internalised in the process of bureaucratic accommodation which was until recently fairly characteristic of the European approach to control of utilities. This does not mean that the actual problems of regulatory capture, which in part led to the radical changes in regulation in the US, were absent in Europe. The classic case was, again, Britain, with a clear 'model' of public ownership which was supposed to deliver public control and accountability and managerial efficiency. It delivered neither, in large part because most of the utilities were ultimately able to 'bounce' their sponsoring ministries and the Treasury, with a whole series of badly designed investment programmes. The rhetoric from the utilities was always about 'political interference' and denial of public funds for necessary investments. The reality was that in the end the industries tended to get what they wanted. (Thus, for example, the British Government is now saddled with an enormously costly nuclear energy industry, which it found impossible to privatise and which necessitates a levy on all electricity consumers into the foreseeable future). Even on

privatisation, the utilities succeeded in maintaining many of the privi-
leges of monopolies, whilst, initially at least, gaining greater freedom to
behave in a more marked-orientated manner. As the National Consumers' Council in Britain commented, in theory privatisation presented an
opportunity to shift the balance of power. Thus:

> the process of privatising an industry provides an opportunity for it to be
> restructured to increase competition where this is possible and to minimise the
> problems involved in regulating the parts of the industry where competition
> is not possible, or is undesirable (NCC 1989: 6).

CHARACTERISTICS OF PUBLIC UTILITY MANAGEMENT

In our Introduction we cautioned against the conventional wisdom that
public and private sector organisations are quite different and that the
fundamental management tasks are therefore very different. Nevertheless, it would be foolish to argue that the managerial styles in say, a
local authority water supply undertaking in England in 1963, are the
same as in the now privatised water companies in 1993. However, the
magnitude of the differences would vary according to the level within
the organisations at which measurement was taking place. Some observers in the water industry in Britain today would argue that the closer
one gets to implementation, the less discernable are the differences in
managerial styles pre and post privatisation. At plant level, life may
be pretty much the same – the managerial equivalent of Hoffmann's
distinction between 'high' and 'low' politics (Hoffman 1966). Clearly,
traditional public utilities – especially in Europe under public ownership
– have developed rather different organisational cultures to, say, the
Ford Motor Company. Whilst reminding us that, in public services, the
appropriate service culture depends on the nature of the service and the
relationship between the organisation and its environment, Flynn stresses
the difference in stakeholders, between public and private organisations,
as follows:

> In the private sector, the most important elements of a service business's
> environment are its customers (existing and potential) and its competitors. In
> the public sector there are many people who have a stake in the organisation:
> politicians, taxpayers, voters, can all have an important influence on what the
> public sector organisation does, how it is funded and how it works. Because
> of the importance of these stakeholders the development of a culture which
> focuses exclusively on customers is not possible (Flynn, 1988: 29).

The implication here is that managing a utility, at least when publicly
owned, is rather different to managing a private company. Even when
the utility is *not* publicly owned, the suggestion that there are more
stakeholders holds true. Because of their monopoly or quasi monopoly
nature, utilities have been subject to either public ownership or to a high

degree of state regulation as a surrogate for public ownership, and/or a surrogate for market competition. In some cases, at least, these surrogates have either delivered good results or have at least not prevented good results. Thus, Alfred Kahn notes that the long-run comparative trends in the costs and rates of US utilities show dramatic results, without a corresponding offsetting trend in profits (Kahn, 1971: 99). Quoting Kendrick's data, he points out that,

> ... the average annual rate of increase in total factor productivity in communications and public utilities was more than twice as great as the private economy generally, and eighty per cent higher than in manufacturing alone, during the period 1899–53. Their margin of superiority in the shorter period 1948–66 was less, but still notable (Kahn, 1971: 99–100).

Whilst noting that these 'impressive accomplishments' reflect, above all, the enormous potential of technology, he reminds us that technology does not develop unassisted by human hands. Thus, 'The data presented, inescapably support a judgement that there have been favourable institutional factors operating in these areas of the economy' (Kahn, 1971: 101). He reviews a range of institutional factors – some of which are more relevant to the US than to Europe – e.g. the threat that a governmental enterprise might be set up in competition with the existing utilities. However, his list includes 'manageralism'. Although divorcing ownership from control can produce worse, rather than better, results he argues that 'the exposure of public utility executives to public scrutiny and criticism, their desire to be associated with growing and progressive companies, to enjoy the approbation that comes from giving a good service, and to avoid unpopular rate increases are motives that are reinforced by the presence of regulation' (Kahn 1971: 1001).

As is clear from the quotations from some of the many critics of the efficacy of regulation in practice (these are matched by the strong criticism in Western European states of the failure of public-ownership to consistently meet the desired goals), this is probably a rather benign view of the managerial achievements of the utilities. However Kahn's observation does point us towards an important feature of utilities management – namely the special motivation of managers in joining utilities. Thus, organisations like a municipal water supply organisation, a gas board, or electricity generating company – particularly when they are in public ownership – almost certainly attract a particular type of individual, with a particular set of values and orientations. These values are often 'community' and 'service' orientated, and emphasise security of employment. They are rather different to values one might expect in a manager deciding to join a highly competitive market-orientated organisation, such as a tobacco or car manufacturing company. Put simply, the type of people who seek employment in a municipal water board are usually rather different to the kind of people who join IBM. Indeed, the post-privatisation experience of utilities in Britain suggests that one of the management problems that they have faced has been that a high percentage of their staff lacked so-called private sector skills. For example, Helm et al. have reviewed the performance of privatised utilities in terms of their acquisition and diversification activities. They conclude that:

> Acquisitions are management decisions and their success therefore depends on the quality of utility managers. Most have come from the public sector with little or no experience in acquisitions and their subsequent control. Importing external management expertise appears to be an important condition of success (Helm et al., 1992: 7).

In a fascinating footnote, Kahn quotes the observations of a perceptive executive of a public utility company:

> I think that the whole trouble is with the concept of economic man (sic) and especially the assumed characteristics of this construct: perfect intelligence and thorough venality (at least within the limits of the law). An instance of the distance between economic man and real man is to be found in the fact that utility people work like mad cutting costs and benefiting consumers, despite the fact that the industry is essentially a cost-plus industry (Kahn, 1971: 101).

Thus an important managerial characteristics of utilities is the type of person attracted to the organisations and the organisational culture which they create and perpetuate. The downside of this 'public service orientation' is, of course, caution and conservatism. As Kahn himself notes, 'By the same token, managerial inertia, a common attribute of public utility monopoly, operates in the other direction' (Kahn, 1971: 102). It is this view, rather than the view that the public service orientations lead to better efficiency and better service, which has underpinned the wave of regulatory reform and privatisation of utilities that has taken place since the mid 1970s in many advanced democracies. Politicians of the right have been happy to portray publicly owned utilities in a stereotyped fashion, as part of the campaign to secure support for deregulation and privatisation. However, there is at least some research evidence that the benefits of the public service orientation can be accompanied by the disbenefits of the type suggested by politicians on the right. Thus, in Britain, Dopson and Stewart suggest that, overall, 'managers in the public sector appear to be less enthusiastic than their counterparts in the private sector about both the possibility and the desirability of change' (Dopson and Stewart, 1990: 38). In the US, one research project has reported that the great majority of public managers

> ... describe their work as bounded by the rule of law, procedure and structure. In this culture, restraints on individual behaviour take on an important symbolic and methodological meaning by being elevated to an institutional status. Where the controls are institutionalised, they cease being negative statements about self-worth and become, instead, devices easily viewed by managers as limiting their ability to manage' (Whorton and Worthley, 1981: 358–9).

Critics of public utilities would argue that this general description of public management could equally be applied to publicly owned utilities and to highly regulated private utilities. Indeed, de-regulation and privatisation in Britain was in part initiated by the utility managers themselves, for these very reasons.

The new conventional wisdom (not really based on scientific analyses of the results of different forms of organisation or different forms of regulation) is that we need a new kind of 'manageralism'. This reflects an ideological belief that a more competitive and consumer orientated management style is necessary. However, it is important to remember that the fundamental feature of utilities – combining public accountability with involvement in market transactions – will remain, irrespective of forms of organisation or regulation (Carter et al., 1992: 139).

MARKETS, CONSUMERS AND CHANGING ORGANISATIONAL CULTURES

In discussing the new situation facing utilities, we need to again remind ourselves that the pressures to which they are now subject are common elsewhere in the public and private sectors. For example, increased emphasis on performance targets, often contained in operating licences, is also to be found in the British commercial TV franchising system, as it is in the creation of the 'internal market' in the (still) publicly funded health service. General Practitioners are now set performance targets for a range of activities such as vaccinations, health check-ups etc. Moreover, contracts can be ended, if some of the budgetary targets are not met. Even the BBC has targets for the percentage of independently produced (i.e. contracted out) TV programmes it screens each year.

In Britain, British Telecom (BT) is the utility which has the most experience of trying to change its managerial culture in response to these broader environmental pressures. On paper at least, BT has been transforming itself from a government department (via public corporation status) to a global company in the private sector. In a perceptive and amusing account of the development of BT, Pitt has concluded that '... BT's efforts at intensive organisational change aimed at giving it a 'crackerjack' image have closely paralleled the experience of AT&T which has, since divestiture, experienced what one commentator has described as a 'cultural train wreck'' (Pitt, 1990: 61).

Pitt goes on to describe the BT equivalent of the 'ramping up' which occurred in AT&T. This cultural transformation (no less) has affected both external and internal relationships. For example, BT has changed its hitherto very cosy relationship with suppliers, who now have to supply internationally competitive products; its corporatist relationship with the unions has been abandoned; and its relationship with its customers (under de-regulation and increasing competition from Mercury) has begun a transformation. Pitt notes that internally:

the imperative of cultural change was given prominence in speech after speech by 'change champions' within the organisation ... aimed at the transformation of the dominant behavioural mores, value system and the 'spirit' of the organisation. Paralleling the American apothegm, 'Ma Bell doesn't live here anymore', BT was intent on conveying the message to staff and the outside environment alike that 'bureaucracy is no longer in residence' (Pitt, 1990: 63).

Despite much continuing criticism of BT, Pitt is surely correct in pointing to the managerial distance already travelled, albeit with a warning that the most difficult tasks are yet to come in escaping the legacy of the past such as under-investment and bureaucratic procedures, etc. (Pitt 1990: 74). The ability to achieve organisational change has surprised many observers, just as 'management by surprise' has been a feature of the post-divestiture stage in US telematics (Pitt, 1990: 69). A similar picture of dynamic structural and cultural change is evident in the British Post Office, (PO). (This was originally in one Government Departmental organisation with telecoms, prior to the separation of posts and telecoms and the eventual privatisation of BT). Thus, Fish suggests that 'since 1983 the Post Office has undergone massive structural changes which have largely gone unnoticed by the outside world' (Fish, 1988: 29). The changes were introduced by a far-sighed top management team, responding to the likelihood of a more competitive environment. Part of this changing environment was a threat to the virtual monopoly of traditional postal services. (This had already been somewhat eroded by special services provided by the private sector). But change was also 'sparked' by the threat of technological changes elsewhere – particularly the convergence of telecommunications and computerisation. According to Fish, the reorganisation team in the PO mapped existing organisational paradigms and their strengths and weaknesses, and concluded that the undoubted strengths '... would not be sufficient in themselves to enable the Post Office to face up to an increasingly turbulent world ...' (Fish, 1988: 30). Our earlier suggestion that 'marketisation' is the key to the organisational and cultural changes in the management of utilities (whether publicly or privately owned) is echoed here. Thus, in the PO, 'The need was to get everyone to think 'market'. A key strategy was to elevate the presence and impact of marketing and to make the organisation look outward to customers and competitors' (Fish, 1988: 31). However, as we suggested earlier, a key research question is whether these 'high management' cultural and organisational changes really percolate through the whole organisation and make very much difference to its actual performance. Thus we need to be aware of the managerial equivalent of symbolic politics. In the case of the Post Office, Fish sounds a warning note, 'The good work needs to be reinforced, particularly below top-management level. The process of seizing the hearts and minds of 170,000 staff has only just started. Customers have yet to benefit fully from what the Post Office has to offer' (Fish, 1988: 33).

In fact, if we were to select one word (some would say symbol!) to capture the essence of the changing behaviour of utility management – particularly in Britain, it would be *customer*. Here there is probably a difference between utilities in the public and private sector. Interestingly, British publicly owned utilities now see themselves as aiming towards the American utility model. They saw the potential of privatisation as allowing them to change the nature of their organisation, from being essentially a public service organisation, to American style utilities providing a product to customers. This shift, it should be emphasised, had begun *prior* to privatisation. For example, as early as 1973, the water industry had begun to see water less as a 'service' and more as a 'commodity' (Saunders, 1985). A whole series of legislative and organisational changes had been taking place, not least of which was that the water industry had gradually become much more technocratic and managerial, with a decline in conventional public accountability (Richardson et al., 1992: 160). These changes were given much greater impetus by the arrival of a few senior managers with private sector backgrounds, appointed by the Conservative Government. In several cases these change agents have been quite crucial in transforming the managerial culture of their organisations. For example, Pitt cites the examples of Sir George Jefferson and Iain Vallance in BT. In the water industry, Roy Watts, from the privatised British Airways, played a crucial role in both the changes in management in the Thames Regional Water Authority (then publicly owned) and indeed in placing privatisation of water on the public agenda.

In Britain, the debate about utility performance has now shifted, post-privatisation, to the area long familiar in the US – namely regulation – and to much broader questions about citizen's rights. In terms of regulation, it is fair to say that Britain is in a regulatory mess, in part because the regulatory framework was part of the bargain between the (then) public sector managers, the Conservative Government, and City financial interests as part of the necessary price for a successful floatation. There is now much conflict between the regulators and the utilities (and, indeed, between different regulators in the same industry), as the regulators have begun to ratchet up the regulatory rules under which the utilities operate. However cosy the regulatory bargain might have been at the time of privatisation, (Veljanovski suggests that regulatory capture took place in Britain in the very formulation of the agencies and the structure of the industry itself – Veljanovski, 1957), this situation has shifted quite radically. The regulators have responded to increasing criticism from the 'attentive publics' surrounding the utilities and to broader consumer pressures (Maloney and Richardson, 1992). An added complication in many western European states is, of course, the European Community – itself a major source of regulatory pressure, particularly on utilities in environmentally sensitive sectors such as water. Nowhere is the regulatory mess greater than in the case of the UK energy sector where decisions by regulators in electricity and gas have had profound consequences for the coal industry – and ultimately for the Government itself.

Whilst the British case might be an extreme case, it is typical of the general destablisation of the environment of utilities, virtually throughout the advanced industrial nations. Thus de-regulation and privatisation (often re-regulation in practice, substituting one set of regulating rules for another) appear to have had a major impact on at least the senior management of these industries. The general response to these pressures appears to be for utilities to behave more and more like 'normal' private sector organisations, within the regulatory constraints, just as firms like IBM, ICI or Volkswagen-Audi have to manage their operations in an increasingly regulated world. Utility managers now see themselves, increasingly, as needing to behave in ways in which they perceive other private companies in the world to behave – particularly in terms of trying to see themselves as dealing with customers. This shift (which is reflected even in the language used within the utilities) is partly self-induced and is partly 'prompted' by the influx of new managers, as suggested above. These internally generated changes have been re-enforced by further pressure from the British Government. Thus the Government published its Citizen's Charter in July 1991. The document's subtitle was 'Raising the Standard'. The Charter aimed to set standards of service across a range of 'services' including the remaining publicly owned utilities – British Rail and the Post Office. In the former case, privatisation was the main solution. In the latter case, amongst a range of proposals, it was announced that performance standards will in future be set by the Secretary of State, not by the Post Office (Citizen's Charter, 1991: 30). Whatever the practical effects of the Citizen's Charter (so far it has been subject to more ridicule than praise), at the level of the utilities so-called 'customer charters' are now common. For example, in March 1993, British Rail published its Customer Charter with promises such as offering an alternative means of transport to an 'appropriate station' if it failed to deliver on its promise to get passengers to their intended destinations. Similarly, London Underground published its Charter in the summer of 1992, covering such matters as improved train services and information, helpful and courteous staff, working lifts and escalators, clean trains and stations, safety, accessibility of stations, responsiveness, refunds, future plans, and customer contacts (Villers, 1992: 111). In practice, evidence so far suggests that some of the benefits to consumers, refunds on British Rail for example, are difficult to secure once the fine print is understood!

Of more importance are the internally generated performance indicators produced by the utility managers themselves. For example, British Rail set up a Productivity Steering Group which produced some 244 performance indicators in the early 1980s. 'Every production department has PIs and each senior manager had about six PIs which increased at each level downwards so that at the disaggregated bottom line level all 244 indicators were in operation' (Carter et al., 1992: 143). The water industry had also become quite experienced in developing performance indicators, well before privatisation (Carter et al., 1992: 157). The British water case is particularly interesting as an example of a utility becoming much more conscious of living in the proverbial goldfish bowl. For example, in March 1993, Thames Water plc (the largest of the ten privatised water companies) took out full page advertisements in the Sunday newspapers, under the slogan 'Thames Water: Running Water for You'. It explained that the company had been spending £1 million per day to improve water services and that it was opening a new £40 million customer service centre, reducing the previous forty telephone numbers to one. In fact, Thames was fairly typical of the new managerial culture in British utilities – moving towards a more centralised and efficient system of dealing with customer queries and complaints, etc., as well as towards targets for meeting regulatory requirements on water quality, etc. Some of these changes no doubt reflect the appointment of a new External Relations Manager who had gained wide experience in the public relations and media field before joining Thames in September 1990. Within the organisation, quite sophisticated customer service monitoring procedures have been set up for such issues as billing queries (total received, response times, throughput of queries, etc.). Similarly, Yorkshire Water plc included improvements in levels of service and customer care as key elements in the strategic objectives contained in its Business Plan. Virtually all British utilities now routinely publish customer guarantee schemes. For example, Thames Water Utilities' Customer Guarantee Scheme includes such items as keeping appointments, dealing with account queries, complaints procedures, interruption of supply and the payment of a (small!) credit when supply conditions are not met. Similarly, BT has customer compensation payments to its customers under specified conditions. In behaving in this way they were no different to those 'services' remaining in the public sector. For example, in the same region as Thames Water plc, Oxfordshire Ambulance Service had a target of responding to 50 percent of town emergency calls within 8 minutes and 95 percent of rural calls within 19 minutes. It then published data on actual performance (51.7 percent and 92.3 percent respectively!). Other health service targets in Oxfordshire included a pledge that no patient should wait longer than 30 minutes past the appointment time.

CONCLUSION: A CHANGING MIX OF 'PUBLICNESS' AND 'PRIVATENESS'

The similar examples of Thames Water Utilities and Oxfordshire Health Authority illustrate Lewis Gunn's reminder that the public/private distinction is often overstated. Thus, in the cases cited, managers in the totally publicly owned Health Service are behaving in exactly the same way as the totally privatised utility, Thames Water plc. In turn, their behaviour was no different to non-utility private sector companies such as banks. They were all under increasing public pressure to raise their often poor standards of service to consumers. The changes in the operating

environments of these different types of organisations – more regulation, more pressure to be consumer-friendly – are pretty well universal.
As Gunn suggests, 'managers of multinational companies, in particular,
ridicule the notion that they operate in a relative non-political milieu'.
Moreover, 'Managers of British companies agree and add that they operate within their own 'fish bowl' and are increasingly held to account
for their actions in relation to investors and other 'shareholders' such
as employees, customers and entire communities' (Gunn, 1988: 24).

As Bozeman also argues, 'all organisations are public because political
authority affects some of the behaviour and processes of all organisations'
(Bozeman, 1987: 83). He formulates a multi-dimensional theory contain-
ing three axioms, the first of which is especially relevant to our discussion
of utilities management.

Axiom 1: Publicness is not a discrete quality but a multi-dimensional property.
An organisation is public to the extent that it exists or is constrained by
political authority (Bozeman, 1987: 84).

The multi-dimensional assumption is central to his theory and he
uses 'publicness' as a shorthand for the location of an organisation on
a publicness-privateness dimension. At the other end of the continuum,
'an organisation is private to the extent that it exercises or is constrained by
economic authority' (Bozeman, 1987: 84). His suggestion that much of the
variation in organisations' outcomes resulting from political acts relates
to the 'buffering' ability of organisations, is especially relevant to our
discussion of utilities. Thus, in the past, utilities have generally managed
to operate under one of two types of 'buffer' – public ownership (either
in government departments or public corporations of various kinds) or
private ownership with a high degree of public regulation. In both cases,
these 'buffers' have produced a relatively stable environment in which
the utilities could operate. Paradoxically, state ownership has proved to
be a more effective buffer, than private ownership + regulation. Public
ownership has provided them with a useful myth of 'accountability' often
disguising the real power of these organisations. In reality, the publicly
owned utilities have been private organisations, given a 'franchise' for
public policy.

Deregulation and privatisation appear to have begun to shift these
organisations towards the economic end of Bozeman's continuum,
changing the mix of economic and political authority. Yet the greater
pressure to be more responsive to their customers – and to be more
socially responsible (e.g. in terms of public safety and environmental
standards) may be pushing in the opposite direction. In practice, the
different patterns of ownership, different degrees of regulation, and
differences in organisation culture mean that public utilities are quite
difficult to locate precisely on Bozeman's 'publicness grid'. This is simply
because it is almost impossible to maintain a clear distinction between

a public and a private utility. The direction of policy and managerial change appears to be uniform, but its particular institutional forms do vary (e.g. in Europe, Britain has been much keener on telecoms de-regulation than, say, Germany, which has been rather more cautious). The destablisation of the existing economic and political authority mix in many utilities has certainly sparked off a new organisational life cycle within them. Just as with conventional 'public 'organisations, such as government departments and local authorities, the 'marketisation' trend is still underway. Its consequences in terms of managerial styles and structures – and more importantly in terms of organisational performance – have yet to be assessed. The irony for utility managers – especially in Britain – is that considerable pressure is mounting for shifting the utilities back along Bozeman's continuum, towards more 'publicness'. If this trend continues (via tougher and more 'intrusive' regulation), utility managers may find themselves with rather less independence than under public ownership! This irony is not lost on managers in the privatised water utilities. They now have to deal with no less than nine regulators – far more than under public ownership. At the same time they have to keep city investors happy!

10

PUBLIC RESOURCE ALLOCATION

Torben Beck Jørgensen

In a static society with only a modestly developed public sector, public management – provided 'public *management*' is a meaningful concept – presumably has very little to do with the survival and growth of the single public organization. Rather, public management has the scope of traditional public administration, e.g. keeping the administrative and judicial machinery in good shape and to some extent taking care of internal efficiency.

By using Hirschman's (1970) concepts one might say that relationships at the upper levels in the administrative pyramid, e.g. between public institutions and their responsible directorates or ministries, could be characterized by *loyalty*. Has this pattern changed in the post-war period of substantial growth in public expenditure? A quick answer is yes.

The growth in the public sector can briefly be characterized as: growth in budgets, tasks, number of organizational units and size of units; growth in expectations towards the problem-solving capacity of the public sector; growth in vested interests in the welfare state, especially in those countries (e.g. in Scandinavia) which have chosen the institutional welfare state concept (Titmuss, 1974).

In this climate of general expansion it is likely that managerial success is not only linked to administrative and judicial criteria but also to the ability to follow the mainstream of growth. It is not a coincidence that in this period we also witnessed a growth in studies of resource allocation, the classic study being Wildavsky's (1965) analysis of budgetary behaviour in which, among other things, he analysed how public agencies tried to defend and expand their budgetary base.

These simple observations may lead us to the conclusion that *loyalty* was replaced by *voice*. However, this conclusion is too hasty. Although we do find some *voice* in the defence of the budgetary base, the model applied by Wildavsky to describe budgetary behaviour was the well known incremental model. Some of the main characteristics of incremental budgetary behaviour are: (a) the existence of relatively stable expectations among the actors; (b) the continuation of activities at a level rather close to that of the previous period; and (c) that changes in the resource allocation will affect the actors on an equal and fair basis (the fair share principle). Consequently, embedded in the incremental method itself we find *loyalty* towards the historical and negotiated pattern of resource allocation.

A decade after Wildavsky's classic study we begin to face a change in what is perhaps a condition for the incremental method: budgetary slack (Wildavsky, 1975; Mouritzen, 1991). In the 1970s the political and economic situation changed: a political reaction towards the public sector emerged and many western democracies became at the same time victims of the fiscal crisis. The interplay of these two factors naturally created a tendency towards retrenchment. The post-growth period began; a period with a much more hostile environment but still with living hopes, ideologies and practices from the growth period (Tarschys, 1981; Whetten, 1984). Public organizations found themselves placed in a much more competitive situation, fighting for better appropriations and avoiding cuts; the rationale of public management in the single organization being survival and if possible further growth. Comparative budget increases became a kind of 'virility index' (Dunleavy, 1991: 155).

In this period *voice* became a much more salient aspect of the budgetary game, and simultaneously *loyalty* decreased in two senses. The producing organizations displayed less *loyalty* towards ministerial policies and demands of retrenchment, and the ministries themselves cared less about the well-being of 'their' organizations and the continuation of the institutionalized pattern of resource allocation.

In this chapter we shall primarily take a closer look at different aspects of the use and consequences of the voice option. In the last section we shall discuss, by way of example, some recent changes in Denmark concerning the political climate and the formal budgetary rules which fit neatly into the third of Hirschman's options: *exit*.

THE THEORETICAL POINT OF DEPARTURE

Public organizations can be conceptualized as organizations placed in two circular flows of contributions/inducements (Simon et al., 1950; March and Simon, 1958). In the upper circuit, the interested actors receive inducements from the organization in terms of degree of compliance to political goals, proper use of appropriations and the like. Stated more generally, inducements are decreasing of the cost of being a politician or a budget authority. The contributions from the interested actors are political support, better appropriations, etc. Consequently, we do not perceive the relation between a ministry and subordinate public organizations as an exercise of authority but rather as an exchange relationship (Wamsley and Zald, 1976).

In the lower circuit, the inducements are the goods or services produced, e.g. transportation, day-care, hospital services, education, social security, etc. The contributions from the clientele are no complaints or

Figure 1   *The public organization and its environment*

Politico-administrative
costs

Interested actors:
budget authorities,
politicians, interest
groups, media

The politico-
administrative
appropriations
market

Political support,
appropriations

The public
organization

Satisfaction of
needs, lack of
complaints, fees

Market of
goods/services

Clientele

Produced
goods/services

expressed satisfaction and in some cases a willingness to pay for the
services.

The two circuits can also be conceptualized as two distinct 'markets': the
politico-administrative appropriations market and the market for goods
and services, the term 'market' here being used more as a metaphor rather
than in a strict economic sense. Accordingly, the public organization is
seen not as an administrative unit strictly following political commands,
but as an organizational entity competing with other public organizations
for better appropriations.

Since the source of money ultimately is the Ministry of Finance and the
Parliament, managerial time and energy in general are likely to be chan-
nelled into the upper circuit. This is even more true in the competitive
climate of the post-growth period. The lower circuit plays a role in budget
negotiations only in so far as an inducement/contribution balance, e.g.
client satisfaction and growing needs from the clientele, is accepted as
a convincing argument by the budget authority. What is a 'convincing
argument'? The cynical assumption underlying this perspective is that
considerations of user needs and political goals only play a minor role in
budgetary allocations. This is not to conclude that user needs or political
goals never has a say, but it is hypothesized that the impact of needs and
goals are conditioned or modified by a number of structural properties of
the politico-administrative market which only coincidentally are related
to society's needs, whether expressed by politicians or users. We could

label this perspective a contingency theory of public resource allocation.

In the next section we shall take a closer look at characteristics of the politico-administrative appropriations market in the post-growth era. The point of departure is which factors determine the possibility of avoiding cuts. Or – putting it another way – what causes more or less organizational vulnerability towards retrenchment demands. The main focus will be on what makes the *voice* option effective on behalf of the public organization. We shall concentrate the analysis on structural conditions of the appropriations market, not on the tactics to survive in terms of micro-behaviour of public managers, although we shall deal with this question later in the chapter.

THE POLITICO-ADMINISTRATIVE APPROPRIATIONS MARKET

A not uncommon method of retrenchment distribution is the so-called scream method. It is essentially simple and can be formulated as follows:

1 One should cut in such a way, that all screams are equally loud.
2 If they are not, re-cut until (1) is obtained.

But what are the presuppositions of this method? To the extent that its objective is a just distribution of cut-backs in the sense that they should be equally painful across the board, the method is based on, among other things, the two following presuppositions:

1 Everyone has the same ability to scream.
2 Every kind of scream is equally legitimate.

To the extent that the method's objective is a just distribution of cutbacks in the sense that the public organizations contributing the least to social welfare should bear the most cuts, the method also presupposes that:

3 There is proportionality between screaming and usefulness: the greater the screaming, the greater the usefulness and vice versa.

There are still more presuppositions that must be realized before we can assume that the method will lead to the desired result. But the three we have mentioned are sufficient for our further analysis. All three presuppositions have this in common, that they assume that all public organizations are equally vulnerable to the political demand to reduce expenditure. My thesis in the following is that this is obviously not so. Before going into the various factors that condition the degree of vulnerability, a few preliminary clarifications are in order.

We can begin by distinguishing four phases in the retrenchment process: (1) formulation of a general demand (amount) for expenditure reduction; (2) identification of potential retrenchment targets; (3)

allocation of cut-backs to specific organizations; and (4) implementation of cut-backs. An organization's vulnerability relates only to the last three phases, since protests against cut-backs in general rarely are directed towards a reformulation of the expenditure reduction demand. We may now distinguish between the following types of vulnerability:

Political vulnerability

Identificational vulnerability: the likelihood of being spotted ('discovered') as a potential retrenchment target.

Allocational vulnerability: the likelihood of being unable to avert a retrenchment demand unequivocally directed to a specific organization.

Operational vulnerability. The likelihood of implemented cutbacks having a detrimental effect on the organization's core activities.

Identificational vulnerability

The question here is the degree of invisibility of certain activities. One of the characteristics that must be taken into account is, of course, the organization's purposes and tasks. What does this have to do with invisibility? I would argue that public organizations which are entrusted with tasks of *central importance* for the functioning of society or which administer values of undisputed worth are, so to speak, invisible to eyes searching for retrenchment targets. There may, in reality, be a large potential for cut-backs, but for psychological reasons they are not seen. They are unconsciously bypassed in the identification phase. Or it may be considered as politically damaging to question the value of the organization.

Pure specimens of the type are not easily found. But the significant growth areas during the 1960s and 1970s, like welfare, health and education, clearly suggest themselves. Subsequent attempts during the 1980s to retrench in these areas were, it should be noted, characteristically were accompanied or preceded by an attack on central values. On a more general level, it may be noted that the ideological conception of administering society's well-being through professionalized institutions has being increasingly subjected to critical scrutiny.

If there is a shift in the centrality of a public organization's tasks, their *controversiality* entails the risk of high vulnerability. This means that it is in no way self-evident that the acitivities may be useful for anybody. Public organizations engaged in cultural pursuits are presumably examples of this. The cultural values administered, for instance, by the Danish National Museum, the State Art Gallery and the Royal Theatre have over the last twenty years hardly attained a centrality which would render these organizations invulnerable, in the sense that they would not be seen during a retrenchment search. Far from fading out because of a total lack of interest (perhaps also a form of invisibility), these organizations have been vulnerable because of controversiality. The more often a public organization's tasks are publicly and critically debated, the more questions are asked in Parliament and the appropriations committee, the greater the likelihood of the organization being pointed out as a retrenchment target.

Organizations may also have certain properties that affect their visibility, e.g. *transparency*. The easier it is to 'x-ray' a public organization, the more difficult it is to conceal slack (pockets of 'fat', reserves and the like). And the simpler the tasks, the greater the difficulty of arguing against cut-backs, since the antagonist, the budget authority, will very likely have as much relevant information as the organization, i.e. the information asymmetry is low (Niskanen, 1971). On the other hand, the more complicated the structure of the organization, and the more opaque its tasks and technology are for outsiders, the greater the reluctance of the budgetary authority to seek it out as a target. It knows beforehand – or will soon learn – that it will there encounter an endlessly long and overwhelmingly incomprehensible case for the defence. Examples may be found in the health sector, particularly, perhaps, in larger hospitals.

It may be added, finally, that not all public organizations, or even all public activities and services, are registered with equal *budgetary clarity*. Wherever tasks are co-administered by several organizations or through the interaction of state and local government authorities, there can be considerable difficulty not only in penetrating what is going on, but also in discovering what the costs really are.

Allocational vulnerability

We now move into the next phase of the retrenchment process and assume that a given organization has been spotted as a potential target. What factors contribute to the organization's ability to avert a cut-back demand?

Whether or not some of an organization's tasks can be deferred without significant political noise is frequently decisive in allocating a cut-back. This is sometime closely related to the *composition of the budget*. If a very large portion of the core budget (Dunleavy, 1991) consist of capital plant investment, allocational vulnerability is high. Postponed investments do not protest. Expenditures mandated by law pull in the opposite direction. The more the mandatory expenditures, the more difficult it is to implement cut-backs because, if for no other reasons, the procedure of legislative revision is long in relation to the usual one-year time perspective of cutbacks.

Presumably, a very decisive factor is the *visibility of the organization's impact* on the societal environment. On condition that the organization's activity is not highly controversial, we may assume that the more visible its product, the less its vulnerability. This is because in such a situation the effects of retrenchment will be more conspicuous. Service-producing organisations in particular have a visible impact. Consider, for example, the visibility of reduced service in organizations such as the Danish State Railway (fewer trains running, fewer carriages on those that do, irregular service, passengers standing in trains and waiting on platforms); the Highway Department (bridges without approaches, half-finished stretches of highway, traffic jams); or the Post and Telegraph Department (closed post offices, longer delivery time, fewer deliveries). Research, on the other hand, is an activity with very indirect effects and little immediate impact visibility. Cut-backs would not be directly noticeable, except in the long term. The tax authority's assessment activity is another example where the effect of retrenchment would presumably be difficult to notice, and in any case the citizens affected would hardly make a fuss.

Closely linked to but not identical with visibility is the distinction between *current and hypothetical demand*. As a rule, service-producing organizations meet a current, even daily, demand for their products, as opposed to some organizations whose main task is to prepare for possible future events. In the broadest sense, the concept can be applied to research, some library functions and various planning activities. It is applicable, in particular, to such emergency organizations as those of the armed forces and civil defence.

Current demand can reduce vulnerability because detrimental effects will be immediately visible. Organizations operating in this area will, therefore, also be able to argue more easily against retrenchment. It is quite the contrary in areas of hypothetical demand. Expenditure reductions will possibly never be noticed. The task of civil defence is to protect civilians in time of war. But what if war never comes? Then the money is wasted. The organization prepares itself for an event which possibly will and possibly will not occur. Thus, demand is hypothetical and in a situation of retrenchment invisible.

Still another factor related to an organization's product and the demand for it is the *distribution of benefits and costs*. Who receives the benefits and who pays the costs? Here the thesis is as follows: the more the benefits are concentrated among a particular group of the population and the more extensive the group that pays the costs, the greater the ability of the organization to avert cut-backs by mobilizing resistance.

The reason for this is that benefit concentration elicits from the recipients a very strong motivation to avoid retrenchment, while those who pay the costs (as a rule, the taxpayers in general) have very little motivation to organize themselves specifically in order to eliminate a tax burden which is extremely marginal in relation to the significance of the benefits for those who receive them.

Moreover, those who benefit are not only the formal receivers of public goods but also the producers. The beneficiaries of national defence are not solely the defended but also those who defend. Consequently, collective goods do in some cases have a taste of private goods (Kristensen, 1980).

For a number of reasons public organizations may vary a good deal with regard to the incentives to avoid budget cuts. Following the typology developed by Dunleavy (1991) one can argue that delivery agencies distribute benefits to a much smaller fraction of society compared to transfer agencies. Moreover, the core budget absorbs a much greater portion of the bureau budget in delivery agencies. Finally, delivery agencies in general are characterized by *client proximity*. In those cases where the production of benefits takes place 'close to the citizen' or in close interaction with citizens or clients, the organization will experience more direct reaction against cut-backs on the part of the benefit recipients. This may tend to constrict the organization's elbowroom, but it may also facilitate the mobilization of clients and their organizations in an effort to avert retrenchment. It is thus a typical trait of retrenchment protest to parade the client consequences. The benefit consumers are pushed up in front of the producers: 'Look, Minister! There's a body on the slab!'

These arguments may be linked to and reinforced by the *degree of professionalization* within the area in question. The more a public organization's production is conditioned or dominated by a highly professional group (e.g. doctors, teachers, social workers and the like), the lesser its vulnerability to retrenchment. This is due to and depends on the profession's legitimacy, status, knowledge monopoly and autonomy. A profession may, moreover, exercise an authorized monopoly; for example, only the services of 'real' doctors are subsidized, as opposed to those of naturopaths. All this can be used to portray the retrenchers as ignorant laymen.

A coalition of a public organization, professional interests and organized clients – elsewhere labelled 'the professional-bureaucratic complex' (Beer, 1977; Kristensen, 1980) – can be highly effective in avoiding cuts, especially perhaps if the motivation for doing so is not solely based on professional and bureaucratic self-interests (institutional imperialism) but also on a genuine interest in contributing to societal welfare.

Vulnerability can be lowered, if the organization has acquired the status of a *quasi-monopoly*. In this case there are no comparable organizations, and low efficiency may be difficult to detect or assess. There are no competitors to offer a better bid or informed criticism that can 'mess up' the process.

A common characteristic of most of the factors that have been mentioned is that in one way or another they are linked to a demand for the production of a public organization. Nevertheless, these factors are indicators neither of 'objective demand' nor 'objective utility'. They are related to certain properties of the public organization and its environment that reduce or enhance the ability of the organization to present its case persuasively for the existence of a demand and the usefulness of its product; in other words, the ability to scream loud and long.

But the screaming must be heard and conveyed to the budget authority (e.g. Parliament or the municipal council). We must, therefore, examine more closely the relevant properties of the politico-administrative sector of which the public organization is a part. An important topic in the Danish debate on sectorism has been the question of the sector segmentation of Parliament. It has been pointed out that many of the permanent committees have been sectorized also in the sense that they are overweighted with members often considered to be 'sector representatives', such as farmers and farm organization officials in the committee for agriculture (Damgaard, 1986; Damgaard and Eliassen, 1978). Similar patterns have been found in local governments (Mouritzen, 1985). If a politico-administrative sector is hallmarked by the dominance of 'professional people' from the top to the bottom, retrenchment vulnerability will obviously be lowered. The same applies if the sector is 'covered' by interest group organizations which are profoundly in accord on the sector's 'mission' in or significance for society.

Operational vulnerability

We move now to the final retrenchment phase, assuming that a given public organization's funds have been effectively cut. What we shall examine more closely is the likelihood of detrimental effects on the organization's core activities as a result of retrenchment, i.e. its operational vulnerability. Operational vulnerability varies greatly according to differences in the properties of the organizations and their environments. In some cases cutbacks can be absorbed without significant operational consequences. In other cases, the effect can be disastrous.

To begin with, such factors as the *organization's size and the differentiation of its tasks and structure* should be noted. The larger its size, and the more differentiated its tasks and structure, the better it will be able – all other things being equal – to absorb retrenchment by internally reordering priorities. Inversely, the simpler the organization, the more difficult it is to allocate the cutbacks without detrimental effects. One of the reasons for this is that reprioritization in a complex organization is difficult to trace, tending to lessen internal resistance.

A factor directly effecting the operational vulnerability of an organization is the very *technology*, the basic works processes, it employs, since they may in themselves be more or less vulnerable. A clear case of vulnerable technology is that employed in the withholding-tax system. There is simply a technically determined threshold for retrenchment, beyond which the tax authority's computerized data system will cease to function. Either it is in running order or it does not run at all. The same is true of the computerized population-registration system and the customs authority's system of controlling excise taxes. It is presumably also the case with regard to archive functions at the National Museum and the State Archives. They are either maintained and kept up to date or they are not. The same argument can applied on organizations with special obligations with regard to due process and legal rights. Even a few mistakes may create a general lack of thrust in the system as such.

Technology is important in another way. Assembly-line technology is presumably very sensitive to expenditure reductions. If an organizations's technology is a long conveyor belt, it will be very sensitive to external irregularities – including a retrenchment demand. Other things being equal, this is the case today with the centralized technology of the main post office in Copenhagen, as opposed to what it might have been if a number of smaller and parallel sorting units had been installed.

Buffer capability is another factor closely connected with the question of technology. An organizational buffer is a mechanism for absorbing external irregularities (Thompson, 1967). To a certain extent, task and structure differentiation can be considered as a buffer, but a more traditional type of buffer is stockpiling. In the context of retrenchment the thesis, naturally, is that the greater the buffer capability, the lower the operational vulnerability.

Buffer capability affords us a good illustration of variations in the significance of the vulnerability factor from organization to organization. Let us compare the postal service with the collection of taxes. To some extent, the tax authorities are able to stockpile tax returns. They can stretch the process of assessment out over one or several years simply by annually skipping over a number of taxpayers and making regular five-year random checks instead, thereby evening out the huge seasonal fluctuations. The tax authorities have the added advantage that very few will notice the stockpile; perhaps only the nervous taxpayers.

The postal service, on the other hand, cannot stockpile letters for a month before delivering them. Its work cycle is short: one day in principle (and, it is hoped, in practice). And a stockpile would be utterly visible. In this regard its operational vulnerability is much greater than the tax authority's.

Budget composition is a further factor affecting vulnerability, since some budget items may be more or less inviolable. If the core budget includes a relatively large plant investment budget, its operational vulnerability will, as a rule, be low in the short run. On the other hand, if its operating expenditures – and especially the wage ratio – are very large, its operational vulnerability will be high, since the burden of retrenchment will fall with a disproportionately heavy impact on the few alterable items.

Finally, organizations vary with regard to their chances of *externalizing costs and problems*. The better the possibilities of passing the cut-backs on to other organizations or clients (e.g. fare raises, cuts in subsidies, service deterioration or externalizing administrative costs), the less 'confined' the possibilities of prioritizing, and the lower the operational vulnerability.

ON THE USE OF VULNERABILITY FACTORS

Despite the sketchy character of the previous considerations on various properties of public organizations as factors of retrenchment vulnerability, let us assume that we are dealing not merely with a number of hypotheses, but with an established body of facts[1]. Then the next question is: To what uses can this knowledge be put?

If the budget authority takes a 'Machiavellian' approach, it will demand cut-backs where political vulnerability is highest. The screams will not be loud , the resistance will be modest, and the level of conflict will be low (Behn, 1978). From a politico-administrative viewpoint the task will be easy. It will affirm the so-called Matthew Effect: to those who have, more will be given; from those who have not, what little they have will be taken from them.

If the budgetary authority takes a 'moral' approach, it will demand cut-backs where political vulnerability is lowest. For it will have reason to suspect that this is where the fat has been able to accumulate for a long time, and the hour of reckoning has come. It will, so to speak, try to even out the screams by putting them on scales with the same zero-base. By so doing, it will not necessarily succeed in bringing about 'equal pain across the board'. If that is the real objective, it must also take operational vulnerability into consideration.

But is there any correlation between allocational vulnerability and operational vulnerability? Before attempting to answer, let us sketch four types of public organizations as related to the two kinds of vulnerability. The 'difficult' cases are not types 2 and 3. Type 2 is easily hit by cuts, but not greatly damaged. Type 3 would be, but it is rarely hit. Type 1, on the other hand, has a hard time. It is frequently hit and suffers severe internal damage. And type 4 gets all the breaks. This is the type that has and to which more will be given – the type the moralist budget authority will be looking for.

Now, is there any correlation between political and operational vulnerability? Is the real world of public organizations mostly of types 1 and 4 or 2 and 3? In general, this is hardly to be expected, since the factors that condition high (respectively, low) political vulnerability are not the same

Figure 2   *Organizational typology based on dimensions of vulnerability*

Operational vulnerability

		High	Low
Political vulnerability	High	Squeezed – 1	Broad- shouldered + 2
	Low	3 Sensitive but secure +	4 Thriving –

as those that condition low (respectively, high) operational vulnerability (aside from budget composition). It can be said, of course, that high operational vulnerability is a good argument for not cutting, but its persuasiveness is conditioned by such factors as professionalization, impact visibility, client proximity and sectoral organization. High operational vulnerability could, quite to the contrary, entail political vulnerability. It is entirely plausible that poor performance (due to cut-backs) could be construed by the public as poor efficiency or bad management which in turn might foster a tendency to subject the organization in question to further cut-backs.

What is now the options left open for the public manager? Levine (1978) discussed how public organizations could resist or smooth cuts. The present analysis leads us to consider as the main strategy the possibility to alter the general conditions on the appropriations market, i.e. the public manager should seek to establish his organization, if possible, as a type 4 organization.

In the 1970s the Civil Defense were severely threatened by cut-backs. Due to a relative lack of international crises the hypothetical demand appeared to be even more hypothetical. The Civil Defense consequently scored high on political vulnerability. After several previous cut-backs on investment and equipment which of course lead to an unbalanced budget composition they scored high also on operational vulnerability. This caused the Ministry of Finance to make detailed studies of the entire civil defense system. Thus, political vulnerability increased once more. The Civil Defense became squeezed (type 1).

As a consequence the management adopted a number of strategies to avoid further retrenchment. They expanded their activities in cases of fire, environmental pollution, snow storms, storm surges and the like. Luckily, in that period Denmark 'suffered' from very warm summers (and an increase in dangerous forest fires) and cold, snowy winters and floodings at the West Coast. In other words, they tried to link their core activities (1) to current and visible demand (fire and flood control) and (2) to a widespread and growing concern for the environment, thereby trying to achieve task centrality (Beck Jørgensen, 1981).

The attempts to reformulate organizational goals and thereby obtaining new support and legitimacy were not entirely successful. To some extent they managed to become 'sensitive but secure' (type 3) but certainly not without problems as they by creating a new policy space faced new competitors guarding *their* organizational domains: the fire service and the environmental agencies[2].

CONCLUSION: A SHIFT IN PUBLIC MANAGEMENT ORIENTATION?

Some recent tendencies point to changed contingencies of resource allocation and thus possibly to a new orientation of public management. First, the described appropriations market has over time displayed itself as a market with a very small degree of free competition. Secondly, the prolonged period of retrenchment with many cut-backs in traditional areas (investment, operational expenses excluding personnel) has forced managers to take a closer look at the internal functioning (Beck Jørgensen, 1987).

Following the three main characteristics of the development outlined at the beginning of this chapter we should expect managers to be more concerned about:

1 Optimizing the composition of available resources (factors of production) instead of only securing growth.
2 Adjusting the expectations of the clientele downwards.
3 Breaking down vested interest, because these will appear to be barriers to reprioritizing and reorganization.

These shifts represent a general change in management orientations towards more concern about internal problems combined with clientele characteristics, the implications being that more managerial time and energy are put in the lower circuit of inducement/contribution (see Figure 1). An illustrative example is the current emphasis on service management both in practice, in management training courses and in the Danish programme on the modernization of the public sector.

But one problem still remains. So far as public organizations are financed through a traditional appropriation system a substantial part of managerial energy will be tied to the upper circuit. However, interesting developments among other things of the formal appropriation system leaves room for a more substantial shift in management orientation in Denmark.

1. During the 1980s budgetary and personnel reforms have been implemented in central as well as local government. First it is worth mentioning the increased use of *frame-budgeting*. This means a firm demand of keeping costs within the fixed frame. A necessary assumption is that the frame is relatively stable, at least in the short run. On the other hand there is less control with details and greater autonomy in experimenting with alternative means of production and with the development of new products.

Second, it is worth noting that public organizations now can engage themselves in production to a 'real money market', keeping a fixed portion of the *profit for themselves*. Third, it is made possible to *save money*. Unused appropriations in one fiscal year can be transferred to the following fiscal year (with a maximum, of four years). Fourth, it is possible to *borrow money* in the budget department to finance specific projects, provided that the expected internal interest is above a certain level. Finally and perhaps most important, is the extended use of *appropriations directly linked to the number of users*, e.g. a fixed amount of money per student, school pupil etc.

Table 1   *Future organizational cultures in the public sector*

	Administrative culture	Business culture
Decision culture	Risk avoiding	Risk taking
Focus on management	Making old systems perfect	Financial planning
Economic rationality	Marginal gimmicks	Optimizing
External source of changes	Interpretation of political goals	Market analysis
Internal source of change	Sporadic	Capability of innovation
Structure	Bureaucratic	Holding companies, joint-stock companies, joint-ventures, internal restructuring
Recruitment capability	Small	Growth of personnel in units not financed by appropriations

2. Beside changes in the appropriation system we can find changes in *organizational status*. Quite a number of traditionally organized public institutions and directorates have been transformed to public enterprises, 'free-agencies' and publicly owned joint stock companies. This trend is very similar to the British 'next step agencies'. Parallel to this development we can point to the increase in the contracting out of many auxillary functions.

3. In some cases citizens have been allowed to *choose more or less freely* among the services of a number of comparable public organizations, e.g. day care institutions, schools and hospitals thereby criss-crossing traditional politico-administrative boundaries.

The interesting point is that these changes in the formal systems seem to be not merely surface adjustments. On the contrary, it can be argued that they go to the heart of traditional public sector organization. So to speak, these changes alter the rules of the game, having one element in common: They are all varying examples of public organizations *exiting* the public sector, because the general implication is less political and hierarchical control, substituted by more 'market control'. We could label this trend *'the new public capitalism'*.

What consequences these changes might cause in managerial behaviour have yet to be seen. The changes do not dictate a certain behaviour but they constitute new possibilities and thereby raise challenges for the management in at least two respects. If greater autonomy is to be utilized there is a demand for management on a *new professional basis* and there is a need for *new management attitudes*.

Therefore, it is not easy to forecast what will be development in the next decade. But we could imagine the development of two distinct types of public organizations. Let us discuss them as extremes. The first type is the organization where management reacts passively and traditionally. The guess would be that in the long run they will suffer repeated cut-backs. The second type is the organization where the management actively uses the new possibilities. In a decade we might see the contours of two separate organizational cultures in the public sector, the administrative and the business culture.

Both cultures raise serious questions. The administrative culture signals public organizations with a decreasing problem-solving capacity, and the business culture, being an intrinsic part of the new public capitalism, might create several tensions (Beck Jørgensen, 1992). Because of decentralization of autonomy public management can be politicized and at the same time formal political responsibility will be eroded. A tension between territorial democracy and the new public capitalism might emerge since citizens in some cases will be part of one local political system (at the county or municipal level) and demand services from public organizations belonging to another political system. With regard to the EC we might even realize this tension on the international level.

Notes

1 A number of the vulnerability hypotheses have been tested by Dunsire and Hood (1989). The test does not support the hypotheses in a definitive way. However, testing such micro hypotheses is not uncomplicated for several reasons, the main reason probably being, that there can be found huge interactional effects between the proposed relationships, i.e. the power of one hypothesis is conditioned by a number of other hypotheses. Forecasting the budgets of a population of public organizations is thus very similar to weather forecasting!.

2 The Canadian Emergency Measures Organization (EMO) faced a strikingly parallel development in the same period (Hannigan and Kueneman, 1977). Although EMO was more succesful in getting accept on their new role as 'peacetime planning for natural disasters' compared to the Danish Civil Defense, the basic challenge and the organizational responses were the same.

PART 3

THE PUBLIC MANAGER

Managers are the core element in the internal management of public organizations. Nevertheless, few studies have been devoted to research into the role of the manager as such. Most of the literature has instead focused on public management and management in general. In this book, however, we have focused on the role, perceptions and attitudes of managers (Strand), the important task of human resource management, both in relation to the managers themselves and in relation to their subordinates (Yntema) and the persons facing the greatest problems in all organizations, particularly when they are involved in a process of change, the middle-managers (Gerding). More generally, all of these studies advise the managers to be aware of, to understand and to try and prepare the conditions for change in their own environment.

In *Bureaucrats and Other Managers*, Torodd Strand observes that public managers see their organizational environment as predictable but complex, in contrast with the views of the private managers who see theirs as simple but changing. He shows how these differences in perception have a heavy influence on their role as managers. In his analysis, he employs a matrix of basic functions in an organization and the corresponding roles.

Strand points out the ambiguity which exists between perceived demands and reported managerial and organizational performance. Public managers do not perform in accordance with their self expressed demands for integration and attention to the external world. They proclaim production to be their favourite function, but are rather meek and vague in stating results and achievements.

In *Public Managers in the Middle*, Gerhard Gerding uses, in part, the same model of different managerial types as Torodd Strand. He investigates the relationship between the context in which management in the public sector is located, managerial styles and effectiveness. The article concludes with some recommendations as to how to reduce the dependency of public managers and increase their influence. With regard to managerial style, the author stresses the need to adopt one specific managerial style, rather than combining elements of many.

Managing Human Resources in the Public Sector is the theme of Paul Yntema's article in which he advocates the need for a modernization of public human resource management. He argues that modernization in this field, is even more important in the public than in the private sector. The public service should adopt more flexible rules, but within a structured framework that combines a centrally determined strategy with decentralized (autonomous) operational managers. This requires the creation of a new type of managerial role and a new type of personnel in institutions providing public services.

11

BUREAUCRATS AND OTHER MANAGERS:
ROLES IN TRANSITION

Torodd Strand

ACTORS AND SYSTEMS

The rising interest in the concept of public management suggests a stronger attention paid to action, actors, and managers. It also explicitly approaches the question of whether the public-private distinction is fruitful or not in describing, analyzing and advising leaders in various types of formal organizations.

Organization theorists and social scientists in general are quick to point to the constraints and systemic conditions under which actors operate, often relegating the actors to the roles of puppets, for all practical purposes determined by external conditions, such as bureaucratic structures and procedures, political mandates, and the imperatives of their professions. The argument seems to be more justifiable for mangers in the public services than for managers in the private sector (Rainey et al., 1976). Pfeffer (1977) points to the apparent failure in leadership studies to reach consistent results and ascribes this to the narrow focus of the studies as they tend to disregard the assumed uniform social selection of leading personnel, the inhibiting nature of organizations and the lack of control of the environment. Carried to its extreme the argument leaves no room for significant individual behaviour or leadership in the sense of acting over and above formal rules and obligations of an organization (Katz and Kahn, 1976). The relationship between actors and system is however, admittedly a dynamic one. The dilemma of actors versus systems is hard to solve in theory and even more difficult to pursue in empirical examinations. There are, however, fruitful suggestions as how to go about it, one being the study of how roles of significant actors are performed, and another studying actors and systems over time (Katz and Kahn, 1976, Poole and van de Ven, 1989).

Applying a conception of organizational role will help to link the social order with characteristics and behaviour of the individual implying that leaders have liberty to act and at the same time are socially bound. Thus we can avoid the dilemma of systems descriptions with no room for actors and actors approaches with insufficient regard for the context.

In this chapter we shall explore these assumptions by describing leadership roles in several types of contexts, private and public, bureaucratic and non bureaucratic and compare data from two time periods. The analysis is based on questionnaire data about Norwegian mangers' perceptions of their role expectations, role performance and other organizational features especially relevant to the interplay between managerial action and organizational structures.[1]

Are the role profiles different in the different contexts? Is there a correspondence between what the mangers define as core demands and their ability to perform? What room is there for leadership in different types of organizations? And finally, when looking at different types of organizations, how are so called functional prerequisites attended to? Can managerial roles be related to typical patterns attributable to the various organizations? The above questions are being analyzed across two time periods.

By reporting data from two time periods we shall be able to say something about stability and potential for change conditioned by the type of organization. Changes in roles are particularly relevant for the period from which our observations are drawn. The eighties have been a period of reform in the public sector and a period of considerable turbulence for those organizations which depend on the market for their existence, in Norway as well as other European countries, and the administrative doctrines have changed (Olsen, 1988; Lægreid, 1992; Hood and Jackson, 1991) .

THE PRIVATE-PUBLIC DISTINCTION

The public-private distinction has been discussed extensively in other parts of this book. The approach taken here is that rather than accepting a list of predefined characteristics of public and private organizations, and hence managerial roles, we propose to explore variations of roles and behaviours across four organizational types. We start out with a simple institutional distinctions of public and private by recording what the respondents declare their organizations to be. State agencies and public utilities as well as local governments are taken as public, and private companies are denoted private. Thus some undetermined cases and voluntary and cooperative organizations are excluded from the sample as hybrid cases. In addition we make a distinction between bureaucratic and other types of organizations in recognition of one fundamental distinction which cuts across the public- private distinction.

Figure 1   *Perceptions of environments: public and private managers*
            (percentages 'very stable' and 'very competitive')

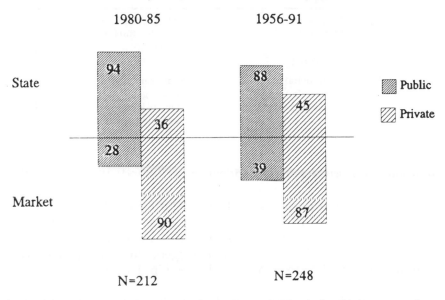

Bozeman argues that the most valid method of classifying organizations as to their 'publicness' is to ascertain their dependence on political authority , i.e. the state, and economic authority, i.e. the market (Bozeman, 1987).

The overriding majority of organizations classified as public, have leaders who report a strong dependence on the state, however, dependence on the market is also admitted. On the other hand the overriding majority of organizations denoted as private recognize their dependence on the market, but also recognizes to a large, and increasing degree the dependence on the state. The data illustrates Bozemans point: even when excluding the obvious 'in between cases' we find that organizations regardless of formal status see themselves as dependent both on the state and the market. The differentiating power of the two dimensions is diminishing. It also underscores Metcalfe and Richards' point that institutional distinctions seldom produce clear cut results (1988: 73).

BASIC FUNCTIONS AND ROLES IN ORGANIZATIONS

Having chosen an actor approach, without discarding organization and environmental contingencies, and having left the public-private distinction as hypothetically useful, we shall define our area of study further by introducing the notion of basic functions or prerequisites in organizations, assuming that such basic functions can be manifested through specific roles. This approach allows us to describe individuals and apply significance to their actions while at the same time considering their

Figure 2   *Basic organizational functions and corresponding roles*

	Internal	External
Change	Integrator Motivating Developing Integrating	Entrepreneur Avoiding threats Exploring opportunities
Stability	Administrator Maintaining and developing structures	Producer Setting goals and standards Achieving results

functions in a broader organizational sense (Strand, 1988). The notion that high level officials may be seen as the embodiment of the organizational values and purposes has been set forth by Selznick (1956). The notion that leaders both act instrumentally towards and symbolizes the core values of an organization has since been elaborated through various approaches, ranging from that of managerial 'ownership' to conceptions of the symbolic preeminence of leadership (Fligstein, 1987; Pfeffer, 1981).

An organizations' variety of needs and purposes, can be embodied more or less perfect in leadership roles, relating both to the internal functioning of the organization, its structural adaptation, and its legitimation towards a wider society. Since Parson's (1959) theory of the AGIL functions, there has been a number of elaborations and suggestions as to what the basic functions in organizations are (Lyden and Freeman, 1975). There are considerable areas of agreement, although the phrasing may be different (Quinn, 1988; Yntema, 1990).

The following scheme is inspired by Adizes (1980) and Quinn (1982; 1988) and has been applied by Metcalfe and Richards (1990) and Yntema (1990). An elaborate version is applied by Quinn (1988). Healthy organizations are supposed to perform all the four functions successfully, although relative emphasis and visibility may vary over time and by the nature of the basic requirements a particular organization must meet. By mapping the role set in an organization at the highest level one may catch some of the basic orientations, weaknesses and strengths of that organization (Tsui, 1984; Gammelsæter, 1991; Strand, 1992). Leadership behaviour as well as theories about organizations and leadership tend to leave one or several aspects out, they have blank spots. In the current writing about public organizations we seldom find the integrator function described or attended to at all (Larsen, 1984). Intuitively one would place the emphasis in public organizations in the lower area of the model with a strong bias towards administration and production. However, this is open to empirical investigation.

We can also place competing theoretical traditions in the separate boxes. Examples are human relation theories, theories about open systems, theories about rational decision making, and theories about stable structures, such as bureaucracies. Quinn emphasizes the fundamentally paradoxical nature of management and introduces the notion of competing values, a map of which can help us to clarify our perceptual biases. (Quinn, 1988: 85–87).

Referring to Figure 2, we find a strong emphasis on internal coordination and maintenance of the system on the left side, whereas on the right side achievements and impact are highlighted. In the lower area of the Figure, order, rationality and authority are emphasized, whereas in the upper sections, innovation, sensitivity to external and internal signals prevail. The functions and orientations, exhibited in Figure 2, may be expressed in an organization through a corresponding set of roles, most likely to be performed by leading personnel.

Co-ordination may take place when managers perform more than one role well, when differences are recognized and formalized procedures for cooperation, such as management teams and, consultation procedures do exist. An obvious pitfall would be to recognize and foster only one style or one type of role.

Furthermore one must ask questions about leadership. Given that there are formal roles to perform the above functions the question of whether the incumbents are given the instruments and social opportunities to fulfil their roles is an open one (Katz and Kahn, 1976: 532). Formalistic, impotent, and even dysfunctional behaviour is a possibility also for leading personnel. The factual conditions for exerting leadership, or in our jargon: performing the vital roles, may vary a great deal between organizations and settings.

To explore the question of how organizations perform the functions of production, administration, integration and entrepreneurship, with a particular view on the organizations managers, we shall present data in three tiers, gradually broadening the perspective from managerial role expectations to organizational profiles: (1) perceived role expectations classified according to the four functions or roles mentioned above; (2) perceptions of role performance compared to role demands and perception of room for leadership; and (3) information about what the organizations have undertaken and achieved in the four areas, independent of the managers' role.

We pose the question of whether there is a relatively stable relationship between the perceptions of roles and environments on one hand and organizational context on the other. It is reasonable to expect that organizations as dissimilar as public bureaucracies and private business firms exhibit quite different patterns of orientations in their management. But given the possibility for contradicting demands and the loose coupling between managerial perception and organizational events, a wholly consistent and stable pattern should not be expected. However, the mapping of inconsistencies, paradoxes and tensions in organizations is also of great interest.

Table 1   *Perceived demands on leader roles* in four types of organizations (percentages adding to 200, double answers. N=446)*

	Bureaucracy		Other organization		
	Public	Private	Public	Private	Average
a. Getting things done, proceeding (PRODUCER)	59	51	60	42	51
b. Controlling, applying rules (ADMINISTRATOR)	20	9	7	4	9
c. Motivating, supporting people (INTEGRATOR)	78	82	73	78	77
d. Exploring opportunities (ENTREPRENEUR)	11	17	15	27	19
e. Scanning environment to be able to adapt (ENTREPRENEUR)	31	40	45	48	43

* Question (translated): *Which of the items below represent the most important demands the job requires from you? (Tick two)* (Item f, 'other answers' omitted).

PERCEIVED DEMANDS ON LEADERSHIP IN DIFFERENT SETTINGS

Roles are constituted by the formal description of a position, the expectations directed towards the incumbent, and the incumbent's interpretations of his/her tasks, constraints and capabilities (Biddle and Thomas, 1966). The data which are presented in this section are responses to a question concerning the managers' perception of core demands of their jobs. Perceived demands will serve as proxy for the core concept of role theory, expectations (Tsui, 1984). The responses will be used as indicators of the relative emphasis on the roles the respondents in fact do perform: administrator, producer, integrator and entrepreneur (see Figure 2).[2] We shall place the patterns of responses into a matrix which distinguishes public from non-public settings and bureaucratic from nonbureaucratic organizations. The suggestion is that the role profiles will be different in the four settings (Table 1).

The most frequent response in all types of organizations was the demand for motivating and supporting people on the job, 'integration'. The least frequently reported demand was, on average, that of controlling and applying rules, 'administration'. The most frequent combination of responses are item a, 'getting-things-done' combined with item c, 'motivating, supporting people' on the one hand, and the combination of item c, 'motivating' and item e, 'scanning the environment' on the other hand. The two combinations together account for about two-thirds of the answers in the sample. Public bureaucracies are typical for the first combination, whereas other private organizations are most typical for the second.

Table 2 *Changes from period 1979–85 to 1986–91 in perceived demands on leader role in four types of organizations (percentage differences)*

	Bureaucracy		Other organization	
	Public	Private	Public	Private
a. Getting things done, proceeding	5	8	–12	–2
b. Controlling, applying rules	–20	5	–5	1
c. Motivating, supporting people	14	2	9	–6
d. Exploring opportunities	1	–12	–1	8
e. Scanning environment to be able to adapt	0	–3	9	–1

The two dimensions along which the answers to each item 'a' to 'e' is distributed, account for some differentiation, but generally give an impression of a high degree of uniformity in managers' perceptions of the core demands towards the role. This observation agrees with conclusions reached by Lau and Pavett in their examination of role profiles in private and public organizations (1980). There also seems to be agreement with Lau and Pavetts findings as to what the major dimension of managerial work content is, '... to guide and motivate subordinates and to integrate individual and organizational roles' (Lau and Pavett, 1980: 457, see also Næss and Strand, 1992).

Some of the differences between organizations, however, are the following[3]: Leaders in public bureaucracies distinguish themselves from those of private non bureaucratic organizations by emphasizing somewhat more 'getting-things-done' (17 percentage points difference) and rule application (11 percentage points difference). The public bureaucrats score marked below average in terms of reporting demand for 'exploring opportunities' and 'scanning the environment'. Only for item c, 'motivating people' is there no notable difference between public bureaucracies and private non bureaucracies.

The gross sum of differences between all 'public-private' pairs is 97 percentage points and the differences between all-'bureaucracy' and 'other organizational form' categories are 72 percentage points.

The differences between the two time periods, 1979–85 and 1986–91, are significant and interesting. By splitting the material and inspecting the data for the two time periods we find that the total variation for the first period, measured as sum of percentage differences is 111, and only 53 for the second period. The changes from the first to the second period are the following (Table 2).

The public and private organizations are becoming more alike, and the major change is that the public bureaucracies are emphasizing 'controlling' to a lesser degree and adding to the frequency of 'motivating people' as a more important demand for leaders. The only difference which emerges to be larger in the second period, is that private-non-

Table 3	*Area of best performance as perceived by role incumbent, by four types of organization (percentages. N=411)*

	Bureaucracy		Other organizations		
	Public	Private	Public	Private	Average
a. Getting things done, proceeding	58	58	48	51	53
b. Controlling, applying rules	24	10	18	7	13
c. Motivating, supporting people	13	22	24	22	21
d. Exploring opportunities	1	1	7	6	5
e. Scanning environment to be able to adapt	4	10	3	14	8

bureaucratic organizations to a larger extent than before emphasize the exploring of opportunities and thus deviates from the common pattern.

DEMANDS AND ABILITY, MATCH OR MISMATCH?

The leaders also assessed the relative strengths and weaknesses of their personal and unit performance in relation to the perceived demands of their jobs by responding to the questions: 'Which of the items 'a' to 'e' indicate the area in which you and your unit perform best? And weakest?' Table 3 has the replies. All types of managers report item a, 'getting things done' most frequently as the area in which they perform best. Item c, 'motivating people', the most frequently reported demand, obtains a weak second, and in the case of public bureaucracies, a third place. Consistently low come items d and e, relating to the environment, where only private organizations exceed 10 percentage points on the last item 'scanning the environment'. The two items relating to the environment are also most frequently reported as weaknesses, by 36 and 21 percent. The public bureaucracies distinguish themselves by scoring considerably higher than average on both counts. The item concerning 'motivating people' is also mentioned in 21 percent of the cases concerning weak performance.

We note the considerable deviance between what mangers perceive as role demands and their perception of what they do best. By cross-tabulating the responses to the 'best performance' question by the responses to the 'demand' questions, we find that there is a considerable correspondence when it comes to item a, 'getting-things-done', in which case 74 percent also mentioned this item as a core demand for their job. We also see a roughly descending degree of correspondence down the list of items, in that the areas which least frequently are mentioned as areas of high ability, items d and e, also have the smallest degree of correspondence between demand and ability. Particularly noteworthy is the poor match between demand and ability for item c, 'motivating' the most frequently mentioned demand, in which case a match was

Figure 3 *Profile of managerial functions in public bureaucracies (cf. Figure 2). Based on question about role demands and ability to act on relevant demand*

INTEGRATION	ENTREPRENEURSHIP
Demands to motivate	Demands to scan env.
low ability, increasing	low ability
emphasis	Little exploration
ADMINISTRATION	PRODUCTION
Rel. high demand	'Getting things
for control activity	done, proceeding'
High ability, decreasing	Frequently demanded
	and high ability

found only in 26 percent of the cases. Further differentiation by type of organization and time period shows that public organizations are below average on all items in the first period. On the important item of motivating people, public organizations improve their score from below average in the first time period to about average in the second period.

In summary the respondents report great discrepancies between what they see as their main demands to the role as leaders and the ability to perform the corresponding functions. Particularly, deviance is found between the demand for motivating people and the ability to do so. The score for public organizations is particularly low here, but it is rising over time, approaching the average for the sample. Also between the demands for orienting themselves towards the environment and the ability to do so the respondents report a conspicuous gap. Again, the public sector stands out as a case of above average deviance between demand and ability.

We can sketch a rough pattern of role profiles, singling out the characteristics of public bureaucracies for special attention. Referring to Figure 3, profile of managerial functions in public bureaucracies, the following pattern emerges. Leaders in public bureaucracies reported demands in the upper left quadrant 'integration', but exhibited their strength in the lower area, where there is a relatively high degree of correspondence between demands and reported ability to act on relevant demands. The public bureaucrats are on average approaching the pattern of other types of organizations in that they in the second time period portrayed here, de-emphasize the demand for controlling and applying rules and in that they emphasized more, like other public leaders, the need for and ability to motivate and support people.

LEADERSHIP, DISCRETION AND PERCEIVED PERFORMANCE

Freedom to act is a distinguishing aspect of leadership. It is commonly assumed that there is less programmed activity the higher up in the organization one reaches. Stewart and others have suggested that the

Table 4 *Percentage of time available for activity chosen by respondent*

	Bureaucracy		Other organization	
	Public	Private	Public	Private
1979–85	27	40	27	37
1986–91	29	32	37	40

area of leadership is 'located' in the space between the core demands of the job and the perceived constraints occurring in the organizational and external environment (Stewart, 1982; Hambrick and Finkelstein, 1987), a view that implies that public bureaucracies leave little or no room for leadership at all. A simple measure of the perceived room to manoeuvre is time available for activities chosen by the manager him or herself (see Table 4).

For the first time period there is some difference between the public and the private organisations in the sample, 13 and 10 percentages points. In the second time period the differences have shrinked to being insignificant. Again we note an indication that the leadership roles in the different types of organisations are becoming more similar over time, although the difference between the extremes, the public bureaucrat and the leader of the private firm is about the same in two time periods, 10 and 11 percentage points.

The question which has not have been answered is whether the constraints are generated by previous choices or just are 'givens'. There is also a question whether managers act as leaders or mainly deal with technical routine or insignificant aspects of the organizational life. Another indication of the managers' leeway is their report about their influence on hiring and on allocating personnel and allotting tasks.

As expected but rarely proven, the public managers experience much less influence on such important aspects of organizational life as hiring and reassigning tasks than do managers in the private sector (Table 5). The differences over time are minuscule (and are not displayed in the Table).

There is support for the notion that leadership is less expressed in mechanistic organizations than in organizations with different structures, located in less stable environments. When asking a general question about the managers' ability to master their jobs, we find some small differences

Table 5 *Influence by respondent in two areas (percentages 'Strong')*

	Bureaucracy		Other organization	
	Public	Private	Public	Private
Choice of personnel (N=469)	57	93	75	93
Reassigning personnel/tasks (N=468)	13	59	28	76

Table 6 *Organizational performance last year as assessed by respondent (percentages 'Very good')*

| | Bureaucracy | | Other organizations | |
	Public	Private	Public	Private
1979–85 (N=204)	21	47	28	43
1986–91 (N=246)	26	38	32	44

between the public and private leaders. The numbers may reflect a reality, or to some extent the difference in legitimacy in reporting success in the two types of settings. However, the above data about time available and discretionary power in important matters reveal differences which clearly go deeper than differences of language.

THE FOUR FIELDS OF ORGANIZATIONAL FUNCTIONING: MANAGERIAL ROLES AND BEYOND

We shall look further into how the four functions are performed by reporting opinions and activities which relate to the functions. These activities and opinions are only indirectly related to the managerial roles, but do reflect upon the managers Together with the role expectation data presented above, they provide a fuller picture of how the managers and their organizations perform concerning the functional prerequisites.

The function of producing and achieving goals

Are public organizations more or less oriented towards goals and specific achievements than other organizations? Selznick (1956) calls goal setting one of the defaults of leadership. It is also a frequent assertion that vagueness of objectives pursued is one of the characteristics of public management and that potentially conflicting interests makes it difficult to pursue a single goal. It is reasonable to hypothesize that the role of the producer, who sets goals and standards for achievements, and who is occupied with achieving goals, is weakly represented in public organizations. However, leaders in public bureaucracies more often than others report that the main demand of the job was to get things done, and a high percentage reported that this is what they are best at. When asked what motivates the managers in their jobs a large proportion in all sorts of organizations, approximately 80 percent, reported that a wish to see the results of their activity was a primary driving force. Judged by the managers self-reported orientations, and given also that many public organizations are populated by professionals there is a considerable attention to the need for producing and achieving standards (Lægreid, 1991). However, when it comes to reporting the results of their efforts, the public leaders are evasive.

Table 7 *'Is your organization well adapted to tasks and products' (percentages 'Yes')*

	Bureaucracy		Other organization	
	Public	Private	Public	Private
1979–85 (N=219)	52	78	70	77
1986–91 (N=254)	70	88	74	81

When asked about the indicators by which they determine their organizations result, 85 percent of the private leaders pointed to economic indicators, whereas leaders in public organizations were uncertain, with client satisfaction as the most frequently reported answer. In the majority of cases 'no answer' and 'miscellaneous' were the only responses given.

The public managers were also more modest when it came to assessing the results of their organization's activity than were leaders in private organizations. The differences between the sectors are significant, although the distance between the public bureaucracy and the private firm shrinks somewhat over time. The public leaders were inclined to report 'satisfactorily' on this general question of performance. Some more specific dimensions of performance have also been measured, of which work effort, quality and efficiency are relevant to the production theme (Appendix: Table 1). These indicators show that public organizations scored lower than private organizations the first period, but caught up with them in the second, by the managers' opinions.

Although it is not confirmed that goal setting and achievement orientation are primary characteristics of public management, the data at least allow for some doubt about the notion that public business is 'aimless'. Clearly there is not one predominant goal or measure of success, on the other hand there is a widely reported orientation towards results and a wish to get things done. In addition, when several dimensions of performance are observed, we get a rather optimistic picture of how the public managers perceive 'results', and over time matching the picture reported from the private.

Administration as structuring of the organization

Are public organizations more rigid and ill suited to their tasks than private organizations, and are public managers more or less passive towards their structural settings? The role of the administrator in public organizations is often conceived of as the role of the bureaucrat, oriented towards authority and routines, while taking the structural limitations for granted. We have observed that rule application was a more predominant feature of managers in public bureaucracies than in other types of organizations, although being no favourite in either type.

Public bureaucracies appear to be deemed less suited for their tasks

Table 8   *Frequency of OD measures last three years (percentages 'Yes')*

| | Bureaucracy | | Other organization | |
	Public	Private	Public	Private
1979–85 (N=219)	52	53	58	59
1986–91 (N=254)	87	59	81	57

than other organizations (Table 7). The answers indicate some pessimism among the public managers, particularly those in bureaucratic organizations, but the frequency of 'agree' answers have increased over time and the distance between private and public bureaucracies have diminished. We found the same response patterns concerning adaption to market demands and client needs.

Our findings indicates that public bureaucrats may be stronger in maintaining structures than in creating and adapting them, although expressed dissatisfaction may represent the degree of insight as well as a factual diagnosis. However, measures are being taken, organization development project have flourished in the public sector (Table 8).

The change over time is striking: Public managers have engaged in organizational development activities during the second time period much more frequently than their private counterparts. Moreover, those who have engaged in OD activities are those most likely to find that their organization is well adopted to the nature of their tasks, on average 73 percent.

Integration

The reported profiles of the public managers' role expectation do not reflect the stereotype of the impersonal bureaucrat. Motivating and supporting people was deemed to be the single most important demand of the job. The high rate of OD activities reported above may also testify to the emphasis on integration, and increasingly so in the second time period studied. Also the high scores on 'morale' and 'recognition by others' support the point of view that public managers strive to deal with questions of interpersonal relations, pride in the work and intrinsic motivation (Appendix, table 1). However, the public managers do not consider themselves particularly competent in their roles as integrators. On the contrary, a high proportion singled out integration as their weakest area of performance. They also consistently report that they were less stimulated than private leaders to develop communication ability, openness, kindness, and empathy. And cooperative efforts across areas of responsibility are deemed as a less important part of their jobs than for other managers. The data suggest that public managers and organizations are prompted to deal with issues of integration, but experience difficulties in realizing the demands.

Figure 4   *Perceptions of environments: public and private managers (percentages 'very stable' and 'very competitive')*

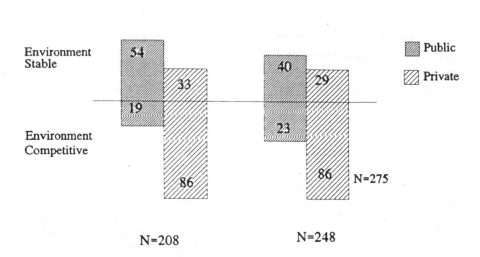

1979-85   1986-91

Environment Stable

Public

Private

Environment Competitive

N=275

N=208   N=248

Innovative and entrepreneurial functions

Entrepreneurial and innovative activities in the public sphere normally is thought of as being the prerogatives of politicians. But some analysts maintain that the focus on structural problems at the system's level is the first distinguishing feature of public management, implying that dealing with units outside ones jurisdiction is necessary to be efficient (Metcalfe and Richards, 1987: 75). The role of the entrepreneur in public organizations is vaguely and infrequently described and judged by the role expectation and role performance indicators the material clearly indicates that entrepreneurial orientations are in little demand and even less well performed. One indicator of entrepreneurship – 'innovativeness', points in a positive direction. Whereas public managers in the first period studied judge their organizations as being considerably less innovative than private organizations, they report an equal level in the second period.

The environment of the public organizations is increasing becoming unstable and competitive. (But for public managers there is a negative relationship between perceived instability and demands for external orientation).

CONCLUSIONS: PUBLIC MANAGEMENT – STABILITY, TENSIONS, AND TRANSFORMATION

The findings of the study can be summarized as follows:

(1) *Managerial roles are perceived to be increasingly uniform.* Our data

support the hypothesis that managerial roles to some extent are shaped by the type of organization of which they are a part. As expected public bureaucrats emphasize rule application more than other leaders and less frequently define their roles toward external demands. But the uniformity of the reported role expectations across various types of settings is striking and somewhat unexpected in that public leaders perceive interpersonal matters as important as other leaders do. The convergence in role expectations between the sectors over time is notable. By and large the public leaders seem to adopt the language of private leaders, 'less rules, soft approach'. Also on other counts, such as perceiving one's organization as well adapted and appreciating specific qualities of one's own organizations, the four groups of managers are becoming more similar over time.

(2) *The four types of organizations are perceived to perform differently.* When we move away from perceived demands and inquire about performance, discretionary powers and specific organizational features, we find that the differences are restored and some times exacerbated. Generally the public managers are very modest in stating the achievements of their organization. Public managers frequently see themselves as having little ability to meet the most frequent demand, integration. Also gross differences are also found concerning the freedom to act and influence in important issues. In public bureaucracies the mangers find themselves in more restrained leadership roles than their private counterparts, in terms of time available and in terms of perceived influence on important events in their organizations. They also express a greater dissatisfaction with the organization they are working in concerning its suitability for the tasks and in terms of performance.

(3) *Ambiguities: There is a loose connection between perceived demands and reported managerial and organizational performance.* It is difficult to depict what managers in various types of organizations 'contribute' in terms of functional prerequisites as compared to what is performed by organizational design. Tensions and ambiguities prevail. There seem to be greater distance between expectations and ability for managers in public bureaucracies than in other organizations. Public bureaucrats do not perform in accordance with self expressed demands for integration and attention to the external world, they proclaim production as a favourite function, but are rather meek and vague in stating results and achievements.

On the other hand, one has to allow for interpretations with a flavour of ambiguity and paradoxes, and both functional and symbolic explanations are imaginable: In public organizations 'producing' is given much attention, but indicators of results are ambiguous and achievements are deemed to be relatively moderate. On the other hand the quality of the processes are deemed to be approaching the level of private organizations. In public organizations managerial roles concerning 'production' are often constituted by procedural and internal references. Faced with a general question concerning performance, the public managers sense an externally given yardstick and safeguard themselves by giving modest answers, whereas they can claim that the quality of the processes is good. Another interpretation of the humble attitude concerning performance may be that the responses are a reflection of linguistic artifacts. Private managers are comfortable with such a word as performance, whereas public leaders may perceive it as something alien or unusual. An alternative to the question of performance would be to ask also private leaders 'how well do your organization serve society'.

Also the observation that public managers report 'integration' as a prime demand, and admit that they do not perform well, lends itself to the idea of admissible language, rather than change in behaviour. Alternatively, when public managers, even in bureaucratic organizations, emphasize integration, a function alien to that structure, a functional remedy may have been introduced as a real ambition (Katz and Kahn, 1978: 263). The fact that bureaucracies are deemed to be increasingly adequate also lends itself to both functional and symbolic explanations.

Finally, the virtually non-existing connection between demand and ability in the area of external relations may be seen as a recognition of the challenges posed by reformers and public opinion, combined with restraints on their implementation (Laegreid, 1992).

A rather pessimistic interpretation of the above observations would be that the changes which are reported are mere changes of language, perhaps reflections of the prevailing ideas in the environment (Røvik, 1991; Czarniawska-Jorges, 1988). But the notion that public organizations are subject to calls for adaptations is strongly supported. The use of a suitable language is one way of mediating between conflicting demands. What mangers say is a weak indicator of what they do, yet a valid representation of their preferred language provides an important cue to understanding how they present themselves and deal with questions of legitimacy, ambiguity and change (Brunsson, 1989).

APPENDIX

Appendix Table 1   *Reported performance of organization unit by sector and time-period (percentage 'Good' and 'Excellent')*

| | 1979–85 | | 1986–91 | |
	Public	Private	Public	Private
Work effort	58	74	62	74
Quality of work	51	68	62	60
Innovativeness	35	51	53	54
Recognition by others	37	62	54	56
Productivity	43	56	47	58
Efficiency	40	52	47	46
Moral	64	60	57	59
N	112	104	76	174

Notes

1 The data reported in this chapter are questionnaire responses from 473 Norwegian top- and high level managers in the private and public sectors. All occur in the sample as a result of their participation in management, training and development programs for public and private personnel: the Administrative Research Foundation's (AFF) nine weeks management/development program and a three months program for higher civil servants sponsored by the Ministry of Administration and Consumer Affairs. The frequently reported distinction between public and private and bureaucratic and non-bureaucratic settings, give the following distribution of respondents.
Number of respondents in each cell:

	Public	Private	All
'Bureaucracy'	114	80	194
'Other organizations'	105	174	279
All	219	254	473

The categories public/nonpublic are established on the basis of unambiguous classification of respondents' organizations. 69 organizations/respondents were excluded from the sample as they could not be classified as either public or private. The categories bureaucratic and other organizations were established by classification of responses to a question concerning the dominant mode of governing the respondents' organizational unit. 'Strictly formal organization governed by rules and regulations' was counted as bureaucratic, all others were counted as 'other organizations'.

2 Methodological remarks: The indicators of the four functional roles, items 'a' to 'e' are not fully adequate measures, one weakness being that item 'd' is unclear as to its position on the internal external dimension. Item 'a' may be interpreted as representing administration as well as production. The entrepreneurial function is represented i two items, and potentially over-represented in the answers. Hence exact mapping is difficult, but differences, changes over time and correspondence between demands and performance can be represented in a meaningful way.
The data have been controlled for background variables, age and sex. Females are over represented among public managers, but count for no variation in the dependent variables. Hierarchical position count for some variation, but is let out of the present analysis (See Naess, 1992).

3 Significant differences between means at .05 level exist between at least three of four groups for each item except 'c', where no significant differences are found in the total aggregate, although for the 1979–85 part of the sample.

12

PUBLIC MANAGERS IN THE MIDDLE

Gerard Gerding

Influencing other people is a vital managerial task. Without contributions from others – whether or not they perform their activities under his ultimate responsibility – a manager fails to realize organizational objectives. When a manager is managing by walking around (Peters and Austin, 1985), he or she tries to influence the behaviour of workers on all kinds of levels in his organization. When a manager is working the network (Mueller, 1986), channels for information and influence are built. When a manager stimulates subordinates to learn 'outside the umbrella' (Mintzberg and MacHugh, 1985), he or she influences their adaptive behaviour and their learning potential, both necessary for long term organizational survival. And when engaging in processes of agenda building (Kotter, 1982) a manager participates in a continuous struggle with other actors inside and outside the organization in order to create favourable conditions for organizational goal-attainment, if not the personal growth and prosperity for the various members of his or her organizational environment.

A manager who needs to influence the behaviour of others is dependent upon these other people. Influencibility and dependence are two sides of the same coin. The obvious nature of this truth not only applies to relationships on the actor level, i.e. between a focal manager, superiors, subordinates and outside constituents. Equally important are relationships, whether or not reflecting some kind of mutual dependency, on the systems level. Organizations – and the units of which they consist – maintain relationships with environments, most often characterized by a high degree of institutionalism. Therefore the concepts of dependence and influencibility can also be useful in analyzing and understanding the exchange processes between organizations – or their building blocks: units – on a systems level. Organizations depend on their environments, but at the same time also shape and reshape environmental elements.

This general description of key aspects of the functioning of managers and their organizations applies, in my opinion, to both the private and the public sector. Public managers not only try to influence their civil service subordinates and societal counterparts, but also aim at changing the behaviour and the agendas of their political masters. They try to anticipate the effects of changes – for instance those brought about by democratic election processes – in the political arena, whilst at the same time promoting the approved policies of their contemporary superiors. Channels of information and influence serve varying and sometimes predominantly 'personal' purposes. Their agencies, on the systems level, are dependent upon each other for developing and implementing policies, both for gaining entry to critical resources and for maintaining checks and balances with other parts of the socio-political system.

ORGANIZATIONAL STRUCTURE AND STRATEGY FORMATION

Choice and determinism

Nowadays, the relationships between an organization and its environment constitute an important field of interest for both managers and management researchers. With respect to the latter, Scott (1981: 164) states correctly that 'since the emergence and increasing prominence of open systems models, investigators are no longer able to comfortably ignore the effects of environments on organizations'. The opposite of this statement, however, is of equal significance. Organizations – as remarked in the introduction to this chapter – are not only influenced by their environments, their actions – if not their mere existence – also shape environmental developments. In this section I will briefly discuss this theme by referring to recent work on organizational structuring and strategy formation processes.

Organizational structure is often seen as an instrument for coping with environmental demands and developments. The degree in which managers can freely choose or adapt this instrument is nevertheless subject to debate. The population ecology school (Hannan and Freeman, 1966) adopts a deterministic view on the relationship between organization and environment and hence on the topic of structure. In this perspective, managerial activity contributes little or nothing to long term organizational survival. Structure can not easily be adapted. Inappropriate structures will therefore in the long run be selected out.

An opposing view, which one might characterize as being of a voluntaristic nature, is embedded in the concepts of strategic choice (Child, 1972) and resource dependence (Pfeffer and Salancik, 1978). Although organizational adaptation can be severely limited by environmental circumstances, organizations – at least to some extent – are considered to be able to reshape their environments, recreate structures and actively seek conditions more favourable to organizational survival. For a long time the perspectives of 'choice' and 'determinism' have been seen as mutually exclusive. In recent years bridges between these antagonistic perspectives on the significance of structural design were constructed by Hrebiniak and Joyce (1985) and Grandori (1987). The latter author stresses the complementary nature of both approaches. When trying to adapt in order to survive, every organization meets with certain constraints. But in her view these deterministic forces are seldom homogeneous or well-balanced. As more trial-and-error learning is required to cope with these forces, network types of organizational structure will become necessary. At a certain point, hierarchy fades away and a market type of structure will emerge. On the other hand, the less trial-and-error is needed, the more a hierarchical structure will be able to deal with environmental demands effectively. Grandori thus explains organizational structure as a contingent outcome of a combatting process between choice and determination. Loosely coupled systems, adhocracies and semi-autonomous units in bigger scaled organizations must be seen as mixed structures, designed to cope effectively with today's dynamic environments.

Hrebiniak and Joyce (1985), in their landmark article, approach the same phenomenon from a different angle. They distinguish between four types of organization-environment relationships. The keyword in their model is adaptation, which is seen as a fundamental managerial task. Adaptation can take place in a situation characterized by low choice and high determinism, but is then labeled as 'minimum choice' or passive adaptation. In a situation of high choice and low determinism ('maximum choice'), the adaptation process is fully amenable to human design. These combinations of choice and determinism both reflect the aforementioned classical debate between population ecologists and the supporters of resource dependence and strategic choice. Hrebiniak and Joyce however also construct two innovating perspectives on the relationship between choice and determinism: 'incremental choice' (low determinism, low choice) and 'differentiated choice' (high determinism, high choice). In the first perspective, coincidence plays an important role in the adaptation process; in the second perspective adaptation takes place within certain constraints.

From an empirical point of view this framework offers several opportunities for analyzing real life organizational adaptation processes. Hrebiniak and Joyce make the interesting observation that lots of so-called quasi-autonomous units in large organizations are actually performing in a situation characterized by differentiated choice. The larger organization to some extent influences the structure and the activities of the smaller unit, but at the same time a certain amount of choice ('intrapreneuring') is encouraged. According to these authors, choice and determinism are both a cause and an effect of each other. They reject a predominantly one way relationship between these variables. Organizations can take up an awaiting attitude towards adaptation, but they have the freedom to try moving themselves to a more favourable situation. On the other hand, regardless its efforts to achieve otherwise, it is conceivable that an organization finally lands up in a situation it perceives as less attractive. But there is always an initial choice (Lawless and Finch, 1989): the decision to start working towards an entry into a more favourable environmental position.

Strategy formation processes

Decisions as those referred to in the previous section are primarily of a strategic nature. According to Miles and Snow (1984: 11), strategy is the basic alignment mechanism between organizational resources, skills and assets on the one hand and environmental characteristics and trends on the other. Strategy, in their view, should bring about a fit between organization and environment and, equally important, should maintain such a state in a dynamic process of adaptation. Strategic decision making has for a long time been seen as the prerogative of top level officials and executives. This thought is clearly on its return. The conceptual and empirical contributions of, among others, Broekstra (1984), Mintzberg and Jorgensen (1987), Shrivastava and Nachman (1989) and Wooldridge and Floyd (1990) all point in the same direction: a top management centered and more or less mechanistic approach to strategy ('the design school') has to be abandoned. Although the strategy theme in itself implies a voluntary perspective on the relationship between environment and organization – a dedicated population ecologist would not bother to see the benefits of strategic managerial activity – the pretentions of strategy theorists have clearly diminished (Mintzberg, 1990). The distinctions between intended and emergent strategies (Mintzberg and MacHugh, 1985), the increasing awareness of the ecological nature of interorganizational relations (Broekstra, 1984) and the development of 'grass roots models' of strategy formation (Mintzberg and Jorgensen, 1987) have all contributed to a more realistic view on the theoretical and practical values of strategic activity. In my opinion, perhaps the most important innovation in strategy conceptualization is the growing understanding among both scholars and practitioners that strategic behaviour not only demands, but also benefits from significant contributions by middle and lower level managers. Nonaka stresses, for instance, the role of middle managers in seeking and maintaining a productive tension between 'abandoning the old and generating the new' (1988: 12). He therefore introduces the concept of middle-up-down management. The same phenomenon is also described by Kanter: 'As managers and professionals spend more time working across boundaries with peers and partners over whom they have no direct control, their negotiating skills become essential assets. Alliances and partnerships transform impersonal, arm's-length contracts into relationships involving joint planning and joint decision making. Internal competitors and adversaries become allies on whom managers depend for their own success. At the same time, more managers at more levels are active in the kind of external diplomacy that only the CEO or selected staffs used to conduct (1989: 89).

As a result of growing interdependencies between organizations and increasing environmental turbulences, our large organizations – whether they are performing in the public sector or in the private sector – have to combine a hierarchical chain of command with some sort of network structure, in which units enjoy certain degrees of freedom to anticipate and adapt to specific environmental demands and circumstances. Before I discuss the research findings derived from relevant empirical studies, in the next section I will outline a conceptual model useful for analyzing strategic managerial activity on the unit level.

A CONCEPTUAL MODEL

Relationships between style and context

The relationships between an organization and its environment can be described in terms of both choice and determinism simultaneously. The next figure can be useful in distinguishing between four archetypical types of such relationships, which I will subsequently refer to as types of context (Table 1).

On the management level, adopting a framework developed by Adizes (1976) and also used by Strand (1987), four archetypical managerial styles can be derived (Table 2).

If management is seen as a balancing process between determinate and indeterminate forces and as ensuring some sort of stability, whilst also remaining sensitive to environmental influence, than each of the four types of managerial style just derived can be seen as a fitting answer to a specific contextual (i.e. organization-environment) problem. Depending on the specific characteristics of the relationship between an organization and its environment, one managerial style might be perceived as being more effective than another. In a contextual

Table 1 *Four types of context*

		DEPENDENCE	
		high	low
INFLUENCIBILITY	high	competitive context	dominated context
	low	dominant context	domain-restricting context

Table 2   *Four types of managerial style*

		ORIENTATION	
		external	internal
	innovation	entrepreneur	team-coach
INTENTION			
	stability	producer	administrator

situation that is defined by high dependence and high influencibility, managers will have to mobilize and use all available resources to cope with various external dependencies. Therefore, a proactive attitude and an orientation towards change have to be adopted. An entrepreneurial style fits into this contextual situation. On the other hand, in a situation of high influencibility but low dependence, managers will realize economies of scale by standardizing operations. In this context the style of the producer might prove effective. If an organization is located in a context which combines low influencibility with low dependence, there is little reason to spend managerial time on innovating strategies and external activities. An administrative style therefore might be appropriate. Finally, when low influencibility and high dependence combine into a specific context, the focal organization will have to change its internal operating capacity in order to meet the demands put upon it by its environment. A team coach type of style, oriented towards internal change, seems best.

Four hypotheses, based on the aforementioned assumptions, contain supposedly effective combinations of style and context: an entrepreneurial style fits into a competitive context; a producer style fits into a dominated context; a team-coach style fits into a dominant context and an administrative style fits into a domain restricting context.

In this conceptual model, effectiveness is treated as the dependent variable, whilst context and managerial style are seen as both independent and intermediary variables. A managerial style, for instance, does not only affect effectiveness, but in my reasoning also influences the contextual situation. This proposition can be reversed: the perceptions of a specific context may induce a manager to change the managerial style in use. Effectiveness, in my opinion, should be defined from a situational perspective and seen as both a state and a process. Notions like 'we are making progress' or 'our performance does not compare positively to yesterday's can be considered as empirical points of reference for a judgement on organizational effectiveness.

The aforementioned model has been put to the test in an empirical investigation into the relationship between managerial style and context within sixteen units (Gerding, 1991). Sixteen case studies built the database for answering the next research question: 'What contribution does the manager on the unit level, given the context in which his unit operates, make towards the creation of fit between his unit and its envi-

ronment?' As one can see, the key notions of contingency modelling, strategy formation and the intermediary role of managerial style are reflected
in the wording of this question.

DEPENDENCE AND INFLUENCIBILITY: THE DUTCH SITUATION

Lagging adaptation

In the past fifteen years a significant amount of empirical data on management practice in Dutch central government has been gathered. The
pioneering work of Kastelein clearly illustrates that at the time 'management and organization are the stepchildren of political enterprise' (1977:
7). Based on a systems/contingency model of organizational behaviour
Kastelein and his associates have analyzed the management profiles of
thirty governmental units. It turns out that coping with environmental
changes meets with grave difficulties. Management's restricted elbow
room, to a certain extent, is a consequence of rigid tasks perceptions of
central staff units, aimed at centralizing various aspects of the managerial process which seriously hampers attempts at a more integrated
managerial policy on the unit level. These perceptions clearly fit into a
model of organizational control that is characterized by standardization,
centralized decision making and an orientation towards procedures, as
opposed to content. Line managers also show a primarily internal orientation. Although the amount of uncertainty in the environment of the
thirty units researched was increasing rapidly, an adequate and timely
adjustment to these changes could not be detected.

As far a the introduction of more advanced management techniques
was an issue at all, a considerable time lag was shown between the
implementation of, for instance, monitoring systems and an increase in
unit effectiveness. Significant measures were only taken when unit performance had deteriorated badly. Kastelein suggests the development of
more advanced monitoring systems, as a means of narrowing the gap
between 'is' and 'ought' situations. A key problem with this suggestion is
that monitoring systems can contribute to the quality of managerial data
required for effective decision-making, but do not necessarily also create
the elbow room needed for strategic adaptation.

In 1980, Maas and Kooiman publish a report on bottlenecks in the management processes within Dutch central government. The problems, perceived by the 654 respondents to their questionnaire, once more illustrate
the lack of fit between governmental operating procedures and structure
on the one hand, and environmental developments and societal problem
solving needs on the other hand. As far as the unit level is concerned,
Maas and Kooiman point out that the input side of the policy making
process is controlled poorly, communication with the political parts of the

government system is still an uphill battle and delegation of authority is lacking. Furthermore, exchange processes between units are typified by a mutual desire to guard off one's own territory. As a result, the structure of central government as a whole, studied at close range, does not merely resemble the classical machine bureaucracy, but also shows a great deal of fragmentation. Although necessary changes in operational practice and managerial style, according to Maas and Kooiman (1980: 6), have to be stimulated and facilitated by political appointees and top civil servants, the lower echelons also have to accept responsibility for their role in the improvement process.

Part-time managers on the middle level

In 1985 Gerding and Sevenhuijsen published five case studies, carried out on the lower unit level of Dutch central government. Their prime focus is on the network, in which the unit manager operates. They draw the following conclusions:

(1) The management tasks of these lower level unit managers only take up part of their available working time. Much time is spent acting as an operational policy-analyst;

(2) Policymaking qualities play an important role in one's career pattern. They seem to be of more significance than managerial qualities;

(3) Unit-managers give lots of attention to the gathering of (external) information. Digesting and condensing information, however, seems to get less thought;

(4) Setting priorities in the day-to-day operations of the unit is an important but laborious and unrewarding task. Time for reflection is always lacking, the inclination to delegate significantly is minimal, and political bosses and top civil servants have little feeling for setting priorities – everything is of great importance at all possible times.

If these results by Kastelein, Maas and Kooiman and Gerding and Sevenhuijsen are compared, a certain development can be pointed out. In terms of dependency and influencibility, the amount of control carried out by central staff units seems to diminish. On the other hand, unit managers tend to have more attention for external relationships and coordination, but this outbreak of managerial assertiveness has not yet resulted in strategic behaviour, aimed at increasing influencibility and decreasing dependence. Government organization looses some of its bureaucratic nature. Its network character, at times, comes into prominence. This ongoing process is described by Gerding (1991). Sixteen units on the middle level of Dutch central government were studied intensively. From this research project, in which the conceptual framework described in a previous section was tested out, I will now present some results. A distinction is made between the description of some general developments, illustrated by the sixteen case studies and the testing of the four hypotheses derived from the conceptual framework.

Towards managerial emancipation

With respect to their political and civil service bosses, phenomena as building top management commitment, channeling disturbances generated by fragmented stimuli from the higher strata and handling the public relations aspects of unit performance take up considerable time and effort of unit managers. Relationships with other units in the government machine turn out to be more complicated as the other unit is situated in the immediate environment of the focal unit. The enemy is often – also in a physical sense – at close range. These problems – when getting top management attention – are often tackled by attempts at structural reform. These reforms tend to be problem-driven rather than strategy-driven. Therefore coordination and mutual adjustment in the long run do not improve significantly, but only change of form. The key to a successful handling of intragovernmental relations seems to be a distinguishing mission or strategy. A unit that succeeds in formulating such an explicit mission – and also creates the support of both top officials and its own members for its internalization – gains a competitive advantage. Remarkably, units with a more or less supportive task are making fair progress in this respect. This is presumably due to their more market like type of core business, their relative distance from the political arena and the contemporary tendency to 'privatize' general supportive activities as consultancy in the field of personnel management, organizational advice, facility management etc.

As far as the relationship between a manager and his or her subordinates is concerned, it turns out that breaking resistance to change is an important prerequisite for improving unit effectiveness. The often desultory character of this kind of opposition has to be dealt with swiftly. Being clear about targets, procedures and mission helps creating a climate in which unit employees with distinctive abilities can really contribute to unit goals. The institutional barriers for introducing these specific kinds of personnel reforms need not be exaggerated. It is therefore concluded that, in general, the elbow room for strategic and operational adjustment to environmental developments is increasing. Unit managers are dependent upon others, but they can create and use their resources for improving influencibility. Managers on the unit level tend to be quite sensitive towards the boundary elements of their managerial role. The research findings on the concept of managerial style illustrate this phenomenon. In the conceptual model four types of style are distinguished: the entrepreneur, the producer, the team coach and the administrator. The typical administrator, the archetype of the Weberian bureaucrat, is threatened with extinction. Unit managers do not significantly try to avoid conflict, their attitudes towards those placed higher up the hierarchy seem quite refined and they do not excessively strive for higher amounts of personnel.

The archetypical 'entrepreneur' is especially concerned with building a portfolio of competitive issues and/or the development and implementation of a strategic vision ('the party line'). The 'producer' turns out to be a perfectionist. Being a typical playing coach, this type of manager will not hesitate to engage in operational activities. His or her knowledge of the production processes at hand is often exceptional, but the ability to delegate is deficient. The 'team-coach' shows considerable skill in enabling a free and fertile flow of information within his unit. This type of manager also is able to assemble high-quality task forces out of the various subordinates.

In the sample, the profile of the average manager contains a significant amount of producer elements. Entrepreneurial and team-coach elements follow at close quarters. Administrative elements only play a minor role.

The average focal unit in the sample makes use of resources one can categorize as information and organization. Their competitive positions are based on the skilful handling of these resources. Their environmental partners, however, prefer the use of 'classic' resources as legitimacy and money. This 'mismatch' between focal and environmental units is explained by the selection of cases studied – it can be argued that the participating focal units were likely to be relatively 'good' performers – and the concept of 'early fit'. The focal units can therefore be seen as precursors of a new, competitive type of governmental unit.

Eleven out of the sixteen units researched operate in a competitive context. They combine a high amount of influencibility with a high amount of dependence. The domain-restricting context (low influencibility; low dependence) has evaporated. A development towards competitive contextual situations seems to be clearly in motion. Units try to develop new types of resources that have to enable them to match increases in dependence with corresponding increases in influencibility.

The test of four hypotheses regarding the relationship between managerial style, context (i.e. dependence and influencibility) and effectiveness only has limited significance. The sample of sixteen units is relatively small and key concepts of the framework are, by nature, difficult to operationalize in an unambiguous way. Nevertheless the preliminary testing results may prove insightful. It turned out that an externally oriented managerial style (entrepreneur, producer) is a prerequisite for effectiveness, but also requires a clear choice for either stability or innovation as a units focal aim. In a context that is characterized by low influencibility and high dependence, the hypothesized style of the team coach does not guarantee effectiveness. In order to enhance long term influencibility, a more externally oriented style (e.g. entrepreneur) is also needed. If a contextual situation is, on the other hand, characterized by low dependence and high influencibility, any style will do, at least in the short run. The contingent style of the producer will do the job, but the adjacent styles of team coach and entrepreneur also perform. Finally, in a competitive context (high dependence, high influencibility) the entrepreneurial style is indeed effective. It however turns out that for the achievement of long-term effectiveness, this style has to be combined with elements of the producer and/or team-coach style.

CONCLUSIONS: SURVIVING AS A PUBLIC MANAGER

A new public manager?

Seen from a systems-oriented point of view the contributions of an individual official should not be exaggerated. Public managers, however, are crucial to processes of organizational adaptation in government bureaucracies. Although in a democratic society public managers will have to respect the decision making prerogatives of their political superiors, their catalytic role in the policy making process should not be underestimated. What in my opinion is overemphasized currently, is the importance of structural reform in the various parts of our governmental system. Government agencies, al least in the Netherlands, seem to engage in permanent processes of reorganization, adding and removing managerial levels and staff activities. As far as I can see these processes of reorganization are mainly problem driven and seldom strategy driven. When a long term perspective is applied, the coordination problems one seeks to overcome only change of form. More radical measures, such as the giving up of certain fields of operation or the formation of semi-autonomous executing agencies ('the Swedish model'), might be needed. Such decisions most often exceed the limits of authority of a public manager. One therefore has to begin with the contextual situations at hand. To the practising public manager five recommendations can be given to facilitate managerial survival.

Five recommendations

Reducing dependence and increasing influencibility requires the engineering of processes of change, both within and outside the focal unit. In order to engineer, a manager needs to be aware of his or her current contextual situation and make an initial choice for change in a specific direction. Based on my research, as outlined in a previous section, I can make the following five recommendations:

1 Adopt a specific managerial style. A middle-of-the-road type of style in the long run will get you nowhere. A classical style of public management, the bureaucratic one, is not exactly suited for bringing about change. In turbulent environmental situations, managerial styles in which the elements of internal change (team coaching) and external change (entrepreneuring) are emphasized, will prove the most effective.

2 A public manager should develop a personal strategic vision on the

future of his unit. On that level the connections between internal strengths and weaknesses and external threats and opportunities have to be made. Without such a vision, a public manager and the unit at hand will find themselves at the mercy of competitive environmental forces.

3 A strategic vision should not only be developed, it of course also needs to be implemented. Of vital significance are acceptance and internalization of this vision by key employees of the unit. A public manager in this respect very often experiences resistance to change. This resistance has to be dealt with swiftly and immediately. A prolonged struggle for power is very detrimental to the external position of the unit. A professional manager therefore likes these clashes short, clean and decisive.

4 Generating the commitment of hierarchical and political superiors is as significant as the cooperation of subordinates. This perhaps is the most difficult task of an ambitious public manager. Superiors are notorious for their lack of commitment to the lower levels of government organization. Keeping their options open is some sort of second nature. Although this attitude can be explained by their contextual situation (dependence and influencibility in the political arena), from the point of view of the public manager it is essential to achieve active support for the mission of the unit. It therefore is necessary to engage in processes of coalition building with other stakeholders inside and outside the domain of the political superior.

5 In order to build coalitions, or to work the network, a public manager needs to create, maintain and continuously improve his or her personal network. This network is the main vehicle for processes of influencing others directly and indirectly. The benefits of such a network in a practical sense express themselves in an improved sight into the arena in which the unit operates. An improved sight enables a manager to use organizational resources in more efficient and effective ways, thereby reducing dependence and increasing influencibility.

Public managers tend to become professional managers. This process of professionalization (or, if one prefers: emancipation) greatly resembles that of managers in the private sector. Teachers, scholars and researchers in public management, like their business counterparts, will have to meet the challenge to facilitate and support this process by all available means.

13

MANAGING HUMAN RESOURCES IN THE PUBLIC SECTOR

Paulus Yntema

Definitions

HRM
Human Resources Management: a personnel management based on the notion that individual needs, values and abilities have to be balanced with the goals and culture of the organisation.

Integrator
That part of the work of an operational manager which involves the managing of human resources, comprising motivating, conciliating, coordinating, coaching, appraising and authorizing staff.

Public Line Manager
A civil servant who has executive responsibility for certain employees and for productivity, as opposed to an official with advisory and staff responsibility.

A NEED FOR CHANGE IN PUBLIC ADMINISTRATION

Public service modernisation has been a theme recurring across the whole developed world during the last decade. The modernisation of public HRM is of great importance because governments recognize the link between public sector performance and the overall performance of the national economy (OECD, 1990: 9). The public sector has a significant effect on economic performance as a buyer and seller of goods and services; its indirect effect on product and labour markets; and the burdens it may place through poor administration. The competitiveness of an economy is influenced by the education of its workforce, the accuracy of forecasts, the efficiency of its law and tax administration and the encouragement of small enterprise. To achieve a more efficient and effective administration reform of public HRM is needed.

In many countries the time is ripe for HRM reform. Three main factors underlie the increased interest in management of human resources of public organisations . One is the necessity of cuts in public expenditures, the second is the growing public demands and expectations regarding the public services offered and the third is the increased complexity and scale of public sector policy-making (e.g. sustaining a partnership between the public and private sectors). Organisational growth, systematic interdependence and the shrinking of the world are the reasons that fewer and fewer consequences of any decisions can be treated as acceptable externalities. In order to reverse the general trend in Western societies, governing capacities must be improved. Reform of public HRM is one important tool to achieve this. The *quality of public service delivery* is increasingly becoming a priority concern of the public sector. The need to cut public expenditure combined with a quest for value for money form a driving force behind HRM reform in the public sector.

Change is needed, discontinuous transformation. There has been a shift towards an increased use of the discretion and initiative of operational line managers, stressing measurable efficiency and effectiveness of public sector activities. Most Western countries now have policies pushing back centrally-held controls over inputs, and delegating financial authority. For example, a provision for savings realised beyond centrally-determined targets to remain with operational units and not be automatically reappropriated by the central budget office. More discretion is also left to managers for input selection, timing of expenditures and the reallocation of funds between activities. Initially, the emphasis has tended to be on financial management but increasingly interest has shifted towards changing personnel management systems by loosening central controls, decentralising HRM functions to ministries and agencies, as well as delegating to line management.

However, moving away from the classic bureaucratic model and mentality is not an easy task for public institutions. 'A system driven by the requirement to achieve equity, consistency and the other bureaucratic virtues is not readily turned into one driven by efficiency and effectiveness criteria (Sue, 1990: 13). However, organisations are no longer satisfied with the bureaucratic model since it is not appropriate for more performance oriented and thus flexible HRM. Even though many ways exist to reform public administration and its HRM, the emphasis in this report is on improvement of HRM by giving the operational manager more personnel tasks and by promoting HRM awareness. This view of a flexible decentralised HRM is based on the experience that public administration faces more and more a need for all-round managers instead of the traditionally specialised civil servants. After all the definition of a manager is one who gets things done through working with people. The personnel management tasks have been insufficiently recognized as part of a typical managerial role. This view of autonomous HRM by the manager is summarized in the model of the Integrator manager later in this report. On the basis of the results from case-studies an action programme is proposed to promote this decentralised HRM which will be called the manager's 'Integrator role'. This HRM approach complements ideas put forward by proponents of so-called 'people-oriented management' (compare, for example, Peters and Waterman, 1984; and Drucker, 1977).

PEOPLE-ORIENTED MANAGEMENT AND THE PERSONNEL OFFICE

Management of people may be the most important task of any organisation. People-oriented management considers individuals as the central asset of an organisation. Only once 'managing people' has gained more significance in the eyes of operational managers can a fruitful partnership with the personnel office develop. HRM has long been a considered a 'soft' branch within the managerial specialisations. Tight budgets and lean staffing has been the result for many personnel departments. HRM specialists earn often less than other professionals of the same level. A consultant study shows that the typical salary of personnel directors in European companies is on average lower (by up to 20 percent) than that of departmental directors of finance, research, marketing or production (*Financial Times*, 26 June 1992).

Part of the reason for this low esteem has probably been their inability to communicate with management in the language of business. One way to tackle this problem is to quantify HRM (Fitz-enz, 1984). This is important so that in the future personnel managers are invited to meetings where performance of the organisation or future programmes are planned instead of being told what their role will be after the fact. People in staff jobs like those in the personnel office, tend to concentrate too much on the process while their focus ought to be similar to that of general management, namely on results.

The public increasingly demands more quality and quantity from government services. Simultaneously, internationalisation of government puts increasing pressure on public management. On the other hand, the individual civil servant also wants more in terms of: freedom, work content, working hours, etc. A HRM which has to harmonise all these demands has to be carried by both line management and the personnel staff. *A partnership with the personnel office* has to be developed. Line managers have to move away from a 'narrow' product orientation by creating a close cooperation with the personnel office. The emphasis has to shift from seeing the personnel department as 'servicing' management rather towards a 'support' role of personnel. Support is a slightly more positive term and there is an image of equality. Personnel staff has to transform its procedure oriented thinking into an attitude of counselling and supporting of the HRM as executed by the line. A coherent HRM strategy has to shake off universal rules to enable the flexibility needed to improve performance. Better knowledge of the behaviour of managers, their motivation and openness to change, could make a great deal of difference. A real 'partnership' between personnel advisors and operational managers could grow in this way.

To de-concentrate HRM tasks to operational managers is also another way to deal with their incomprehension about the traditional personnel tasks. This transformation of the role of the personnel office does not render it less important, though a reduced number of man-hours may be required. Issues of counter-dependency are likely to continue since neither managers nor personnel staff may be clear about their new roles and responsibilities.

DIFFERENCES BETWEEN PRIVATE AND PUBLIC SECTOR HRM

Similarities outnumber the differences when comparing HRM in the private and public sectors. In both sectors the objective is to provide quality services or goods with as few resources as possible. However, the existing distinctions are important. The profit motive in private companies encourages automatically the minimization of personnel expenditure. Public administrations tend to be labour intensive and higher ethical standards are imposed on civil servants. Managers in the private sector may have greater freedom in personnel matters such as hiring and firing than do public managers. In government the lines of authority are often more confused and diluted than in the private sector. The single purpose of a private company is contrasted with the multiple objectives of the public sector. A number of obstacles make public management practice more complex than private sector management. The possibilities are limited to hold public managers accountable for achievement of non-financial performance. A lack of incentives causes aversion to risk-taking, public managers rather tend to follow prescribed administrative procedures than to act as managers. Often little managerial discretion for inter-organisational responsibilities exist. Also the political agenda of the leadership is short-term not allowing for long-term planning by the manager. Finally, public managers have no say in determining why their organisations exist, the formulation of policy being beyond their authority.

These differences supply the rationale for treating HRM separately for its application in the public sector. The private sector has been influential as a source of many of the ideas to convert administrative cultures into managerial ones. It is interesting to note that there is an opposite movement of senior public officials to top positions in the private sector, while trends towards flexible personnel management have moved from the private sector to public administrations.

HRM REFORM IN NATIONAL ADMINISTRATIONS

Implications of a flexible HRM are relatively simple: *objectives, results and means have to be interlinked*. The execution of this is more complicated however. In various countries experiments are taking place with these linkages among decentralised competences and responsibilities: performance linked to a *performance contract* at the unit level. OECD has studied to what extent public administration has introduced such performance-linkages. For example, in Denmark productivity trends are being measured and – where possible – compared to those of the private sector. While in Sweden, it appeared that productivity of the public sector declined in the period from the 1960s to the 1980s compared with the private sector. Since 1980 the trend in Sweden has been reversed. For the 1990s a three year budget process is foreseen whereby departments will have a larger degree of freedom and the yearly budgeting has been converted into rigorous performance reviews. In the USA a broadly defined productivity programme is operative in the federal public sector in which the emphasis lies on quality, punctuality and output with a link to systematic reporting on the basis of the present situation contrasted to aspired levels over a number of years. Also in this set-up a part of the productivity gain can be kept by the department concerned. In the UK measurable reporting of performance is desired at all levels (i.e. including policy work at the top). In Canada and Australia the emphasis has shifted from input controls to improved management performance.

National administrations of OECD countries have started to pay more attention to HRM and the related administrative structure. A new public management culture is gradually developing with improved management training and career planning, more flexible career patterns, increased mobility, the introduction of open competition for posts, and promotion of a performance-oriented culture. National cultures have influenced the development of modernisation programmes in particular ways, and it is therefore difficult to generalise about public service modernisation programmes. Innovations range from changing recruitment procedures and the conditions of employment of civil servants, re-examining their pension schemes, to privatising entire services.

THE INTERNATIONAL DIMENSION

A new element with which HRM in public administrations has to deal is the growing internationalisation of government work. In the public sector, the ending of the cold war, the development of international forums such as the Conference on Security and Cooperation in Europe (CSCE) and ongoing regional economic integration continue to augment intergovernmental co-operation (economic communities or free trade areas exist or are being negotiated in Western and Northern Europe,

North and Central America, Latin America, the Caribbean, the Far East and in the Commonwealth of Independent States). As a result, the number of international officials is likely to proliferate. Demand for international mobility of professional people is growing. In the context of the supranational objectives, calls have been made for the creation of an International Civil Service. Currently four main groups of international civil servants can be distinguished: the United Nations and related agencies (52,000 staff), the European Communities (employing 25,000), the international development banks ((around 14,000 staff members) and the so-called Co-ordinated Organisations (i.e. 11,000 staff at NATO, OECD, ESA, WEU, ECMWF and Council of Europe). A plethora of other small international organisations exists.

Globalisation does not only offer new challenges to the business world but also implies new demands on officials in the context of intergovernmental cooperation and supranational decision-making. A kind of international competition is starting to take place in the public sector as well, namely, which public sector organisation – international or national – will do which tasks since so many tasks start to have supranational implications (compare the debate on subsidiarity in the European Community). This globalisation of government administration warrants some attention in the context of HRM.

The increasing volume of technocratic and policy-making work done at an intergovernmental or supranational level is gradually creating a strain of new public officials, working partially outside the civil services – in international organisations – and partially inside it –in national ministries. In this spirit, the United Kingdom, for example has started to recruit civil servants with the slogan 'Could you help to influence economic policy in either Westminster or Brussels?'(*The Economist*, 21.11.1992) National public HRM has to ponder at ways to produce officials effective at international negotiations.

The management of expatriate human resources in an international organisation implies a great deal of new questions for the public sector. Recruiters in the public sector will increasingly face a worldwide labour market for example, while any manager in an international organisation has to deal with customs originating in various national administrative cultures. Furthermore compensation managers have to offer comprehensive expatriate pay packages to cover needs and demands of employees from vary diverse origins. Pay policy of international organisations has to take account of the varying degrees of expatriation depending on the expatriate employee's: (a) geographical and/or socio-cultural distance between home and host country, (b) time spent in the same duty station, and (c) family situation (possible loss of spouse's job in home country). It is important to keep in mind this international dimension when studying HRM in the public sector. Little research has been devoted to the problems of international HRM in a complex of multi-cultural and multi-lingual public administration systems. In the next paragraph a summary is given of some main personnel management techniques as used both in the private and public sector.

MAIN HRM ACTIVITIES

An overview of various tasks and tools of personnel management is given without going into details of execution or application. These are general HRM activities that are usually engaged in by both personnel staff officials and operational line managers. The managing of human resources is viewed as a *'system'* with a number of HRM activities as interacting functions. The enumeration of HRM activities in the four tables is of course not exhaustive.

The division of HRM activities over four different groups is somewhat arbitrary. The underlying thought is that if a unit would need to be set up from scratch, probably the HRM activities would present themselves in this chronological order. Once the desired output (a mission statement for example) for the new unit has been determined, personnel activities can start. First, part of the HRM preparatory work is related to creating a distribution structure of power and tasks over a number of posts. HRM has to deal with the following inputs for organisational development strategies: *people, output, job design, work rules, structure and pay.* Once jobs have been established, the planning about placement of the human resources (present and future needs) can begin. Next, a number of HRM activities having to do with recruitment can be grouped together. Selection procedures for example, are needed. Further, civil servants can possibly be seconded at a different government department or an international organisation. A third group of HRM tasks is made up the traditional mainstay personnel activities focused basically at keeping employees satisfied and productive at their jobs: remuneration, training & development, promotion, co-determination, etc. The fourth group consists of some examples of less practised HRM tools. HRM literature and HRM practice suggest an enormous number of new HRM instruments aimed at improvement of motivation and output of employees. A brief description of these four groups of HRM activities is given below.

DISTRIBUTION OF POWER AND TASKS OVER POSTS

Organisational development (= OD) involves structuring the overall work situation with a focus on efficiency. One element is position classification which implies examination of work performed in various jobs in order to group similar jobs/positions into classes. This classification is especially important because of its link to an equitable pay plan. OD often focuses on a choice between either top-down or bottom-up approach.

Top-down approach involves starting at the top of the organisation and its mission statement and from there onward create units and sub-units. The disadvantage of this most commonly used approach is the tendency to focus on structure without considering purpose. The bottom-up method is the reverse. The objectives of the organisation are assumed and attention is focused first on designing individual jobs. This approach is important in the context of improving the organisation through decentralisation since at the bottom of the hierarchy are often the people in closest contact with the organisation's customers.

Once defined, the jobs are clustered into organisational units. The danger of this approach is that jobs may be done efficiently but remain non-effective in reaching the objectives. If problems occur with the organisational structure, complicated and expensive reorganisation may be necessary. A number of issues, therefore, will be looked at by an analysts of an organisational structure: (a) the appropriate span of control (number of persons reporting to a superior), (b) the number of hierarchical levels, (c) interrelations among personnel, budgeting and planning, (d) regional or functional set-up, (e) centralisation or decentralisation, (f) directions of the work-flow, (g) roles of specialists and generalists, (h) in-house or privatisation.

More often a manager will have to deal with *job design*, i.e. arranging tasks to be performed by an individual. Job design is a continuous dynamic activity requiring regular adjustments because of changes both in the work and the person. Perhaps a different combination, distribution of tasks of a unit over the available human resources can enrich the job of individuals. In many civil services the classical problem remains that people are employed in a grade rather than for a particular job. Therefore mobility and training are even more essential in these administrations in order to ensure generalist skills or prepare employees for changing specialisms. After all, organisational life is changing rapidly because of economic, socio-political transformations and particularly information technology innovations.

HIRING OF APPROPRIATE PEOPLE

In certain countries *recruitment* to the public sector is a rigid procedure based on comparative entrance exams (more or less selective depending on the country and/or the organisation). In some countries the opinion has prevailed that government may settle for capable but not necessarily superior workers. Expensive extensive recruiting efforts are not often undertaken in the public sector. Another factor that sometimes enters into recruiting is the concept that government job opportunities should be available to a wide spectrum of people. The public service often is the show case of liberal public policy (e.g. positive discrimination). Secondment from national civil servants is a recruitment method often used by international organisations. A civil servant with a proven expertise acquired in a national administration is then attached for a number of years to work at the international level. Selection of future managers in the public sector overall will have to be adjusted so as to recruit people who can deal with both a specialized content field and general HRM tasks.

TRADITIONAL PERSONNEL MANAGEMENT TASKS

Remuneration and promotion policy linked to an employee appraisal system can help motivate employees if some kind of merit pay or negative sanction exists as a function of performance of either an individual or team of workers. A modern HRM will make good use of all the above mentioned personnel tasks. *Training and development* are however particular useful for orienting managers and staff towards a different role and managerial mentality. Several public services have introduced training courses to prepare for entry to top management positions. Staff development is a concerted effort in creating a learning environment for employees so that they adapt themselves to the evolving orientation of the organisation, can be offered real possibilities for self-improvement, mobility and thus provide greater job satisfaction. A staff development plan for a certain service could be set up as follows. First, the needs of the service have to be defined; for example: programme objectives, a mission statement or reorganisation. Second, one has to consider which instruments to use: e.g. training, types of learning tools, exercises, outside fellowships, courses and seminars. Third, guiding principles and prerequisites have to be selected. Finally, management has to anticipate the expectations of participants.

An example from a service in an international organisation gives an idea of the needs (defined in a staff development plan) for improvement of: (a) managerial capacities in the service; (b) integration of work areas; (c) team spirit; (d) internal communications; (e) quality of the output content and/or format (= meetings, documents); (f) awareness of cultural differences; (g) potential mobility within the service and the organisation; (h) capacity for dealing with content matters of the section; (i) use of information technology (software, etc.). Although management development and training are classical personnel management tools, they can play an important role in the pursuit of flexible HRM.

EXTRA TOOLS OF MODERN HRM

Mobility and performance-related pay are the two most discussed tools in public administration today. These two instruments are discussed here because they are essential for flexible personnel management. Increasing the mobility of staff both within the public service and between the public and other sectors is a way to match resources to shifting policy demands as well as a way to prepare managers for the complexities of modern administration. It can also enrich an individual's career in a public organisation. Whether mobility schemes are always appropriate in the public sector is a question: do the needs of government justify more 'generalist managers' (possibly different from the private sector). Government might need experts in legal and administrative affairs requiring more than two years on the job. Nevertheless, considering the lack of mobility of most officials in public administration, it is probably desirable to pursue an internal and possibly external mobility policy.

Remuneration policy is relatively more important for an organisation which wants to recruit and retain high quality staff capable of coping with more flexible performance-oriented HRM. Organisational demands on employees augment but also vice versa. In the private sector (especially in the USA) performance pay has been the rule for quite some years. Usually trends go from the private to the public sector in these management matters. In the public sector, unlike the private sector, seniority is usually still the main factor in determining an employee's pay. Over the past decade some public administrations have started to replace *partially* service and age criteria from the remuneration system and replacing them by systematic assessments of the staff member in order to relate pay to performance. Usually only pay increases – not basic pay levels – are concerned.

The main two objectives of performance related pay that are mentioned in the literature are increased motivation (of both manager and subordinate) and efficiency. A newer trend is towards group bonuses, because of the difficulty to quantify individual employee's contribution to a collective output and also team pressure tends to stimulate the low performers. Performance measurement is better done of a group, a team. Measurement in the end has to be directed at *effectiveness* (at the level of the organisation) not just *efficiency* (at the individual level). It can be recommended also to separate the performance element from the pay structure, i.e. a one-off bonus rather than a merit award which is consolidated into salary. The performance element would, in this way, be more clearly identifiable and distinguished from market factors and inflation.

Successful performance appraisal systems are always a two-way process. The appraiser and the subordinate agree on specific ways the latter contributes to the organisation's objectives and these are set up as targets for individuals or teams; during formal annual (or more often, if necessary) interviews, both agree on how close the subordinate has come to achieving the targets and assess the reasons for possible failure; finally new targets are agreed and an assessment is made of the individual's training needs and scope for promotion.

Some elements are needed in order to design a performance pay scheme: cross-organisation measurement of performance, reliance on managerial discretion, integration into HRM and overall reward policy of the notion, some linkage of organisational performance to that of individual or team.

The most widely adopted method of performance appraisal is MBO (= management by objectives) with for example, an annual 5 point rating, based on achievements against job goals. MBO works if the employee is judged in his own right (comparing his performance history). Comparison across jobs or units allows less for comparable standards. A number of empirical studies conclude that complicated systems to measure the quality of individual white collar employee performance still remain inadequate (Wood, 1991). Many OECD countries are examining ways of making public sector pay systems more flexible. For example, in the United States, Canada, Japan, Australia, New Zealand, France, Norway and The Netherlands, Spain, Switzerland and the United Kingdom performance based pay regimes have been operating (OECD, 1992: 11). The premiums involved vary from less than 1 to 50 percent of the base salary.

QUANTIFYING HRM

For most of these modern HRM tools mentioned some kind of quantification of HRM is absolutely needed. For these reasons as well as for the sake of upgrading the personnel task as compared to the other management functions, attention for quantifying HRM is essential. A measurement system also promotes productivity in general by focusing on important issues, tasks and objectives. The personnel function has to be instrumental in design and communication of measures of efficiency and productivity such as standards of performance. The feasibility of HRM reform and introduction of tools such as performance pay depend on whether the relevant factors can be quantified.

As general indices for quantified measurement the following elements can be identified: (a) cost, (b) time, (c) quality, and (d) quantity. One major tool for implementation is report drafting: communicating achievements. Whether a report is meant to inform or persuade it has to be clear, concise, accurate and appropriate. If general standards (e.g. about report form and output objectives) are developed and accepted, comparisons can be made. If in the end the processing of the quantifiable information is done, an impression and possible remedies could be distilled as regards to double work, lost time, absenteeism, etc.

Some of the following activities can help to quantify HRM: planning an annual human resources plan describing the staff not only in terms of size, ages, sexes, and races, but also in terms of levels of education, experience, performances, work preferences and potential. Such a plan can, for instance, help for effective replacement. Often the existing internal work force is not fully utilized to find replacement in case of vacancies. A similar systematic and detailed HRM databank on jobs or establishments in the organisation can also help inform which jobs are becoming obsolete, redundant or inappropriate.

Also the specialist HRM work in the personnel office can be quantified. Recruiter effectiveness, for example, depends on whether he fills jobs promptly, cuts hire costs to a minimum and maintains a high quality of hire. Sometimes the quantification will be limited to word-of-mouth reports on orientation and counselling's effectiveness: for example, was the problem solved? Measuring training and development (basically by judging improved task performance resulting in improved department output) has to be considered important so as to justify its cost to management.

THE INTEGRATOR MODEL

In public administrations a great deal of ideas exist about how to improve the management of personnel. After a number of years of experience with decentralisation and deregulation, the conclusion appears to be that one major obstacle for an effective flexible and decentralised HRM is the lack of preparedness of individual managers. Public managers are particularly ill prepared for the growing diversity of their tasks. Government departments are looking more and more for officials who can manage instead of for lawyers and engineers. Meanwhile, little research has been done into the actual management of the public sector or how to meet this need.

Research indicates that a new approach for dynamic HRM based on a 'fit' between the individual on the one hand and the managerial job on the other could be developed (Yntema, 1990). FIT stands for: a New (F)it of (I)ndividuals and their (T)asks. The idea is that one should not try to adjust the individual to a specific job (as traditionally happens by way of training, etc) but one should strive after a simultaneous matching of job requirements and individual needs (see model on next page).

The central approach is to look at how management can be improved by giving operational officials more responsibility for their staff. The most important personnel tasks should be in the hands of this line manager, while the personnel staff unit should retain a strongly advisory and a professional supporting role. The so-called model of the Integrator manager implies managerial autonomy in HRM. Managerial delegation is implied which is distinct from functional and/or spatial decentralisation which also occurs in public administration in a number of countries. Middle level managers, who are often professionals and specialists working at an operational level, seem less attracted by these managerial responsibilities., sometimes seeing them as a necessary chore. This unwillingness on the part of some managers to take up the Integrator role can leave personnel managers whether located centrally or not, in an ambivalent position in terms of authority, responsibility and influence. Still too often (public) managers are promoted to line responsibilities only on the basis of their expertise in a field without giving proper attention to their communicative and managerial potential. When managers have to become personnel managers as well, new skills are required.

A number of hurdles have to be taken to implement this Integrator management style. Fear of traditionally trained managers has to be expelled. Resistance to change has to be overcome. A withdrawal of

Figure 1   *The Integrator model of a manager*

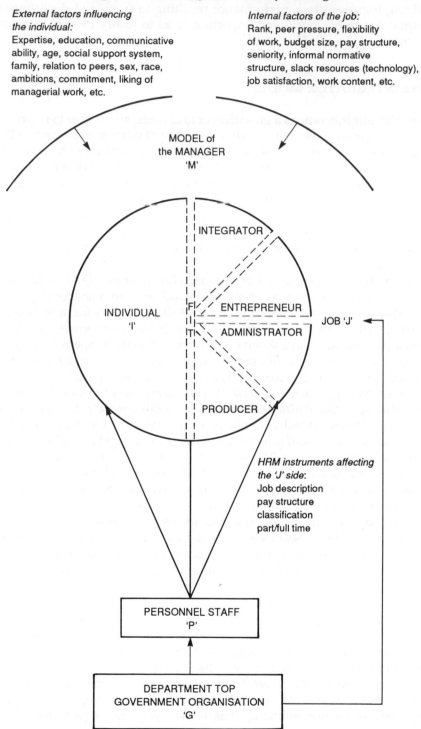

External factors influencing the individual: Expertise, education, communicative ability, age, social support system, family, relation to peers, sex, race, ambitions, commitment, liking of managerial work, etc.

Internal factors of the job: Rank, peer pressure, flexibility of work, budget size, pay structure, seniority, informal normative structure, slack resources (technology), job satisfaction, work content, etc.

MODEL of the MANAGER 'M'

INTEGRATOR

ENTREPRENEUR

ADMINISTRATOR

INDIVIDUAL 'I'

JOB 'J'

PRODUCER

HRM instruments affecting the 'J' side: Job description pay structure classification part/full time

PERSONNEL STAFF 'P'

DEPARTMENT TOP GOVERNMENT ORGANISATION 'G'

traditional frameworks may give rise to uncertainty over span of controls. A variety of contracts (tenured, contract, full-time, part-time) may pose problems in relation to work planning/programming and progress, and in terms of motivation and morale.

A COMPARATIVE MODEL

Personnel management will be analyzed with the help of a model. The focus of this model is on the Integrator role of the manager, which coincides with the human resources management tasks. Usually, this role is less developed than the other three managerial roles distinguished. These three other roles defined by Adizes are those of (Strand, 1986): Administrator (= creating and maintaining rules and structures); Producer (= setting of goals and delivering products); and Entrepreneur (= external public relations and exploration of opportunities).

A premise is that managers can be measured by the efficiency and effectiveness of the units they manage. The Integrator role comprises the manager's set of tools to produce an optimal output with the human resources input of the unit in question. The Integrator Role consists of a number of managerial tasks (i.e. subroles if you wish). The activities which make up the Integrator role we have defined as follows: Motivating; Conciliating; Coordinating; Coaching; Evaluating and Acting as personnel authority. Each of these tasks is described below.

The first Integrator activity of motivation consists of inspiring, stimulating employees to work effectively in teams. An organisation has to express a philosophy so that the employee can determine whether he can find his happiness in this organisational statement of purpose. After all from this philosophy will flow certain values and thus a number of expected, acceptable behaviours. This is the general basis for worker motivation. From our research, six types of motivation methods can be deduced. A manager can motivate employees by way of:

– *Giving result-oriented work*; for example, giving a challenging task to a staff member rather than a bonus;
– *Commenting on a job well-done*; this is easily done in staff units but it is as important in more operational units, too often only the negative criticism surfaces;
– *Management by wandering about*; trying to personally see all employees from time to time, keeping a birthday list of one's staff, etc.;
– *Playing the role of inspirator*; one interviewed manager said: 'I try to make my people feel important, the manager has to radiate positivism; he has to give his unit a goal';
– *Image-building for the unit*; creating professional pride: civil servants often prefer their work over private sector jobs because they recognize their work in the newspaper headlines each day;

– *Maintaining social (not just work-related) contacts with staff*; government departments in The Netherlands for example, often have obligatory excursions for all personnel of a directorate, in public administrations of other countries such an event is not yet feasible.

The second Integrator task, (re-)*conciliating* implies the creation of an ambience of open communications and the anticipation of personal conflicts. The manager, often, can prevent worse by intervening at an early stage. *Coordinating* consists of work-planning involving a maximum responsibility at the team level. *Evaluating* implies a continuous process of appreciating tasks and in particular the way they are being executed. The Integrator's task of *coaching* reminds the manager of how important it is for him to be involved in the on-the-job training of new subordinates and in implementing new technologies. Finally, the manager also plays the role of *authority* when interpreting personnel rules and when matching people with tasks.

AN ACTION PROGAMME FOR HRM REFORM

An action programme is distilled from survey results in order to promote development of this Integrator role (OECD, 1992: 11). The underlying notion is that personnel management tasks of the average *line*-manager are insufficiently recognized. The recommendations from this action programme can be applied to all organisations where personnel management tends to be bureaucratic or centralistic.

The list of recommendations for improvement of HRM can be summarized in a more general framework around the theme 'how to do more with given human resources. The action programme to develop Integrator management consists of four phases.

Phase 1. Development of an Integrator Role Consciousness: Managers need to become aware of their 'Integrator role'. Management of people, motivating them to perform has come to be seen as the line manager's responsibility. A *decentralised* HRM is required. This puts new demands on the average civil servant with managerial tasks, since quite often he or she is rather a specialist than a manager. On the one hand , the manager has to have adequate managerial autonomy and on the other hand his control over the work process has to increase. By asking every employee what his or her product is and for whom it is intended, the manager is forced to think strategically within the responsibilities of his own unit. Furthermore a continuous inventory of the available and needed managerial potential for the unit has to be made.

Phase 2: Using HRM-tools: In order to carry out the Integrator role, a manager has to be taught how to use personnel management tools. The interviewed manager have suggested a number of improvements in these HRM-techniques. Some examples are: – image building for the own unit within the organisation; – the choice of candidate to be recruited should lie with the line manager; – collecting information about managerial needs in the organisation; – placing decentralised personnel consultants in the operational field units; – well-equipped information systems that are adjusted to the human resources planning (e.g. keeping record of work preferences and experience of employees); – flexible work organisation; – granting more room to subordinates to participate; – emphasis on teamwork; – staff development; – performance pay (possibly for teams or projects) based on systematic evaluation.

Step 3: Deregulation and Decentralisation: In order to create a climate where 'managers can manage' it is essential to relax the operational environment and remove or at least lessen the bureaucratic strait-jacket which at times hampers decision-making in public administration. A lean, flat and flexible command structure is indicated. Specialized tasks can be privatised as much as possible or otherwise put in a special unit. In this manner, the United Kingdom Civil Service will put out to tender 40,000 jobs in 1993. A great variety of Civil Service functions are to be contracted out such as collection of statistics, running the Treasury's economic model, helicopter maintenance, ship repairs for the armed services, computer servicing, audit, accountancy, typing, secretarial, payroll and legal services. Privatisation can allow an agency to offer the public (= consumers) differentiated products such as quicker service or fancy car registration numbers at a certain premium. Managers are free to set their objectives concerning output, speed of issuing licenses and permits as well as prices of these government products.

Step 4: Moving towards a People-Oriented Managerial Culture: Maintaining a people-oriented HRM requires an organisation-wide commitment to a new managerial philosophy. Administrative culture – of which managerial culture makes up a part – is obstinate, refractory and difficult to manipulate. The 'managerial ethic' imported from the private sector is not suitable for transfer into the public sector unless it is used to *complement* existing value systems. A new system of values has to be carefully promoted: a focus on individual qualities, open communications, flexible work organisation, etc.. New managerial attitudes need to be developed. Management development has moved ahead in most of the industrialised countries, including staff development and training programmes and promotion of mobility. Special attention is given to the ranks of senior executives in many public services, especially through better training.

The integrator role in practice: three administrations compared

A survey we held in 1990 in the Italian and Dutch public sectors and the European Commission provide three case-studies to measure the degree to which public managers (i.e. directors in ministries) and their managerial instruments are prepared for a new approach to HRM, as promoted by the Integrator role model (Yntema, 1990).

Figure 2   *Management style (a graduated scale based on the average of the responses)*

```
┌─────────────────────────────────────────────────────────────────┐
│                                                                   │
│  innovative/participative/people-oriented                         │
│  ─ ─ ─ ─ ─ ─ ─ ─ ─ ─ ─ ─ ─ ─ ─ ─ ─ ─ ─ ─ ─ ─ ─ ─ ─ ─ ─ ─ ─ ─    │
│                                                                   │
│  1    2    3    4    5    6    7    8    9    10                   │
│                                                                   │
│               The Netherlands                                     │
│                           European Commission                     │
│                                           Italy                   │
│                                                                   │
│  1    2    3    4    5    6    7    8    9    10                   │
│                                                                   │
│  ─ ─ ─ ─    ─ ─ ─ ─ ─ ─ ─ ─ ─ ─ ─ ─ ─ ─ ─ ─ ─ ─ ─ ─ ─ ─ ─       │
│                          authoritarian/conservative/product-oriented │
│                                                                   │
└─────────────────────────────────────────────────────────────────┘
```

The attitudes of the interviewed public managers and personnel offic-ers have been measured on the basis of a set of criteria. This produced an average management style per organisation. This characterisation gives us an idea of how HRM-minded these three public organisations are. In the chart below, one can see the innovative/participatory style corre-sponding with Integrator management and at the bottom, one sees the opposite, traditional personnel management approach.

In the Dutch ministries both the personnel office and the line manag-ers are quite individual oriented; it's generally accepted that employees participate in certain decision-making. Also in some Dutch government departments, personnel offices start to take a strongly advisory role recep-tive to Integrator management in the line.

In the European Commission a majority of the managers are also HRM-minded but the personnel office here remains strongly procedure-oriented. Communications about personnel matters go almost exclusively through hierarchical channels but since a couple of years initiatives have been undertaken to modernise personnel management.

Compared with the Dutch and EC administrations, the Italian public administration still remains the least prepared for the optimal fit between individual and job, open communications and a flexible work organi-sation. Individual managers show – on average – a more conservative attitude and in general a tendency exists for hierarchical personnel con-tacts. However, enthusiastic reform plans from the Italian Civil Service Ministry are currently being studied in Parliament.

The Integrator role of the manager is intended to provide a counter-weight to centralist, bureaucratic tendencies in organisations whereby for example the balance of attention is shifted too much into the direction of either a desired product or application of new technologies without think-ing of the human infrastructure and the organisation of these people each day so as to bring about the desired results in the most effective way.

CONCLUSION

The action programme presented above shows how a HRM-culture can be adjusted so as to allow the new managerial role of the Integrator to install itself. The Integrator manager is only one model to promote flexible HRM, many other models are imaginable. The message which should come across however is that the public service has to adopt more flexible rules, but within a structured framework that combines a centrally determined strategy with decentralised (autonomous) operational managers. This coincides with current trends towards 'empowerment' or 'self-management': shifting responsibility to individuals of all ranks in the organisation (see, for example, Kanter, 1989). Horizontal organisation rather than an emphasis on vertical hierarchical control. This re-distribution of initiative in the organisation should enable a better utilisation of individual creativity.

The main difficulty remains that in the non-traded part of the public sector, the guiding principle is central resource allocation, which determines the human and financial resources of a service. Thus an all-powerful central resource allocator has to be convinced to give up control to operational service providers. On the contrary, in the private sector and the traded part of the public sector the consumer plays a central role in enabling HRM reform. The process of HRM reform in the public sector is decidedly slow. In the Netherlands, for example, despite forty years experience of a steady decentralisation of HRM responsibilities, the Dutch public service is still introducing changes designed to reinforce the central co-ordinating framework, and to overcome the lack of preparedness of individual managers for their HRM role.

Reform of both HRM tools and mentality in the public sector could have enormously beneficial effects in the long run. Passive adjustment to the way human resources develop themselves independently is undesirable and presents great risks. Rather than lagging behind business in innovation of HRM or adjusting to change, public administration could prepare the conditions for change. Too often still the public sector as an employer has a negative un-dynamic image, attracting rather risk-averting people. Introduction of elements such as performance-related pay and more individual responsibility of public officials, in spite of their many implementation hurdles, might be able to enhance an adequate change for the better. At the same time, it needs to be realized that the issue is sensitive for the public servants involved, particularly when the pursuit of flexible HRM is leading to a reduction in the traditionally high levels of job security offered in the civil service. Moreover, the drive for efficient administration and rational HRM should not hurt the public service tradition of equity. Public service remains the custodian of weaker citizens.

PART 4

REFORMING PUBLIC MANAGEMENT

In the 1980s and even more so in the 1990s, a desire for management reform has been sweeping across the public sector in all West European countries. The reasons behind this drive for reform have been more or less the same in all countries. The inability to meet old and, in particular, new public sector tasks as described in Section One of this book, has created the main stimulus for reform. The political importance of the more general ideas surrounding the creation of higher efficiency and effectiveness through private management and the importance of deregulation and goal oriented management in the public sector, has been much more predominant in some countries such as Britain than in others such as Norway. The reform strategies and principles of reorganization which have been employed have varied from one country to another and from the early phases of managerial reform in the 1980s to the more recent phases.

There are several dimensions to the differences in reform patterns which exist across countries and time. One important dimension is one the existence of on the one hand political and to some extent experienced-based eagerness towards managerialism whereas, on the other hand, there has existed scepticism towards employing private management principles in the public sector. At one extreme we find in nearly all countries major privatization program and the introduction of the market economy into the public sector. Over time, we have seen a gradual decline in the unconscious use of private sector management mechanism in public management reforms.

In the first chapter in this section, *Restructuring Central Government: The 'Next Steps' Initiative in Britain*, Brian Hogwood gives an interesting description of an attempt to introduce managerialism and private management logic into the public sector. This initiative established agencies as discrete areas of work with a chief executive personally responsible to the minister, with a delegated budget and with rewards for success and penalties for failure. This high degree of autonomy and managerial independence in public agencies should create a semi private environment for providing public services. The main question is the problem of accountability versus autonomy as with many of these managerial reforms in public sector.

The Efficiency of Public Service Provision by Rune Sørensen addresses one of the main reasons for management reform in the public sector; the assumed inefficiency. Is the public sector inherently susceptible to inefficiency or do governments pursue a more complicated set of societal objectives, resulting in necessarily different criteria for efficiency? In order to answer these questions, the author assesses six reform strategies, hypothesising about the necessary preconditions for efficiency and the preconditions for improvement in each case. The main conclusion which he draws from this assessment is the need for differentiated reforms. Due to the different tasks carried out by the various institutions, it is impossible to present a universal approach to public management reform.

Public Administration, Regulation, Deregulation and Reregulation by Vincent Wright addresses the question of the extent to which the regulators in the public sector have converged in their response to the problems they are confronted with. The chapter looks at the various dimensions of regulation and the traditional styles and instruments of regulation. It then goes on to investigate the various pressures which have reshaped the regulatory environment. After outlining the current problems and dilemmas in the area of regulation, the chapter discusses the extent and the way in which the different countries have converged in their use of regulatory strategies.

Aaron Wildavsky in his chapter, *Budget Games are Ready for Reform*, argues that there is a season for budgetary reforms, moving in the direction of spending controls, including entitlements to reduce the budget deficit. It is nothing new for the conservative right wing to be in favour of this. However, what is new is that the left now sees this as the only possibility to try out new social welfare programs. In Wildavsky's opinion there is an argument for reform based on the fact that the left do wish to alter their priorities. However, they are unable to do this if the budget is driven by increases in entitlements. The inability to meet new public tasks is again seen as the main stimulus for reform.

14

RESTRUCTURING CENTRAL GOVERNMENT: THE 'NEXT STEPS' INITIATIVE IN BRITAIN

Brian W. Hogwood

WHAT IS 'NEXT STEPS'?

The Next Steps initiative in British central government raises a number of important issues about management autonomy in the public sector, financial and political accountability, the use of performance indicators and responsibility to customers or consumers of public services. These issues will be explored after outlining the introduction of the Next Steps initiative.

The Next Steps initiative, publicly launched in February 1988 following a report to the Prime Minister the previous year, has involved the establishment of 'executive agencies' to deliver public services. The official announcement (*House of Commons Debates*, 18 February 1988, vol. 127, col. 1149) refers to the establishment of 'units clearly designated within Departments', though as we shall see some agencies do not fit easily into such a description. This chapter will also show that there is considerable variety in the characteristics of agencies.

Why 'next'?

The Next Steps initiative is a major development in British public administration, but is it a completely fresh start? Next Steps is an incremental development from the pre-existing structure of government, at least in the tactics of its introduction, if not in its ambitions. It can be seen as following on from other developments concerned with public expenditure and public management introduced by the Conservative government which came into office in Britain in 1979. These included the Rayner exercises, named after Lord Rayner, who headed an efficiency unit in the Cabinet Office. The exercises were largely concerned with carrying out existing activities more effectively rather than reviewing policies (see Gray and Jenkins, 1985: 116–22).

The Rayner scrutinies looked at individual areas of government activity, but the next development, the Financial Management Initiative (FMI), was concerned with management across central government. The Financial Management Initiative, launched in May 1982, was designed to be flexible in its implementation, but was concerned with: (a) clearer setting of objectives and where possible measurement of outputs and performance; (b) clearer responsibility within departments for costs; and (c) improvement in financial information within departments.

Although it might be an exaggeration to talk about a managerial revolution within Whitehall as a result of the Financial Management Initiative, there was certainly a dramatic change in awareness of the running cost implications of government activities (see Gray and Jenkins, 1986).

The Next Steps Report was explicitly seen as the further development of the FMI. This is shown in its title, *Improving Management in Government: The Next Steps* (Jenkins, Caines and Jackson, 1988). The Next Steps Report is also commonly referred to as the Ibbs Report, after Sir Robin Ibbs, the Prime Minister's adviser on efficiency, even though the published version does not list him as one of the authors! The Next Steps initiative takes its name from the title of Ibbs Report. The roots of the idea of separate executive units, though, can be traced back to the Fulton Report of the 1960s (Cmnd 3638, 1968; see also Goldsworthy, 1991: 2). Even leaving aside non-departmental bodies, there is a long tradition of non-ministerial executive departments, of which Inland Revenue and Customs and Excise are the most important.

The main recommendation of the Report was the establishment of agencies as discrete areas of work with a chief executive personally responsible to the minister for day-to-day management. The minister would delegate managerial independence within a preset budget. An important focus was on results, with rewards for success and penalties for failure, applying to the chief executive at least. This emphasis on results did include concern to satisfy the 'customers' of government services, though the main targets continued to be costs and throughput. Another consideration was the view that individual employees would be able to identify and feel responsible for agency activities to a greater extent than those of the broader department or the Civil Service as a whole (for evidence on the effectiveness of this last point, see Price Waterhouse, 1992: 12–13). It is important to stress that Next Steps agencies remain part of the departments (though to confuse matters some of them were already separate non-ministerial departments). Though dramatic in a British context, the establishment of agencies simply brings Britain closer to the Swedish and United States models.

Why 'steps'?

There was no attempt to bring about an immediate and complete changeover to agencies throughout the government. Nor was there a grand plan

Table 1   *The development of Next Steps agencies*

Year (April)	Number of UK agencies	In agencies	UK civil servants Including 'Next Steps lines'*	As % of all UK civil servants
1989	3	5,800	5,800	1
1990	26	60,800	60,800	11
1991	48	177,000	204,000	37
1992	66	197,000	287,000	51

Source: derived from *Civil Service Statistics* (HMSO, annual).
* The 'Including Next Steps lines' column adds staff of Customs and Excise (from 1991), which has 30 executive units, and Inland Revenue (from 1992), which has 34 executive offices. These units and offices are not included in the count of number of agencies. Excludes 6 Northern Ireland agencies by April 1992 and staff of agencies who are not UK civil servants.

with a timetable of named agencies to be set up by each date. Instead sections of departments were identified for their suitability as agencies on an *ad hoc* basis. Not surprisingly, some of the early agencies covered already clearly defined activities with specialist technical or administrative tasks. But 'steps' also because there was not a single burst of agencies, but a continuing establishment of batches of them. The growth of agencies and the number of civil servants employed by them is shown in Table 1. The first agency to be established was the Vehicle Inspectorate, which was set up on 1 August 1988. The target for all executive activities to be in agencies by end of 1993 was first set in 1991 in the Citizen's Charter White Paper (Cm 1599, 1991).

The step-by-step approach to establishing agencies caused some concern for the Treasury and Civil Service Committee of the House of Commons, which said 'It would not be satisfactory if a major change in the structure of the civil service were to be introduced piecemeal, without proper opportunity for full public discussion' (HC 496, 1990–1: xii).

FEATURES OF THE INTRODUCTION OF NEXT STEPS

Style of introduction

The British Civil Service is notorious for allowing reforms directed at it to evaporate without outright resistance. Since the Next Steps initiative did not involve a clear blueprint there was a danger that this would happen if responsibility for implementation lay solely at departmental level. A related danger is that the formal requirements of a reform are complied with, but the underlying commitment to the substance is lacking or subsequently evaporates. To avert these dangers a Project Manager for Next Steps, Peter Kemp, was appointed with second permanent secretary status, with a small Next Steps team working under him. This clear identification of 'ownership' of the initiative was important in itself, but also important was the committed and vigorous approach of Peter Kemp, who was prepared to argue the case for Next Steps to audiences of civil servants, MPs or academics. Peter Kemp's style was clearly important in giving impetus to the launch of Next Steps, but eventually proved too abrasive for the British civil service, and he was put into early retirement in July 1992. His place as Project Manager and permanent secretary was taken by Richard Mottram. The momentum of establishing agencies has been maintained, and the expectation is that all agency candidates will be announced by the end of 1993 and be launched as agencies by the middle of 1995 (Cm 2111, 1992: 7). More difficult to assess is whether the change of Project Manager will affect the enthusiasm of agencies to develop innovative management styles.

The political commitment at Prime Ministerial level was also important and had also been a factor in the implementation of the FMI. The Prime Minister has regular meetings with the Project Manager (see Goldsworthy, 1991: 33). The Project Manager also submits six-monthly written reports to ministers. The Head of the Civil Service has also given frequent public support to the initiative. Just as the initiative has survived a change of Project Manager, it also survived the change of Prime Minister from Margaret Thatcher to John Major in November 1990.

No legislation required for move towards agencies

It may seem strange to continental European countries with strong traditions of public law that no legislation was considered necessary to achieve approval or a legal basis for Next Steps agencies. The approval and implementation was entirely a matter for the Executive, though as we will see below, the establishment of agencies has important implications for concepts of accountability to Parliament. The only modest exception to this was the passage of the Government Trading Act 1990, which made it easier to set up trading funds for some agencies (Goldsworthy, 1991: 31).

Not only was legislation not considered necessary, but there was not even a full debate in the House of Commons until May 1991, more than three years after the initiative had been launched. Commons interest was expressed largely through the Treasury and Civil Service Committee, which has carried out a number of investigations into the initiative (of which the most recent was HC 496, 1990–1). Although critical of particular aspects of the introduction and operation of Next Steps agencies, the Committee was broadly supportive and encouraging of the initiative. Individual departmental select committees within the House of Commons have also begun to investigate the relationship between parent department and agencies.

VARIATIONS IN AGENCIES

One of the problems in presenting a brief overview of Next Steps agencies – and one of the problems in devising appropriate frameworks of finance and accountability – is the huge variation in the size and characteristics of agencies. There is no such thing as a typical Next Steps agency.

Size

There are huge variations in the size of the staff of agencies, from 30 (Wilton Park Conference Centre) to 65,600 (Social Security Benefits Agency). Some individual agencies are larger than the total size of some other departments, including core departments plus all their agencies. For example, the Social Security Benefits Agency is double the combined size of the Department for Education, the Department of Health, the Foreign and Commonwealth Office, the Department of Trade and Industry, the Department of Transport, and the Welsh Office, including the 20 agencies within those departments.

Status of agency chief executive

Although size and managerial requirements are not necessarily directly related, there is also a considerable variation in the rank and salary of agency chief executives. The highest salary (£140,000) is paid to the chief executive of the Defence Research Establishment. This is substantially higher than the salary of a permanent secretary or the Prime Minister, so agency heads can be accountable to civil servants and ministers who are paid less than they are. Within the civil service equivalent ranks, chief executives range from Grade 1A, (Second Permanent Secretary equivalent), for example, the Central Statistical Office, to Grade 6 (Senior Principal equivalent), for example, the Rate Collection Agency in Northern Ireland. Some of the Defence Support Agencies are headed by military officers. An important feature of the Next Steps initiative is that chief executive posts should be open to competition from outside the civil service. Of the appointments made up to the end of March 1992, about one-half of chief executive posts were open to competition, and about sixty percent of those open to competition were filled by existing civil servants, though not always people who had previously worked within the same department.

Origin

Any idea that Next Steps agencies are only about carving out separately identifiable executive tasks from previously monolithic departments should be abandoned immediately. The history of individual agencies varies widely from bodies which were already separate non-ministerial departments (Intervention Board), through already separate units within departments (such as the Driver and Vehicle Licensing Agency), to units which were indeed not previously a clearly identified part of a department. Some of the Defence Support Agencies within the Ministry of Defence combine civil servants with other civilian employees and military personnel. Two agencies (the Planning Inspectorate and the Agricultural Development and Advisory Service) are made up from parts of two separate departments and are still considered to be 'owned' by two departments, with interesting implications for accountability.

Some agencies had already been operating as Trading Fund Organizations (TFOs), that is with their own accounts which could retain receipts to offset expenditure.

Other agencies had previously not been part of a government department at all but were derived directly or indirectly from non-departmental bodies (sometimes referred to as 'quangos'). For example, the Training and Employment Agency (Northern Ireland) absorbed a number of non-departmental public bodies. The Employment Service in Great Britain, while immediately previously part of the Department of Employment, had before then been part of the Manpower Services Commission, a non-departmental public body (though one staffed by civil servants).

The treatment of Customs and Excise and Inland Revenue is distinctive: they were already executive non-ministerial departments given responsibility for the day-to-day management of tax collection, but have been internally 'reorganized' along 'Next Steps lines'. In Customs and Excise the executive units were largely based on the already existing regional structure. Thus, for Customs and Excise and Inland Revenue there are agency structures within what are already non-ministerial executive departments. It is worth noting that there are still a number of other non-ministerial departments, mostly of a regulatory nature, which are not Next Steps agencies.

Funding

Next Steps agencies vary along the whole range of funding, from 100 percent government funding of their activities to fully covering all their costs from fees or charges. Related to this is the difference in trading status, with some agencies (such as Cadw, the Welsh Historic Monuments Executive Agency) being Supply financed and required to pay any income into general government funds, some (such as the Vehicle Certification Agency) are Supply financed but operate on a 'net running costs regime', while others (such as the Royal Mint) have trading fund status, which enables them to retain receipts to offset expenditure. As noted above, some, though not all, such agencies already had trading fund status before becoming Next Steps agencies.

Staffing

Most employees of Next Steps agencies are civil servants, but not all. Of the 227,000 employees of Next Steps agencies at 1 April 1991, 8,000 were Armed Forces personnel in Ministry of Defence agencies and 1,300 other staff. In the case of Service Children's Schools (North West Europe), 1,300 of the 2,330 employees were not civil servants. Agencies vary in the extent to which they consist solely of 'non-industrial' (that is, administrative) civil servants, or include a mixture of industrial and non-industrial. (Since a few non-departmental bodies do employ civil servants, it can be seen that employee status cannot be used as an absolute criterion for distinguishing Next Step agencies from non-departmental public bodies.)

Existence of boards

A number of Next Steps agencies have 'steering boards' or 'advisory boards' or 'councils', whereas some others have management teams consisting solely of staff from within the agency. Some of these boards are chaired by the chief executive, some by a senior civil servant from the parent department, and some by a junior minister. Boards vary in the extent to which they have private sector representation, and in the extent to which civil servants from outside the agency are members. Some private sector representatives are clearly there as a 'managerial peer group', while others represent the 'customers' of the services delivered by the agency. While most boards are concerned with supervising or advising management, some are given an explicit policy advisory role. The roles of these boards, and their implications for accountability, are very neglected issues.

Monopoly status

Agencies vary in the extent to which they are a statutory or de facto monopoly or are simply one of a number of potential suppliers of a service. The Buying Agency within the Department of the Environment provides a service which can also be provided by agencies or departments themselves or purchased from the private sector. The Benefits Agency, on the other hand, is the sole supplier of social security benefits which it administers. These variations have implications for the development of comparative performance indicators and potential for privatization, and also the extent to which customer or client orientation should be a matter of public concern rather than commercial prudence.

Task focus

Not all agencies are the smallest identifiable unit with a single definable task. Some are single-function agencies, such as the Military Survey, while others, such as the Social Security Benefits Agency, have a range of functions, some of which are on a larger scale than have elsewhere been delegated to separate agencies. In addition to its core task of paying out benefits, the Social Security Benefits Agency provides a number of services to other statutory authorities and government departments (including other parts of the Department of Social Security) (Cm 1760, 1991: 570). This varying pattern reflects in part the importance in the early stages of the initiative of getting agreement from those at senior levels in the would-be agency. From the perspective of civil servants in the Next Steps team, some of the original framework agreements can be seen as 'holding operations', and will be subject to reconsideration when framework documents come up for review after three years.

Typologies

The nature of the activities of Next Steps agencies also varies substantially in the centrality of their activities to the policy functions of departments. The Fraser Report (1991: 22–5) suggested that there were four main groups of agencies:

Mainstream agencies, which are fundamental to the mainstream policy and operations of their departments, such as the Employment Service or the Social Security Benefits Agency. *Regulatory and other statutory agencies*, which execute in a highly delegated way statutory functions derived from the main aims of a department, such as the Vehicle Inspectorate. *Specialist service agencies*, which provide services to departments or other agencies, such as the Information Technology Services Agency in the Department of Social Security. *Peripheral agencies*, which are not linked to the main aims of a department but report to its minister, such as HMSO.

The Fraser Report did not derive a separate group for the large number of Defence Support Agencies, suggesting that it should be possible to fit all such agencies into one or other of the four groups. The report noted that even within one department, the relationships with agencies would not necessarily follow a common format.

Greer (1992) has developed an alternative typology based initially on whether agencies are self-funding and whether they are monopolies. She notes (1992: 91) that non-monopoly self-funding agencies are those which have the greatest potential for development as autonomous business units.

IMPLICATIONS FOR NATURE OF PUBLIC SERVICE

Because the Next Steps initiative did not involve any legislative change, the civil service status of the employees of government departments was not affected (except for chief executives, about three-quarters of whom are career civil servants). This was deliberate, to avoid setting trade unions against Next Steps. However, the establishment of agencies with greater managerial flexibility clearly has implications for the existence of a unified civil service with standard pay structures and conditions of service.

Currently, agencies maintain the Civil Service structure of 'Whitley' negotiating committees with unions. HMSO has been an exception in breaking away completely from civil service pay and conditions, but HMSO had been a separate trading fund organization for a decade.

Sir Angus Fraser, the Prime Minister's Adviser on Efficiency (who in 1991 had prepared a report on Next Steps for the Prime Minister), told the Treasury and Civil Service Committee of the House of Commons that 'a "unified civil service" really is not compatible with the way we are going' (HC 496, 1990–1: 49). By this he appeared to mean that uniform pay and conditions would disappear, but he still seemed to see a need for 'codes and principles, of things like loyalty, impartiality, fair and open competition in recruitment, promotion on the basis of merit and performance' (HC 496, 1990–1: 48). He also appeared to see some need for central overview of career management for those with senior management potential.

The debate in the British literature about the impact of Next Steps for a unified Civil Service (see e.g. Drewry, 1990: 328–29), overlooks the wider implications of grouping civil servants with other staff, such as military staff and civilians not in the UK civil service within the agencies. The extent to which there was in any case a unified civil service can be overemphasized. The Diplomatic Service remains distinct from the Home Civil Service. The Ministry of Defence is staffed by an amalgam of civil servants and military staff which does not fit neatly into the classic model of departmental chains of command. Northern Ireland Departments, which are not part of the United Kingdom civil service, do have Next Steps agencies. Advocates of Next Steps pointed out that the bulk of civil servants did not identify with the civil service as a whole or even the department they worked for, but the particular part of the department or even local office in which they worked.

Observers from outside Britain should note that the British concept of civil servant does not include many categories of persons working for government agencies or funded by the state (such as university lecturers) who might be classified as civil servants in some other countries. None of these remarks detracts from the fact that many of the *top* civil servants, amounting to about 27,000 out of 565,000, do have a genuine commitment to a concept of public service rather than simply emulation of private management, and see themselves as having a lifetime career within that service. We have already noted the implications of the separation of agencies from core departments for career paths.

A PARTISAN OR CONSENSUS DEVELOPMENT?

The attitude of the Opposition to Next Steps became of interest in the approach to the General Election eventually held in April 1992. The government itself was anxious to stress the non-partisan nature of the reforms. The then Labour Party Treasury spokesman (now Leader of the Labour party), John Smith, made it clear in May 1991 that he would not attempt to reverse the initiative (quoted in HC 496, 1990–1: ix). The Treasury and Civil Service Committee of the House of Commons has been concerned to sustain and develop all-party support for the initiative. By the time of the next election, due by 1997, the initiative, at least in terms of the establishment of agencies, will be complete.

Elements of the market-oriented 'New Right' are not keen on Next Steps because it diverts attention from the possibility of privatizing some activities which are instead being given to agencies. Activities are supposed to be considered for termination or possible privatization before becoming Next Steps agencies, though it is recognized that some potentially privatizable activities do not yet have the managerial and financial structure to make them attractive to purchasers (Goldsworthy, 1991: 18). Agency status is not seen as ruling out future privatization, though further immediate change was thought unlikely (Goldsworthy, 1991: 19). Greer (1992) has pointed out that the prime candidates for privatization are those which are self-funding non-monopolies. In terms of functions discussed above, agencies engaged in the delivery of specialist services are the most likely candidates for future privatization.

IS THERE REALLY MUCH AUTONOMY?

There has been some increase in managerial discretion, but still Treasury involvement over details. There is conflicting evidence about the extent to which the agencies themselves desire autonomy. Price Waterhouse (1992: 10) found that agencies would welcome the freedom to introduce more flexible pay and reward systems and that they had strong feelings on this issue. However, Goldsworthy (1991: 32) found that few agencies were pressing for more freedom to hire and dismiss staff or to develop their own pay arrangements, at least in the initial preparation of agency proposals.

As might be expected in the initial stages of establishing Next Steps agencies, working out relationships with the parent departments was a major preoccupation. A survey by Price Waterhouse (1992: 7) found that this has become significantly less dominant by early 1992 compared to a year previously. However, a number of the other preoccupations of chief executives, such as 'Business/corporate planning' and 'New Financial Regime', also involved substantial contact with the parent department. More discussion between agencies and departments took place on budgets than anything else, with personnel matters and agreeing targets also featuring (Price Waterhouse, 1992: 11).

It is clear that the relationship between agencies and parent department is not one of annual discussions over targets followed by a 'hands off' relationship for the next twelve months. Price Waterhouse (1992: 11) found that about half the agencies had daily contact with officials and the rest mostly weekly. Rather than declining, this frequency of contacts had increased compared to a year earlier. This level of frequency of contacts raises the question of whether the line has clearly been drawn between policy and operational matters. Unfortunately, we lack data on frequency of contacts between civil servants in sections of departments prior to the establishment of agencies, so we have no baseline for comparison. Price Waterhouse (1992: 12) suggests that agency managers are no longer absorbed in the work of the department as a whole and place less focus on their relationships with ministers and senior officials.

At least as relevant as the evidence of such surveys is the attitude of chief executives. It is clear from listening to presentations which chief executives have made to mixed audiences of civil servants and academics that some, including those heading the largest agencies, are personally committed to using the greater flexibilities available within their framework documents to provide a more customized service to the relevant members of the public and to involve their staff in arrangements to do this. This enthusiasm has been evident in the early years after the establishment of agencies, and it remains to be seen whether there will be a continuing innovation.

Moves towards greater pay flexibility within agencies were set back by the government's pay policy for the public sector announced in November 1992, which limited pay rises to a maximum of 1.5percent. This did still allow some flexibility for performance pay for individual employees, though it clearly precludes some kinds of flexible pay arrangements.

ROLES OF CENTRAL POLICY CORE OF DEPARTMENTS AND 'CENTRAL DEPARTMENTS'

Although the roles of departments and of centre of government (especially the Treasury) were briefly mentioned in the Ibbs report, the scale and structure of the central policy core of departments was not discussed. The implications for the scale and structure of departments came rather as an afterthought (see Fraser, 1991). Some 'central' staff of departments have been transferred to agencies' books and their services have to be bought back by departments and other agencies.

The discussion of the relationship between departments and the Treasury in the Ibbs report was very tentative and the possibility of direct or triangular relationships involving the Treasury, agencies and departments was totally neglected. In November 1991, the government agreed that the role of the Treasury and the Cabinet Office should be clarified in the light of the Next Steps Initiative (Cm 1761, 1991).

Crucial issues include the policy roles of core and agencies, and the question of direct bargaining by agencies with the Treasury over resources. Some agencies are given an explicit remit to offer or comment on policy advice. In others a civil servant below the level of permanent secretary is given this policy advice role. For agencies which are already separate departments, the whole notion of there being a 'core department' to which they relate is problematic. A general issue is how does the 'centre', whether core of spending departments or the Treasury, assess agencies when special expertise is concentrated in the agencies?

There are also implications for personnel management in terms of career development. Are two different strands of executive and policy core civil servants to develop, or will involvement in an agency be seen as a prerequisite for a top posting in a core department?

Some departments are already used to thinking of themselves as 'holding companies' for separate units. The Department of Employment had separated out functions by the mid 1970s to such an extent that it referred to itself as the Department of Employment Group. Other departments, such as Social Security, have a more monolithic past and have to work out a different style of relationship between core and agencies.

IMPLICATIONS FOR 'ACCOUNTABILITY'?

Much of the existing academic literature on Next Steps which has raised the issue of accountability has done so on a relatively narrow range of issues and often on the assumption that there are generic issues of accountability applying in a similar way to all agencies. The variations between agencies already noted should suggest that varieties of formal and informal accountabilities need to be explored.

Of agencies to departments and ministers

An important development for agencies which are part of departments has been the extent to which civil servants in identified posts have been publicly specified as being responsible for the supervision of agencies, ranging from grade 3 to the main permanent secretary of the department (grade 1). Just what is implied by the responsibility of such civil servants for supervising agencies and advising ministers about matters relating to the policies delivered by such agencies is not clear. Agencies which are themselves non-ministerial departments are directly accountable to ministers, though the top civil servants from the minister's 'main' department may have an explicit role to advise the minister.

Of agencies to central departments, such as the Treasury

Most agencies are required to go through the principal finance officer for their departments in negotiations with the Treasury about finance, and agencies which are part of departments are still dependent on the way in which departments carve up the allocation achieved in public expenditure negotiations. One of the possible developments to watch for the future of agencies is whether they seek to increase direct contact with the Treasury. Agencies which are departments and certain other agencies already have the right to discuss finance directly with the Treasury. A related underexplored area where accountability issues arise is that of spending departments to central departments for their agencies.

Of agencies and ministers to Parliament

We have already noted that Parliament had little role in the introduction of the Next Steps initiative, with interest largely confined to the Treasury and Civil Service Committee. The accountability of specific agencies and ministers to Parliament is certainly a set of issues which has aroused substantial debate given the centrality of the doctrine of ministerial accountability to Parliament in the informal British constitution (see Judge, 1993). However, much of that debate has assumed that the issues are the same for all agencies. Particular concerns have arisen over questions from MPs about agencies:

(1) A lack of clarity about when issues are about matters of policy and therefore directable to ministers; one MP who tabled a series of questions about agency budgets found that nine departments referred the question to the relevant agency for answer and seven answered on behalf of the relevant agencies.

(2) The question of the availability of answers to MPs' questions. Answers from agencies have been sent to the MP concerned, with a copy normally being placed in the House of Commons Library. However, this meant that the replies were not easily available to those outside the House of Commons, even when the answers have wider implications than the particular case about which the question was asked. The Procedure Committee of the Commons recommended that answers from agencies should be included in the Official Report of the House of Commons (HC 178, 1990–91). The government accepted that there had been practical difficulties and that access to replies from agency chief executives needed to be improved (Cm 1761, 1991). The solution adopted conformed to the request of the Procedure Committee that answers from chief executives should be included in the Official Report of the House of Commons, a solution which disappointed civil servants who want to emphasize that ministers should not be politically accountable for day-to-day managerial actions by agencies.

In British constitutional convention, one of the key features of the accountability of government to Parliament is financial accountability. In contrast to political accountability of ministers for the policies on which expenditure is incurred, responsibility for ensuring that expenditure is properly incurred (and increasingly for ensuring the efficiency and effectiveness of expenditure) has lain with an 'accounting officer', normally a permanent secretary. As the Treasury and Civil Service and the Public Accounts Committees of the House of Commons pointed out, this arrangement did not accord well with the responsibilities of the chief executives of agencies. The government accepted this point (Cm 914, 1989), and announced that where appropriate agency chief executives would be designated as 'agency accounting officers', and would accompany the accounting officer when the Public Accounts Committee was examining an agency's affairs. However, in some cases the chief executive is the full accounting officer for all the expenditure by an agency where that agency has its own expenditure 'Vote'. In some cases chief executives are full accounting officers for part of the expenditure of their agencies and agency accounting officers for other parts! Whatever the Next Steps initiative has done, it has not produced uniform patterns of financial accountability.

Of matters affecting agencies and the broader public

There has certainly been the publication of a greater degree of information about the detailed activities of those parts of departments which have been put into agencies. There are framework documents, corporate plans and annual reports for each agency. Framework documents are freely available, though some corporate and annual plans are considered commercially sensitive and are not released. The availability of this mass of documents itself makes it difficult to cope with the flood of information and identify general issues affecting agencies. There have been various government reports about developments in the progress of the Next Steps initiative, and the government now publishes an annual review summarizing each agency's achievements and plans. However, the information is not provided on a consistent basis as expenditure for some is given for the previous year, for others in a future year, and information about other sources of funding is not provided on a consistent basis. Further, there is a tendency in these summaries about individual agencies to put a positive gloss on results, even where there have been major problems. It is only if the reader is aware of the detailed background to the agency that he or she can interpret the comments.

The 1992 review dropped the summary table about staff and operating costs (not total expenditure) which had appeared in the 1991 review. The government's annual publication *Civil Service Statistics* only lists the staff of agencies who are members of the United Kingdom civil service, and therefore omits the staff of agencies who are other civilian staff, members of the armed forces, or members of the Northern Ireland civil service. Despite the mass of detailed material available, the government does not publish complete summary information about staffing or expenditure of all agencies on a consistent basis, or data about individual agencies which would facilitate comparisons across time and between agencies.

PERFORMANCE INDICATORS AND THEIR PROBLEMS

The emphasis on 'results' is clearly central to the Next Steps initiative and to issues of accountability. The government has produced a guide to setting targets and measuring performance in Next Steps agencies (HM Treasury, 1992). This guide makes it clear that its recommendations are not mandatory and that the choice of targets and levels is for individual ministers in the light of proposals submitted by chief executives. There are very substantial variations in both the total number and the types of targets set for different agencies. The Treasury and Civil Service Committee (HC 496, 1990–1: xxi–xxii) pointed out that not all agencies had targets in the three key areas of financial performance, quality of service and efficiency. This continued to be the case in the 1992 Review (Cm 2111, 1992).

Agencies are meeting three-quarters of their targets according to Sir Peter Kemp (*Economist*, 21 Dec 1991: 28). Is this good or bad? Weiss (1972: 32) refers to the 'fully/only' school of analysis which, in the absence of direction about how much progress towards the goal marks success, will (to adapt Weiss) come out with different conclusions: 'Fully 75 percent of the targets ...' boasts the promoter; 'Only 75 percent of the targets ...' sighs the detractor. Do we need targets for targets? For what it is worth, the author has calculated from summary tables in the annual reviews that 77 percent of targets were met in 1991–92, up from 72 percent in 1990–91. The summary tables give no information about the percentage underachievement (or overachievement) of targets, though information on this is given in the summaries for individual agencies, some of which also discuss the extent to which failure to meet targets was a result of factors (such as economic recession) beyond the control or predictive ability of the agency. No information is given about the consequences for agencies or chief executives of failures to meet targets, though this is at the heart of issues of accountability.

Elizabeth Mellon, an academic at the London Business School who has studied five agencies, has been quoted as stating: 'What tends to happen is that the agency asks for targets it feels safe with, the department adds some more, and the agency aims for the ones it can achieve' (*Economist*, 21 December 1991: 28).

CONCLUSION: NEXT STEPS IN CONTEXT

Was Next Steps really necessary? Flexibility in employing types of staff did not require Next Steps as such and the same is true of other minor delegations (HC 496, 1990–1: viii). However, even those making these points accept that tactics can be used to bring about significant changes beyond the small changes which agency status on its own requires (see comments by Mellon in HC 496, 1991: 110).

It is important to place Next Steps agencies in the context of other recent organizational developments in British government. Although the Conservative government came into office in 1979 committed to the reduction of non-departmental bodies or 'quangos', research currently being undertaken by the author shows that, while the number of such bodies may have declined, their significance in terms of finance has grown. Particularly worth noting are the number of organizations in urban development and education which administer functions previously the responsibility of local authorities. The government has also set up a number of bodies, notably the Training and Enterprise Councils, which the government does not count as government bodies, even though they are publicly funded and some include civil servants. Single-industry regulatory offices (with non-ministerial departmental status) have been established to regulate privatized utility industries. Issues of the accountability and autonomy of Next Steps agencies are only part of such issues affecting the range of bodies which are involved in the delivery of British government policy.

The study of Next Steps agencies must take account both of this broader context and of the wide variety of different forms and functions of agencies themselves. How similar are (some) Next Steps agencies to other bodies with a formally different constitutional status? What are the implications of some of the very substantial differences among agencies (such as the fact that some are separate government departments!) for issues such as accountability, policy advice, and bargaining for financial resources? The debate to date on accountability in particular has tended to assume that there is a generic issue, whereas the evidence presented in this paper points to the need for micro level analysis to plot the operation of accountability in practice in a variety of forms. The Next Steps initiative has introduced many new issues for exploration, but it has also served to highlight some of the previously neglected issues in public administration, such as the roles and function of non-ministerial departments, which account for about a quarter of the total UK civil service. The diversity of agencies has not replaced some mythical age of uniform departmental structure, activities, and accountability. Rather it has revealed and built on the diversity of activities in which central government was already engaged.

For many readers the interest in the Next Steps initiative will lie in the possibility of policy transfer to other countries. It should be clear by now that there is no single model of a typical Next Steps agency which can form the basis of any generalised transfer. Is the interest in the type of agency which reports direct to a minister and negotiates directly with the Treasury for its budget, or is it in the those which report through a medium-level civil servant and have to channel all budget requests through the core department? Is the interest in arrangements for largely self-funding units which are more appropriate than the conventional bureaucratic model, or is it in units which rely entirely on funding from taxation to provide services according to standard rules to citizens? While there are some general features, such as the relatively explicit statement of expectations through framework documents and annual plans, we have seen that almost every other aspect of the scale, structure and relationships of agencies varies substantially. This variation results not from a clear typology for application but on the ad hoc development of agency arrangements, albeit with some learning as the initiative has developed.

Another trap for policy transfer is the substantially different agendas on issues such as accountability of officials to politicians which can exist in different countries, and the substantially different relationship which can exist between units of the bureaucracy and the core executive and between units of the bureaucracy and the legislature. These would affect how any agency-like reforms would operate in other countries.

The Next Steps initiative in Britain is interesting for the way that it raises issues about the management of the public sector rather than for any simple answers which it has produced.

15

THE EFFICIENCY OF
PUBLIC SERVICE PROVISION

Assessing Six Reform Strategies

Rune J. Sørensen

1. INTRODUCTION

Is the public sector inherently susceptible to inefficiency? The conventional view holds that the absence of a self-adjusting mechanism similar to that of the market system causes an inefficient public sector. Inefficiencies are reinforced by soft budgetary frames, by inadequate assessment of performance, by deficient reward systems and by bureaucratic waste. Others counter to the contrary, and argue that these are ill-founded charges. Governments pursue a more complicated and less tangible set of social objectives than that of the private company, and the efficiency criteria are different from those of private business.

An understanding of the underlying causes of ineffective resource use is a prerequisite to reform proposals. The analysis must take into account the special characteristics of the public sector and its objectives. We start out in section (2) by addressing the economic performance criteria, and their place in the evaluation of government institutions. Section (3) presents a brief survey of the Scandinavian background that is the main empirical reference in the following discussion of efficiency.

Surprisingly little theory and empirical evidence exist about the causes of cost inefficiency. We offer six hypotheses about the reasons for an inefficient public sector, and the preconditions for efficiency improvement: The first interpretation is presented in section (4). Comparisons of the public and private sectors suggest that private sector producers deliver services at lower costs than do public producers. The institutional diagnosis derived from this is that of separating the responsibility for providing and producing public services. We discuss the generality of these findings, and suggest some of the limitations of this strategy.

Section (5) outlines the second hypothesis, namely that inefficiency stems from the 'soft' budget constraints of government agencies. It is the lack of a tight resource constraint that inflates costs and undermines the efficiency objective. The proper strategy is that of imposing a firm budget limit. Efficiency can be improved by putting pressure on the government institutions by means of a centralized budget-control. The question remains as to whether this is possible and, if it is, whether the strategy impairs other important goals of public policy.

The third proposition relates to the micro-level of budget making. Section (6) states that inefficiency is due to lack of proper information systems. Budgetary researchers repeatedly claim that performance measurement is impossible, that it induces damaging conflicts, and that it generates potentially counterproductive incentives. We present evidence that modifies these claims, and emphasize the beneficial motivational effects. The fourth proposition states that performance measurement is a necessary condition for efficient service provision, but not a sufficient condition. Section (6) employs agency theory to explore the possibilities for designing incentive schemes that promote efficiency without impairing other goals.

The fifth hypothesis relates to bureaucratization. The point in section (7) is that political institutions tend to accumulate an excessive administrative overhead, which subverts the efficient operation of the public enterprise. According to this line of argument, the proper strategy is to curb the administrative component of public agencies.

The sixth strategy focuses on the preconditions for active leadership. We argue in section (9) that regulations and democratic governance constrain the public leader, and that relaxing these limitations is an essential factor in inducing a more dynamic form of leadership. We also acknowledge the inherent implementation problems as well as the negative side effects of this strategy.

2. THE PRECONDITIONS FOR EFFICIENCY ASSESSMENT

Herbert Simon (1945 (1976: 179)) suggests that 'the criterion of efficiency dictates that the choice of alternatives that produces the largest result for the given application of resources'. Efficiency means getting the most out of scarce resources to achieve whatever goal the organization wishes to pursue. The economic definition compares benefit and costs or, in other words, it relates the usage of resources to the results obtained.

Simple as this may seem, the usage of efficiency criteria in the public sector is claimed to be more complex than in profit enterprises. The difficulties stem from the inherent differences between public and private organizations. The public sector must submit to legal and formal constraints and political influences. Government agencies have a coercive or monopolistic nature; their goals are complex and public authorities affect the society as a whole. People expect public authority to be

Figure 1   *Preconditions for using efficiency criteria in public organizations*

		Clarity of public sector objectives	
		HIGH	LOW
Knowledge about cause-effect relations	CERTAIN	A: Economic efficiency	C: Institutional legitimacy
	UNCERTAIN	B: Judgmental criteria	D: Institutional legitimacy

fair, responsive and accountable to democratically elected bodies. This has a fundamental impact on the choice of authority relations between stakeholders (citizens, elected representatives) and the operative agencies (Allison, 1979).

We acknowledge the differences which exist between the two sectors, but what is the relevance to efficiency criteria? Which attributes of the government sector delimit the application of efficiency criteria? Are the points summarized by Allison relevant in this respect? Following Thompson (1967), we suggest that the application of economic efficiency criteria depends on: (a) the degree of goal clarity and measurability and (b) the extent to which cause-effect relationship is known. These distinctions are outlined in Figure 1.

Goals can seldom be precisely defined, and measurements are subject to random and systematic measurement errors. Knowledge of cause-effect relations is always deficient. The above classification must therefore be applied with some degree of pragmatism. For the sake of argument, we shall distinguish among the four ideal situations outlined in Figure 1, and discuss the proper evaluation criteria for each of the four cells.

First, the case for an efficiency evaluation is presented in cell **A**. The usage of efficiency criteria assumes a definition of the objectives of public agencies. The administrative leadership and elected bodies can assess efficiency only if there is an explicit definition of the goals of government programs. The existence of objectives is not sufficient; they must be translated into operational definitions that facilitate measurability of service output, and the stakeholders must approve of both the theoretical and operational definitions.

Even if we can observe a degree of goal attainment, decision makers need to know the factors that produce the desired output. The ideal situation is a formal production function. A production function outlines the relevant resource inputs, interacting to yield a particular quantity of output. It provides a benchmark from which we can evaluate service production.

There are two types of economic criteria: *Cost efficiency* means that organizations minimize the usage of input resources to provide a given amount of (public) goods. X-efficiency (Leibenstein, 1966) implies that there are no slack resources available. Cost efficiency denotes that production is X-efficient, that it exploits the best technology available, and that the production factors are combined in the best possible way. Given the amount of a particular society's available resources, *allocative efficiency* implies an optimal mix of outputs as defined by the preferences of the citizens/ consumers. Allocative efficiency implies that the mix of all goods – public and private – is Pareto-optimal (Samuelson, 1954).

Second, cell **B** represents a situation of well-defined goals and inadequate knowledge of cause-effect relations. This means that we can assess the degree of goal attainment, but have little knowledge of the degree to which government activities contribute to this. An example from the educational sector may illustrate the point. There are several studies of the input factors that contribute to the pupils' knowledge and skill development. It is a matter of controversy whether small classes and a high teacher-pupil ratio improve student performance. Studies made in the USA and Sweden do *not* appear to show any significant difference between the ability, well-being and social adjustment of pupils in small classes as compared with those in larger classes (Hanushek, 1986; Chubb and Moe, 1990). Nevertheless, Scandinavian countries have reduced the teacher-pupil ratio considerably during the last decade. Since cause-effect relations are uncertain, and they can be controversial, decision-makers fall back on qualitative interpretations and less precise judgmental criteria.

Third, cell **C** depicts states in which goals remains ambiguous, while cause-effect relations are known. Decision-makers know how to achieve different goals, but they have not specified which social states they what to realize. Some scholars maintain that public sector objectives are complex, vague, intangible, and internally inconsistent (Wildavsky, 1979; Rose, 1984). Efficiency means that we compare input resources with goal attainment. Since we do not know which target we are aiming at, it is impossible to know whether we hit the target or not. An accurate weapon is of little interest if you do not know whether you actually need it. The full implications of this situation are further described below.

Fourth, cell **D** illustrates situations where goals are obscure, and there is little knowledge of how to reach them. This would make the concept of economic efficiency totally inappropriate. Managers have only vague notions of what they are trying to do, and unclear knowledge of the factors that improve goal attainment (March and Olsen, 1976). Institutional theorists (Meyer and Scott, 1983) suggest that, in the absence of approved performance indicators, organizations should be evaluated by the appropriations of their organizational structures and decision-making processes. Organizations are efficient if outside observers regard the institutional framework and the decision-making procedures as appropriate. This is the criterion of *institutional legitimacy*. This criterion seems particularly appealing to government institutions. Legitimacy means that public sector activities are in harmony with fundamental societal objectives. However, legitimacy is not a straightforward criterion. Who is the relevant outside observer? Should the elected representatives, the user groups (patients, students, criminal offenders, etc.), or the general public

Table 1   *Government final consumption expenditure as a percentage of GDP 1960–1990. (Government employment as a percentage of total employment in parenthesis.)*

	1960	1974	1980	1990
Denmark	13.3 (mis)	23.4 (22.2)	26.7 (28.3)	25.2 (30.5)
Norway	12.9 (mis)	18.3 (19.0)	18.8 (23.2)	21.0 (27.7)
Sweden	16.0 (12.8)	23.4 (24.8)	29.1 (30.3)	27.1 (31.7)
Finland	11.9 (7.7)	15.2 (13.8)	18.1 (17.8)	21.1 (22.4)
Total OECD-Europe	13.4 (11.0)	16.4 (15.3)	18.1 (17.3)	18.2 (18.1)
Total OECD	14.4 (11.2)	16.2 (14.1)	16.8 (14.9)	16.8 (14.8)

Source: OECD Historical Statistics

(the taxpayers) assess the results? The choice of observer is in itself a question of legitimacy, and it is often a controversial issue.

A further problem is that of how disagreement between legitimate observers should be handled? Should the institution or its processes be considered illegitimate if all observers believe they are unacceptable? Is the legitimacy criterion linked to consent by a majority of the citizens or the elected politicans?

A final objection to this criterion is misinformation. Should the institution be considered legitimate if outside observers are misinformed about relevant aspects of its activity? For example, most citizens have a vague knowledge of the unit costs of important services such as kindergartens, schooling, health care and care for the elderly. They are badly equipped to evaluate quality relative to the costs of the service. The consent of observers who lack the basic prerequisites for evaluation cannot be considered a reasonable criterion.

This suggests that goal clarity and cause-effect control are fundamental prerequisites for efficiency evaluation. These preconditions are more difficult to satisfy in the public than in the private sector, and we may need to supplement economic efficiency with other evaluation criteria. It does not mean that the criteria of economic efficiency, judgmental assessment and institutional legitimacy are incompatible. Judgmental evaluation may be seen as a less precise and formal way of estimating efficiency, while legitimacy can be regarded as a complementary rather than an alternative criterion. Indeed, economic efficiency may be one of the factors that promotes general consent.

3. INEFFICIENCY PROBLEMS OF PUBLIC SERVICE PRODUCTION

The public sector holds principal responsibility for providing education, welfare services and health care. Table 1 provides data detailing public consumption and government employment in the Scandinavian countries compared to the OECD averages. Services are considered public when they are financed by taxes, and are subject to central or local government management.

Public consumption accounted for an increasing share of the national products in all OECD-countries in the period 1960 to 1980. The right-wing resurgence of the 1980s imposed constraints on the public sector. Post war economic growth resulted in stable public consumption levels relative to the national product. Comparing the Scandinavian countries with the OECD-average shows that there were relatively modest differences. During the 1960s and 1970s public consumption expenditures grew considerably faster in the Scandinavian countries than in the OECD-area. This is evident in the Swedish and Danish cases and is also true for Norway and Finland but to a lesser extent.

One explanation of the almost universal increase in public consumption expenditures relative to the national product (and government employment relative to total employment) is Baumol's model of unbalanced growth. Baumol (1967) suggests that the expansion of government spending results from the technological differences of public and private production processes. In private production, such as in manufacturing, labor is an instrument for the attainment of the final product. Baumol argues that labor is an aim in itself for public services. He refers to teaching as a clear-cut example of a labour-intensive production with a zero (labor-) productivity growth. Assuming that the wage rates of the two sectors grow in parallel, Baumol suggests that the costs per unit of the public sector will rise, while the unit costs of the private sector will remain constant. If consumers and citizens demand a constant ratio of public and private services, an increasing fraction of the labor force will be transferred to the non-progressive public sector. The relative costs of the public household will continue to grow (Baumol, 1967: 419).[1]

Several studies support Baumol's contention of the increasing unit costs of public goods. For example, Bradford and Oates (1969) demonstrate that most of the spending growth of US local government in the period from 1902 to 1966 is due to rising unit costs. In line with the Baumol proposition, they find that technology has often led to higher quality services, but not to cost-reducing measures. Subsequent econometric modelling of the growth of public consumption suggests that the productivity explanation accounts for a significant portion of public sector growth in most Western countries (Lybeck and Henrekson, 1988; Mueller 1989: 326)

According to Baumol's approach, the relative decline of public sector productivity is an inescapable reality. Public administrators cannot improve efficiency by institutional redesign, information about public performance or the development of incentive schemes. The fact that public sector productivity lags behind the productivity growth of the private sector does not mean that public service production is inefficient.

Cross-sectional analyses of public agencies reveal substantial differences in efficiency. A rough indication of managerial problems can be

Table 2   *Unit costs of public services in the Nordic countries, 1980. Sweden =*
100

Services[a]	Denmark	Finland	Norway
Day-care centers	50	46	51
Family day care	77	76	151
Social home services	57	47	49
Nursinghomesfortheelderly	139	50	mis.
Hospital care	85	49	86
Basic education	69	61	77
Judiciary	mis.	51	45
Police	mis.	56	56
Prisons	mis.	33	53
Employment exchange	mis.	23	35
Road maintenance	mis.	148	187

[a] The unit costs are calculated per registered child (day-care centers and family day-care), per household (social home services), per service unit (hospital care), per pupil for basic education, per day in custody (prisons), per inhabitant (judiciary and police), per unemployed (employment exchange) and per kilometer road (road maintenance).

Source: Statskontoret. Kostnader för offentlige tjänster i Norden. Kron-prosjektet. Stockholm 1983

seen in the considerable variation of unit costs in the Scandinavian countries. Table 2 measures unit costs relative to the Swedish case (100).

The higher unit costs are a major explanation for the relatively high public consumption expenditures in Sweden. With the exception of road maintenance, nursing homes for the elderly (Denmark) and family day care (Norway), the costs in Sweden are greater for all services reported in Table 2. The higher quality of Swedish services may account for some of the difference, but it cannot account for all of it. In spite of the obvious problems of comparison (variations of output quality, differences in cost accounting, fluctuation of currency rates, differences in environmental conditions such as climate), the unit cost variations indicate significant efficiency differentials.[2]

4. HYPOTHESIS I: LACK OF PRODUCER COMPETITION

If Baumol's explanation of technology differentials is valid, we would expect minor and random differences in public and private production of identical services. It is the nature of the output, and not institutional factors that account for differences of cost efficiency. Welfare economics would also point to the fact that the market place is ineffective in providing certain goods and services; notably those characterized by public goods properties (non-excludable, non-rivalness). The public sector has a place where the market fails.

Public choice theorists take the argument a step further, maintaining that we should balance the merits and failures of the market system and the government institutions. Inefficient service production is an inherent feature of the public sector, which suggests that we should compare the efficiency loss of public provision with the potential gains of providing optimal amounts of public goods.

It is the lack of incentives that causes inefficiency. The owners of the private firm seek to maximize profits, there is a market for corporate control and there is a bankruptcy constraint on financial achievement. This is not the case in a publicly owned organization, and managerial incentives are affected accordingly. Private managers are more inclined than public administrators to maintain efficiency.

We have, therefore, the main stream argument. However, the empirical support is somewhat inconclusive. In a survey of about 50 studies, Borcherding et al. (1982) found that the private enterprises were more cost efficient than their public counterparts. Similarly, Dunsire et al. (1991) survey the impact of ownership and performance on ten British organizations that have changed legal status. The tests for performance in productivity, employment and financial ratios showed no clear impact of ownership. Vickers and Yarrow (1989: 39–43) propose that most investigations of the efficiency performance of public and private enterprises have focused on electricity supply, the water industry and refuse collection. There is no clear-cut advantage in having private ownership of the electricity or water supplies, while the findings on refuse collection are more supportive of the private alternative. We are therefore led to conclude that the private alternative is superior in some, but not all, cases. As to be expected, the characteristics of the goods supplied are important for the relative performance of the market and the public alternative.

Competition or the existence of contestable markets may be more important than the type of ownership. Following Borchering et al. (1982: 136), it seems that, given sufficient competition between public and private producers, the differences in unit costs are insignificant.[3] This is also the interpretation presented by Vickers and Yarrow (1989). The electricity and the water industry have significant economies of scale and scope, and there are significant entry barriers. Changing from public to private ownership does not alter this, and we would not expect privatization to improve efficiency. Refuse collection is different. Savas (1977) found that differences in unit cost levels vanished when controlled for competition.

Competition does not necessarily imply the existence of several firms in the market place. Contestable markets mean that additional firms are allowed to enter, not that they necessarily do so. Public firms may improve efficiency if their monopoly positions are threatened. For example, Dunsire et al. (1991: 23) suggest that British Airways might have improved performance in anticipation of tougher competition.

Empirical issues aside, what is the proper role of competition in the public sector? Several authors point to the potential for using private enterprises in the actual production of goods and services, while relying on government financing to fund the products (Kristensen, 1987). Others emphasize the potential for price competition among public producers, such as publicly owned TV-companies, public hospitals and schools. Even when this potential has been fully exploited, there will be a certain minimum amount of public production. There are certain parts of the government sector that must be subject to direct state control, such as the police, the military forces and parts of the administrative apparatus. This does not imply that competition is irrelevant; it merely signifies that we do not use a traditional form of market competition. The competition for positions among civil servants promotes efficiency (Stinchcombe, 1974), as does the budgetary rivalry among the public agencies.

It can be concluded that the claim that public agencies are less efficient than private enterprises is not generally correct. It appears to be the case for certain goods and services, but not for them all. In so far as public production is more expensive than private (such as for refuse collection), there is considerable scope for employing the market mechanism to provide public goods. Thus, there is little support for the public choice type of tradeoff between cost efficiency and allocative effectiveness.

5. HYPOTHESIS II: LACK OF A FIRM BUDGET CONSTRAINT

The soft budget constraint signifies that the initial appropriations are negotiable. This is reasonable in the case of an output contract, that is the sponsor declares that it will buy any quantity of a particular good for a fixed price. It is also rational to allow for supplemental appropriations when unexpected and uncontrollable incidents occur. It is difficult to separate exogenous shocks from inefficient production. If an agency learns to expect additional resources whenever a need arises, it will hardly strive to minimize resource output. This suggests that it is the lack of a strict budget constraint that subverts efficiency in the public sector.

The health care sector is an interesting case, particularly the recent experiences of the Canadian and US systems. The Canadian scheme is one of publicly financed health care and universal coverage, while the US-structure is based on a market system of voluntary health insurance. The Canadians changed from a market approach to a public system in 1971, at a time when both countries used a similar proportion of their GNP for health care purposes. Health care spending has risen significantly faster in the US than in Canada, although it is hard to find evidence indicating that service levels differ substantially (Evans et al., 1989; see also Contandriopoulos, 1986; Maarse, 1989). It seems that it is the combination of universal coverage and centralized cost control which constrains the Canadian system into being more cost efficient than the US system.[4]

The US-Canadian comparison fits nicely with the Scandinavian experience. A striking finding of the Swedish productivity studies (performed

by the ESO-group) was that some sectors (e.g. law enforcement) managed to maintain efficiency, whereas other fields experienced a productivity decline (e.g. education, health care). There seems to be a pattern in the results that led Murray (1987) to suggest that:
– A slower rate of increase of resources improves the productivity performance of the agency, a faster rate of increase worsens it.
– In periods of fast increase of output – mostly exogenously determined, from the point of view of the agency – productivity increases (or falls less). (Murray, 1987: 193)

If this is correct, there are two rather different cures for public sector inefficiency. We may expand service demand so that output increases by a given amount of resources, or we may constrain resources by using global spending limits. The latter is the simple efficiency strategy of cutting slack. Schick (1986: 127–8) reports that a number of Western countries have defined expenditure targets before the agencies develop spending requests for the next year. The frame is a restricted sum of real resources appropriated for a program or sector, frequently defined as a multi-year strategy. The agency is required to develop its spending proposals within the centrally defined frame, explicitly justifying proposals exceeding the limit. However, Scandinavian studies also suggest that top-down cost control has its limitations. First, Christensen (1982: 142) describes the operation of expenditure ceilings at the Danish central government level. He repeatedly finds the limits to be overruled as 'exceptional' situations arise. The reforms have neither made government better equipped to withstand pressure for additional appropriations nor made it easier to implement cutback goals in general. In a subsequent study (1992), he proposes that the major deficiency is the lack of proper incentives in the public sector. There are few incentives to hold back on spending and improve efficiency. For example, there is almost no risk of activating negative sanctions by overspending relative to approved frames.

Second, Brunsson (1988) examines the impact assuming a particular productivity growth (2 percent per year) in the Swedish central government. She investigates the implementation of this policy, and finds that the policy has met a series of obstacles similar to those described by Christensen. Though it was complicated to calculate the degree of goal attainment, the author suggests that the program exerted a very modest impact on public spending. One explanation is that government has no effective ability to impose sanctions upon those bodies that exceed their budgetary limits.

Third, we performed a study of Norwegian local government (Sørensen, 1992) to compare authorities that used (a) bottom-up procedure of budget making, (b) annual expenditure frames and (c) preset spending limits derived from a multi-year budget. The analysis showed that the budget-frames were repeatedly renegotiated. Many of the agencies subject to spending frames were able to get supplemental appropriations or they simply spent more money than that which had been formally approved.

Nonetheless, we found that politicians and agencies are more disciplined under a frame system compared to traditional budgetary systems.

Fourth, this result is in line with experience from the Norwegian health care sector. Hagen (1991: 154–55) examines the relation between a DRG-cost index (based on the system of Diagnoses Related Groups) and the budgetary growth rate. Using data for twelve Norwegian hospitals he finds that the DRG-costs per patient per day are greater the higher the growth of appropriations.

This does not signify that higher spending levels or expenditure generate an efficiency loss. An evaluation study of Norwegian social service agencies suggests that increasing the number of positions can cause improved efficiency. In a quasi-experimental design, Nervik (1991) found that the agencies that received additional resources managed to diminish outlays for social assistance, and decrease the duration for which clients received social security contribution. They rehabilitated more social clients, and the cost savings of the experimental agencies were greater than the increased expenses incurred by the experiment. The efficiency improvement was obtained by a combination of additional personnel, agency reorganization and a clearer managerial orientation towards a specified set of objectives. This example points to the importance of managing by a broad set of performance criteria, and it underscores that the blind cutback strategy is as likely to induce inefficiency as it is to improve performance. It seems that (at least) two conditions must be met in order for top-down spending limits to induce greater efficiency: First, the frames must be *firm*. Credibility is essential; the decision-making institutions must commit themselves to maintaining the top-down spending limits. If initial budgetary limits are renegotiated and significantly increased according to agency proposals, the system will degenerate towards the traditional, incremental procedure. Second, the frames must be *realistic*. Advance limits must be based on realistic notions of what is attainable. Consider the case of moderate cutbacks. If appropriations are moderately low compared to last year, output may not decrease in proportion to expenditures. Professional norms can induce the 'street-level bureaucrats' to improve efficiency as a means of maintaining a minimum supply. Consider the strategy of severe cutbacks. Popular protests will arise, and unions and client-organizations will pressure politicians to increase appropriations. Large cutbacks may even undermine the morale of service-suppliers, and cause negative reactions such as loss of loyalty and problems of communication. A deterioration of budgetary discipline may manifest itself in declining efficiency.

6. HYPOTHESIS III: LACK OF PERFORMANCE MEASUREMENT

It follows from our discussion in section (2) that goal clarity and appraisal is fundamental to efficiency management. Attempts to evaluate the results and costs of government programs are not new. Taylor's scientific management represents the first wave of this process; the application of PPBS (Planning-Programming-Budgeting System) constitutes the second wave of reform; whereas the third wave of managerial reform takes a more diversified approach to public sector performance evaluation. The basic aims of the reforms remain the same, to improve efficiency by means of policy analysis. We restrict our discussion to two assertions about this strategy.

The first argument holds that comprehensive quantitative evaluation is *impossible*. One of the sharpest critics of the PPBS-reforms, Wildavsky (1969) suggests that policy analysis should be rescued from PPBS. The fact that, *in principle*, it is a good thing to determine the efficiency of public programs, does not imply that governments should perform a systematic and quantitative analysis of benefits and costs relating to alternative policy measures. The fundamental problem with this approach is that 'no one knows how to do program budgeting.' It was possible to employ this technique in the US Department of Defence because goals could be easily specified, there was a comfortable margin of error, and the substantial costs of the analysis could be justified. However, these prerequisites are not met in other policy areas, the most notable examples being those of health care, education and welfare programs. Analytic studies are only possible in more narrowly defined areas.

Nevertheless, governments have recommenced evaluation. The 1980s was a decade of renewed focus on cost-efficiency. Several countries have taken initiatives to establish performance measures, both at the central and local levels of government. However, the reliability and comprehensiveness of these performance measures is debatable. A study of Norwegian local government agency heads revealed that productivity measurement is relatively rare (Sørensen, 1992). No more than 20 percent of the agencies calculate unit costs or estimate productivity quantitatively. The other agencies use qualitative and verbal descriptions to evaluate efficiency.

The Swedish ESO-group attempted to assess the productivity development of the entire Swedish public sector to investigate the national accounts assumption of a zero productivity growth. By means of relatively crude output-indicators for about 70 percent of public consumption, productivity could be assessed over a 20 year period. It turned out that the productivity growth was negative, about –1.5 percent *per year*. This dramatic figure has triggered a controversy over the validity of the output indicators. The ESO-report is based on simple, quantitative proxies of output, and they do not represent all relevant objectives or the qualitative dimensions of the public supply.

Both studies underscore and support Wildavsky's assertion about the problems of ambitious and general performance evaluation similar to the PPBS programme. However, even imperfect and relatively simple measurement may facilitate an increased awareness of productivity issues. The fact that measurement is difficult in many areas does not imply that it is impossible or fruitless in all segments of the public household. Some agencies can assess cost-efficiency.

The second assertion claims that performance measurement causes *conflict* rather than efforts to improve efficiency. Dror (1967) claims that performance evaluation provokes anti-innovation forces that oppose reforms. The direct usage of simple productivity indicators can stir up devastating conflicts between management, policy researchers and professionals. Although this may be the case in some areas, some evidence runs counter to this claim.

The publication of cross-sectional productivity data can, in itself, help to improve productivity. Johnson (1985) demonstrates that measurements of performance in Swedish social insurance offices have led to competition to promote efficiency. Those offices that initially were below average improved their positions most. Similar results have been obtained for Norwegian public hospitals (NIS, 1992). Since the development of a statistical system for comparing hospitals, productivity has improved and the efficiency variation declined.

These results derived from performance measurement seem to be favourable ones. However, define service quality to those dimensions of the service supply that increases consumer satisfaction. The quality dimensions do not necessarily coincide with quantitative indicators of output; hospital efficiency can be measured by classifying patients using the DRG-system (Diagnostic Related Groups). Such efficiency measures fail to tap potentially important aspects of service quality. The patient appreciates physicians who take time to talk, and nurses who have time to be concerned. Similarly, the personnel input is likely to improve the quality of social services, child care, and, education services.

Efficiency evaluations should in principle be made by contrasting service outputs of equal quality. Quality data are expensive, and the data is inadequate for efficiency analysis. To the extent that efficiency is measured by simple, quantitative indicators, and the service producers maximize measured efficiency, the end result can be inadequate quality and consumer welfare.[5] This does not imply that service quality should be maximized. Higher quality standards in public services normally (but not always) means higher costs. Optimal quality means that the marginal benefit to the consumer equals marginal costs.

Hence, the experience with performance measurement highlights limitations as well as possibilities. It is not fruitful to implement an ambitious measurement on all public programs, it is not constructive to apply the same approach throughout the public sector, and it is potentially counterproductive to link imperfect measurement with a reward system. It seems worthwhile, however, to develop performance indicators for some parts of the public sector; the publication of efficiency indicators can improve efficiency; and policy analysis can provide important guidelines for government policy formation.

7. HYPOTHESIS IV: LACK OF INCENTIVES

Incentives are implicit in most of the previous discussion. Price competition forces the producers into minimizing inefficiency, a firm budget constraint induces cost restraint, while performance measurements put the sponsor as well as the agency in a position to assess efficiency. We may distinguish between two types of incentive schemes: the *behavior-oriented contracts* based on fixed salaries and frame budgets, and *outcome-oriented contracts* of commissions and price arrangements (Eisenhardt, 1989). There is no doubt that the behavior-based contracts dominate the public sector, while the output-oriented incentive schemes are more common in the private sector. Rainey (1979) reports a comparison of questionnaire responses by US public and private middle managers. Government managers generally perceive a weaker relationship between performance and pay, promotion and job security than do business managers. This suggests that government employees have weaker incentives than business employees to improve performance, which might indicate that a revision of the reward system is required.

The fourth strategy suggests that government efficiency can be improved by replacing the traditional budgetary mode of resource allocation with a price contract. The contract specifies that the sponsor (such as an elected body) should purchase certain goods and/or services at a fixed price. However, the agency theory suggests a more careful examination of the preconditions for this to occur. The principal-agent contract is conditioned by several circumstances (Allison, 1989), of which two factors are of particular significance to the public sector.

Measurability of outcomes and behavior is the first criterion of contract design. When outcomes can be easily and accurately measured, the outcome oriented contract is preferable. On the other hand, easily observable behavior means that the behavior contract is appropriate. In line with the argument in section (2), we may point to the fact that public institutions provide 'intangibles' (such as cultural activities), and that they pursue multidimensional objectives (for example health care provision and religious services). The better the outcomes measurement, the more efficient the outcome-based contract. To the extent that the information systems yield information about agency behavior rather than outcomes, the behavior-based contract is preferable.

A price contract encourages producers to focus on measurable results, and to ignore the potentially important intangibles that are not an observable part of the contract.

Outcome uncertainty is a second criterion, requiring an extension of the discussion of cause-effect knowledge begun in section (2). Outcome uncertainty is low when goal attainment results from the agent's effort, while outcome uncertainty is high when outcomes fluctuate significantly due to outside influences. The risk averse agent will only be willing to bear the risks of an outcome-based contract when the price is high, whereas the behavior-based contract will be more attractive to the principal. The outcome-based contract is more efficient when uncontrollable variations in outcomes are *low*, while the behavior-based contract is preferable when there is substantial outcome uncertainty.

Outcome uncertainty may be considerable in government activities, such as in education and law-enforcement. The output of a school depends in part on the teachers' efforts and qualifications, but socio-economic background, parents' support and pupils' motivation and talent are critical to improve knowledge and skills. Similarly, the level and type of police activity used to prevent and detect crime depends on the criminal activity and the attitudes of the general public. Since these activities are subject to uncontrollable factors, the behavior-based contract is more effective (Perry, 1986).

8. HYPOTHESIS V: LACK OF ADMINISTRATIVE CONSTRAINT

Service provision depends on a mix of operative resources and administrative coordination, monitoring and leadership. There has been a steady growth in the relative size of administrative resources in most Western countries. This applies to both the public and private sectors (Melman, 1951). One explanation for the declining productivity in the private sectors, and even more so in the public sector, is overadministration. The fifth proposition suggests that the supraoptimal administrative intensities decrease the efficiency of public service provision.

We may first observe that administrative intensities have increased. Local government is the main provider of public services in the Scandinavian countries. Central administration in Norwegian local governments took about 3 percent of the local budgets in 1885, it increased to 5 percent in 1935, and reached a stable level of 6–8 percent in the post-war period. Similar patterns are found in Swedish and Danish local government (Lane, 1986).

The fact that administrative costs have increased does not in itself imply inefficiency. Crossectional studies of administrative intensity suggest that administration does not vary in proportion to the operative level of activity. Some authorities have administrative *slack*, meaning that they are in a position to reduce administration without impairing service output (Kalset, Rattsø and Sørensen, 1992). Other studies indicate that parts of the university sector suffer from overadministation (Lane, 1989).

Why are government institutions subject to bureaucratization? The public choice scholar would point to the self-interested bureaucrat who maximizes administrative outlays (Mueller, 1989). Since managers are close to the decision-making apparatus, they are in a good position to further their interests. The agency theorist might point to the fact that administrative output is more difficult to observe than the actual service output, which puts the monitoring principal in a difficult managerial position.

Organizational theory points to the role of economies of scale. Since administrative intensity tends to fall with increasing organizational scale, efficiency can be improved by consolidating government agencies. There is a trade off to be made. Increasing size tends to facilitate complex structures that require greater administrative resources. If the amalgamation strategy is pushed too hard, the administrative costs required to coordinate and monitor will outweigh the economies of scale (Mintzberg, 1983).

9. HYPOTHESIS VI: LACK OF ACTIVE LEADERSHIP

Leadership has a significant impact on efficiency. One of the major lessons to be learned from Japanese management style is that it matters; Japanese manufacturers can produce their cars just as effectively in the UK or the USA as they can in Japan. The Toyota-type of leadership style can be implanted in non-Japanese cultures in Europe and in the US. It has been used to upgrade the efficiency and quality in one of General Motors' least effective plants (Pfeffer, 1992: 317). The key to success appears to be a leadership style based on non-authoritarian values, the conscientious development of skills within relatively small work-groups, and a commitment to continuous organizational learning, product improvement and quality production. If this strategy works well in the private sectors, why not put it to work in the public sector?

A principal difference between public and private leadership is the nature of constraints imposed on leaders. The first limitation is caused by *democratic governance*. The primary leaders are not professional managers, but elected representatives subject to electoral controls. Several observers of the public sector note that efficiency reforms are a direct product of the political commitment to promote that aim. Politicians do *not* oppose efficiency *per se*, as it is the societal side effects that make politicians refrain from efficiency measures. For example, it is necessary to lay off personnel to tap the efficiency gains of technological innovations in public telecommunications services. The rate of personnel reductions has been slower than necessary to tap the full efficiency potential. Public managers are not free to pursue efficiency objectives.

The second limitation is *bureaucracy*. The discretion of the public leader is restricted by rules and regulations that control product development, innovation and the management of human resources. For example, the director of a public school cannot diversify the supply of products or change the criteria for recruiting teachers to the school. The public schools are subject a system of formal budgetary control, centralized modes of production, rigid pay schemes, and formalized decision-making procedures. Chubb and Moe (1990) argue that it is this aspect which makes the market system superior in the provision of education in the United

States. They find that there are three major determinants of student achievement: student ability, school organization and family background. It is the bureaucratic, top-down controls which impair efficiency in the public sector: 'Direct democratic control stimulates a political struggle over the right to impose higher-order values on the schools through public authority, and this in turn promotes bureaucracy – ..' (Chubb and Moe, 1990: 167). The autonomy of public schools is subverted by administrative controls of the educational programs, and by restrictive and union-dominated personnel policies.

Could public management be improved by sheltering the service providing institutions from political influence, and by deregulating public service provision? First, allocative effectiveness requires that electoral demands are transformed into management decisions. The elected politicians are the major instrument through which this ambition can be reached. Sheltering the service providing agencies from elected influence may easily impair effectiveness. Second, laws and regulations restrict managerial discretion. Yet, the recent experience with deregulation demonstrates that rules serve a legitimate purpose. For example, the abolishment of service quality standards, or the relaxation of criteria for the distribution of services would not necessarily comply with citizens' preferences.

10. CONCLUSIONS

There is scope for efficiency improvement in the public sector, and that institutional factors affect efficiency. Figure 2 summarizes the main findings, and offers some further observations about the six strategies discussed:

The first message derives from conventional welfare economics. When the conditions for market provision are sufficiently fulfilled, private production is more cost efficient than production by government agencies. This is not primarily due to public ownership, but stems from the contestability and competition of the market system. Lso the limitations follow from welfare economics. The public sector could perform better when production involves economies of scale, as illustrated by studies of the electricity and water industries. Asymmetrical information may enable private producers able to induce demand, and thereby overexpand of the supply. In these situations we find that privatization generates allocative inefficiency.

The second observation is that the 'soft' budget limit weakens efficiency. Top-down spending frames can improve efficiency, which is documented by studies of public hospitals. The professional units tend to maintain output with less resources. However, it is difficult to enforce strict budgetary frames. If budgetary growth is socially desirable, there is a tradeoff between efficiency and (allocative) effectiveness.

The third strategy is that of measuring performance. The government

Figure 2   *Assumed impact, potential implementation obstacles and potential side effects of efficiency strategies*

PROPOSITION	ASSUMED IMPACT	IMPLEMENTATION PROBLEMS	SIDE EFFECTS
H$_1$: Let public and private producers compete to deliver public services	Public agencies improve efficiency at the market level level	Limited to certain types of services	Allocative effectiveness (supplier induced demands
H$_2$: Establish 'hard' budgetary limits	Improves cost consciousness, and cost efficiency	Hard to establish credible frames	Impairs allocative effectiveness (cost constrained output)
H$_3$: Implement performance measurement	Information about efficiency improves performance	Performance measures are controversial	The costs of appraising outputs and outcomes
H$_4$: Reward agencies according to performance	Incentives spur efforts to improve efficiency	Outcome uncertainty Inadequate measurement	Undermines the norms of the civil service
H$_5$: Constrain the administrative component	Lower administrative while maintaining output	The 'privileged' position of administrative executive	Undersizing of the administrative component
H$_6$: Induce a more active leadership by deregulating service supply and by reducing political interference	Efficiency improvement by a committed and professional public management	Opposition from unions, professional groups and interest organizations	Impairs allocative effectiveness, quality standards, and distributing criteria

managers have weaker incentives to improve efficiency than business managers. Information about the performance of comparable agencies encourages all of the agencies to improve their achievements. Information systems and the regular assessment of outputs and resources enhance comparisons and competition within the public household, which in turn promotes efficiency. The essential question is therefore not whether performance measurement promotes efficiency. The question is one of feasibility. Measurements are often controversial in the sense that some aspects are difficult to quantify, particularly the quality aspects of public services. There is also the question whether a full-scale measurement is economically feasible.

The fourth hypothesis is that of rewarding performance. Efficiency should be stimulated by a price contract. This yields better results that the lump sum appropriations and the top-down monitoring of behavior. If output can be measured, and if output results from agents' efforts rather than exogenous factors, the output-based contract is preferable. The lack of performance or output based incentive schemes are, to a considerable extent, justified by the intrinsic characteristics of public activity. A potential side-effect of this strategy is the abolishment of a modest and committed civil service culture.

The fifth argument is that bureaucratization subverts efficiency. Administrative slack accumulates due to the problems of monitoring administrative performance, and due to the 'privileged' power position of top-managers in government agencies. The fact that administrators have the dual position of producers and advisers put the elected representatives in a difficult position. They may suspect that administration is oversized, but lack the guidelines for determining the optimal amount. Finally, this chapter suggests that inefficiency is due to a lack of active leadership, and that public management must be spurred by greater professional discretion and protection from *ad hoc* political initiatives. Yet, even this strategy faces formidable implementation problems. This approach affects the basic values of democratic governance, and important stakeholders are likely to protest. Deregulation may weaken legitimate concerns for quality standards, and cause a less equitable distribution of scarce public resources.

If there is a general lesson in all of this, it is the need for differentiated reform (cf. Dwons and Larkey, 1986; Premchand, 1987). Sweeping statements about public sector strategies ignore the fact that public institutions provide vastly different services, and that they seek to achieve dissimilar outcomes. All reform proposals have limited applicability and they generate side-effects. We should reject universal approaches to public sector reforms, and seek a combination of strategies that adapt to local and practical problems.

Notes

1 This proposition is in agreement with the figures of Table 1. Public consumption and public employment takes about the same share of GNP and total employment. Note that about 20–25 percent of public provision of goods and services in the OECD-countries are purchased from the private sector (Oxley, 1991).

2 See for example the interpretations of the annex to the Swedish government long-term plan of 1987 (Bilage 21 till Långtidsutredningen, 1987).

3 Recent studies of US hospitals are based on the DEA-approach (Data Envelopment Analysis). These analyses indicate that public hospitals are more efficient that private hospitals (see, for example, Valdmanis (1992)).

4 This conclusion does not take into account efficiency losses due to heterogenous preferences in a system of regulated standards of quality and quantity. Neither does in consider the impact of a tax-financing versus a private, insurance based system of finance. The former induces an excess burden due to a lower overall production. It has been estimated that moving an additional dollar from the private to the public sector

reduces GNP by about 20 percent (Pauly, 1992). These effects favour the US system of health care.

5 The number of refereed articles in international journals may serve as a measure of research output in the University sector. This gives an indication of quality and quantity in research (Kyvik, 1991). Using such indicators as the only criterion for evaluating research may generate perverse incentives, i.e. it may motivate easily printable articles by mainstream methods and conventional approaches.

PUBLIC ADMINISTRATION, REGULATION, DEREGULATION AND REREGULATION

Vincent Wright

The basic purpose of this chapter is to attempt to answer two broad questions: what are the major problems currently confronting public regulators and, more especially, those in the public administration? to what extent have these regulators converged in their responses to the problems? The chapter opens with a brief look at the various dimensions of regulation in order to underline the extent, the diversity and complexity of regulatory activity (I). It then turns to an examination of the traditional instruments and style of regulation to show the wide and contrasting variety of experiences (II). An account follows of the various pressures which have been reshaping the regulatory environment since the early 1980s – pressures which have singularly complicated the task of the regulators. (III) After outlining the current problems and dilemmas of administrative regulators (IV), the chapter directly addresses the question of convergence (V).

THE REGULATORY JUNGLE

Regulation is 'a notoriously contested concept'(Hancher and Moran, 1989) – a concept which has different connotations on both sides of the Atlantic and, indeed, on both sides of the English Channel. In Europe it is used to encompass a vast domain of legislation, governance and social control, whilst in the USA the concept is deployed in a more specific sense: 'it refers to sustained and focussed control exercised by a public agency over activities that are generally regarded as desirable to society.' (Majone, 1990) The French use of *réglementation* is intended to cover the entire juridical and normative framework which constrains public and private actors (see the brilliant essay by Chevallier, 1988) whilst their British neighbours fall between the narrow conception of the Americans and the all-embracing sense of the French.

In defining the relationships between public administration and regulation it is important to unravel its various strands. For Llewellyn, 'in the final analysis the role of regulation is to offset market failures which would work to the detriment of consumers if market mechanisms were allowed to operate unfettered' (Lewellyn, 1981). Whilst for Minick, 'regulation is the public administrative policing of a private activity with respect to a rule prescribed in the public interest' (Mitnick, 1980). Pelkmans and van Nie, on the other hand, define regulation as 'the interference of the government in the market sector by means of statutory requirements, relating to production processes, production factors and products.' (Perklmans and van Nie, 1985). But these definitions help little in attempting to disentagle the many-faceted activities of the adminsitrative agents of regulation. Hancher and Moran are more helpful in distinguishing between regulation as 'the making and enforcement of legal and administrative rules' on the one hand, or alternatively, regulation as 'system maintenance, a process of eliminating distortions or disequilibria' (Hancher and Moran, 1989: 129). Stephen Elkin, on the other hand, contrasts regulation as a method of achieving *efficiency* with regulation aimed at overall system stability (Elkin, 1986).

Given the focus of this chapter the first useful distinction is that between regulation which aims to correct economic failures of the market and that which is concerned with the social failures of the market (i.e. with non-economic goods produced 'inefficiently', provoking, for instance, discrimination against minorities or deprived regions). The two forms are, of course, linked. Indeed, one of the drives to economic deregulation were the allegedly heavy costs of social regulation: the exigencies of fairness and efficiency are not automatically met through regulation – one of the major problems confronting regulators. A second useful distinction for our purposes is that proposed by Kay and Vickers who distinguish between *structural regulation*, which determines which actors may engage in which activities (i.e. the number of actors and their qualifications), and *conduct regulation* concerned with how the actors behave in their chosen activity (Key and Vickers, 1988). Thus, structural regulation covers restriction on entry, single capacity rules, rules against individuals providing services without appropriate qualifications, whilst conduct regulation involves measures to protect against anti-competitive behaviour by monopolistic or dominant incumbent firms, price control or rate of return control. As a refinement on the above it is possible to denote three other forms of regulation: price and entry regulation of monopolistic industries, sectors or firms (railways, postal services, water industry); price and entry regulation in industries with competitive or potentially competitive structures (taxis, pharmacies which are regulated by licences); quality regulation which attempts to cover various kinds of other market failure problems (for instance, in environmental, health and workplace security regulation there is a plethora of activities ranging from occupational licensing and product safety standards to detailed health regulations). A final typology of regulation for our purposes would also distinguish between sectors: industrial, financial and professional. Whatever typology is chosen, it is clear that administrative agents are involved in an omnipresent, complex, multi-layered and overlapping set of activities of very diverse and potentially conflicting character.

It follows logically that deregulation also involves a range of diverse overlapping and potentially conflicting activities. And this has proved to be the case in practice. It has affected all sectors – industrial, financial and professional – and has taken many forms, ranging from the privatization and liberalization of public sector industries to a vast programme of 'debureaucratisation' – the easing or dismantling of rules, based on the principle that regulation should never create more intervention and compliance costs than are strictly necessary for the fulfilment of the objective being pursued.

It is important, therefore, to recognise that there are various forms of regulation, and regulation and that deregulation are not mutually exclusive. Indeed, one of the arguments of this chapter is that the administration is involved in an ever-changing game of regulation and deregulation because they impact upon each other in a dynamic and often unpredictable way.

THE TRADITIONAL INSTRUMENTS AND STYLE OF REGULATION

The nature and intensity of regulatory activity varied widely across countries and within each country across sectors. It is, therefore, highly misleading to make generalisation in comparing the 'regulatory culture' of the USA and European countries. Broad assertions, if correct, that the French state was *dirigiste* in its relations with industry and finance, that West Germany combined corporatism and market-orientation, that the United Kingdom and the US governments were generally 'hands-off' in those relations, and that Sweden and Austria were corporatist may capture some of the general style of regulation and provide vital clues about the total configuration of forces likely to be involved in the process of regulation (Schubert, 1988). But they tell us nothing about the precise role of the regulatory agencies. That France and Italy had very extensive public sectors and hence a potential for enhanced regulation reveals nothing about the complex and troubled relationship between the nationalized firms and their sponsoring ministry and the Treasury: in other words, the size of the public sector tells us nothing about the willingness or ability of the state administration effectively to control it. West Germany's market-orientation did not preclude heavy state interventionism in some sectors and a high degree of sectoral self-regulation in industry. The American free-market tradition did not prevent massive trade-distorting subsidies to industry and agriculture and a long tradition of detailed regulatory activity. Britain's 'hands-off' administrative culture was rooted in a willingness to entrust private agents with public service regulatory obligations: this was most noticeably the case in the City (see below).[1] But it was combined with a constant willingness to manipulate its extensive public sector in the pursuit of macro-economic objectives. Whatever the difficulties it would not be impossible to construct a continuum with, at one end, the loosely regulated Stock Exchange of Italy and at the other the tightly regulated (yet nominally private until 1981) steel industry of France.

Industrialized countries differed widely not only in their propensity to intervene. They differed, too, in the range of instruments at their disposal. Six major instruments of regulation may be identified:

– *nationalization*, involving direct state ownership of sectors characterised by universal service obligations, statutory prohibitions or restrictions on entry, the scrutiny of corporate strategies and investments, the setting of financial targets, the establishment of rates of return, and the control of borrowing and tariffs. Of course, the size, nature and autonomy of public enterprises differed greatly. Some European countries (notably Austria, France and Italy) had very extensive public sectors, parts of which belonged to the international competitive market, which were clearly instruments of industrial and macro-economic policy and which were heavily politicised. On the other hand, the USA and some European countries (Sweden, West Germany, Switzerland and the Netherlands) had relatively small public sectors;

– *hybridization* which took two major forms: mixed public-private ventures (for example, the *société d'économie mixte* in France), and self-regulation by groups – but within a tight statutory framework imposed by the state;

– *administrative* regulation of a functional (environmental protection) or purely sectoral nature, and performed by the Treasury, a central bank or a bureau of the appropriate sponsoring ministry. This form of regulation, which was particularly evident in states of the Napoleonic tradition with its emphasis on *tutelle*, shielded from judicial review and public scrutiny.

– *public agency* regulation, with agencies again being defined either functionally or sectorally. The USA, with its wide range of federal and state independent regulatory commissions (IRCs), has the longest and widest experience of this form of regulation. One of the most important IRCs, the Interstate Commerce Commission, dates from 1887, and continues to play a vital role in controlling prices, routes and service conditions of surface transportation companies. A number of important IRCs, including the Federal Communications Commission, the Securities and Exchange Commission and the Civil Aeronautics Board, go back to the New Deal period. These IRCs have wide-ranging legislative, judicial and executive powers. In Europe, it is possible to trace public agency regulators to long before it became fashionable to create them in the 1970s. However, few acquired the expertise, the powers, the autonomy or the flexibility of their American counterparts;

– *self-regulation*, either through the professional peak trade associations, chambers of commerce or of agriculture, or even exclusively private organizations (the so-called 'pigs' or private interest governments. One of the best examples of this form of regulation was the City of London which was governed rather like a 'gentlemen's club', with unspoken rules dictating entry and conduct. The professions – law, accountancy and medicine – also provide clear illustrations of self-regulation, with their restrictions on entry, advertising and fees;

– *regulation within private firms or groups*, a form which is common in major accounting and financial groups, and which is designed to ensure a strong competitive position by guaranteeing a quality higher than that demanded by the official regulator.

An examination of the traditional regulatory 'mix' across countries brings out the great variations: in the extent and nature of the public sector; in the role of corporatist semi-corporatist, meso-corporatist or private regulatory arrangements; in the legal framework of regulation; in the relative weight attached to indirect and direct forms of regulation. However, there are two common features of all country systems. Firstly, whatever the emphasis, each country had multiple instruments at its disposal: the public administration, far from holding a monopoly, was frequently a minor regulatory agent. Secondly, public administrators were involved at different, and potentially conflicting, levels of regulatory activity.

Perhaps the greatest contrast lay between the USA and European countries. This contrast was highlighted less by the absence of an extensive public sector in the USA (this was the case with several European countries) than by the heavily 'judicialized' American system of regulatory decision making. In Western Europe there was little reliance of judicial review in regulation: even in European states with heavily legal traditions in their administration there was a reluctance to have recourse to litigation as a normal method of regulation. A non-litigious industrial culture, the time and costs involved, and the availability of more politicised and more negotiated means combined to reduce the regulatory role of the courts in most West European countries.

The USA, with its emphasis on regulatory agencies and on the courts, differed, therefore, from European countries in its regulatory form and style. But it shared an important feature with those countries: the relationship between the regulators and the regulated was problem-ridden, even if the nature of the problems was not always comparable. In the USA the significant role played by the regulatory agencies raised profound political and constitutional issues relating to their status and accountability. Similarly, the self-regulatory role of corporatist bodies or professional associations (which frequently governed the entry, voice and exit of their members) provoked a debate about the transparency of their operations and the democratic legitimacy of their power. Furthermore, the two major forms of state regulation – through nationalization and administrative bureaux – were especially fraught with difficulties. At bottom this may have been a reflection of the inherent tensions between state and market, with the agents of each pursuing conflicting objectives. This was frequently the case with nationalized industries which were 'regulated' in a politicised manner, and became the instruments of wider, macro-economic, industrial, regional, social, and even politically partisan objectives. All too often they were saddled with shifting and inconsistent requirements. Alternatively, they were accused of having become 'states within the state', autonomous baronies ruled by managers who tolerated overmanning and inefficient work practices as the price of a quiet life with their powerful unions. If nationalized industries were defective tools of state regulation, so, too, were the administrative bureaux exercising *tutelle*. There was a gulf between the stable, ordered, hierarchical, formalized, bureaucratized world of the public official and the unstable and unpredictable universe of the businessman. In many countries, public officials lived 'a monastic existence', cut off from the world they administered. They were, moreover, often imbued with objectives and a general ethos which was totally at odds with most of the business community. Certainly, there was very little interchange of personnel: top public officials in some countries, such as France, might occasionally be seduced into the private sector, but businessmen were very rarely enticed into public administration. The tensions between state and market actors were to be accentuated during the 1980s.

THE CHANGING REGULATORY ENVIRONMENT

Several changes since the early 1980s have served singularly to complicate the task of public officials as market regulators. Some of these changes have squeezed them towards convergent responses.

The first change relates to the intellectual and ideological climate. Since the economic crisis of the mid-1970s the West has indulged in a far-reaching debate about the proper relationship between state and market. At the centre of this debate is the issue of regulation, triggered by an assessment of the relative costs of government and of market-regulation failure. This issue has raised fundamental and inter-related questions about the motives and the outcomes of state regulation. Apologists for regulation continue to point to the persistent need to remedy various kinds of market failure or imperfections (monopoly power abuse, externalities, asymmetric information, destructive competition when firms sell products below cost price) or to ensure certain social goods (services for the disabled or for rural areas) and they claim that in certain sectors (notably banking and financial services) regulation has been efficient because it has provided confidence and predictability. Critics of regulation, on the other hand, have argued that state failures have far outweighed market failures, have claimed that the private sector is intrinsically more efficient than the public sector, have criticised the inability of insensitive and ignorant state bureaucrats to appreciate the complexities of the market place, have denounced the heavy administrative, monitoring and compliance costs, and, more importantly have questioned 'the logic of collective action' (i.e. the outcome of the interplay of individualised 'rational' activities may produce 'irrational' or sub-optimal outcomes for the community).

A series of inefficiencies – technical, internal or X-inefficiency, allocative and innovative – are attributed to the heavy hand of the regulators. For the critics inefficient outcomes must be sought in the initial motives and in the structures of regulation. The Public Choice School sees regulation as the result not of the will of politicians or the attempt to translate into practice some abstract notion of the public good, but rather as the consequence of the pressure of strategically-placed interest groups on compliant bureaucracies. From Stigler to Olson there has been a constant critique of the ill-effects of this situation. Allied to this is the theory of 'capture', based on the closed and collusive relationship between regulator and regulated, which was popularized by Stigler and diffused by others of the Chicago School. However, doubtful their empirical underpinning (the weight of evidence suggests that regulation may maximise the achievement of the interests of many groups, and agencies are not automatically captured – they are responsive, in varying degrees, to wishes of political principal) the ideas of the Chicago School were unquestionably influential in the 1980s. They had a strong normative bias, and fed wider controversies about democratic accountability, individual freedom and equality. They were taken up by neo-liberals seeking a rationale for their policies and by groups searching for a legitimising discourse in pressing governments for 'regulatory relief'.

The second major change in the regulatory environment has been the change of heart of many governments towards some traditional forms of regulation. Not only Reagan's America or Thatcher's Britain were sceptical about the role of the state in the regulation the economy. The economic crisis of the mid-1970s provoked a debate not only about state intervention but more specifically about the efficiency and cost of traditional regulatory tools. Under pressure from 'modernising coalitions' other governments, to a greater or lesser extent, have also attempted to withdraw the state from the economic sphere: deregulation, marketisation, liberalization and privatization have been pursued with varying degrees of enthusiasm by almost all governments – either overtly or covertly. It is important to note that deregulation and privatization in one country often has the effect of squeezing or enticing other countries into similar policies. Thus the deregulation of air transport in the USA had an immediate impact across the Atlantic, whilst the 'demonstration effort' of the British privatization programme was to be felt throughout Europe.

For the regulators several interconnected consequences have flowed form this 'state withdrawal'. Firstly, there has been a widespread disenchantment with the public sector as an effective regulatory tool: inefficient, captured by politicians (because the patronage system or) powerful unions, inflexible. There has been a reduction in the state industrial sector in most countries, but particularly in Britain which has disposed of most of the sector, including 'strategic' industries and public utilities such as telecommunications, water, electricity and gas. Secondly, even in those countries without a radical privatization programme there is a greater awareness of the limits of nationalisation as an effective instrument of regulation: indeed even socialist governments in France and Spain have underlined their limitations by granting far greater autonomy to public sector managers by encouraging them to act as if they were private entrepreneurs. From the mid-1980s we witness, therefore, a reshaping of the relationship between the nationalised industries and their sponsoring ministries. Whilst this should not be exaggerated – state officials continue to interfere in the decisions of these industries (as in France and Italy) – the tendency is undeniable, and has led to a loosening of direct state regulatory leverage.

The third major consequence of state retreat has been the progressive dismantling, through administrative regulation, of a vast panoply of controls and constraints, (for example, currency exchange, planning regulations and prices) The consequences are far reaching. Thus, financial market deregulation which has swept the world, had had the effect of abolishing, or drastically easing, exchange controls, thus facilitating the free flow of capital. It has also, and more immediately, led to the abolition of fixed commissions and of single capacity the separation of broking and jobbing as well as to the dissolving of traditional frontiers in financial institutions and the creation of financial supermarkets. Thus, major banks diversified, often unwisely, by buying up stockbrokers and jobbers with a view to dealing in equities and gilt-edged government securities. Insurance companies have taken to lending money, and banks to selling insurance policies. Even retail supermarkets are now involved in insurance and banking activities. This lowering of the barriers between traditionally segregated financial sectors ('decompartmentalisation') threatens to produce conflicts of interest between interlocking markets within the financial conglomerates. Governments are increasingly worried about the danger of 'chaotic competition' which destabilize markets, as well as about new market distortions, with dominant actors intent of restricting competition – and this has heightened the need for new forms of regulation. Since the late 1980s there has even been a spate of marriages between banks and insurance companies (what the Germans can *Allfinanz* and the French *bancassurance*). An even greater challenge to regulators has been the growth of off-balance sheet activities (the global market in financial derivatives such as swaps and options) and the nature of credit, price and settlement risk they entail. Regulators are keen but not always able to monitor these operations closely.

In most countries we see a tightening of the regulatory framework and the creation or strengthening of regulatory agencies. Thus, in the UK, there has been a move to more statutory regulation of the City and away from the self-regulation of the gentlemen's club – particularly when a series of scandals demonstrated that some of the gentlemen were capable of very ungentlemanly behaviour.

Deregulation has, therefore, sometimes called forth reregulation (Khoury, 1990). So, too, have certain forms of privatization. The problem has been particularly acute when the privatized industries hold, or threaten to hold, oligopolistic or monopolistic positions. This is especially the case in the United Kingdom which simply transferred the great public utilities of gas, electricity and telecommunications into the private sector with their monopolistic positions virtually or totally intact. As a result, new regulatory agencies such as OFTEL, OFGAS and OFWAT had to be created. The early evidence suggests that they are beginning to interfere in the life of their industries much more than the sponsoring ministries ever dared to do in the operations of the nationalised industries, and relations between the regulatory watch dogs and the privatized industries have been characterised by persistent bouts of ill-tempered public exchanges. Each of the regulatory agencies has sought to expand its control, each has sought to obtain greater information, each has not hesitated to mobilise outside support in its struggle with its respective privatized industry. Curiously, therefore, deregulation in one respect has merely led to reregulation in another: loose structural regulation has been replaced by tighter conduct regulation.

The third major pressure which is recasting the regulatory environment is the *increase* in the role of the state, but not as producer of goods and services which has decreased. Rather, this increase relates to the state's role as protector of the consumer and of the environment – previously neglected areas. In some countries deregulating the labour market is some aspects (over, for example, flexibility) has been accompanied by heightened regulation in others (e.g. over participation and redundancy). In many cases, deregulation and reregulation have been part of the bargained compromises. Since the 1980s there have, therefore, been very conflicting pressures at work: different modes of regulation have been triggered by new demands and by deregulation.

The fourth major pressure for change, which is linked to the previous ones, lies in the changing nature of the policy environment since the mid-1980s. This is not the place to indulge in a debate on corporatism, neo-corporatism, meso-corporatism – whether or not it ever existed and, if it did, whether it was a phenomenon of pre-oil crisis Western Europe. Suffice to note that, for a variety of reasons, ranging from financial squeeze to stock exchange scandals, there has been a greater reluctance on the part of governments to rely on some of the actors who traditionally formulated and delivered public policy, including regulating much of the sectors to which they belonged. The Thatcher and Reagan governments were not the only ones to dismantle some of the comfortable and collusive relationships which had grown up between the state and certain social and economic groups – many of whom were committed to the market-distorting *status quo*. The economic policies of many other governments since the mid-1980s have required the elimination or marginalisation from the decision-making process of previously significant groups as well as the mobilisation of new coalitions. Whilst corporatist-style self-regulation persists everywhere in Western Europe, it would appear to be less prevalent than in the 1950s and 1960s.

The fifth complicating pressure for the regulators has been the accelerating pace of the internationalization of financial and industrial circuits. Exchange controls have largely been abolished and stock exchanges have been opened to foreign firms and investors. No less significantly, international securities trading has exploded since the 1980s, leaving regulators, notably the International Organization of Securities Commission (IOSCO) ill-equipped to deal with a rapidly changing market (Khourgh, 1990: 226). The consequences cannot be overstated. For instance, major multinational conglomerates have highly diversified activities which span the responsibilities of several national regulatory agencies. The traditional problem of fragmentation of regulation has, therefore, been accentuated. Many companies are listed on several stock exchanges (the London's screen-based market) where regulations listing requirements, treatment of minority shareholders, takeover bids may vary widely. Indeed, respecting the rules of one stock exchange may involve the violation of the rules of another.

Internationalization, coupled with liberalization, poses in acute form, the problem of *extra-territoriality*. There is a need for international regulatory co-operation to combat international cartels (uranium), conspiracies against competition (the Laker affair), insider dealings, money laundering and financial fraud (the BCCI affair). At present, there is some cooperation (see below) but also overlap and not a little conflict. One of the basic problems is that there is sometimes a premium for domestic regulators not to cooperate, for a common regulatory framework may harm home-based firms.

There has also been an internationalization of some politically sensitive problems, because of severe externality problems: pollution provides the best example. Cross-border or international regulatory activity is crucial but immensely difficult to achieve because of potentially disproportionate compliance costs.

The Europeanization of many industrial and financial activities presents the sixth major pressure on regulators. The emergence of European-level industrial and financial actors together with the internally-driven regulatory interventions of the Commission raise complex problems about the level at which regulation should take place (Neumann et al., 1984). European-wide regulation flows quite logically from competition policy – itself rooted in liberalization and the unification of the internal market. Thus, the drive to create an EC-wide market in banking and related services requires the definition of a coherent framework embracing regulatory issues such as the capital adequacy of banks, ownership, rules of market access and contestability. Regulatory harmonization and attempts to ensure the mutual recognition of rules has a direct and obvious impact on domestic regulators. National governments, not unnaturally, negotiate regulatory issues in the light of their own interests: hence the conflicts over reciprocity led by the United Kingdom, or the stonewalling of the Germans over insurance. Yet pressure from the Court, the Commission and some member States on certain issues has led to an undoubted spread of European-level regulation – presenting domestic regulators, and not only in the Community, with new and highly complex challenges.

The seventh major pressure which has affected the role of the regulators has been the changing nature of the corporate structures of major firms. Large multinational firms have developed complex internal markets, in an attempt to minimize costs and maximise the economies of scale. Such firms, aided by new technologies, may transfer capital across national boundaries without any recourse to national officialdom.

The eighth major pressure which has had a real impact on the task of the regulators has been changing technology. To explore all its ramifications would require a chapter in itself. Two examples may be cited to illustrate its significance. Firstly, technological innovation unquestionably facilitates integrated global trading in the financial markets: technological change and liberalization are integrally linked. Second, technological change has altered the fundamental nature of some industries, transforming single-product monolithic natural monopolies into multi-product, fragmented and unnatural ones: the case of telecommunications comes to mind. One of the principal arguments for nationalisation – the need to supervise a natural monopoly, and one cited by the governments of Italy, France and the market-loving Germans – has sometimes been removed by technological innovation. In a very direct way, therefore, its consequences for regulation were quickly felt. The final pressure on the regulators has been the growing political pressure for greater transparency in decisionmaking. This has caused problems in countries such as Britain and France with their administrative 'culture of secrecy' and in highly corporate countries used to binding agreements between elites. This pressure has been accompanied by the growing demand in some countries to depoliticise regulatory decisionmaking. Traditional American arguments in favour of independent regulatory agencies have found an echo in many European countries which have created such agencies. In Britain, bodies such as the Independent Broadcasting Authority, the Civil Aviation Authority, the Commission for Racial Equality and to the Equal Opportunities Commission were creatures of the 1970s. Elsewhere in Europe, independent regulatory agencies were created rather later. France, with its long tradition of *tutelle*, began creating such commissions in the late 1970s: by 1993 there were seventeen including the Commission Bancaire, the Commission des Opérations de Bourse and the Commission de Controle des Assurances.

To summarize, deregulation, liberalization, privatization, increased concern for consumer and environmental rights, the globalization of industry and finance, the internationalization of certain issues, changing

corporate structures, technological innovation and political pressures – all interconnected in mutually reactive fashion – have remodelled the regulatory environment. In this new environment there has been:
– a weakening of regulatory control through traditional public ownership and state regulatory instruments;
– a need for reregulation in some sectors;
– a requirement to regulate new sectors;
– a change in the nature of regulation to a somewhat more indirect form;
– a growing mismatch between national modes of regulation and the internationalized and Europeanised actors and problems to be regulated.
– a reshaping of the policy communities involved in regulation;
– a persistence in the ambiguous behaviour of governments, keen to promote regulation at the domestic level, but often reluctant to do at the international level in order to protect their own industrial and financial concerns.
In short, in the age of deregulation the need for regulation or reregulation has in no way diminished, it has merely become more complex and difficult.

PROBLEMS AND DILEMMAS OF PUBLIC ADMINISTRATIVE REGULATION

There are inherent tensions in the relationship between regulatory administrations and their clients. The source of these tensions lies in the role, the structure, the culture and the general ethos of public administration.

Traditionally understood, public administration was government administration, and it was forged by a number 'elaborative theories' (Hood, 1990: 108–9):

– *executive government performs well when policy responsibilities are monopolized by a single and accountable bureau.* However, regulation has never been monopolized by a single and accountable bureau. Rather, there has always been a proliferation of administrative agents, often pursuing conflicting objectives (conflicts between finance ministries, central banks and sponsoring ministries have always been endemic). This is unavoidable. Thus, regulating any particular industry necessarily involves officials from the sponsoring ministry and the finance ministry as well as from the health, the environment and the trade ministries. The regulation of a multinational enterprise or even national multi-product conglomerate requires the mobilisation of officials from several ministries.

– *executive government is organized most efficiently in hierarchical style, with one person responsible at each level of oversight.* However, regulation is organized by multiple ill-coordinated agencies, with overlapping and often imprecise or ambiguous jurisdictions.

– *'good government' is most effectively achieved by life-time career officials.* This is an area requiring empirical research, but the evidence suggests

that most administrative bureaux responsible for regulation are characterized by great instability, with many officials viewing their bureau as
merely a temporary step in their career progression.

– *'democratic' government hinges on drawing lines between policy and administration: ministers decide, officials implement.* But, regulation is an area in
which it is intrinsically difficult to draw distinctions between the political
and the administrative spheres. The uncertainty of the boundary presents a problem everywhere. 'Who regulates the regulators?' is a question
increasingly asked in the USA, and goes to the heart of the issue of
democratic accountability. The problem, is compounded by the profound
schizophrenia which characterizes politicians' views on regulation. Many
of the latter will the end but baulk at the means: this may be seen in their
attitude to certain powerful producer groups which resist regulation.
It may also be seen in their postures at EC level where they indulge
in the rhetoric of regulation for enhancing competition but provided it
does not harm their home industries. In other words, far from providing
a relatively stable and predictable set of policy objectives for regulators,
politicians put them under cross pressure and obfuscate their objectives. It
should be pointed out that this ambivalence is shared by many domestic
regulators themselves: they are not unaware of the political consequences
of their regulatory activities and they are also sensitive ot the need to
maintain the stability of the market they are regulating.

– *sound administration requires not only good management techniques but also
planning and specialization.* Here, we touch upon a particularly acute problem for the administration. Predictability and planning may shape the
normative universe of the public official but they are not the most obvious
features of the modern market place. Furthermore, the specialization of
the administration is rarely directly related to the workings of private
business or finance. Public officials are often particularly ignorant of private sector processes – and by recruitment and training they are unlikely
to acquire the necessary knowledge. More importantly, the degree of specialization of public regulators rarely provides them with the kind of data
they require to carry out their monitoring work effectively. Most administrative regulatory bureaux are over-worked and understaffed, and do
not have the time or ability to acquire access to vital information. Hence,
the problem if asymmetric information which so exercises observers of
the regulatory scene. At its most extreme, lack of knowledge completely
incapacitates the administration: combating insider trading, for instance,
is an 'unwinnable war'. It also points to the fact that regulators, for
bureaucratic reasons, may tolerate cartels (the case of the Bank of England
the banking cartel in the 1960s and 1970s) with which it has built up a cosy
relationship.

– *public administration is national state administration which functions within
identifiable,* if not always stable territorial boundaries. Yet, to emphasise a
point which is made above, regulation is becoming increasingly extrater-
ritorial in character.

– effective administration requires drawing a line between public and private interests. Indeed, the culture of the civil servants of some countries is embedded in a philosophy of the need to protect the 'public interest' against particularist private interests, whilst in other countries, officials have a 'monastic tradition' built on the need to ensure distance form the private clients they service. However, regulation frequently totally erases the conventional divisions between public and private spheres; public bodies such as sponsoring ministries routinely represent special interests whilst formally private bodies such as trade associations frequently carry out public service obligations in the implementation of particular regulations. The intermeshing of public and private spheres does not imply inevitable 'capture', as argued by Bernstein (1955), although the danger is ever present, but it does require constant exchange, bargaining and compromise – and even a degree of compliance and collusion.

Some of the problems confronting administrative regulators have already been mentioned – for example, the fact that they have generally to compete with other regulators; that they have vague and often conflicting objectives (social and economic aims, fairness and efficiency, competition and stability); that the increase in the number of independent regulatory agencies is causing problems of democratic accountability; that measuring the costs of social regulation is intrinsically difficult because it is frequently a normative and essentially political exercise.

Regulators have internalised many of the conflicting objectives and the constraints inherent in regulation: environmental regulators are aware of the employment implications of their decisions; economic regulators realize that their policies may lead to an expansion of the black economy; financial regulators understand the impact of their regulation on the international competitive position of their banks. Regulators are, therefore, locked into a profound persistent and uncomfortable ambivalence.

This section brings out some of the other problems. Firstly, there is the need to adjust inflexible and bureaucratized administrative attitudes and structures to the requirements of regulation, with its emphasis on trade-offs and bargaining. In many cases, it is no longer a question of imposing the rules but of seeking a negotiated compromise. Some administrative systems and officials are more flexible than others, as attitudinal studies have shown. However, too great a degree of flexibility could lead to 'capture'. This problem is aggravated by that of asymmetric information, since regulators may trade off information for a less rigorous pursuit of regulatory objectives. Secondly, administrative regulators belong to a fragmented and ill-coordinated world. Often they take decisions in their own sphere which have spill-over effects on other spheres. They become dependent, therefore, on other regulators whose goodwill or cooperation is far from ensured. Thirdly, the spill-over effect of a decision within a particular sector may be felt in another unregulated part of the same sector. This can easily lead to extending regulation to the previously unregulated part (the case of OFTEL, the watchdog of the British telecommunications industry, is highly instructive in this respect). The mismatch between internationalized regulatory problems and nationally-based agents presents the fourth major problem.

The relationship between 'the administrative system' and the regulated has, therefore, always been a peculiarly complex one: they are separate in some important respects (there is little or no interchange of personnel, their patterns of authority and work methods differ widely) yet they are locked into an interdependence based on the sharing of responsibilities and resources. The traditional administrative system fits uneasily in an environment marked by overlapping jurisdictions between multiple actors, representing a hybrid of public and private institutions, with unclear lines of authority, and fudged and often conflicting policy goals.

CONVERGENCE

In some important respects the political, economic, financial and technological pressures of the 1980s and 1990s have left the administrative regulatory landscape untouched. Some of its traditional features persist and have, in some cases, been somewhat accentuated. The administration remains fragmented, ill-coorindated, ill-equipped and often ill-informed, competing with a host of other regulatory agencies, sometimes of a private nature, sometimes placed outside the country, and it has to contend with ambiguous, incoherent and inconsistent state regulatory policies. The BCCI affair and the clutch of scandals on the London and New York Stock Exchanges and the Bourse underline the inadequacy of existing regulatory instruments.

Common pressures and similar problems continue to be mediated in each state through strong institutional forces within the politico-administrative system, ensuring certain continuities, persistent exceptionalism and perhaps even divergence – especially in policy styles; the looseness or even absence of regulatory arrangements in Greece and Italy; the reliance on private agents in certain sectors, notably the City, in the United Kingdom; the omnipresence of the *Trésor* in France; the recourse to corporatist-style regulation in Germany; the importance of the courts in the USA.

Yet there are discontinuities compared with the 1960s and 1970s, some of which are leading to convergence. A flurry of activity, perhaps unprecedented in its scope and intensity, has reshaped the regulatory environment: there are new objectives, new rules, new or modified instruments and sometimes even new outcomes and new styles. Examples about, and several have already been mentioned: new *objectives* which are more market and consumer sensitive; new *rules* for banking, stock exchanges and key sectors such as telecommunications have been introduced everywhere.

Scepticism (even on the Left) towards the traditional *instruments* of regulation through public ownership has been accompanied by the creation of new (e.g. the utility watchdogs in the United Kingdom), or the reshaping of old (e.g. the various stock exchange regulatory agencies everywhere) instruments; new *outcomes* include more effective international efforts to regulate the Third World debt crisis and the attempts, not always successful, to stabilize currencies (most notably in the EC), limited policies designed to harmonize the regulation of capital markets and a greater drive at EC level to regulate a range of sectors; new *styles* may be illustrated by the less consensual, less socially-exclusive, less personalized system aof financial market regulation in the United Kingdom and the less explicitly interventionist habits of the French administration.

When turning to the question of convergence, analytical problems are numerous (Bennet, 1991):

- during which time span? Clearly, the point of departure becomes critical;
- convergence towards what? A common pre-conceived goal based on a mutually-agreed end? An exogenously-driven move towards a dominant model?
- convergence in what respect? Policy convergence may mean one of five things: convergence in policy *goals*; convergence in policy *content* (statutes, rules, regulations, court decisions); in policy *instruments* – the institutional tools of formulation, formalization, legitimation, implementation and evaluation; convergence in policy *outcomes* – the results of implementation; convergence in policy styles – the methods by which public policy is processed (consensual or conflictual, incremental or rational, anticipatory or reactionary, corporatist or pluralist). It is perfectly possible to have convergence in one respect and not in the other: thus, convergent policy objectives may be implemented by strikingly dissimilar policy instruments and styles – the case in point in the area of financial regulation when countries such as the United Kingdom and Italy are compared. And, apparently different policy instruments may disguise convergent goals and objectives (Brickman, Jasanoff and Ilgen, 1985; Bennett, 1988): the student of comparative public policy has constantly to search for functional equivalents.

It has been argued (Bennett, 1988) that convergence may come about by essentially four processes, and all four may be discerned in the case of regulation:

- *convergence through emulation*: most public policy, it is alleged, is imitative: it builds on the experience of models – real or supposed – borrowed from overseas, and nowhere is this more true than in the field of regulation (Llewellyn, 1988).
- *convergence through elite networking* – either of an official or unofficial nature. One of the striking features of sectors such as the international civil aviation policy community is the existence of an elite which constantly exchanges information and helps set regulatory standards.

Loose networks of professionals and academics have been the diffusers – albeit unwitting on occasions – of regulatory models.
- *convergence through harmonization* as the result of interdependence. Examples would include the bilateral and multilateral agreements at the international banking level, such as the 1987 agreement by all the leading industrial nations to ensure that by the end of 1992 all their banks would maintain capital at least equal to 8 per cent of their assets, weighted according to risk. It was signed by Belgium, Canada, France, Germany, Italy, Japan, the Netherlands, Sweden, the United Kingdom, the USA, Switzerland and Luxembourg. The committee on banking supervision of the Bank for International Settlements in Basle is vigorously pursuing plans to strengthen consolidated supervision to cope with the growing number of diversified financial companies that include banks. It is, of course, at the EC level that convergence through harmonization and the more flexible form of mutual recognition is most marked. Key sectors – agriculture, telecommunications, transport, energy, banking – have come under supranational regulation.[2] However limited, inadequate and ignored (Italy has yet to implement a 1976 insurance directive ...) the process may be, it has had a profound effect on national systems of regulation.
- *convergence through penetration*: convergence is often imposed by the pursuit by a dominant country of a set of policies which other countries are, in practice, obliged to adopt: American policies of deregulating telecommunications and financial markets provide a good illustration of the phenomenon (Hill, 1986).

To conclude, the homogenising, pressures of the 1980s and 1990s have produced convergence in the challenges to be met, in some of the tactics and strategies adopted and in many of the policies implemented. There has been some convergence in the policy instruments and style of regulation though mainly of a negative sort (less reliance on nationalized instruments). Whether or not there has been institutional convergence of a positive sort can be shown only by probing behind apparently dissimilar institutions to evaluate their functions. By analysing, over a twenty year period, the regulation of a sector, the activities of a set of regulatory agencies in a sector (the SIB, the COB and the CONSOB, for example), or the treatment of a particular problem (insider dealing, for instance) we may more effectively explore the relationship between institutional forms and public policy-making, as well as the vexed question of the convergence of the relationship in Western Europe.

Notes

1 There is a useful literature on regulating the City of London. See, notably, M. Clarke, *Regulating the City: Competition, Scandal and Reform*, Milton Keynes, 1986; M. Reid, *All-Change in the City: the Revolution in Britain's Financial Sector*, London, 1988.
2 *The Harmonization of European Public Policy: Regional Responses to Transnational Challenges,*

L. Hurwitz (ed.), Newport, Conn., 1983; P. Cullen and G.N. Yannopoulos, 'The redistribution of regulatory powers between Governments and international organizations; the case of Euorpean airline deregulation', in *European Journal of Political Research*, 17, 1989, 155–168; A. Liberatore, 'Problems of transnational policymaking: Environmental policy in the European Community', in *European Journal of Political Research*, 19, 1991, 281–305; P.A. Vipond, 'The liberalization of capital movements and financial services in the European single market: a case sutdy in regulation, in *European Journal of Political Research*, 19, March–April, 1991, 227–244; J. Erdmenger, *The European Community Transport Policy*, Aldershot, 1983; P. Montagnon, 'Regulating the Utilities', in P. Montagnon, *European Competition Policy*, London, 1990, 52–75.

17

BUDGET GAMES ARE READY FOR REFORM

Aaron Wildavsky

By now one would think that budgeting was a big bore: the same game being played in the same stultified way by the same team under the same rules with the same outcome – the central treasury always loses. There are only two sides, spenders and savers. The spenders are literally what their name suggests, executive branch agencies whose purpose it is to provide more aid to those who presumably benefit from their programs. Thus the people in society who actually get to spend the money are not unnaturally called beneficiaries while those who supply these funds are, as we have seen, called spenders. This alliance between spending departments and their client beneficiaries is at the heart of contemporary budget politics and, because of its extraordinary sameness, budget boredom: everyone knows what is coming (spenders want more money for their clients, savers less) but, out of embarrassment, pretends it's all new.

'Savers' have an institutional home, finance ministries or treasury departments in parliamentary systems, an Office of Management and Budget or Bureau of the Budget in presidential systems. Their task is to keep spending down or at least within revenues or within a modest deficit as a proportion of gross domestic product (or some such measure of national economic product). Thus they are the nay-sayers of the budget process.

Budget ritual is as formalized as any court etiquette. The spenders, taking care to spend up to and a bit beyond the previous year's appropriation to show need, ask for incrementally more than they received. The savers cut back this bid below the asking price, but above actual spending outlays. Thus the two budget roles are performed successfully, the spenders by getting to spend more and the savers by marking down, as it were, the spenders' mark-ups.

Each budget strategist also counters the other's moves. When spenders thrust with the coercive deficiency, by deliberately running out of money for purposes widely regarded as essential, like completing a road or feeding children, savers counter with quarterly or monthly apportionments to control the pace of spending. When spenders attach their activities to whatever good is going – national defense, the environment, ending poverty – savers argue that the deficit is destroying the country, that it is more important to tax more and spend less than to serve these other subordinate purposes.

The steps in this budget minuet are well choreographed; each side can anticipate the moves the others will make while fully expecting the other to anticipate its own moves. Why, we may ask, has this stereotyped game persisted so long? Why do the players persist with the pretense? What sustains this game? And why are both players and spectators now tired of it?

INCREMENTALISM

The game of incremental budget moves, as described in the 1964 first edition of *The Politics of the Budgetary Process*, was based on assumptions deeply buried in the practices of the time, so deeply buried, indeed, that I had to undertake historical reconstruction in order to resurrect them (Webber and Wildavsky, 1986; Wildavsky, 1983). (By incrementalism, I mean a regular pattern of relationships between spenders and savers as well as modest percentage changes from year-to-year (Dempster and Wildavsky, 1979). The budgetary base is the product of repeated interactions during which expectations arise and are maintained as to the level of funding).

The assumptions of budget incrementalist practice may be approached by asking what would render its practices inoperative. Basically, economic growth and public spending would have to keep within hailing distance of each other. If not, if spending leaped ahead or growth lagged behind, whichever, the result would be growing deficits that would either lead to calls for much greater taxation, which would make the practices unpopular, and might itself dampen economic growth by diverting resources from the private sector, or calls for draconian cuts in spending, unpopular and, due to their severity, exceedingly difficult to achieve. In short, it was the results of incremental budgeting, either budget balance or small deficits, that justified its practices in the eyes of practitioner and public alike. For balance meant all was well with the world. Balance meant that the system was working. Balance meant that savers and spenders were in balance and, as far as anyone knew, all was well with the world. But we know now that it wasn't and isn't. What happened?

In the past, through the 1930s and, in many places, the 1950s, most large expenditures were not recurrent. Governments might buy battleships but they did not keep buying them, at least not at the same pace. Social service schemes, medicare for the elderly, medicaid for the poor, and unemployment compensation (whatever the names under which they were known in the various Western, capitalist industrial democracies, including the social democracies of Scandinavia) broke their respective budgets. As populations grew and citizens aged, as they began to retire and suffer more from illness, and as the 'uptake' of those eligible and of benefits rose, entitlements outdistanced economic growth. Why did budget controls fail in regard to entitlements (programs in which everyone who qualifies has a right to payment), we may ask, whereas they apparently succeeded in regard to the rest of the budget?

It was well said in medieval times that a lender who loaned a king a little had a lot of control over his monarch; but a lender who loaned a lot had mortgaged himself to his king. By their regularity and automaticity, entitlements attracted tens of millions of beneficiaries. Maybe they were once grateful and dependent on government. Soon enough, public officials were dependent on them. It became easy to increase benefits and automatic cost of living adjustments. And it became difficult to reduce benefits and allow inflation to erode them.

Sharing in growth meant rising benefits; protection against inflation meant maintenance of purchasing power. Consequently, when economic growth stagnated or declined, the revenue base to support entitlements was inadequate.

If one asked the always important political question – Who will bear the costs of change? – the answer was not the citizen but the state. Unfortunately, this shifting of the burden of taxation proved unsatisfactory. Citizens felt that the state that was supposed to support them not only now but in the future was being improvident by running big deficits. Worse, the indulgent parental state was being cowardly by failing to impose limits on its children. If the state keeps each individual citizen stable, the question is, who will keep the collective, on which each of us depends, stable?

'Not me,' comes the cry from each and every interest group. As government grew in size and scope, the number and size of clientele groups dependent on government also grew. Consequently, in every cabinet the vast majority of ministeries (or secretaries, as they are called in the United States) favor spending. Within the executive branches of modern governments, spenders overwhelmingly outnumber savers.

Indeed, one of the most consistent relationships in all government is that central budget controllers (finance ministers and directors of OMB) always lose. Even when they win for a year or two, over time entitlements continue to grow. Why, then, realizing what is happening, do the various spending ministries whose collective fortunes are, after all, tied together, not change their behavior?

DEFICITS

In trying to answer this question, let us inquire into the view of burgeoning deficits held by conservative and progressive parties. Economic conservatives are outraged by big government and big spending. But they are politically too weak. When strong, as with Ronald Reagan as president of the United States, their preferred strategy is to cut tax rates so as to try to force spending down. If not, they will choose big deficits over big government.

Social conservatives abhor large deficits but they favor entitlements as demonstrating that existing institutions take care of their people. They are willing to impose fiscal discipline but have so far proved unwilling to impose it on entitlements. Yet they fear that large deficits (at, say, three to six percent of GDP) will lead to system failure or, nearly as bad, perception of system failure.

Progressive parties (European social democrats, American liberal Democrats) have suffered worst from large deficits. They used to like small deficits so as, in their view, to help secure full employment. But when Reagan showed them what a real, Marlboro man deficit was like, they realized some home truths. One of these is that big deficits drive out future Democratic party programs. Indeed, unless President Clinton seeks to and succeeds in slowing future entitlement increases, they will absorb all future resources, leaving no room for him to impose his and his party's imprint on government. Yet it is precisely his constituents who have most to lose from cuts in entitlements. What to do?

Turning to European social democracy, we find widespread support for the welfare state. If they could continue to borrow, they would not hesitate to incur larger and larger deficits. But they can't. Deficits cannot be incurred without willing lenders. Big debt encourages currency speculations to pick off weaker currencies, which in turn encourages Europeans to seek smaller deficits, a phenomenon now called, according to the provisions of the Maastricht protocols, budgetary convergence. Now that there is a common awareness of the importance of reducing deficits in the Western world, either because big deficits have bad effects or because they are wrongly but widely believed to do so (see White and Wildavsky, 1990), the question arises of what can be done to curb deficits? As the end of the cold war is resulting in much lower military spending (in the United States from 14 percent of GNP at the end of the Korean War in 1955 to 9 percent at the height of the cold war during Reagan's military buildup in 1983 to 5 percent and dropping now), the question is whether entitlements will be cut or revenues raised or both?

NEW RULES

My predictions follow: Bill Clinton will try to follow the European lead. *Rule one: means-tested entitlements,* that is, give to people with the lowest incomes, less or nothing to those with higher incomes. Hence, universalism, as a welfare principle, will decline. At least 85 percent of social security earnings (instead of 50 percent as today) will be taxed, and medicare and unemployment compensation will also be graded by income. *Rule 2: income tax rates will move* marginally *higher,* say two to three points, above certain incomes, at first $200,000, as per campaign promise, later $100,000 and lower in recognition of the fact that most of the people have most of the money. At the same time, capital gains taxes on investments will be reduced for those who act according to governmental desires. Despite these efforts, and despite the draw down in defense, the Clinton administration will discover that it has not raised enough money to pay for the even more rapid increase in entitlements. *Rule three* it will borrow from Britain: *no inflation premium, no 'volume budgetinq,' no 'current services'* budget. Whereas at present in the United States federal government, last year's outlays are multiplied by the inflation level to provide the current services to which an agency and its clientele are entitled to begin the year, under the new budget rules they will start from the prior year's outlays (actual spending) and have to explain why they have not increased efficiency to make up for inflation.

When the American administration discovers that its supporters are not willing to curb the rise in entitlements, and that numerous other factors – many Americans believe that one day they too will be rich, other nations followed the Reagan administration's lead in reducing top tax rates, the incentive to avoid-evade high marginal tax rates distorts the economy and lowers average moral behavior – reduce the political and economic value of high progressive taxes, they will turn to a new *rule four, a value-added tax*, a sales tax levied on each stage of production. This is a huge money maker, although European experience shows that entitlements *can grow even* faster than VAT. Now it is the Europeans' turn to show what they can do to reduce deficits after VAT. What will they do? They will build upon American experience.

Rule five is an intensification of European experience (not possible under separation of power systems like the United States): *strengthen executive governmental authority to have budgets voted up or down as a whole.* This rule strengthens governmental ability to reject numerous disabling amendments that increase spending and hence deficits. The U.S. version would be some form of line-item veto for the president. Power to diminish sums, experience has shown, is more efficacious than outright elimination, which is often impractical.

Next, European governments will adopt an American device, practiced in the United States Senate, known as PAYASUGO. This application of the economic doctrine of opportunity costs (in which the value of a good is what one has to give up to get it), has proved efficacious where it has been tried. PAYASUGO does make it harder to get at spending in the base. But the deficit problem is with increases. Over time, PAYASUGO will drive spending down as a proportion of GNP or GDP. First, in *rule six an overall ceiling for government* is established in order to keep spending from growing faster than GDP. Then, in *rule seven, this ceiling is subdivided among governmental accounts.* Any department within these accounts that wants to spend more than its sub-ceiling must then PAYASUGO, either by getting other departments to spend less or by getting the government as a whole to raise revenues. Instead of budgeting by addition, in which spending supposed to be good for some clientele is added to other such spending, without concern for where the resources came from, budgeting turns back to resource allocation in which some clients receive less so others may receive more.

By following these seven rules, budgetary processes in Europe and the United States will look much more alike than they have for the past century. But the problem posed by entitlements, in the presence of a rapidly aging population and a growing welfare population, has not yet been seriously confronted. Just as entitlements, with their cost of living adjustments (COLAs), drive spending budgets, they also propel the fortunes of politicians who will learn how to drive or be driven by them. Cutting them down to what is affordable runs up against political objections; raising revenue to cover them runs up against economic objections

How might this miracle be achieved? In three ways: raising revenues via the methods discussed, *decreasing the increase* in entitlements (by cutting back COLAs, raising retirement ages, starting new entrants somewhat lower), and economic growth. There is a tendency to denigrate the contribution of growth. In view of the already historically high level of per capita GDP, quite modest growth rates, around 2 percent a year, would double income in around 35 years. Whatever we wish would be a lot more affordable at double our present incomes in relation to constant purchasing power. Whether the growth in the economy will cover the growth in entitlements is the great economic question. Whether the political system will be able to adjust the rate of growth in entitlements so as (a) to reflect the government's desires, while (b) avoiding adverse effects (slowing economic growth, unemployment, inflation), so as (c) to increase public satisfaction, is one of the great questions of our time. From an ideological perspective, economic conservatives want to solve the problem by reducing spending, egalitarian progressives, by increasing revenue while maintaining or increasing spending, and social conservatives by a bit of both.

At present, the entire political stratum (witness the popularity of term limits and the unpopularity of European bureaucracies) suffers from failing to control entitlements. In order to avoid or lessen this damage to democratic politics, I have suggested the creation of 'quasi-entitlements,' allowing governments to vary the amount paid by 5 percent a year. The entitlement would be real, at least 95 percent of the stipulated amount but government would have the flexibility to keep costs within the sustainable growth of the economy. When and if it is recognized that no party, whatever its ideology, can long prevail when it is being controlled by (instead of controlling) entitlements, more substantial measures like quasi-entitlements may be undertaken.

As things stand, it is not worthwhile for any substantial interest to make sacrifices by lowering its budget aspirations because there is no way of guaranteeing that the sacrifice will be worthwhile unless everyone contributes their share. The PAYASUGO principle should cure that. Taken together, quasi-entitlements and ending the inflation premium should give politicians greater control over budget allocations and, equally or of greater importance, give the appearance that, for better or worse, they and not those nefarious special interests are in control of government.

CONCLUSION: CONVERGENCE UPON BUDGET REFORM

Now we are in a position to understand why the game of budgeting has come into disrepute. It is not that the budget minuet is rejected because of its repetitive character. It is in disrepute because it no longer performs its essential dual functions of (1) relating expenditure to revenue such that (2) participants in the process and the attentive public is satisfied that the government is well-balanced.

Incrementalism has seized control of budgeting with a vengeance. With the agreed base so large, a rapid succession of increments adds up to an enormous cost. It is no longer tolerable to say that these costs are incurred by automatic mechanism.

Nowadays, the simple arithmetic is that entitlements, including farm price supports, are about 55 percent of the budget, defense is down to 20 percent and dropping, interest on the debt is at 15 percent, and all the rest is around 10 percent. As entitlements grow to absorb the decline in defense, there is not much point in ostensibly being in charge of government to dispose of, at most, 10 percent of the budget.

What makes me think that this is a season for budget reform in the direction of controlling spending, including entitlements? The center wishes to limit spending to reduce the deficit. The economically conservative right has always wanted smaller government. What is new is that the egalitarian left sees that its desire to try new social welfare programs is being crowded out by incremental advances of its old social welfare programs now called entitlements. Its adherents do not wish to reduce the size of government but they do wish to alter their priorities and they cannot do that if the budget is driven by increases in entitlements. Thus all factions are ready for reform.

18

CONCLUSIONS

Kjell A. Eliassen

MAJOR THEMES

The previous chapters in this volume have dealt with various aspects of managing public organizations, ranging from the governing of the public sector as such, to the internal management of public institutions. The two levels of management are, however, closely linked.

Firstly, the management of public institutions is different from private management due to the raison d'etre of a public activity and the public fulfilment of various societal tasks. An understanding of the management of resources and personnel, implies an understanding of the functions performed in ministries, agencies and municipalities. At the same time, the culture, functions, organization and processes of public agencies have important implications for the overall governing capacity in the public sector.

Secondly, the ambitions and handling of external management by politicians, the principal agents in public organizations, are often responsible for the internal management problems of the public sector.

Most chapters in this book deal with the relationship which exists between management and the environment, focusing on either public sector governance, the management of public organizations or the public manager. However, they still emphasise the importance of analysing both types of management, the governing or steering of society at large and the leadership of managers in public agencies, in order to understand the particular characteristics and the future challenges facing the public sector and its governing institutions.

The authors have discussed different perspectives of public management, the leadership function, the role conceptions of public managers, and the possibilities of using different managerial tools in order to strengthen management functions in public sector organizations. The various chapters reveal that the range of problems confronting public sector organizations is substantial and that the solutions to these problems are often of a highly experimental nature. This has to do with both the lack of systematic scientific knowledge about public management and with the great uncertainty which exists with regard to what the more general solutions to these problems should really imply.

In this volume, the authors have employed a wide range of perspectives on public management, using a large variety of concepts, theories and empirical evidence. There are, however, a few 'common themes' among the various contributions which I will discuss in this concluding chapter.

Firstly, all of the authors emphasise a growing scepticism towards the importing of concepts, ideology and managerial tools from the private sector to the public. Up until now, many public managers have, to a large extent, borrowed solutions to their problems from the private sector. Most consultants and students of public management have also agreed to use elements from the rapidly changing management ideas of the private sector, in an attempt to strengthen the management function in public sector organizations. In addition to a growing hesitation, this volume also presents elements of new management philosophies, based on experiences from the public sector.

Secondly, most contributors emphasise the role of management culture in both explaining existing management patterns and as a tool for changing the internal and external management of public organizations. In particular, the idea of integration, of a mission statement, and of human resources development has taken on a growing importance in internal management.

A third recurring theme and one which the contributors are in disagreement over, is how to view the future prospects of public sector management. Should we be pessimistic or are there some foundations for optimism? Some of the contributors are optimistic and stress the ability of the public sector to adapt and meet the challenges of the future. Others stress the basic problems of public governance as such and see the public sector as having no ability to meet the challenges of the future.

Finally, the question arises as to what can be learned from the nature of management behaviour reported in this book? We have seen that, basically, the same type of management problems occur in different countries. The politicians and the administrators, however, have tried a large variety of different solutions. The managers and their advisors have little, if any, information on the solutions developed and tried in other countries. If they make any use of experiences from public agencies and the public sector in other countries, they often resort to rather uncritical and superficial use of strategies based more on hope than on research and a sound matching of proposed solutions to assumed problems.

However, with a growing scepticism towards borrowing private sector solutions, the need to draw more extensively on experiences from the public sector in other countries, is increasing. Various national public sector organizations in different countries are perhaps more similar than public and private sector organizations within each individual country.

PUBLIC MANAGEMENT IN THE PUBLIC SECTOR

There are several dimensions to the differences in reform patterns which exist across countries and time. On the one hand, there is a politically and often experienced-based eagerness towards managerialism as such and, on the other hand, a degree of scepticism towards employing private management principles in the public sector. At one extreme we find, in nearly all countries, major privatization programs and the introduction of the market economy into the public sector. Over time, however, we have seen a gradual decline in the unconscious use of private sector management mechanisms in public management reforms.

The main reason for this has been described by Guy Peters as lying in the fact that the new economic conceptualization of government '... tends to substitute one narrow concept of efficiency for the more fundamental values of accountability and responsiveness that should be inherent in a democratic system'.

Thus, management reform in the public sector has to be based on the particular characteristics of public sector organizations. Studies have shown that public managers see the rules and regulations as governing their level of productivity in their organizations. The decisive importance of official rules as the basis for activities in public bureaucracies, is highlighted as being significant for public management. These types of steering mechanisms are used extensively at both the state and local level and a new strategy would imply both an improvement in how these mechanisms are used and an attempt to reduce the role of hierarchy and regulations as working tools in public organizations.

Another important element of public management, when compared with private, is the dual relationship which exists between the public manager and, on the one hand, the politicians who are his superiors and who set the goals and, on the other hand, his subordinates, the bureaucrats, who implement these goals. The character of this double-sided and complex relationship also helps to differentiate the public sector from the private. The logic of politicians, their goals and the duration of their office have particular effects on public managers. Public managers need to react to sudden shifts in the priorities of the political leadership, their numerous and often conflicting goals, and their short time perspective which is defined by the number of years in which they hold office.

One other important difference between public and private management lies in the rules governing the activities of managers. In the public sector, both the goals of the activities and, to a large extent, the organizational structure and functioning of the different agencies are laid down in laws and regulations. These imply such characteristics as bureaucratic standards, hierarchy and lifetime employment. As a result, the room for manoeuvre is much more restricted in public-owned agencies.

These problems with regard to goal-setting in the public sector have to be taken far more seriously when trying to develop new strategies for governing the public sector. Attempts to set goals and priorities have to be included as important elements in management strategy. The politicians have to realize that they are part of the managerial team in public organizations. Forcing them to do the job of setting goals and priorities is a crucial part of the task of top level bureaucrats. These factors also underline the need for a reduction in the use of traditional ways of governing the public sector and an increased use of other steering systems more oriented towards managing uncertainty and shifts in goals and priorities in the public sector.

Finally, the surroundings of the public sector are changing or will change rapidly in the future. This is also an important reason as to why a new management strategy has to include mechanisms which allow for a continuing process of redefining goals and reordering priorities at all levels of public bureaucracies. However, in order to create this type of administrative system, one has to use other steering systems in addition to hierarchy and regulations.

Public management is an inter-organizational and not an intra-organizational activity as it mainly is in private organizations. Thus, in the public sector, the managerial strategies of control and culture have to be developed within the framework of the inter-organizational character of the tasks of these types of organizations. This point is well illustrated by Kooiman and van Vliet in their chapter on Governance and Public Management.

As far as the more internal dimensions of public management are concerned, the cultural dimension of the public sector has important characteristics which are different from those of private firms. This has to be taken into account when we analyse management in the public sector.

CULTURAL VALUES AND ORGANIZATIONAL IDENTITY

Here we want to draw attention to a phenomenon that, for a long time, has been neglected as an element of serious scholarly analysis, although the 'special' character of public organizations has often been implicitly described as having factors of a cultural nature. The dominance of the structural and procedural aspects of public bodies has somewhat over-shadowed the just as important cultural variables in the proper functioning of these organizations. It seems that 'culture' as a variable has been more or less taken for granted. This has not, however, satisfied everyone; one only has to mention the often 'bureaucratic' traits present in the attitudes and behaviour of public officials. Nevertheless, this dissatisfaction has not served to stimulate the idea that these traits could be easily changed.

Several authors, including Strand, Beck Jørgensen, Gerding and Metcalfe and Richards, show that the attitudes of public officials can be changed, albeit within certain limits. However, the values, even ethical ones, upon which they are based must be changed if anything fundamental is to be expected from a new approach to managerial problems in the public sector. This is not something which can be achieved overnight. Many of the attempts at introducing new concepts, methods and techniques into the public arena have failed because, either they were introduced in a purely technical sense, or they did not take values and attitudinal aspects sufficiently into consideration. These attitudinal aspects, as we know so well, have a lot to do with resistance to change. However, even where there was a willingness to adapt, if it was not fed into a more basic cultural bedding, it often wore out rapidly under the strain of 'back to normal'.

Cultural changes are needed and the cultural dimension is certainly one of strategic value. Les Metcalfe and Sue Richards argue that changes and developments in public sector management are cultural phenomena, based on learning processes. In our view, this means that culture is the most internally oriented dimension of public management and it holds the greatest opportunities for the future. However, specific strategies are needed to put these opportunities to their best possible use.

An important part of the cultural element in improved public management is its ability to change the orientations of public managers. In the words of Torodd Strand, there is a need for a change in role orientation towards entrepreneurship and integration. As Torben Beck Jørgensen comments, public managers will have to: change their orientations in the direction of optimizing the composition of available resources (factors of production) instead of only securing growth; adjust the expectations of the clientele downwards; and break down vested interests, because these will be seen as barriers to reprioritizing and reorganization. At the same time, Yntema argues that there is a need to modernize public human resource management. He claims that modernization in this field is even more important in the public sector than it is in the private sector.

These shifts in direction imply a change in management orientation from a focus on issues, rules and regulations, to a greater emphasis on strategies directed at goal fulfilment and the establishment of a creative and change-oriented atmosphere, both internally in the organization and externally in relation to the agency's clientele.

More managerial time and energy will then have to be put into what is called, in Beck Jørgensen's terminology, the 'downwards' relationship. An example is the current emphasis being put on service management. This shift in orientation takes place, however, in an organization which is still highly dependent upon financial appropriation from the 'upper' political level and not on financial support supplied by the customer in a market situation. Thus, a substantial amount of energy has still to be redirected to either the customers or to the organization itself. A new strategy for public management is needed, but the change will be gradual and the rewards for the successful manager will come in the long term rather than in the short run. The bureaucratic system itself and, in particular, the government appropriation and reward system are only going to change slowly and gradually.

This emphasis on management roles, conflicts, dilemmas, ambiguity and change implies a focus on culture, as we have seen in several recent studies of management strategies. There seems to have been a major shift in the orientation of both managers and, in particular, management consultants, from techniques of management to the management of culture. We support this inclination for change but not in terms of 'quick and easy' results, as we so often see in fashionable studies in private management. Focusing on how the cultural dimensions of an organization can be changed with regards to such aspects as values, integration, social learning and attitudes, in order to improve management capabilities in the public sector, constitutes a fundamental and major adaptation.

Public managers should see cultural change as a major source of organizational flexibility. As Metcalfe and Richards argue, the core values around which public management cultures should develop include learning, experimentation, adaptability and flexibility. The need for these values arises from the rate of change with which government will have to cope in the future. With a high level of change, the need to establish a continuing learning process is as important as carrying out predefined goals. In order to establish a functioning learning process in an organization, one has to change the total organizational climate, the culture of the organization. Is this possible? Do we, on the basis of a need for cultural change, have a foundation for optimism in the public sector?

MANAGING PUBLIC ORGANIZATIONS IN THE FUTURE: OPTIMISM OR PESSIMISM

Nearly all of the contributors to this book have some views on how bad or good the prospects are for meeting the challenges of the public sector in the future. Some of them, like Keeman, are very optimistic stating that, 'Contrary to the widespread ideas that both the development of the welfare state and the growth of the public sector are difficult to control, let alone to change, we did not find evidence to sustain this argument.' Others, like Guy Peters in his chapter, Managing the Hollow State, share an attitude of pessimism and question whether the new economic conceptualization of government really helps to improve management.

At the same time, Metcalfe and Richards voice some doubts as to whether the cultural - and structural - conditions present in the modern welfare state are such that the embedded resistance to change, inherent in public bureaucracies, can be overcome.

The internal situation is, in nearly all of the chapters, described as difficult in relation to both the effectiveness and efficiency of public management and Yntema, Strand and Gerding place great weight on this, providing examples to illustrate this point. Management tools are, to a large extent, inadequate and ineffective. In addition, hierarchical structures, rules and public regulations are overused as steering systems within the public sector itself and in the implementation of public policies. With regard to the managers, their roles are not well defined or developed and they have only a restricted space in which to manoeuvre.

Moreover, societal development will necessitate new types of strategies. In his chapter, Carl Böhret takes societal development as the starting point for a discussion of the future of public management. He links the need for management reform to two distinct types of societal change: the development towards a post-industrial society and the development towards a post-modern society. Within these two scenarios there are differences with regard to what the important tasks for the public sector will be and what tools will be needed to manage public organizations. These two directions of societal change will, however, tend to go together in the future development of western societies, and public management will have to take the implications of both these scenarios into account.

Whatever the views of such authors as Kooiman and van Vliet on societal development in the future, the need for radical management reforms in the public sector is stressed in all of the chapters and the authors have indicated several different opportunities for improving the management capabilities of public sector organizations.

What consequences do the different aspects of public sector management have for the opportunities of developing new strategies in the future? First and foremost, public managers, when developing new strategies, will have to pay more attention to the general frameworks which structure their activities. Secondly, they will have to acknowledge the fact that these frameworks limit the possibilities which they have of importing role conceptions, managerial tools and strategies directly from the private sector. Specific strategies for the management of public organizations will have to be developed. Our investigation of the character of public management has indicated some of the possible strategies which could be followed and the main elements which these strategies should contain.

WHAT WE CAN LEARN: NEW STRATEGIES FOR PUBLIC MANAGEMENT REFORM

We shall now examine some of the main types of strategy which could be implemented in order to help improve the standard of management in public organizations. The various strategies which were indicated previously can be condensed into three main categories.

First and foremost, there must be a development of new tools within the framework of hierarchy and regulations used as management steering systems.

Secondly, a reduction in the overall steering ambitions of government must be implemented. The total level of both public involvement in society and the detailed regulation of the structure and activities of public

organizations are currently so extensive that the efficiency and effectiveness of the steering mechanisms are highly questionable.

Finally, there must be an increase in the use of alternative steering systems such as the market and increased democracy, both as a supplement
to bureaucracy and regulations and in place of them. One of the main
reasons for the managerial problems which exist in public organizations,
is the over-emphasis on bureaucracy and regulations in the management
of public tasks.

The reasons behind this drive for reform have been more or less the
same in all countries. The inability to meet old and, in particular, new
public sector tasks as described in Section One of this book, has created
the main stimulus for reform. The political importance of the more general ideas surrounding the creation of higher efficiency and effectiveness
through private management and the importance of deregulation and
goal oriented management in the public sector, has been much more
predominant in some countries such as Britain than in others such as
Norway. The reform strategies and principles of reorganization which
have been employed have varied from one country to another and from
the early phases of managerial reform in the 1980s to the more recent
phases.

The first of these strategies to improve the traditional tools of the
bureaucratic steering system in the public sector is one of the core themes
of several chapters in this book. The question concerns how more effective
use can be made of a bureaucratic structure and its traditional ways of
governing public organizations and the delivery of public services. We
have discussed in detail how the tools of design, personnel, information and financial management could be employed more consciously
and more in accordance with the specific character of the public sector, in order to improve public management. In addition, in order to
provide an account of the possibilities implied in these different types
of management strategies, various chapters have also used examples,
demonstrating new ways in which these strategies could be implemented
in different organizational settings within the public sector in Europe.

Another important lesson which can be learned from the chapters in
this book, is that most perspectives on public management tend to ignore
or at least to undermine the role and importance of the public manager.
This is true to a much larger extent than in theories and studies of management in private enterprises. We believe that increased emphasis has to
be placed on the role and function of public managers in order to acquire a
better understanding of the future needs of public management and find
viable solutions to management problems in the public sector.

The main resource in both private and public organizations is the
employees. Thus, the leadership of people, or human resources development, is of crucial importance. An improvement in the 'management of
people' is certainly needed in the public sector. This type of management
requires a completely new attitude to personnel management in the public

sector and the use of other types of incentives than those which we normally find in state, regional and local public organizations. However, first of all, managers in the public sector must be made to understand that, first and foremost, they are leaders of other people and not just experts in their particular field of professional knowledge within the public sector.

More specifically, several changes have to be made in personnel management in the future, in order to improve the functioning of public organizations. First of all, personnel management has to take on a more strategic perspective, in order to translate changes in environmental conditions into specific personnel policies. Secondly, the day-to-day functioning of personnel management has to be decentralized to line managers. Thirdly, new evaluation and reward systems have to be developed in the public sector. Finally, the employer function in public organizations has to be strengthened, both by reducing the role of politicians in personnel management, and by developing a more harmonized personnel policy at the state and local level. All of these tasks which are confronting personnel management require both a more professional personnel agency in public organizations and more professional personnel managers in the public sector.

Furthermore, the increased focus on top- and middle-level civil servants as managers, implies a new attitude towards leadership roles in public organizations. Torodd Strand has, in his chapter, elaborated on the implications of a role approach in his study of public management. Following the ideas put forward by Adizes, he discusses the managerial roles of a producer, an administrator, an integrator and an entrepreneur. His analysis shows that, among public servants, a clear bias is demonstrated towards the producer and administrator roles.

However, the potential strength of the public sector lies in an increase in the emphasis on the integrator role, and perhaps also on the entrepreneurial role of the bureaucrat. Furthermore, in public management, one has to pay more attention to the creation of leadership teams with complementary roles, instead of looking for one particular type of leader.

These changes in the role of public managers are necessary in order to obtain a better standard of management within the framework of bureaucracy as a steering system in the public sector. However, they are also important as a means of increasing the use of other types of steering systems in managing public tasks.

In his chapter, Böhret discusses, in more general terms, the tools for public management in a future post-industrial and post-modern society. He also identifies specific public tasks, with the different alternative scenarios for societal development and different tools of public management to be used to meet these tasks. At a rather general level, he links such elements as cost-benefit analyses, prognostics, public regulations and assessment studies with post-industrial society. Post-modern society he identifies with scenarios, acceptance studies, negotiations and bargaining processes, in addition to strategies outside the framework of traditional bureaucratic steering systems, such as laissez-faire direction, partial social legislation and direct public participation in the planning process. The post-modern society necessitates the use of management mechanisms other than bureaucratic steering systems in the public sector.

The second strategy for managerial improvement, designed to reduce the steering ambitions of public organizations, has also been covered in this book. The level of public steering and management in society has been taken for granted. This problem has been raised in several chapters and most explicitly by Böhret, Sørensen and Wright. My main argument is that, in most western European countries, we have now reached a critical limit on the total level of public steering in different aspects of society. The reason for this is both that the population will not accept any more government interference and that the effect which further public steering would have, is highly questionable. It is impossible to implement further rules and regulations in an effective way and one type of regulation often creates problems for or eliminates the effects of other regulations.

The third type of strategy for improving the managerial and steering mechanisms of the public sector, is to use elements of other steering systems such as the market and increased democracy and negotiations, as a supplement to bureaucracy and regulations or in place of the traditional mechanisms discussed by several of the authors in this book, including Wright, Richardson and Wildavsky. The most radical change in the way that public services are provided involves the employment of private organizations as suppliers meaning, as a result, privatization. A less dramatic change is the attempt at building elements of market mechanisms into bureaucratic procedures. Price, competition and rewards have been inadequately used as managerial mechanisms in the public sector.

In recent years, European governments have increasingly used other types of organizations to deliver public goods and services. The main argument in favour of this is that the effective and efficient management of public services is easier to obtain within a private than within a public organization.

The question is, however, to what extent and in what way the management of public services differs from the management delivering the same services within private organizations. Richardson concludes that, in actual fact, the level of public regulation is not necessarily less but, in some cases, even greater in private utilities than in public. Without public ownership, the need for regulations seems to increase.

There is some evidence in the literature that private organizations are more effective and efficient, but this seems to depend to a large extent on the type of services provided. The benefits of using private production of public services are greater with regard to simple services such as cleaning, refuse collection and fire protection, than they are with regard to more institutionalized services such as hospital treatment and education. The most important aspect of a renewed interest in private production is, however, not a general use of this type of production as such, but the opportunity which it provides to evaluate and compare in a systematic manner, the costs and benefits of both private and public production. Only when this type of analysis has been carried out, will it be possible to know the exact cost of public production and thus to evaluate what we have to pay for the other benefits such as job security which is linked to public production of public services.

By way of a conclusion, it can be said that public management is currently focusing heavily on the combined challenge of, on the one hand, the need for improved public sector efficiency and effectiveness and, on the other hand, the growing scepticism towards the importing of concepts, ideology and managerial tools from the private sector. The authors in this book emphasise the important influence which the purpose of public activities and the way in which they are carried out, have on the management of resources and personnel. In addition to highlighting the growing scepticism, this book also presents elements of new management philosophies, based on experiences drawn from the public sector.

This challenge is closely linked to the disagreement over the future prospects of public sector management which are discussed in this book. Some of the contributors are optimistic and stress the ability of the public sector to adapt to and meet the challenges of the future. Others underline the basic problems of public governance and see the public sector as having no ability to meet the challenges of the future. However, the need for radical management reforms in the public sector is stressed in all of the chapters as being a necessity to meet the public sector challenges. This volume has indicated some of the changes which are needed, the obstacles to such development and various possible strategies for managing the public sector in the future.

REFERENCES

Aberbach, J.D. and Rockman, B.A. (1988) 'Image IV Revisited: Executive and Political Roles', *Governance*, 1: 1–25.

Aberbach, J.D., Derlien, H.U., Mayntz, R. and Rockman, B.A. (1990) 'American and West German Federal Executives – Technocratic and Political Attitudes', *International Social Science Journal*, 123: 3–18.

Aberbach, J.D., Putnam, R.D. and Rockman, B.A. (1981) *Bureaucrats and Politicians in Western Democracies*. Cambridge, MA: Harvard University Press.

Aberbach, J.L., Putnam, R.D. and Rockman, B.A. (1981) *Bureaucrats and Politicians in Western Democracies*. Cambridge, Mass.: Harvard University Press.

Adizes, I. (1976) 'Mismanagement Styles', *California Management Review*, 19 (1): 5–20.

Alchian, A.A. (1950) 'Uncertainty, Evolution and Economic Theory', *Journal of Political Economy*, 48: 211–221.

Alchian, A.A. and Demsetz, H. 'Production, Information Costs and Economic Theory', *American Economic Review*, 62: 777–795.

Allison, G.T. (1979) 'Public and Private Management: Are They Fundamentally Alike in All Unimportant Respects?' *Proceedings* for the Public Management Research Conference, November 19–20 (Washington D. C.), reprinted in Shafritz, J.M. and Hyde, A.C. *Classics of Public Administration*. Chicago: The Dorsey Press.

Alt, J. and Chrystal, K. (1983) *Political Economics*. Berkeley and London: University of California Press.

Anderson, C.W. (1977) 'Political Design and the Representation of Interests', *Comparative Political Studies*, 10, 1.

Aquina, H. and Bekke, H. (1993) ' Governance in Interaction: Public tasks and Private Organizations' in J. Kooiman (ed,) *Modern Governance*. London: Sage.

Armstrong, P., Glyn, A. and Harrison, J. (1984) *Capitalism since World War II. The Making and Breakup of the Great Boom*, London: Fontana.

Ashby, R.W. (1960) *Design for a Brain*. London: Chapman and Hall.

Aucoin, P. (1988) 'Contraction, Managerialism and Decentralization in Canadian Government', *Governance*, 1: 144–161.

Barach, P., Baratz, M.S. (1970) *Power and Poverty*. New York: Oxford University Press.

Barker, A. and Peters, B.G. (1992) *Advising West European Governments*. Edinburgh: University of Edinburgh Press.

Barkovich, B.R.(1989) *Regulatory Intervention in the Utility Industry. Fairness, Efficiency and the Pursuit of Energy Conservation*. Westport: Quorum Books and Greenwood Press.

Barzel, Y. (1982) 'Measurement Cost and the Organization of Markets', *Journal of Law and Economics*, 25: 27–48.

Baumol, W.J. (1967) 'The Macroeconomics of Unbalanced Growth. The Anatomy of Urban Crises' *American Economic Review*, 57: 415–426.

Beck Jørgensen, T. (1981) *Når staten skal spare*. Copenhagen: Nyt fra Samfundsvidenskaberne.

Beck Jørgensen, T. (1987) *Models of Retrenchment Behavior*. Working Paper no. 24. Bruxelles: International Institute of Administrative Sciences.

Beck Jørgensen, T. (1992) 'Den ny offentlige kapitalisme', *Administrativ Debat*, 3: 6–9.

Beer, Samuel H. (1977) 'Political overload and federalism', *Polity*, 10: 5–17.

Behn, R.D (1978) 'How to Terminate a Public Policy: A Dozen Hints for the Would-be Terminator', *Policy Analysis*, 4: 393–413.

Bendor, J. (1990) Formal Models of Bureaucracy: A Review, in N. Lynn and A. Wildavsky (eds), *Public Administration: The State of the Discipline*. Chatham, NJ: Chatham House.

Bennett, C.J. (1991) 'What is policy convergence and what causes it?' in *British Journal of Political Science*, vol. 21 (2), April: 215–233.

Bennett, C.J. 'Different Processes, One Result: the Convergence of Data Protection Policy in Europe and the USA', *Governance*, 1: 415–41.

Berg, S.V. and Tschirhart, J. (1988) *Natural Monopoly Regulation. Principles and Practice*. Cambridge: Cambridge University Press.

Bernstein, M.H. (1955) *Regulating Business by Independent Commission*. Princeton.

Blau, P.M. (1974) *On the Nature of Organizations*. New York: John Wiley and Sons.

Bodiguel, J.L. and L. Rouban (1991) *Le fonctionnaire detrone?* Paris: Fondation Nationale de Science Politique.

Borcherding, T.E., Pommerehne, W.W. and Schneider, F. (1982) 'Comparing the Efficiency of Private and Public Production: The Evidence from Five Contries', *Journal of Economics*, Supplement 2: s.127–156.

Bozeman, B. (1987) *All Organizations Are Public. Bridging Public and Private Organizational Theories*. San Francisco: Jossey-Bass.

Boston, J., Martin, J., Pallot, P. and Walsh, P.(1991) *Reshaping the State*. Auckland: Oxford.

Bradford, D.F., Malt, B.A. and Oates, W.E. (1969) 'The rising cost of local public services: Some evidence and reflections', *National Tax Journal*, 22: 185202.

Brickman, R., Jasanoff, S. and Ilgen, T. (1988) *Controlling Chemicals: the Politics of Regulation in Europe and the USA*. Ithaca, N.Y. 1985.

Broekstra, G. (1984) 'Mama: Management by Matching. A Consistency Model for Organizational Assessment and Change', in R. Trappl (ed.) *Cybernetics and Systems Research 2*, Elsevier (North Holland): 413–420.

Bromley, D.W. (1989) *Economic Interests and Institutions*. Oxford: Blackwell.

Brunnsson, K. (1988) 'Hur stor blev tvåprocentaren? Erfarenheter från en besparingsteknik', *ESO-Rapport* 1988: 34 Stockholm: Almänna forlaget.

Brunsson, N. (1989) *The Organization of Hypocrisy. Talk, Decisions and Actions in Organizations*. New York: John Wiley and Sons.

Buckley, W., Burns, T.R. and Meeker, D. (1974) 'Structural Resolutions of Collective Action Problems', *Behavioural Science*, 19: 277–97.

Böhret, C. (1988) 'Allgemeine Rahmenbedingungen und Trends des Verwaltungshandelns', in Reinermann, H. et al. (ed.), *Neue Informationstechniken – Neue Verwaltungsstrukturen*. Heidelberg: Verlag Decker u. Müller.

Böhret, C. (1990) *Folgen Entwurf für eine aktive Politik gegen schleichende Katastrophen*. Opladen: Leske und Budrich.

Böhret, C. (1992) 'Innovationsbündnisse', *Politische Ökologie*, 10: 67–70.

Böhret, C. and Franz, P. (1982) *Technologiefolgenabschätzung*. Frankfurt and New York: Campus Verlag.

Böhret, C. and Hugger, W. (1980) *Test und Prüfung von Gesetzentwürfen*. Köln and Bonn: C. Heymanns Verlag.

Caiden, G.E. and Siedentopf, H. (eds.) (1982) *Strategies for Administrative Reform*. Lexington: Heath.

Cameron, D.R. (1978) 'The Expansion of the Public Economy', *American Political Science Review*, 72: 1243–1261.

Cameron, D.R. (1982) 'On the Limits of the Public Economy', *Annals of the American Academy of Political and Social Science*, 1982, vol. 459: 46–62.

Cameron, D.R. (1985) 'Does Government Cause Inflation? Taxes, Spending and Deficits', in Lindberg and Maier (eds): 224–279.

Carter, N., Klein, R. and Day, P. (1992) *How Organisations Measure Success. The Use of*

Performance Indicators in Government. London: Routledge.

Castles, F.G. (1985) *The Working Class and Welfare. Reflections on the political developments of the welfare state in Australia and New Zealand, 1890–1980.* London: Allen and Unwin.

Castles, F.G. (1988) *Comparative Public Policy Analysis*: Problems, Progress and Prospects, in: Castles et al. (eds): 197–224.

Castles, F.G. (ed.) (1982) *The Impact of Parties. Politics and Policies in Democratic Capitalist States.* London and Beverly Hills: Sage.

Castles, F.G. (ed.) (1989) *The Comparative History of Public Policy.* Oxford: Polity Press.

Castles, F.G., Lehner, F. and Schmidt, M.G. (eds) (1988) *Managing Mixed Economies.* Berlin and New York: Walter de Gruyter.

Cevallier, J. (1988) 'Les Politiques de Déréglementation' in *Les Déréglementations: Etude Comparative,* Paris: 11–74.

Child, J. (1972) 'Organizational Structure, Environment and Performance: The Role of Strategic Choice', *Sociology,* 6: 1–22.

Christensen, J.G. (1982) 'Growth by Exception: or the Vain Attempt to Impose Resource Scarcity on the Danish Public Sector', *Journal of Public Policy,* 2: 117–144.

Christensen, J.G. (1992) 'Hierarchical and Contractual Approaches to Budgetary Reform', *Journal of Theoretical Politics,* 4: 67–91.

Chubb, J.E. and Moe, T.E. (1990) *Politics, Markets and America's Schools* Washington: The Brookings Institution.

Cm 1599 (1991) *The Citizen's Charter.* London: HMSO.

Cm 1760 (1991) *Improving Management in Government – The Next Steps Agencies: Review 1991.* London: HMSO, November 1991.

Cm 1761 (1991) *The Next Steps Initiative. The Government Reply to the Seventh Report from the Treasury and Civil Service Committee, Session 1990–91.* London: HMSO, November 1991.

Cm 2111 (1992) *The Next Steps Initiative: Review 1992.* London: HMSO, December 1992.

Cm 914 (1989) *HM Treasury, The Financing and Accountability of Next Steps Agencies.* London: HMSO, December 1989.

Cmnd 3638 (1968) *Civil Service* (Fulton Report). London: HMSO.

Cmnd 3638 (1968) *Civil Service* (Fulton Report). London: HMSO.

Coase, R.H. (1960) 'The Problem of Social Cost', *Journal of Law and Economics,* 3: 1–44.

Coase, R.H. (1988) *The Firm, the Market and the Law.* Chicago: University of Chicago Press.

Cogan, J.F., and Timothy J.M. (1990) 'The Great Budget Shell Game', *The American Enterprise,* November/December: 35–41.

Contandriopoulos, A-P. (1986) 'Cost Containment Through Payment Mechanisms: The Quebec Experience', *Journal of Health Policy,* 7: 224–38.

Crozier, M. (1964) *The Bureaucratic Phenomen.* Chicago: University of Chicago Press.

Crozier, M. (1987) *Etat modeste, Etat moderne.* Paris: Fayard.

Cupei, J. (1986) *Umwewltverträglichkeitsprüfung.* Köln and Bonn: C. Heymanns Verlag.

Czarniawska, J.B. and Bernard J. (1990) *Organizational change as materializations of ideas.* Stockholm: The study of power and democracy in Sweden. Report no. 37, January.

Dahl, R. (1985) *A Preface to Economic Democracy.* Berkeley: University of California Press.

Damgaard, E. (1986) 'Causes, forms and consequences of sectoral policy-making: Some Danish evidence', *European Journal of Political Research,* 14: 273–287.

Damgaard, E. and Eliassen, K.A. (1978) 'Corporate Pluralism in Danish Law-making', *Scandinavian Political Studies,* 1: 285–313.

Day, P. and Klein, R. (1987) *Accountabilities.* London: Tavistock.

Dempster, M.A.H., and Wildavsky, A. (1979) 'On Change ... or, There Is No Magic Size for an Increment', *Political Studies,* September, 217, 3, 371–389.

Den offentliga sektorn productivitet och effektivitet *Bilalag* 21 til Långtidsutredningen 1987 Stockholm: Finansdepartementet.

Derlien, H.U. (1984) 'Einstweiliger Ruhestand politischer Beamter des Bundes 1949–1983', *Die Öffentliche Verwaltung,* 37: 689–99.

Derlien, H.U. (1985) 'Politicization of the Civil Service in the Federal Republic of Germany – Facts and Fables' in F. Meyers, (ed.), *The Politicization of Public Administration.* Brussels:

International Institute of Administrative Sciences.

Derlien, H.U. (1988) 'Repercussions of Government Change on the Career Civil Service in West Germany: The Cases of 1969 and 1982', *Governance*, 1: 50–78.

Derlien, H.U. (1991) ' Historical Legacy and Recent Developments of the German Higher Civil Service', *International Review of Administrative Sciences*, 57, 385–401.

Deutsch, K. (1981) 'The Crisis of the State', *Government and Opposition*, 16, 3: 331–43.

Dienel, P.C. (1978) *Die Planungszelle*. Opladen: Westdeutscher Verlag.

Dierkes, M., Weiler, H. and Antal, A.B. (eds) (1987) *Comparative Policy Research. Learning from Experience*. Aldershot, Gower.

Dopson, S. and Stewart, R. (1990) 'Public and Private Sector Management: the case for a wider debate', *Public Money and Management*, vol. 10, no. 1, 37–40.

Downs, A. (1967) *Inside Bureaucracy*. Boston: Little, Brown and Company.

Downs, G.W. and Larkey, P.D. (1986) *The Search For Government Efficiency*. Philadelplhia: Temple University Press.

Drewry, G. (1990) 'Next Steps: the pace falters', *Public Law*, 332–9.

Dror, Y. (1967) 'Policy Analysts: A new Professional Role in Government Service', *Public Administration Review*, reprinted in Shafritz, J.M. and Hyde, A.C. *Classics of Public Administration*. Chicago: The Dorsey Press.

Drucker, P.F. (1977) *People and Performance: The Best of Peter Drucker on Management*. New York.

Dunleavy, P. (1991) *Democracy, Bureaucracy and Public Choice. Economic Explanations in Political Science*. New York and London: Harvester Wheatsheaf.

Dunleavy, P. (1991) *Democracy, Bureaucracy and Public Choice*. London: Harvester Wheatsheaf.

Dunsire, A. and Hood, C. (1989) *Cutback Management in Public Bureaucracies: Popular Theories and Observed Outcomes in Whitehall*. Cambridge: Cambridge University Press.

Dunsire, A. (1988) ' Bureaucratic Morality in the United Kingdom', *International Political Science Review*, vol. 9, 179–191.

Dunsire, A. (1993) 'Modes of Governance' in Kooiman, J. (ed.) *Modern Governance*. London: Sage.

Economist, 21 November 1992.

Eggertson, T. (1990) *Economic Behaviour and Institutions*. Cambridge: Cambridge University Press.

Eisenstadt, S.N. and Ahimeir, O. (1985) *The Welfare State and Its Aftermath*. New York: Barnes and Noble.

Eliassen, K.A and Kooiman, J. (1993) 'Editors' introduction' in Eliassen et al. *Managing Public Organizations*. London: Sage Publications.

Elkin, S.L. (1986) 'Regulation and Regime: A Comparative Analysis', *Journal of Public Policy*, vol. 6 (1), January–March, 49–72.

Emery, F.E. and Trist, E.L. (1965) 'The Causal Texture of Organizational Environments', *Human Relations*, 18: 21–32.

Esping-Andersen, G. (1990) *Three Worlds of Welfare Capitalism*. Cambridge, Polity.

Esping-Anderson, G. (1985) *Politics against Markets. The Social Democratic Road to Power*. Princeton and New Jersey, Princeton University Press.

Evans, R.G. et al. (1989) 'Controlling Health Expenditures – The Canadian Reality', *The New England Journal of Medicine*, 320: 571–577.

Fesler, J.W. (1983) 'Politics, Policy, and Bureaucracy at the Top', *AAPSS*, 466, 23–41.

Fish, Martin, (1988) 'The Post Office: strategy of a programme for change', *Public Money and Management*, vol. 8, no. 3, 29–33.

Fisher, R. and Ury, W. (1984) *Das Harvard-Konzept*. Frankfurt and New York: Campus Verlag.

Fitz-enz, J. (1984) *How to measure human resources management*. McGraw Hill.

Fligstein, N. (1987) 'The Intraorganizational Power Struggle: Rise of Finance Personnel to Top Leadership in Large Corporations, 1919–1979', *American Sociological Review*, 1987, 44–58.

Flora, P. (1983) *State, Economy, and Society in Western Europe 1815 – 1975.* vol. I, *The Growth of Mass Democracies and Welfare States.* Frankfurt/London and Chicago: Campus and Macmillan and St. James.

Flora, P. (ed.) (1986) *Growth to Limits. The Western European Welfare States Since World War II* (Volumes 1 to 4). Berlin and New York: Walter de Gruyter.

Flora, P. and Heidenheimer, A.J. (eds) (1981) *The Development of Welfare States in Europe and America.* New Brunswick and London: Transaction Books.

Flynn, N., (1988) 'A Consumer Orientated Culture?', *Public Money and Management,* vol. 8, no. 3, 27–31.

Fraser, A. (1991) *Making the Most of Next Steps: The Management of Ministers' Departments and their Executive Agencies: Report to the Prime Minister.* London: HMSO.

Fry, J.K. (1988) 'The Thatcher Government, the Financial Management Initiative, and the 'New Civil Service'', *Public Administration,* 66, 1–20.

Furubotn, E.G. and Pejovich, S. (1972) 'Property Rights and Economic Theory: A Survey of Recent Litterature', *Journal of Economic Literature,* 10, no. 4: 1137–1162.

Gammelsæter, H. (1991) *Organisasjonsendring gjennom generasjoner av ledere. En studie av endringer i Hafslund-Nycomed, Elkem og Norsk Hydro.* Molde: Møreforskning.

Gawthrop, I., (1984) *Public Sector Management, Systems, and Ethics.* Bloomington: Indiana University Press.

Gerding, G. (1991) *Unit Management bij de Rijksoverheid. Het verband tussen manage- mentstijl en context onderzoek bij zestien units* (Unit Management in Dutch Central Government. An investigation into the relationship between managerial style and context within sixteen units). Delft: Eburon.

Gerding, G. and Sevenhuijsen R.F. (1985) *Middle Management Onderzocht, verslag van een praktijkonderzoek,* (Middle Management Researched, report on an empirical investigation). Rotterdam: Erasmus University.

Goldscheid, R. and Schumpeter, J. (1976) *Die Finananzkrise des Steuerstaats. Beiträge zur Politischen Ökonomie der Staatsfinanzen.* Frankfurt: Suhrkamp.

Goldsworthy, D. (1991) *Setting Up Next Steps: A Short Account of the Origins, Launch and Implementation of the Next Steps Project in the British Civil Service.* London: HMSO.

Gough, I. (1979) *The Political Economy of the Welfare State.* London and Basingstoke, MacMillan.

Grandori, A. (1987) *Perspectives on Organization Theory.* Cambridge: Ballinger.

Gray, A. and W. I. Jenkins (1985) *Administrative Politics in British Government.* Brighton: Wheatsheaf.

Gray, A. and W. I. Jenkins (1986) 'Accountable management in British central government: some reflections on the Financial Management Initiative', *Financial Accountability and Management,* 2: 171–86.

Greer, P. (1992) The Next Steps initiative: an examination of the agency framework documents, *Public Administration,* 70(1): 89–98.

Gunn, L. (1988) 'Public Management: a third approach?', *Public Money and Management,* vol. 8, no. 3: 21–25.

Hagen, T. (1991) 'Moderne kommunale styringsmodeller' *NIBR-rapport* 1991: 5.

Hales, C.P.(1986) 'What do managers do ? A Critical Review of the Evidence', *Journal of Management Studies*: 88–115.

Hancher, L. and Moran, M. (1989) 'Introduction: Regulation and deregulation', *European Journal of Political Research,* 17: 129–136.

Handy, C. (1981) *Understanding Organizations.* London: Penguin Books.

Hannan, M.T. and Freeman, J. (1966) 'The Population Ecology of Organizations', *American Journal of Sociology,* vol. 72 (November): 267–272.

Hannigan, J.A. and Rodney M.K. (1977) 'Legitimacy and public organizations: a case study', *Canadian Journal of Sociology,* 2: 125–135.

Hanushek, E.A. (1986) 'The Economics of Schooling', *Journal of Economic Literature,* 24: 1141–77.

Hargreaves, H.S. (1989) *Rationality in Economics.* Oxford: Basil Blackwell.

Harrison, R. (1972) 'Understanding Your Organizations's Character', *Harvard Business Review*, May–June: 119–28 .

HC 178 (1990–91) *Parliamentary Questions* (Select Committee on Procedure, Third Report). London: HMSO.

HC 496 (1990–91) *Treasury and Civil Service Committee, Seventh Report, The Next Steps Initiative*. London: HMSO, July 1991.

Heald, D. (1983) *Public Expenditures*. Oxford, Martin Robertson.

Heclo, H. (1977) *A Government of Strangers. Executive Politics in Washington*. Washington, DC: Brookings.

Hedberg, Nystrom and Starbuck (1976) 'Camping on the Seasaws'.

Heidenheimer, A.J., Heclo, H. and Adams, C.T. (1983) *Comparative Public Policy. The Politics of Social Choice in Europe and America* (2nd edition). New York: St. Martin's Press.

Helm, D., Aveline, M. and Lawrence, R. (1992) *Acquisition and Diversification: The Record of Privatised Utilities*. Oxford: Oxford Economic Associates Ltd.

Henning, R. (1991) 'Målstyrning och resultatuppöljning i offentlig förvaltning' *Rapport til expertgruppen för studier i offentlig ekonomi* (Stockholm: Ds 1991: 19).

Henry, N. (1992) *Public Administration and Public Affairs*. New Jersey: Prentice Hall.

Hicks, A. and Swank, D. (1984) 'On the Political Economy of Welfare Expansion: A Comparative Analysis of 18 Advanced Capitalist Democracies, 1960–1971', *Comparative Politcal Studies*, (17) 1: 81–119

Hill, J. (1986) *Deregulating Telecommunications: Competition and Control in the U.S., Japan and Britain*. London.

Hirschman, A.0. (1979) *Exit, Voice and Loyalty*. Cambridge, Mass.: Harvard University Press.

Hirschman, A.O. (1970) *Exit, Voice and Loyalty. Responses to Decline in Firms, Organizations and States*. London: Oxford University Press.

Hjalmarsson, L. (1991) 'Metoder i forskning om produktivitet och effektivitet med tillämpninger på offentlig sektor', *ESO-rapport* 1991: 20.

HM Treasury (1992) *Executive Agencies: A Guide to Setting Targets and Measuring Performance*. London: HMSO.

Hoffmann, S. (1966) 'Obstinate or Obsolete: The Fate of the Nation State and the Case of Western Europe', *Daedalus*, 95, 3: 862–915.

Hogwood, B. and Peters, G.B. (1985) *The Pathology of Public Policy*. Oxford: Clarendon Press.

Hood, C. (1990) 'Public Administration: Lost an Empire, not yet found a role', in A. Leftwich, *New Developments in Political Science*, Aldershot: 108–109.

Hood, C. (1986) *The Tools of Government*. London: Macmillan.

Hood, C. and Schuppert, G.F. (1988) *Delivering Public Services in Western Europe*. London: Sage.

Hood, C. M.W. Jackson, M.W. (1991) *Administrative Argument*. Aldershot: Dartmouth.

Hood, C., Dunsire, A. and Thomson, L. (1988) 'Rolling Back the State: Thatcherism, Fraserism and Bureaucracy', *Governance*, 1: 243–270.

Hoogerwerf, A. (1977) 'Government Growth in the Netherlands since 1900: Size, Development, Imbalances and Overload', ECPR Joint Sessions Paper, Berlin.

Howlett, M. (1991) 'Policy Instruments, Policy Styles and Policy Implementation', *Policy Studies Journal*, 19: 1–21.

Hrebiniak, L.G. and Joyce, W.F. (1985) 'Organizational Adaptation: Strategic Choice and Environmental Determinism' *Administrative Science Quarterly*, vol. 30 (September): 336–349.

Income Data Service (1991) *IDS Focus Quarterly: Performance Pay*, December.

Jenkins, K., Caines, K. and Jackson, A. (1988) *Improving Management in Government: The Next Steps: Report to the Prime Minister* [Ibbs Report]. London: HMSO.

Jones, C.O. (1988) *The Reagan Legacy*. Chatham, NJ: Chatham House.

Jonsson, E. (1985) 'A Model of a Non-Budget-Maximizing Bureau', in Lane, J.-E. *State and Market. The Politics of the Public and the Private*. London: Sage Publications.

Jordan, G. (1990) 'Sub-governments, Policy Communities and Networks: Refilling Old Bottles', *Journal of Theoretical Politics*, vol. 2: 319–38.

Jordan, G. (1990) 'The Pluralism of Pluralism: an Anti-theory?', *Political Studies*, (38): 286–301.

Judge, D. (1993) *The Parliamentary State*. London: Sage Publications.

Jungk, R. and Müllert, N.R. (1981) *Zukunftswerkstätten*. Hamburg: Rowohlt Verlag.

Kahn, A. (1971) *The Economics of Regulation: Principles and Institutions* (vol. 11). New York: John Wiley.

Kanter, R. M. (1989) *When Giants Learn to Dance*. London.

Kanter, R.M. (1989) 'The New Managerial Work', *Harvard Business Review*, (November–December): 85–92.

Kastelein, J., Attema T., Blindeman Krabbenbos, K., Klanderman, J.E. and Bellaar Spruyt, M.J. (1977) *Management in de Rijksdienst. Een vergelijkende verkenning in 30 eenheden van de centrale overheid* (Management in Dutch Central Government. A comparative exploration into 30 units of central government). Amsterdam: Instituut voor Bestuurskunde.

Kaufman, H. (1979) 'Fear of Bureaucracy: A Raging Pandemic', *Public Administration Review*.

Kaufmann, F.X., Majone, G. and Ostrom, V. (eds) (1986) *Guidance, Control and Evaluation in the Public Sector*. New York: De Gruyter.

Kay, J. and Vickers J. (1988) 'Regulatory Reform in Britain', *Economic Policy*, 71, October: 286–351.

Kelsen, H. (1961) *General Theory of Law and State*. New York: Russel and Russel.

Keman, H. (1987) 'Welfare and Warfare. Critical Options and Conscious Choice in Public Policy', in Castles et al. (eds): 97–141.

Keman, H. (1988) *The Development toward Surplus Welfare. Social Democratic Politics and Policies in Advanced Capitalist Democracies (1965–1984)*. Amsterdam: CT-press.

Keman, H. (1990) 'Social Democracy and Welfare Statism', *The Netherlands Journal of Social Sciences*, 26/1: 17–34.

Keman, H. (ed.) (1993) *Comparative Politics. New Directions in Theory and Method*. Amsterdam, VUUP.

Keman, H. and Lehner, F. (1984) 'Economic Crisis and Political Management: An Introduction to Political Economic Interdependence', *European Journal of Political Research*, 12(2): 121–130.

Keman, H., Paloheimo, H. and Whiteley, P.F. (eds) (1987) *Coping with the Crisis. Alternative Responses to Economic Recession in Advanced Industrial Society*. London: Sage Publications.

Kemp. P. (1990) 'Next Steps for the British Civil Service', *Governance*, 3: 186–96.

Khoury, S.J. (1990) *The Deregulation of the World Financial Markets*. London.

Kiewiet, D. Roderick, and Mathew D. McCubbins (1985) 'Appropriations Decisions as a Bilateral Bargaining Game between President and Congress,' *Legislative Studies Quarterly*, May, X, 2: 181–201.

Kingdon, J.W. (1983) *An Idea Whose Time Has Come; Agendas and Public Policies*. Boston: Little, Brown.

Kirschen, E.S. et al. (1964) *Economic Policy in our Time*. Amsterdam: North-Holland.

Kohl, J. (1984) *Staatsausgaben in Westeuropa. Analysen zur langfristigen Entwicklung der öffentlichen Finanzen*. Frankfurt and New York: Campus Verlag.

Kooiman, J. (1988) *Besturen: Wisselwerking tussen Overheid en Maatschappij*. Assen: van Gorcum.

Kooiman, J. (ed) (1993) *Modern Governance: New Government-Society Interactions*. London: Sage Publications.

Kooiman, J. and Eliassen, K. (eds) (1987) *Managing Public Organizations*. London: Sage Publications.

Korpi, W. (1983) *The Democratic Class Struggle*. London: Routledge and Kegan Paul.

Kotter, J.P. (1982) *The General Managers*. New York: The Free Press.

Kristensen, O.P. (1980) 'The Logic of Political-Bureaucratic Decision-Making as a Cause of

Governmental Growth', *European Journal of political Research*, 8: 249–64.

Kyvik, S. (1991) *Productivity in Academia*. Oslo: Norwegian University Press.

Laegrid, P. (1993) 'Rewards for High Public Office: The Case of Norway', paper prepared for a comparative research project coordinated by Christopher Hood and Guy Peters.

Landau, M. and Stout, R. Jr. (1979) 'To Manage is not to Control: Or the Folly of Type 11 Errors', *Public Administration Review*, March/April: 14–56.

Lane, J.-E. (1989) *Institutional Reform*. Aldershot: Dartmouth.

Lane, J.-E. (1993) *The Public Sector. Concepts, Models and Approaches*. London: Sage Publications.

Lane, J.-E. (ed.) (1985) *State and Market: The Politics of the Public and the Private*. London, Sage Publications.

Lane, J.-E. and Ersson, S.O. (1990) *Comparative Political Economy*. London: Pinter.

Lane, J.-E. (1993) 'Relevance of new institutionalism', in Eliassen et al. *Managing Public Organizations*. London: Sage Publications.

Lawless, M.W. and Finch, L.K. (1989) 'Choice and Determinism: A Test of Hrebiniak and Joyce's Framework on Strategy – Environment Fit', *Strategic Management Journal*, vol. 10: 351–365.

Leeuw, A.C.J., de (1986) *Organisaties: Management, Analyse, Ontwerp en Verandering: een systeemvisie*. Assen: van Gorcum.

Lehning, P.B. (1991) *Beleid op Niveau*. Meppel: Boom.

Leibenstein, H. (1966) 'Allocative Efficiency vs X-Efficiency', *American Economic Review*, 56: 392–415.

Levine, Charles H (1978) 'Organizational Decline and Cut-back Management', *Public Administration Review*, July/August: 316–25.

Levine, Charles H. (1988) 'Human Resource Erosion and the Uncertain Future of the U.S. Civil Service: From Policy Gridlock to Structural Fragmentation', *Governance*, 1: 115–143.

Lindberg, L.N. and Maier, C.S. (eds) (1985) *The Politics of Inflation and Economic Stagnation*. Washington D.C.: The Brookings Institution.

Lindblom, C.E. *Politics and Markets*. New York: Basic Books.

Llewellyn, D.T. 'The Changing Structure of Regulation in the British Financial System', in K.J. Button and D. Swann: 189–216.

Llewellyn, D.T. (1981) 'The Changing Structure of Regulation in the British Financial System', in K.J. Button and D. Swann (eds) *Studies in Public Regulation*. Cambridge, Mass.

Lybeck, J.A. and Henrekson, M. (eds) (1988) *Explaining the Growth of Government*. Amsterdam: North-Holland.

Lyden, Fremont J. (1975) 'Using Parsons' Functional Analysis in the Study of Public Organizations', *Administrative Science Quarterly*, 20: 277–294.

Lægreid P (1991) Rofesjonsbakgrunn og leiaratferd i offentleg sektor. Bergen: Los-senter notat 91/15.

Lægreid P. (1992) Tendensar i utviklinga av offentleg sektor. Bergen: Los-senter notat 92/37.

Maarse, J.A.M. (1989) 'Hospital budgeting in Holland: aspects, trends and effects', *Health Policy*, 11: 257–276.

Maas, A.J.J.A. and Kooiman, J. (1980) *De departementen onder Druk* (Departments under Pressure). 's-Gravenhage: Ministerie van Binnenlandse Zaken.

Mackenzie, G.C., (ed.) (1987) *The In-and-Outers. Presidential Appointees and Transient Government in Washington*. Baltimore and London: Johns Hopkins University Press.

Maddison, A. (1982) *Ontwikkelingsfasen van het kapitalisme*. Utrecht and Antwerpen: Het Spectrum.

Maddison, A. (1991) *Dynamic Forces in Capitalist Development. A Long Run Comparative View*. Oxford and New York: Oxford University Press.

Majone, G. (1990) *Deregulation or Regulation*. London.

Malloy, J.M. (1993) 'Statecraft and Social Policy in Latin America', *Governance*, forthcoming.

Maloney, W. and Richardson, J.J., (1992) 'Post-Privatisation Regulation in Britain', *Politics*, 12(2): 9–14.

Manion, J.L. (1991) 'Career Public Services in Canada: Reflections and Predictions', *International Review of Administrative Sciences*, 57: 361–72.

March, J. and Olsen, J.P. (eds) (1976) *Ambiguity and Choice in Organizations*. Oslo: Universitetsforlaget.

March, J.G. and Olsen, J.P. (1983) 'Organizing Political Life: What Administrative Reorganization tells us about Government', *American Political Science Review*, 77: 281–95.

March, J.G. and Olsen, J.P. (1989) *Rediscovering Institutions*. New York: Free Press.

March, J.G. and Olson, J.P. (1983) 'Organizing Political Life: What Administrative Reorganization Tells Us about Government', *American Political Science Review*, 77: 281–96.

March, J.G. and Simon, H.A. (1958) *Organizations*. New York: John Wiley.

Matthews R.C.O. (1986) 'The Economics of Institutions and the Sources of Growth', *The Economic Journal*, 96: 903–918.

Mayntz, R. (1983) 'Politisierung der Bürokratie', in Hartwich, H.-H. (ed.) *Gesellschaftliche Probleme als Anstoss und Folge von Politik*. Opladen: Westdeutscher Verlag.

Mayntz, R. (1984a) 'German Federal Bureaucrats – A Functional Elite between Politics and Administration' in Suleiman, Ezra N. (ed.) *The Role of Higher Civil Servants in Central Governments*. New York: Holmes and Meier

Mayntz, R. (1984b) 'The Political Role of the Higher Civil Service in the German Federal Government' in Smith, Bruce L.R. (ed.) *The Higher Civil Service in Europe and Canada: Lessons for the United States*. Washington, D.C.: Brookings.

Mayntz, R. (1993) 'Governance Failures and the Problem of Governability' in J. Kooiman (ed.) *Modern Governance*. London: Sage Publications.

Mayntz, R. and Derlien, H.U. (1989) 'Party Patronage and Politicization of the West German Administrative Elite 1970–1987 – Towards Hybridization?', *Governance*, 2: 384–404.

Mayntz, R. and Scharpf, F.W. (1975) *Policy-Making in the German Federal Bureaucracy*. Amsterdam, Oxford, New York: Elsevier.

Melman, S. (1951) 'The Rise of Administrative Overhead in the Manufacturing Industries of the United States: 1899–1947', *Oxford Economic Papers*, 3: 62–112.

Metcalfe, L. (1974) 'Systems Models, Economics Models and the Causal Texture of Organizational Environments', *Human Relations*, 27: 6393.

Metcalfe, L. (1981) 'Designing Precarious Partnerships', in Nystrom, Paul C. and W.H. Starbuck *Handbook of Organizational Design* (vol. 1). Oxford: Oxford University Press.

Metcalfe, L. (1993) 'Public Management: from Imitation to Innovation', in Kooiman, J. (ed) *Modern Governance*. London: Sage Publications.

Metcalfe, L. and McQuillan, W. (1977) 'Managing Turbulence', in Nystrom, Paul C. and W.H. Starbuck (eds) *Prescriptive Models of Organizations*, pp. 7–23. New York: North-Holland.

Metcalfe, L. and Richards, S. (1984) 'The Impact of the Efficiency Strategy: Political Clout or Cultural Change?', *Public Administration*, 62 (4).

Metcalfe, L. and Richards, S. (1987) *Improving Public Management*. London: Sage.

Metcalf, L. and Richards S. (1990) *Improving Public Management*. Enlarged edition. London: Sage Publications.

Meyer, J.W. and Scott, W.R. (1983) *Organizational Environments: Ritual and Rationality*. Beverly Hills, CA: Sage Publications.

Meyers, F. (1985) *La Politisation de l'Administration*. Brussels: Institut International des Sciences Administratives.

Miles, R.E. and Snow, C.C. (1984) 'Fit, Failure and the Hall of Fame', *California Management Review*, 26 (3): 10–28.

Milward, H.B. and G.L. Walmsley (1985) 'Policy Subsystems, Networks and Tools of Public Management', in Hanf, K. and Toonen, T.A.J. (eds) *Policy Implementation in Federal and Unitary Systems*. Dordrecht: Kluwer.

Mintzberg, H. (1983) *Structure in fives: Designing effective organizations*. Prentice-Hall.

Mintzberg, H. (1990) 'The Design School: Reconsidering the Basic Premises of Strategic Management', *Strategic Management Journal*, vol. 11: 171–195.

Mintzberg, H. and Jorgensen, J. (1987) 'Emergent Strategy for Public Policy' *Canadian Public Administration*, 30 (2): 214–229.

Mintzberg, H. and MacHugh, A. (1985) 'Strategy Formation in an Adhocracy' *Administrative Science Quarterly*, vol. 30 (June): 160–197.

Mitnick, B.M. (1980) *The Political Economy of Regulation*. New York.

Moe, T.M. (1984) 'The New Economics of Organization', *American Journal of Political Science*, 28: 739–777.

Moe, T.M. (1990) 'Political Institutions: The Neglected Side of the Story' in *Journal of Law, Economics and Organization*, vol 6: 213–253.

Montricher, N. de (1991) 'The career public service in France: problems and prospects', *International Review of Administrative Sciences*, 57, 373–384.

Moore, C. and Richardson, J. J., (1988) 'The Politics and Practice of Corporate Responsibility in Great Britain', in Preston, Lee, E. (ed.) *Research in Corporate Social Performance and Policy*. Greenwich and London: JAI Press Inc.

Mouritzen, P.E (1985) 'Local Resource Allocation: Partisan Politics or Sector Politics', *Research in Urban Policy*, 4: 442–456.

Mouritzen, P.E. (1991) *Den politiske cyklus*. Århus: Politica.

Mueller, D.C. (1986) *The Modern Corporation*. Brighton: Wheatsheaf.

Mueller, D.C. (1989) *Public Choice II*. Cambridge: Cambridge University Press.

Mueller, D.C. (1989) *The Political Economy of Growth*. New Haven: Yale University Press.

Mueller, R.K. (1986) *Corporate Networking. Building Channels for Information and Influence*. New York: The Free Press.

Murray, R. (1987) 'Productivity measurement in bureaucratic organizations' , in Lane, J.-E. (ed.) *Bureaucracy and Public Choice*. Sage Publications.

Naess S. (1992) Ledelse i offentlige og private organisasjoner. En kvantitativ studie av vektleggingen av ledelsesfunksjoner i perioden 1983–91. Bergen : Institutt for administrasjon og organisasjonsvitenskap. Mimeo.

Naess S. og Strand, T. (1992) Kommunale ledere. Forskjeller og likheter mellom ledere i ulike sektorer og innenfor kommunal sektor. Bergen: LOs-senter rapport 9209.

National Consumers' Council, (1989) *In the Absence of Competition. A Consumer View of Public Utility Regulation*. London: HMSO.

Nervik, J.A. (1991) Flere stillinger – lavere utgifter? Evaluering av forsøket 'Bedre bruk av sosialhjelpsmidlene', Oslo: INAS-rapport 91: 6.

Neumann, M.J.M. et al., (1989) 'The appropriate level of regulation in Europe: local national or community-wide? A roundtable discussion', *Economic Policy*, 9 October: 467–481.

Niskanen, W.A. (1971) *Bureaucracy and Representative Government*. Chicago: Aldine Publishing Company.

Nonaka, I. (1988) 'Toward Middle-Up-Down Management: Accelerating Information Creation', *Sloan Management Review*, (Spring): 9–18.

North, D.C. (1990) *Institutions, Institutional Change and Economic Performance*. Cambridge: Cambridge University Press.

Nowtotny, K. (1989) 'The Economics of Public Utility Regulation: An Overview', in K. Nowtotny, D.B. Smith and H.M. Trebling (eds) *Public Utility Regulation: The Economic and Social Control of Industry*. Boston: Kluwer.

OECD (1981) *Welfare State in Crisis*. Paris: OECD.

OECD (1985a) 'The Role of the Public Sector', *Economic Studies*, 4. Paris: OECD.

OECD (1985b) *Social Expenditures 1960–1990. Problems of Growth and Control*. Paris: OECD.

OECD (1987) *Administration as Service: Citizen as Client*. Paris: OECD.

OECD (1990) Public Management Service *Public Management Developments Survey 1990*. Paris: OECD

OECD (1992) *Historical Statistics 1960–1990*. Paris: OECD.

OECD (1992) PUMA *Public Management Developments Update 1992*. Paris: OECD.

Olsen, J.P. (1988) The Modernization of Public Administration in the Nordic Countries. *LOS senter-Notat* 88/2.

Olsen, J.P. (1991) Rethinking and Reforming the Public Sector, LOS-senter Notat 91/33. Bergen: LOS Senteret.

Olson, M. (1965) *The Logic of Collective Action.* Cambridge, Mass.: Harvard University Press.

Olson, M. (1982) *The Rise and Decline of Nations.* New Haven and London: Yale University Press.

Oxley, H. (1991) 'Rainbows and pots of gold: The search for public sector efficiency', *Paper* to Public Sector Workshop, Helsinki 14.03.91.

Parsons, T. (1959) 'General Theory in Sociology' in Merton, R., Brown, L. and Cotrell, L.S. Jr. (eds) *Sociology Today: Problems and Perspectives.* New York: Basic Books: pp. 3–38.

Pauly, M.V. (1992) 'Fairnes and the feasibility in national health care systems', *Health Economics* 1: 93–103.

Peacock, A. and Forte, F. (1981) *The Political Economy of Taxation.* Oxford: Basil Blackwell.

Peacock, A. and J. Wiseman (1961) *The Growth of Public Expenditure in the United Kingdom 1890–1955.* London: George Allen and Unwin.

Pekonen, K. (1993) Governance and the problem of Representation in Public Administration' in Kooiman, J. *Modern Governance.* London: Sage Publications.

Perlkmans J. and Martijn van Nie (eds) (1985) *Privatization and Deregulation: The European Debate.* Maastricht: European Institute of Public Administration.

Perry, J.L. (1986) 'Merit Pay in the Public Sector: The Case for a Failure of Theory', *Review of Public Personnel Administration,* 7: 57–69.

Perry, J.L. and Rainey, H.G. (1988) 'The Public – Private Distinction in Organization Theory: A Critique and Research Strategy', *Academy of Management Review,* 13, no. 2, 182–201.

Peters, B.G. (1991) 'Morale in the public service: a comparative inquiry', *International Review of Administrative Sciences,* 57, 421–440.

Peters, G. (1978) *The Politics of Bureaucracy.* London: Longman.

Peters, T. and Austin, N. (1985) 'MBWA (Managing by Walking Around)', *California Management Review,* 28 (1): 9–34.

Peters, T.J. and Waterman, R.H. (1984) *In Search of Excellence. Lessons from America's Best-run Companies.* New York.

Peters, T.J. and Waterman, R.H. (1982) *In Search of Excellence.* New York: Harper Row.

Pfeffer, J. (1977) 'The Ambiguity of Leadership', *Academy of Management Review,* 2, no. 1.

Pfeffer, J. (1981) 'Management as Symbolic Action: The Creation and Maintenance of Organizational Paradigms', *Research in Organizational Behavior,* 3, 1–52.

Pfeffer, J. (1992) *Managing With Power. Politics and Influence in Organizations.* Boston, Mass.: Harvard Business School Press.

Pfeffer, J. and Salancik, G.R. (1978) *The External Control of Organization.* New York: Harper and Row.

Piekalkiewicz, J. and Hamilton, C. (1992) *Public Bureaucracies Between Reform and Resistance.* Zurich: Anton Berg.

Pitt, D., (1990) 'An Essentially Contestable Organisation: British Telecom and the Privatisation Debate', in J.J. Richardson (ed.) *Privatisation and Deregulation in Canada and Britain.* Aldershot: Dartmouth.

Pollitt, C. (1990) *Managerialism in the Public Sector.* Oxford: Basil Blackwell.

Poole, M.S and van de Ven, A. 'Using paradox to build management and organization theory', *Academy of Management Review,* 14, no. 4, 562–578.

Powell, W.W. and DiMaggio, P.J. (1991) *The New Institutionalism in Organizational Analysis.* Chicago: University of Chicago Press.

Premchand, A. (1987) 'Government Budgeting and Productivity', *Public Productivity Review* 41: 9–19, reprinted in Hyde, A.C. (1992) *Government Budgeting. Theory, Process, Politics.* Pacific Grove, Calif.: Brooks and Cole Publishing Company.

Price Waterhouse (1992) *Executive Agencies: Facts and Trends*, edition 4. London: Price Waterhouse.

Provan, K.G. and Milward, H.B. (1991) 'Institutional Level Norms and Organizational Involvement in a Service-Implementation Network', *Journal of Public Administration Research and Theory*, 1, 391–417.

Pugh. D.S. and Hickson, D.J. (1976) *Organization Structure in its Context: The Astyon Programme I*. Farnborough: Saxon House.

Putnam, R.D. (1973) 'The Political Attitudes of Senior Civil Servants in Western Europe', *British Journal of Political Science*, 3, 253–79.

Quinn, R. E. and McGrath, M.R. (1988) 'Moving Beyond the Single-Solution Perspective: The Competing Values Approach as a Diagnostic Tool', *The Journal of Applied Behavioral Science*, 18, no. 4, 463–472.

Quinn, R.E. (1988) *Beyond Rational Management: Masting the Paradoxes and Competing Demands of High Performance*. London: Jossey Bass.

Raab, C. (1993) 'The Governance of Data Protection', in Kooiman, J. (ed.) *Modern Governance*. London: Sage Publications.

Rehfuss, J. (1991) 'The Competitive Agency: Thoughts from Contracting Out in Great Britain in and the United States', *International Review of Administrative Sciences*, 57, 465–82.

Reich, R.B. (1985) 'Public Administration and Public Deliberation: an Interpretative Essay', *Yale Law Review* (vol 94) 1617–1641.

Reich, R.B. (1988) 'Policy Making in a Democracy', in Reich, R.B. *The Power of Public Ideas*. Cambridge (Mass.): Harvard University Press.

Richardson, J. (ed) (1982) *Policy Styles in Western Europe*. London: George Allen and Unwin.

Richardson, J.J., and Jordan, A.G., (1979) *Governing Under Pressure*. Oxford: Martin Robertson.

Richardson, J.J., Maloney, W.A. and Rüdig, W. (1992) 'The Dynamics of Policy Change: Lobbying and Water Privatisation', *Public Administration*, vol. 70, no. 2, 157–175.

Ridley, F.F. (1985) 'Politics and the Selection of Higher Civil Servants in Britain', in Meyers, F. (ed.) *The Politicization of Public Administration*. Brussels: International Institute of Administrative Sciences.

RIPA (1991) *The Civil Service Reformed: The Next Steps Initiative* (Proceedings of an RIPA Research Seminar held on 28 June 1991). London: Royal Institute of Public Administration.

Robertsen, K. og Friestad, L.-B. (1990) 'Effektiviseringsmuligheter i grunnskolen', *FOU-rapport nr.72*, Agderforskning: Kristiansand.

Rose, R. (1976) 'On the Priorities of Government: A Developmental Analysis of Public Policies', *European Journal of Political Research*, 4/2: 247–290.

Rose, R. (1980) 'British Government: The Job at the Top', in Rose, R. and Suleiman, E.N. (eds) *Presidents and Prime Ministers*. Washington, DC: American Enterprise Institute.

Rose, R. (1984) *Big Government*. London: Sage Publications.

Rose, R. (1985) 'Steering the Ship of State', *Ms.* 85/46

Rose, R. (1985) 'The Program Approach,' in Lane, J.-E. (ed.) *State and Market*. London: Sage Publications.

Rose, R. (1988) 'Loyalty, Voice, or Exit? Margaret Thatcher's Challenge to the Civil Service', *Jahrbuch zur Staats- und Verwaltungswissenschaft* (Yearbook of Government), 2, 189–218.

Rose, R. and Peters, B.G. (1978) *Can Government Go Bankrupt?*. New York: Basic Books.

Rose, R. and Suleiman, E.N. (eds) (1980) *Presidents and Prime Ministers*. Washington, DC.: American Enterprise Institute.

Ross, S.A. 'The Economic Theory of Agency: the Principals's Problem', *American Economic Review*, 64: 134–9.

Rouban, L. (1989) 'The Civil Service and the Policy of Administrative Modernization in France', *International Review of Administrative Sciences*, 55: 445–465.

Rubin, I. (1993) *The Politics of Public Budgeting: Getting and Spending Borrowing and Balancing*, 2nd ed. Chatham, NJ: Chatham House.

Røvik, K.A.(1992) Den 'syke' stat. Myter og moter i omstillingarbeidet. Oslo: Universitets-forlaget.

Samuelson, P.A. (1954) 'A Pure Theory of Public Expenditure', The Review of Economics and Statistics: 387–389.

Saunders, P., (1985) 'The Forgotten Dimension of Central-Local Relations: theorizing the "regional state"', Environment and Planning C: Government and Policy, 3: 149–62.

Scharpf, F.W. (1987) 'A Game-Theoretical Interpretation of Inflation and Unemployment in Western Europe', Journal of Public Policy, 7: 227–258.

Schein, E. (1985) Organisational Culture and Leadership: A Dynamic View. San Francisco: Jossey Bass.

Schick, A. (1980) 'Budgetary Adaptations to Resource Scarcity,' in Levine, Charles H. and Irene Rubin (eds), Fiscal Stress and Public Policy. Beverly Hills and London: Sage Publications: 113–134.

Schick, A. (1988) 'Proposed Budget Reforms: A Critical Analysis,' in Congressional Research Service, Library of Congress, and the Congressional Budget Office, Proposed Budget Reforms: A Critical Analysis, Washington, DC: U.S. Governnment Printing Office, April: 1–70.

Schick, A. (1990) 'Budgeting for Results: Recent Developments in Five Industrialized Countries', Public Administration Review, 50: 26–34

Schick, A. (1990) The Capacity to Budget. Washington, DC: The Urban Institute Press.

Schmalensee, R., (1986) paper presented to National Economic Research Associates Inc. Electric Utility Conference: Surviving An Era of Changing Regulation. Scottsdale, Arizona, 12–15 Feb 1986.

Schmidt, M.G. (1983) 'The Welfare State and the Economy in Periods of Economic Crisis: A Comparative Analysis of Twenty-three OECD Nations', European Journal of Political Research, 11/1: 1–26.

Schmidt, M.G. (1988) 'The Politics of Labour Market Policy', in Castles et al. (eds): 4–53.

Schmidt, M.G. (1989) 'Learning from Catastrophes. West Germany's Public Policy', in Castles, F.G. (ed.) (1989): 56–99.

Schmidt, M.G. (1992) Lexikon der Politik. Westliche Industriegesellschaften. München: Beck Verlag.

Schon, D.A. (1971) Beyond the Stable State. New York: Norton.

Schubert, K. (1988) 'Politics and Economic Regulation', in F.G. Castles, F.G., Lehner, F. and Schmidt, M.G. (eds) Managing Mixed Economies, Berlin, 169–196.

Scott, W.R. (1987) Organizations: Rational, Natural, and Open Systems. Englewood Cliffs, NJ: Prentice Hall.

Scott, W.R. (1981) Organizations: Rational, Natural and Open Systems. Englewood Cliffs (N.J.): Prentice-Hall.

Selznick, P. (1956) Leadership in Administration. University of California Press.

Shepsle, K.A. (1989) 'Studying Institutions. Some Lessons from the Rational Choice Approach', Journal of Theoretical Politics, vol. 1, no. 2: 131–147.

Shrivastava, P. and Nachman, S.A. (1989) 'Strategic Leadership Patterns', Strategic Management Journal, vol. 10: 51–66.

Simon, H. (1945, 1976) Administrative Behavior. A Study of Decision-Making Processes in Administrative Organization. New York: The Free Press.

Simon, H.A. (1947) Administrative Behavior. New York: Free Press.

Simon, H.A. (1957) Administrative Behaviour (2nd ed.). New York: Macmillan.

Simon, H.A. (1976) Administrative Behavior. New York: The Macmillian Company.

Simon, H.A., Smithburg, Donald W. and Thompson, Victor A. (1950) Public Administration. New York: Knopf.

Smith, M.J., (1990) ' Pluralism, Reformed Pluralism and Neopluralism: the Role of Presuure Groups in Policy-Making', Political Studies, 38: 302–322.

Spann, R.M. (1977) 'Public versus private provision of governmental services', in Borcherding, T.E. (ed) Budgets and Bureaucrats: The Sources of Government Growth. Durham, NC: Duke University Press.

Stahlberg, K. (1987) 'The politicization of public administration: notes on the concepts, causes and consequences of politicization', *International Review of Administrative Sciences*, 53: 363–382.

Stephens, J.D. (1979) *The Transition from Socialism to Capitalism*. London and Basingstoke: MacMillan.

Stigler, George, (1971) 'The Theory of Economic Regulation', *Bell Journal of Economics*, 2.1: 3–21.

Stiglitz, J.E. (1988) *Economics of the Public Sector*. New York: W.W. Norton and Company.

Stinchcombe, A. (1974) *Creating Efficient Industrial Administrations*. New York: Academic Press.

Strand T. (1992) Kva gjer rektor for skolen? Om rektor-rolla i den norske grunnskolen. Bergen: Los-senter notat 92/44.

Strand, T. (1986) 'The Public Manager. Bureaucrats or Contingent Actors?', T. Strand *Managing Public Organisations*, vol II, no. 6.

Strand, T. (1988) 'On extending leadership theory: Leadership attributions and beyond' in Hunt J.G. et al. (eds) *Emerging leadership vistas*. Lexington Mass.: Lexington books.

Strand, T. (1987) 'Bureaucrats or contingent actors?', in Kooiman, J. and Eliassen, K.A. (eds) *Managing Public Organizations. Lessons from contemporary European experience*: 87–101. London: Sage Publications.

Strand,T. (1993) 'Bureaucrats as Contingent Actors' in this volume (ch. 12).

Strasser, K. A., and Kohler, M.F. (1989) *Regulating Utilities With Management Incentives*. New York: Quorum Books and Greenwood Press.

Sue, R. (1990) in OECD, Public Management Studies *Flexible Personnel Management in the Public Service*. Paris.

Tarschys, D. (1975) 'The Growth of Public Expenditures: Nine Modes of Explanation', *Scandinavian Political Studies*, 10: 9–31.

Tarschys, D. (1981) 'Rational Decremental Budgeting: Elements of an Expenditure Policy for the 1980s', *Policy Sciences*, 4: 49–58.

Tarschys, D. (1983) 'The Scissors Crisis in Public Finance', *Policy Sciences*, 15: 205–224.

Taylor, C.L. (ed.) (1983) *Why Governments Grow. Measuring Public Sector Growth*. London: Sage Publications.

Thiemeyer, T. (ed.) (1983) *Öffentliche Bindung von Unternehmen*. Baden-Baden: Nomos Verlagsgesellschaft.

Thompson, J.D. (1967) *Organizations in Action*. New York: McGraw Hill.

Thuillier, G. (1982) *Les Cabinets Ministeriels*. Paris: Presses Universitaires de France.

Thurmaier, K. (1992) 'Budgetary Decisionmaking in Central Budget Bureaus: An Experriment', *Journal of Public Administration Research and Theory*, 2, 4: 463–487.

Titmuss, R. (1974) *Social Policy*. London: Allen and Unwin.

Tollison, R.D. (1982) 'Rent Seeking – A Survey', *Kyklos*, vol. 34: 575–602.

Tsui, A. (1984) 'A Multiple Constituency Framework of Managerial Reputational Effectiveness', in Hunt, James et al. (eds). *Leaders and Managers*. New York: Pergamon Press.

Tullock, G. (1965) *The Politics of Bureaucracy*. Washington, DC: Public Affairs Press.

Valdmanis, V. (1992) 'Sensitivity analysis for DEA models. An empirical example using public vs. NSP hospitals' *Journal of Public Economics*, 48: 185–205.

Vanberg, V. and Buchanan, J.M. (1989) 'Interests and Theories in Constitutional Choice', *Journal of Theoretical Politics*, vol. 1, no. 1: 49–62.

Veljanovski, C., (1987) *Selling the State. Privatisation in Britain*. London: Weidenfeld and Nicholson.

Veljanovski, C.G. (1982) 'The Coase Theorems and the Economic Theory of Markets and Law', *Kyklos*, 35, no. 1: 66–81.

Vickers, J. and Yarrow, J. (1989) *Privatization. An Economic Analysis*. Cambridge, Mass.: MIT-press.

Villiers, C. (1992) 'London Underground's Customer Charter. A Comparison with British Rail', *Utilities Review*, Autumn 1992: 111–112.

Voelkner, J. (ed.) (1992) *Planungsmethoden in Verwaltung und Wirtschaft*, 2nd ed. Regensburg: Walhalla.

von Hagen, J. (1992) 'Budgeting Procedures and Fiscal Performance in the European Communities', Indiana Center for Global Business, Graduate School of Business, Indiana University.

Wagener, F. (1971) 'The Structure of Management', in Speyer Academy of Administrative Sciences, *Current Problems of the Organization of Government Departments*: 1–24.

Wamsley, G. L. and Zald, M.N. (1976) *The Political Economy of Public Organizations*. Bloomington: Indiana University Press.

Weber, M. (1919) *Politik als Beruf*. München, Leipzig: Duncker and Humblot.

Weingast, B.R. (1989) 'The Political Institutions of Representative Government', *Journal of Institutional and Theoretical Economics*, 145: 693–703.

Weingast, B.R. and Marshall, W.J. (1988) 'The Industrial Organization of Congress; or Why Legislatures, Like Firms, Are Not Organized as Markets', *Journal of Political Economy*, 96: 132–163.

Weiss, C. (1972) *Evaluation Research*. Englewood Cliffs, NJ: Prentice Hall.

Whetten, D.A. (1984) 'Organizational Decline. A Neglected Topic in Organizational Science', in Barry Bozeman and Jeffrey Strausman (eds): *New Directions in Public Administration*. Monterey: Brooks and Cole Publishing Company.

Whiteley, P.E. (1986) *Political Control of the Macro-economy*. London: Sage Publications.

Whorton, J.W. and Worthley, J.A., (1981) 'A Perspective on the Challenge of Public Management: Environmental Paradox and Organizational Culture', *Academy of Management Review*, vol. 6, no. 3: 357–361.

Wildavski, A. (1979) *Speaking Truth to Power: The art and craft of policy analysis*. Boston, MA: Little, Brown and Co.

Wildavsky, A. (1965) *The Politics of the Budgetary Process*. Boston: Little, Brown.

Wildavsky, A. (1969) 'Rescuing Policy Analysis from PPBS', *Public Administration Review*, reprinted in Shafritz, J.M. and Hyde, A.C. *Classics of Public Administration*. Chicago: The Dorsey Press.

Wildavsky, A. (1975) *Budgeting: a Comparative Theory of Budgetary Processes*. Boston: Little, Brown.

Wildavsky, A. (1979) *Speaking Truth to Power: The Art and Craft of Policy Analysis*. Boston: Little, Brown and Co.

Wildavsky, A. (1989) *Searching for Safety*.

Wilensky, H. (1975) *The Welfare State and Equality. Structural and Ideological Roots of Public Expenditures*. Berkeley: University of California Press.

Wilensky, H. (1981) *Democratic Corporatism, Consensus and Social Policy: Reflections on Changing Values and the 'Crisis' of the Welfare State*, in OECD (1981): 185–195.

Williamson, O. (1975) *Markets and hierarchies*. New York: Free Press.

Williamson, O. (1985) *The Economic Institutions of Capitalism*. New York: Free Press.

Williamson, O. (1986) *Economic Organization. Firms, Markets and Policy Control*, Brighton: Wheatsheaf.

Wilson, G.K. (1991) 'Prospects for the Public Service in Britain. Major to the Rescue?', *International Review of Administrative Sciences*, 57: 327–344.

Wood, R. (1991) OECD, Public Management Studies *Performance Pay and related compensation practices in the Australian state public sector organisations* (by R. Wood) PUMA Occasional Papers, Paris.

Woodside, K. (1986) 'Policy Instruments and the Study of Public Policy', *Canadian Journal of Political Science*, 19: 775–94.

Wooldridge, B. and Floyd, S.W. (1990) 'The Strategy Process, Middle Management Involvement and Organizational Performance', *Strategic Management Journal*, vol. 11: 231–241.

Yntema, P. (1990) *Managing human resources. The role of the public manager in Italy, the Netherlands and the European Commision*. Delft: Eburon.

Zimmerman, (1986) *Neokorporative Politikformen in den Niederlanden. Industriepolitik, kollektieve Arbeitsbeziehungen und hegemoniale Strukturen seit 1918*. Frankfurt and New York: Campus Verlag.

SUBJECT INDEX

AUTHOR INDEX